ABOVE WASHINGTON

by

ROBERT CAMERON

A Collection of Nostalgic and Contemporary
Aerial Photographs of the District of Columbia

Cameron and Company, San Francisco, California

Making this book required the expertise of many people in many ways. The author extends gratitude for their efforts to the following: Hatsuro Aizawa, Fred Bell, Ken Detwiler, Joseph diGenova, Don Dunaway, Robert Eckstrand, Ben Forgey, John Goy, Larry Imrich, Richard Kimmel, Robert Lautman, Ken Leong, George Lukes, Vern Mastin, James Reston, Robert Richardson, Robert Scurlock, Wolf Von Eckardt, and Fred Ward.

For assistance in researching the historical aerial photography, acknowledgement is made to:

District of Columbia Public Library
Department of the Interior
Library of Congress
National Aeronautics and Space Administration, Ames Research Center
National Archives and Record Service
Smithsonian Institution

I am especially indebted to Senator Charles MacC. Mathias, Jr. for his encouragement and assistance.

I asked my friend Bob Wormhoudt to write captions for my pictures. I asked Nancy Hatheway Noyes, the Washington architectural writer, for technical and aesthetic background. I am grateful to them both.

A vital ingredient in aerial photography is the right helicopter pilot. The right helicopter pilot was Daniel P. "Captain Dan" Rosenson. His expertise comes from 15,000 hours "Above Washington."

CAMERON AND COMPANY
543 Howard Street
San Francisco, California 94105

Library of Congress Catalog Card Number 79-89078
Above Washington ISBN 0-918684-08-0

First Printing, 1979
Second Printing, 1980
Third Printing, 1980
Fourth Printing, 1981
Fifth Printing, 1982
Sixth Printing, 1984
Seventh Printing, 1985

Book design by
JANE OLAUG KRISTIANSEN

Color film processing by Customcraft, Washington, D.C.

Typography by Techni-Process, San Francisco, California
and Spartan Typographers, Oakland, California

Color separation and printing by Dai Nippon, Tokyo, Japan

TABLE OF CONTENTS

THE MAKING OF WASHINGTON, D.C.
by
ALISTAIR COOKE

Washington, like Canberra or Brasilia, is a capital city created on a chosen site as the center of government, instead of having the honor of "capital" imposed at some late date on a city whose natural advantages—as a great port, or an intersection of continental highways, or whatever—made it predestined to become the center of things.

In 1787, when the Constitutional Convention had invented a nation and written its constitution, the Continental Congress looked around for a place to call the capital. It was a delicate problem. The North was not inclined to add the costs of construction to the debts it carried from the Revolutionary War, and yet, as the cradle of the Revolution, it was touchy about seeing the government decamp to the South. The South had the money but was quick to resent the suggestion that it should now take on the burdens of a federal city.

Both sides were pacified by an agreement to set aside 100 square miles as a so-called District of Columbia, a neutral zone independent of state influence and one whose costs should be borne by the federal government. (This agreement dictated, down many decades of controversy, the present status of the city as one governed by an elected mayor and city council with a budget controlled by Congress; though the uniqueness of the arrangement might be challenged today by New York City, a chronic bankrupt regularly bailed out by Congress).

The question now was where to locate the neutral zone. The Congress had wandered from Philadelphia to Princeton to Annapolis to Trenton and New York. The final choice was settled, as many political hassles are, by a dinner party. At this one, Thomas Jefferson and liberal helpings of Madeira wine persuaded Alexander Hamilton, in exchange for the support of a bill he was sponsoring, to deliver enough Northern votes to approve a site proposed by President Washington. It was a plot of land, a peninsula formed by the Potomac and Anacostia rivers, to be ceded to the federal government by Maryland and Virginia.

Accordingly, a commission appointed one Major Ellicott to lay out the new city, and he arrived in February, 1791, with his assistant, Benjamin Banneker, a Philadelphia Negro with a high reputation as a surveyor and astronomer. Within a month, however, they were followed by a Frenchman, Pierre Charles L'Enfant, who was directed to "assist" the surveyors. L'Enfant's assistance took the form of obliterating the plans and talents of Ellicott and Banneker and taking over the whole project with a panache that excited the admiration of President Washington.

L'Enfant was an Eighteenth Century architect and military engineer. He at once drew up a plan, lovingly reminiscent of Versailles, of great diagonal avenues crossing a gridiron or rectangular network of long streets. The regular punctuation of "circles" would provide majestic "prospects" or vistas, in three directions. As a point of tactics, they would allow for the placement of cannon. The landowners were at first alarmed by a plan that confiscated more than 3000 of the city's 6000 acres for preposterously wide avenues, anything from 160 to 400 feet wide. But the reassessment of the remaining acres as city lots boosted the value of the original acreage by 1,000 percent. The only other opponents of the plan were men who, having recently shed a monarchy, were shocked on principle by the regal grandeur of L'Enfant's design. But George Washington, in this as in other matters, amply justified Jefferson's persistent criticism of his taste in public show and ceremony as "tending toward monarchy and away from republican simplicity." Washington might privately deplore the arrogance of L'Enfant but he backed his plan and it went forward. (L'Enfant's triumph was swift and short. He over-reached himself when he ordered the largest landowner of the District to tear down a manor house that obstructed a proposed "vista." The man refused to do it, so L'Enfant demolished it himself. He was instantly dismissed from the commission's service and languished into obscurity and a pauper's grave. In all, he had commanded the project for only ten months, but in that time he took hold with such authority and diligence that the master plan was indestructible. In retrospect, it is a blessed thing, for it still gives to Washington whatever it retains of splendor and spaciousness).

It was not originally thought of as a residential city but as a seasonal meeting place for the conduct of the national government. Jefferson called it "that Indian swamp in the wilderness." For most of the year its climate was atrocious. Business would go on through a dank and rheumy winter. The summer was, and still is, one of infernal heat. And in those days, the town was plagued by malaria and yellow fever. So the three branches of government would perform from the fall into the spring and then take off briskly for their home towns and their families. The only permanent residents would be servants, laborers, merchants and the remnants of the thirty Indian tribes still in evidence when Congress set up shop there in 1800. It was conceived, in effect, as a sort of convention city. Consequently, it had a hard time getting itself built, getting lighting and paving and sewers and a water supply and so on. People were loath to put up money to prolong anybody's stay in a mess of shacks on a plain that rose only forty feet above the noxious Potomac. For fifty years or more, the streets were paved exclusively with mud.

For the first half of the Nineteenth Century, L'Enfant's immense avenues were a joke to all visiting Europeans. To get on or off them you had, like the exasperated Harriet Martineau, to hoist your skirts, climb a stile or two and slush through bogs. In the 1840s, Dickens, on his first visit, described Washington as a place "of spacious avenues that begin in nothing and lead nowhere; streets a mile long that want only houses, roads and inhabitants; public buildings that need but a public to be complete." The great turning point in the city's growth came with a war, with the Robber Barons, and with a man.

During the Civil War, Washington, as the base of the Northern armies, swarmed with everybody who had a gun or a favor to sell, a bridge or a shipment of food to contract for, any sort of influence to peddle that claimed to help the Union and might incidentally coin a fortune. During those years, and in the lush days of Reconstruction, with its burgeoning fortunes in steel, railroads, copper, silver and the rest, Washington became the year-round headquarters of the government and an army of civil servants, but also a permanent base for pressure groups, lobbyists and fixers who conceived of a capital as a city dedicated to the proposition that wealth is most successfully manufactured by intimidating the goverment. Some of their heirs are with us still.

If the physical growth of the city can be attributed to one man more than another, that man is Alexander Shepherd, the city's boss during its first fling at "home rule." He gave the city paved streets, workable sewers, a pure water supply, and a gas line. Luckily for all of us, one of his purer drives was a passion for trees, and he went on a rampage of planting sycamores, oaks, lindens and willows. He forever defeated L'Enfant's vistas with avenues of English elms. He made Washington surely one of the leafiest capitals on earth. In the process of all this "development", he bankrupted the city and retired discreetly to a lifetime's exile in Mexico. He had entertained wistful dreams of a great city park, but nothing came of it until Congress, abandoning an appeal to aesthetics, gave out broad hints that a large park within the city confines would greatly increase real estate values. But it took Congress a quarter of a century to acquire as a public "pleasuring ground" 1800 acres of grass and forest and create Rock Creek Park, to which—said Lord Bryce—"there is nothing comparable in any capital city of Europe."

Toward the end of the century, the lust for Athens and Rome consumed the capital's architects, so that today you cannot match in any city of Greece such an imposing stack of porticoes and rows of Ionic columns and saucer domes, and inset-arches, and such sleek piles of white stone cement. This collection of Greek and Roman wedding cakes provided harmless fun for two generations of foreign diplomats, until the increasing tattiness of their home capitals made them wonder whether, after all, the classical orders of architecture were not as graceful a background to living as any.

In this century, as the United States has developed its industrial muscle and so its international power, the capital city inevitably attracted the appurtenances of power and prestige: one of the world's great libraries, several universities, medical research centers, an army of lawyers, lobbyists of every economic interest, a national newspaper, television and radio stations, three great art galleries. Only recently has it abdicated its status as a provincial backwater of the performing arts: the Kennedy Center solicits the performance of first-rate orchestras and occasionally challenges New Haven, Conn. and Boston as the place to try out plays intended for Broadway. Under the reign of Jimmy Carter, the White House has broken two centuries of Presidential abstinence by actually inviting instrumentalists and dancers of international rank to give private performances for the pleasure of the President and his guests.

And, of course, the city has—since Franklin Roosevelt's headlong creation of "alphabet agencies"—spawned a huge and proliferating bureaucracy of government employees. Nowhere else in the United States do so many people (including half a million civilian and military employees of the government, one-third of the city's work force) hold more or less permanent jobs, with the result that the city has racked up the highest average of family spendable income—$22,000—in the nation. Washington, in a word, is the phenomenon of a capital city, preponderantly black, with the largest population of government workers and the highest average annual income of any capital city in the world.

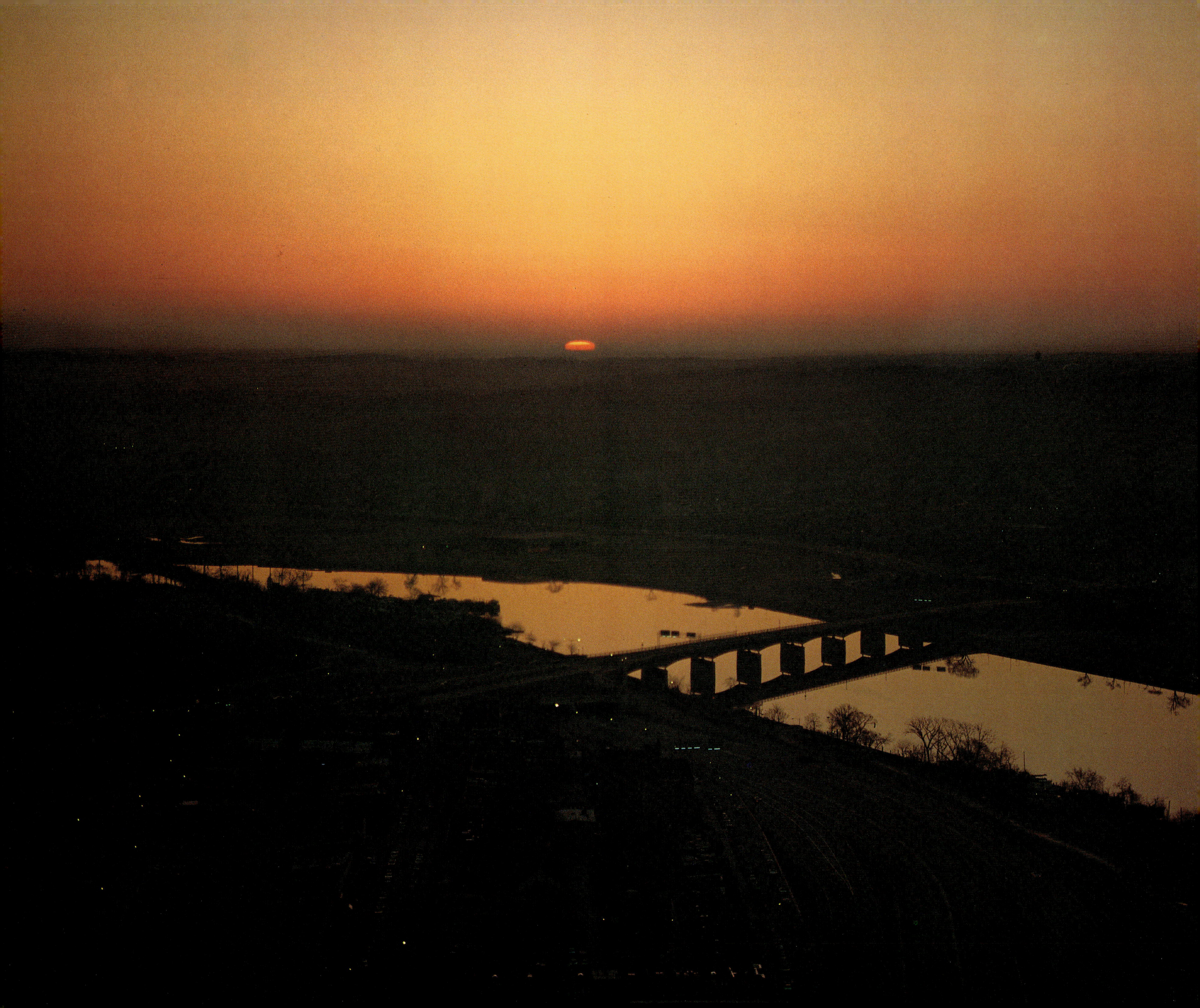

THE FEDERAL CITY

Sousa Bridge at dawn above the Anacostia River.

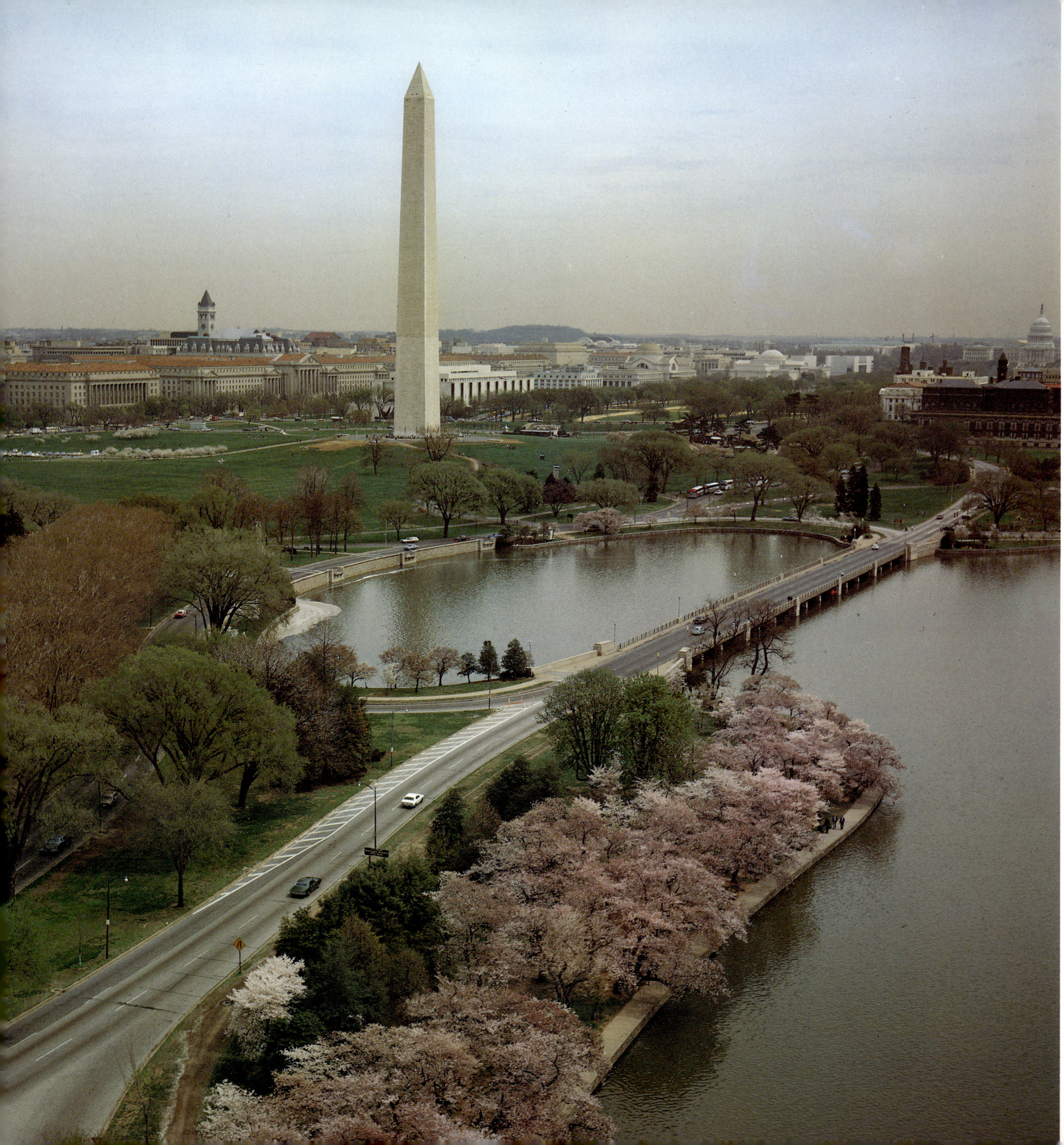

Two sharp verticals are framed and related here to the low-scale aspect of Washington, with distant domes, and the edge of water integral to so much of the city's beauty. The Washington Monument and, in the distance, the tower of the old Post Office Building cut the sky. The cherry trees, the gift of Japan, are beside the Tidal Basin. The prominent domes are those of the Museum of Natural History and, beyond it, the National Gallery of Art. The "water mark" on the Washington Monument indicates the hiatus in construction from 1855 until 1880.

When we approach by air we are often bewildered by large cities. They seem anonymous. We know that when we land we will return to commonplaces. We will be taken to an address we give the cab driver. But where are we? What we see as we near National Airport makes us think we know where we are, or that we ought to.

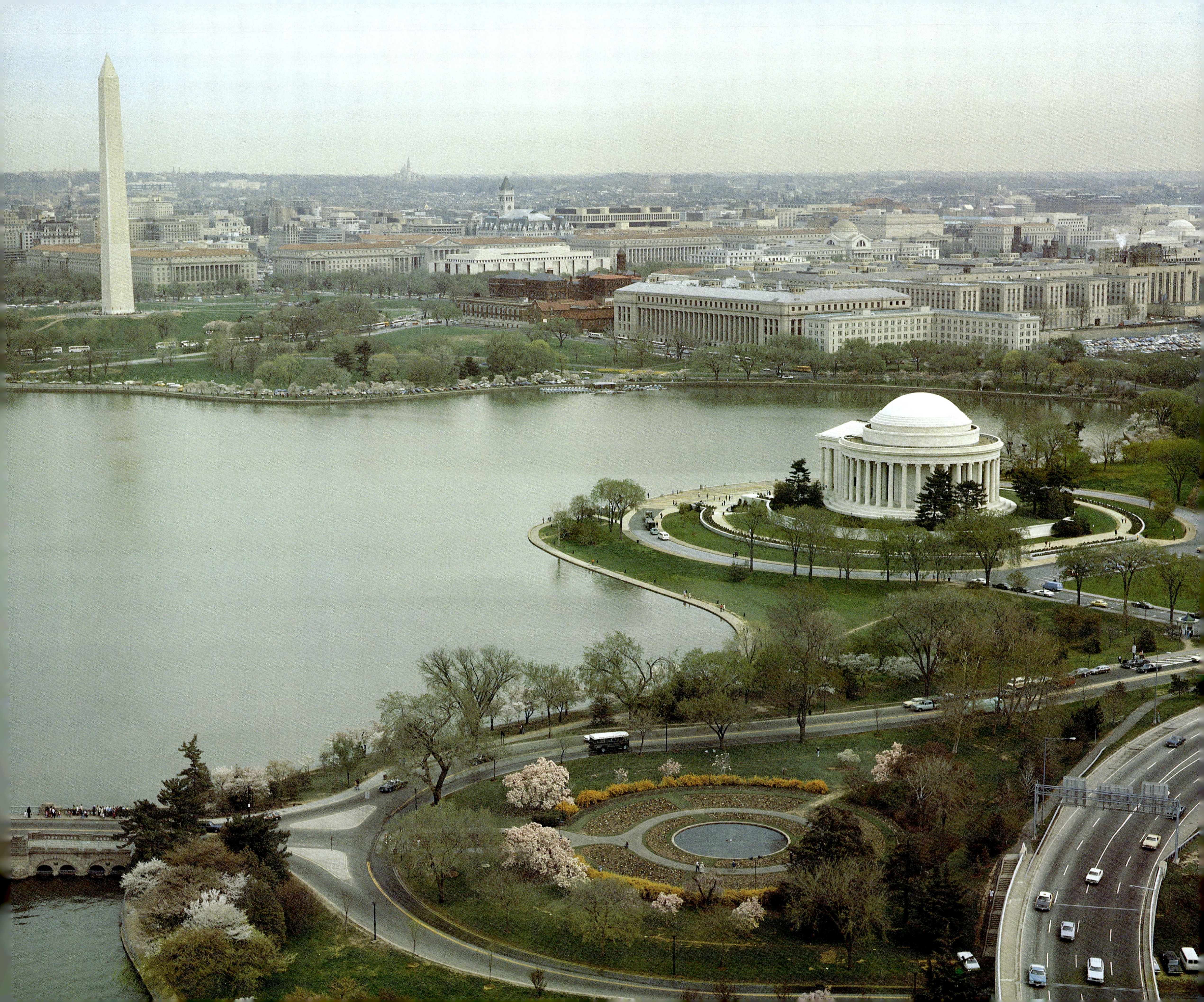

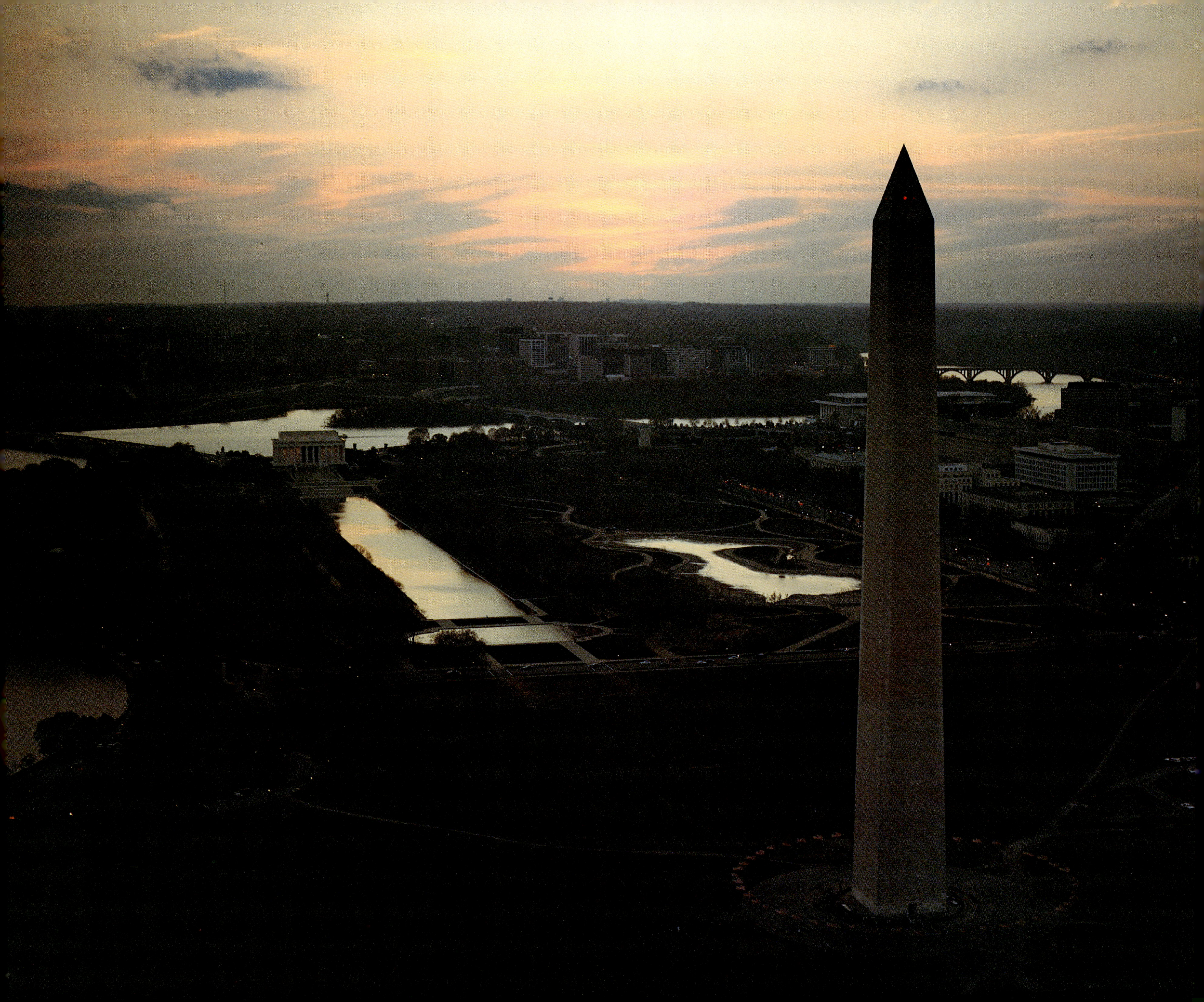

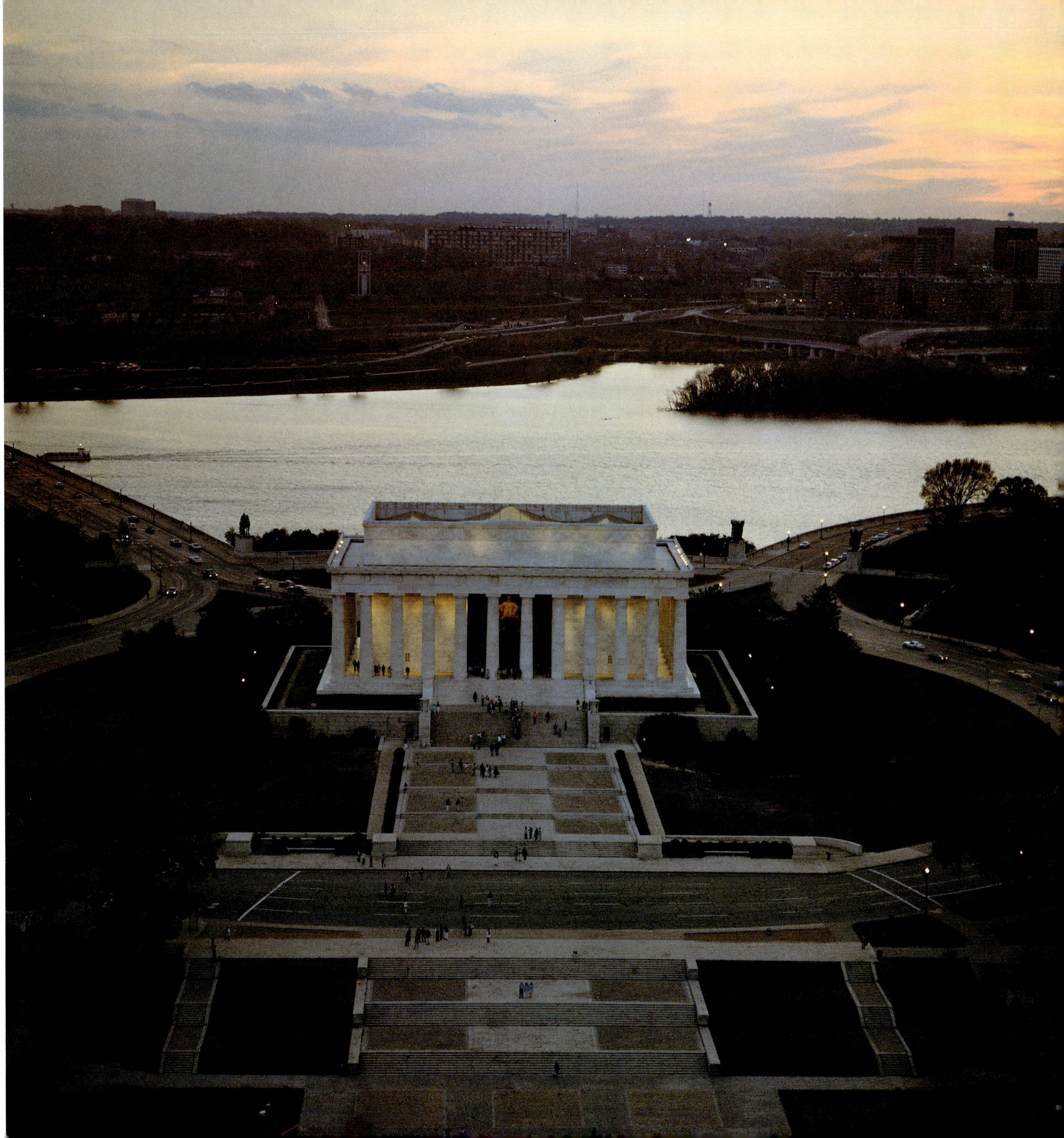

The lights of Northern Virginia sparkle beyond the Potomac. The Francis Scott Key Bridge is above right. The Memorial Bridge is far left. The Lincoln Memorial and the reflecting pool answer to the plan of the McMillan Commission of 1901 which sought to revive essentials of the great design of L'Enfant.

The exterior of the Lincoln Memorial is Colorado marble. The interior floor is pink Tennessee marble. The walls are Indiana limestone. The statue within, by Daniel Chester French, is carved from crystalline Georgia marble. The Union's soils are met, "to bind up the nation's wounds" and "care for him who shall have borne the battle."

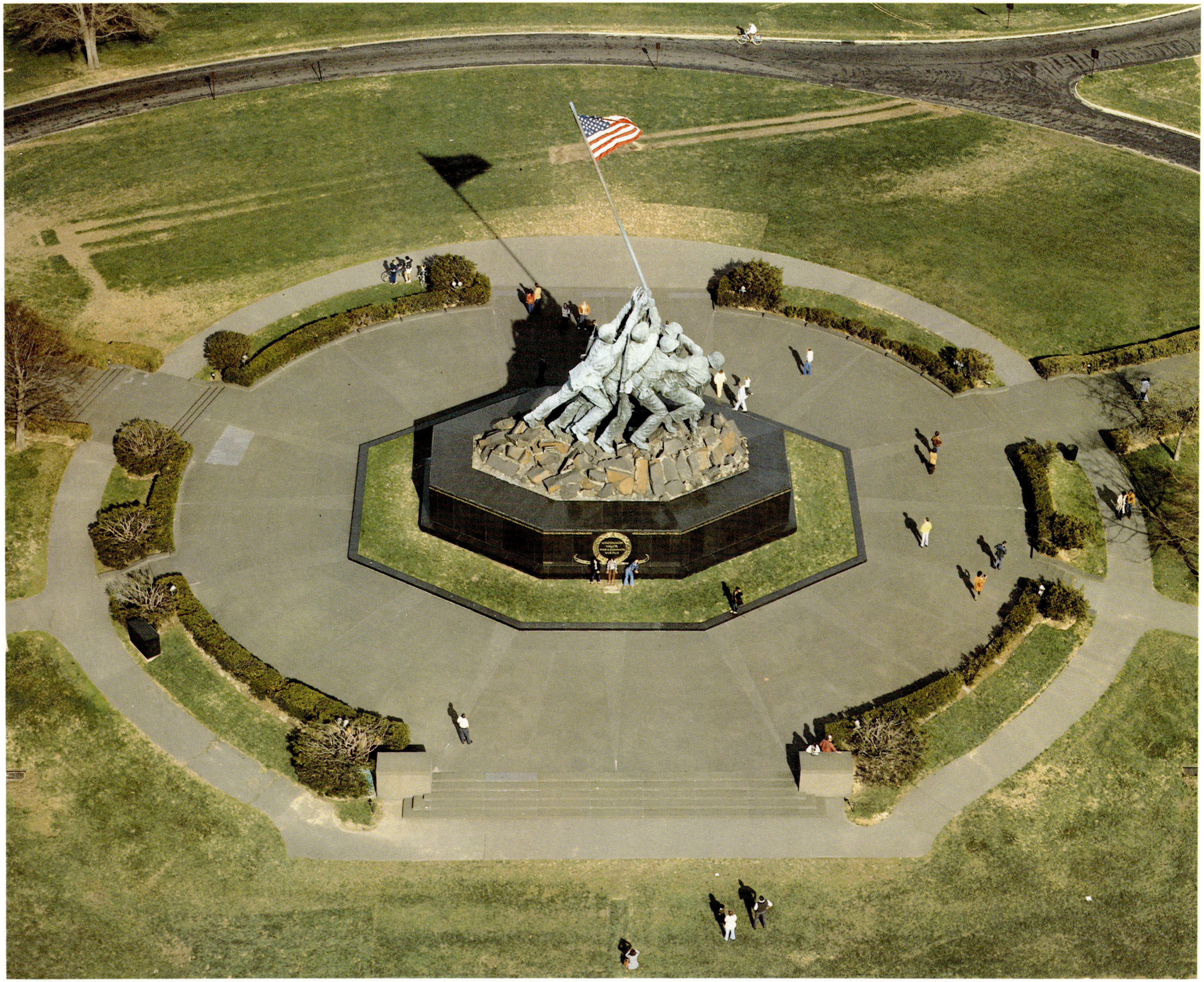

Completed in 1954 by sculptor Felix W. de Weldon, the Marine Corps Memorial is also known as the Iwo Jima Memorial. The design is literally derived from a Pulitzer prizewinning photo by AP photographer Joe Rosenthal of a group of Marines erecting the U.S. flag on Iwo Jima Island in 1945.

Normally hidden from ground-level view by the lush tree cover of Roosevelt Island, the sculpture by Paul Manship dates from 1967. The island is now a wildlife refuge with nature trails and abundant birds. Formerly Mason's Island, it was the home of John Mason ca. 1790-1834. Last remains of the farmhouse and old structures here were removed in 1937 to make way for this nature-oriented use and the memorial to Theodore Roosevelt.

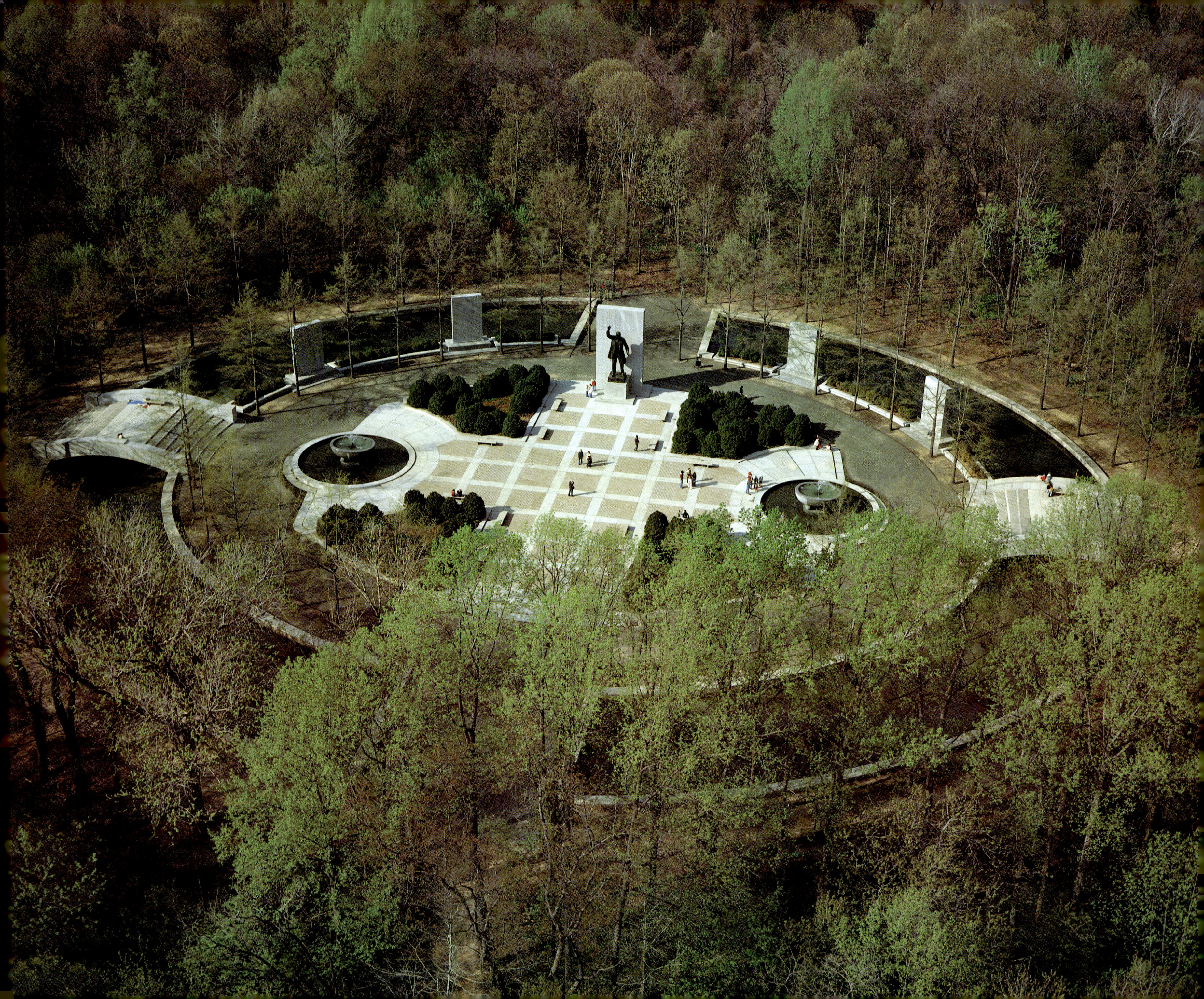

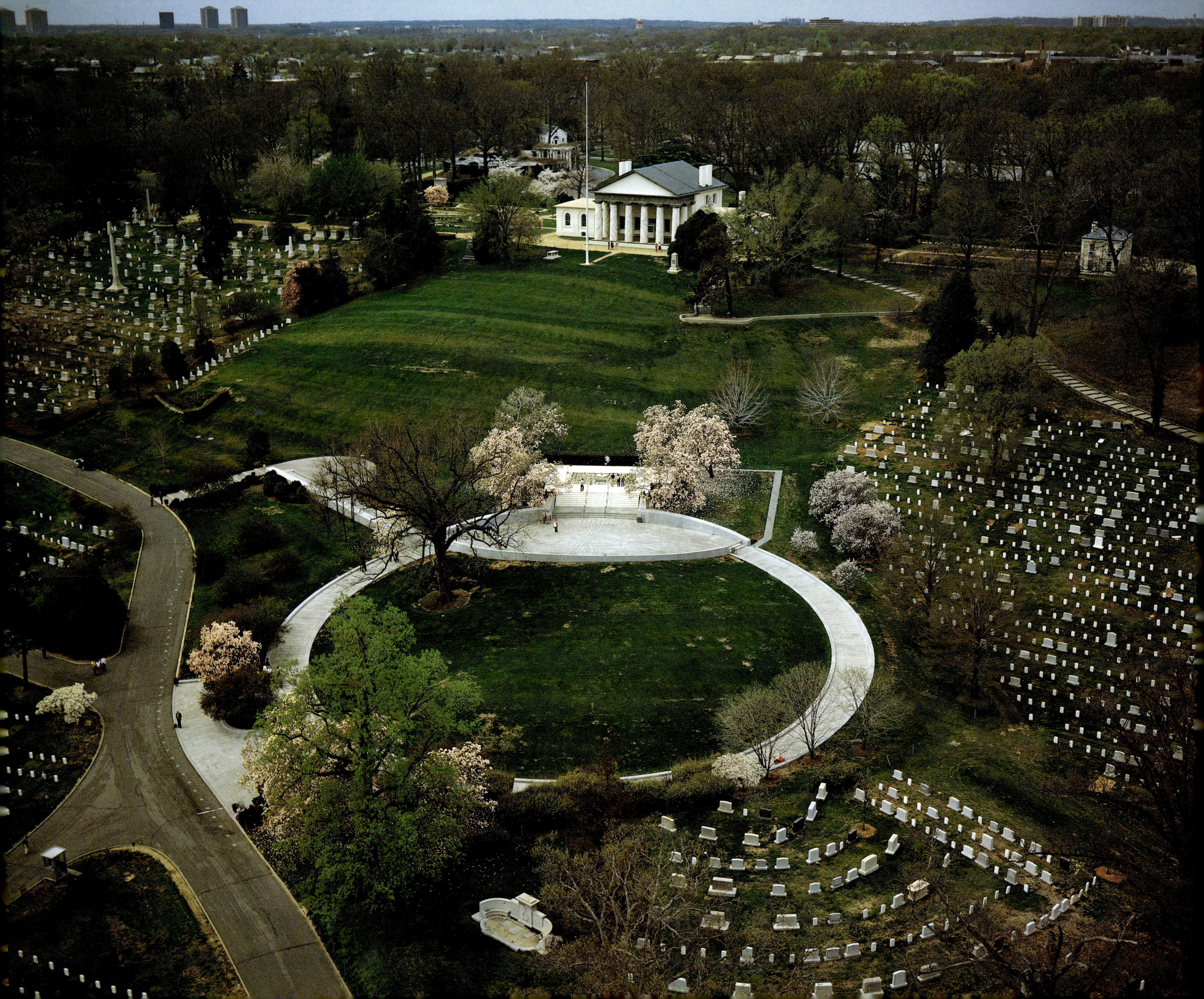

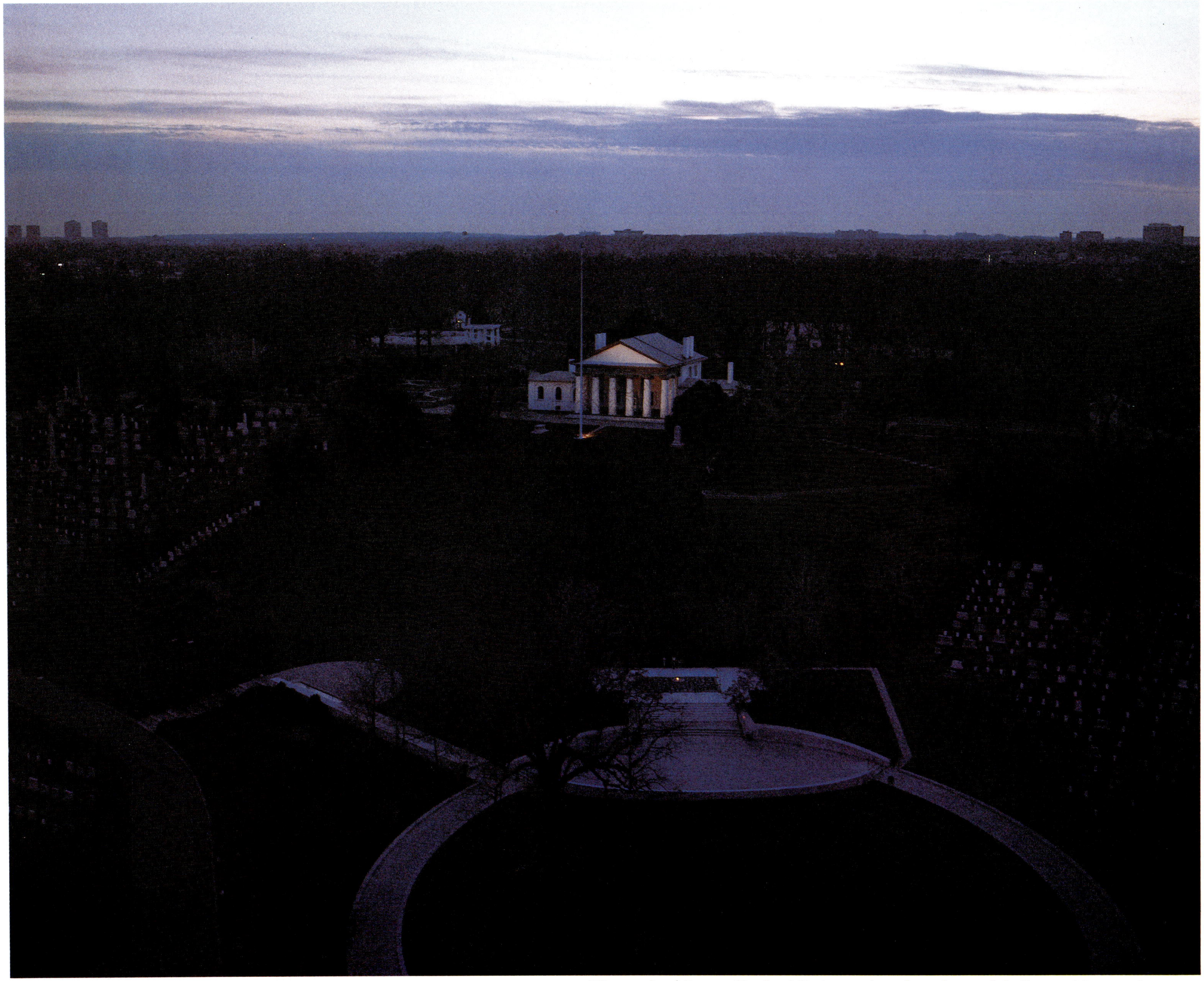

The Greek revival Custis-Lee mansion in Arlington Cemetery was built by a grandson of Martha Washington. It was later the home of Robert E. Lee who married the only child of the house, Mary Ann Randolph Custis. In his bedroom here Lee wrote to resign his commission as Colonel of the First United States Calvary Regiment. From here he rode, in civilian clothes, to offer himself to Virginia. Union soldiers, soon after, were buried in these grounds.

The tomb of Pierre Charles L'Enfant is directly in front of the house. His grand conception in 1790 is now a realized plan, in part, of the nation's capital so spectacularly viewed from this site. Below us in the foreground of the picture is the tomb of John Fitzgerald Kennedy and the eternal flame. Nearby a simple white cross marks the burial place of Robert F. Kennedy.

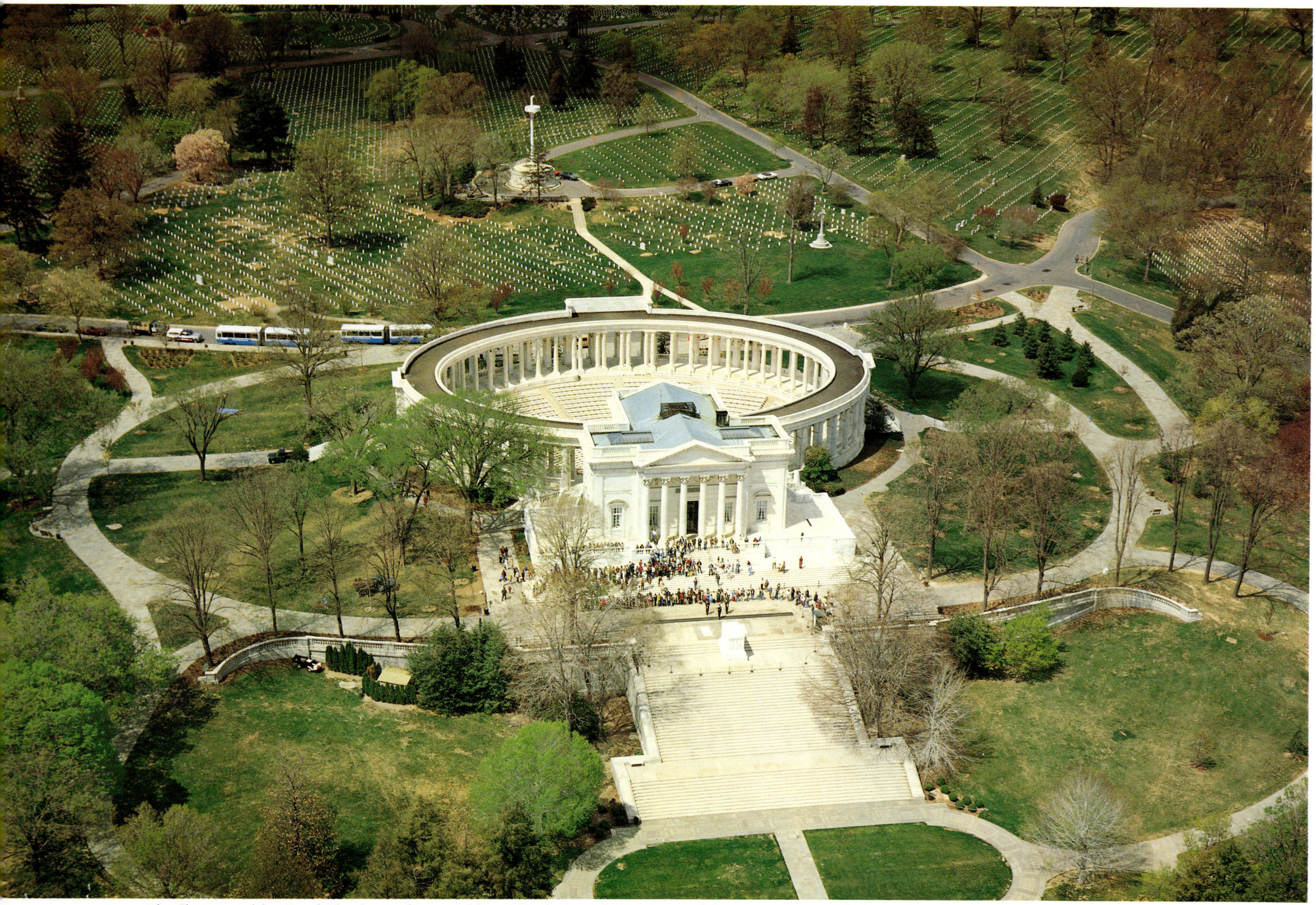

The Changing of the Guard. The three unknown soldiers entombed in Arlington National Cemetery are never left alone. A sentinel from the Old Guard, the United States Third Infantry, paces before the graves, relieved by day every hour on the hour, by night in tours of two hours. The inscription on the tomb reads: "Here rests in honored glory an American soldier known but to God." Although there are no "unknown" dead from Vietnam a reference to those deceased in this conflict will eventually join them memorially to those of World War I, World War II and Korea.

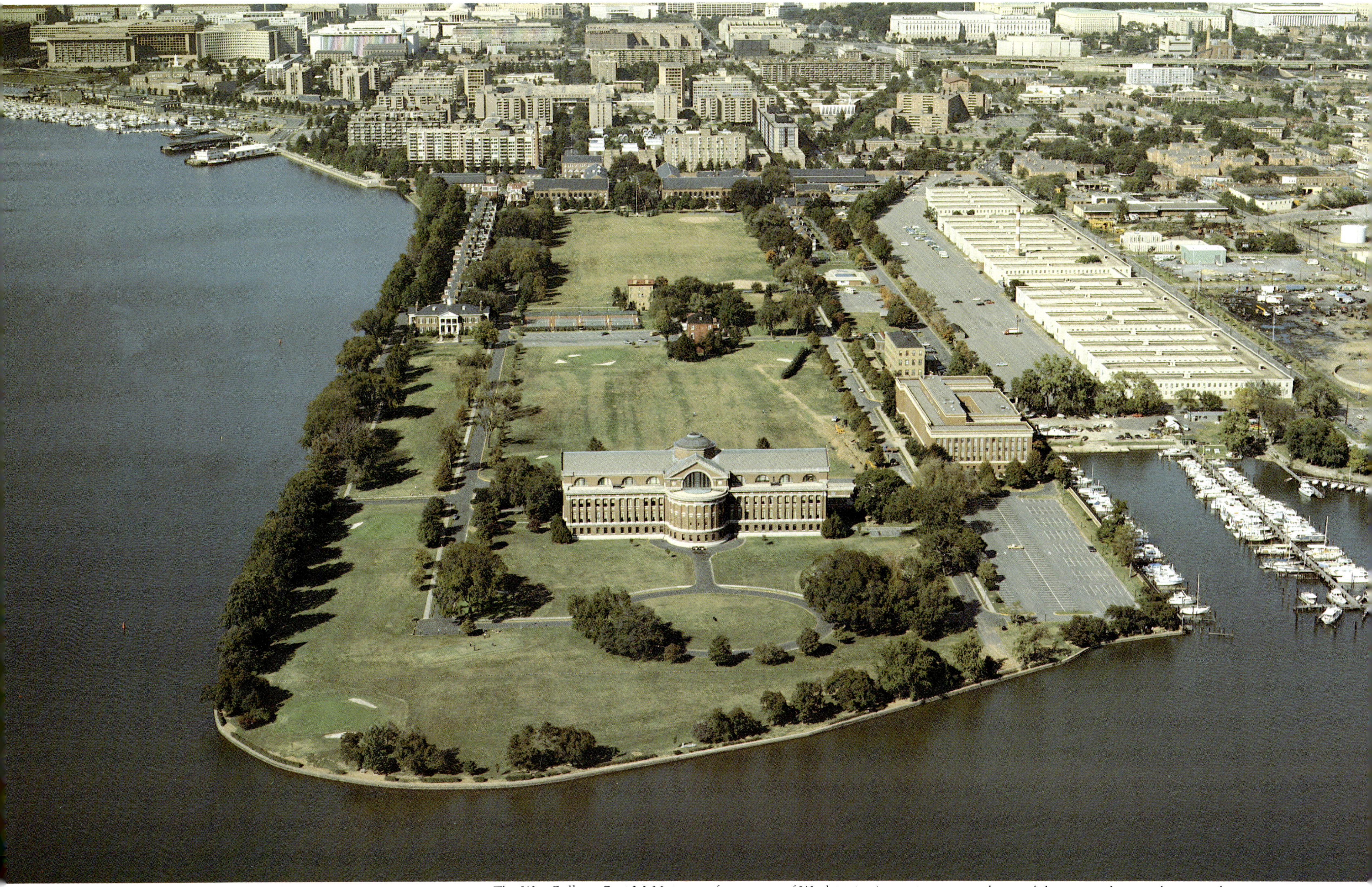

The War College-Fort McNair area forms one of Washington's most serene and peaceful aspects, despite the martial implications of its name. The buildings and the greensward are at Greenleaf Point, the confluence of the Potomac and the Anacostia. Only Great Britian's military library is larger than the collection here, which goes back to Philadelphia and the Continental Congress. Perpetrators of Lincoln's assasination were imprisoned and hanged in the small red brick building at center.

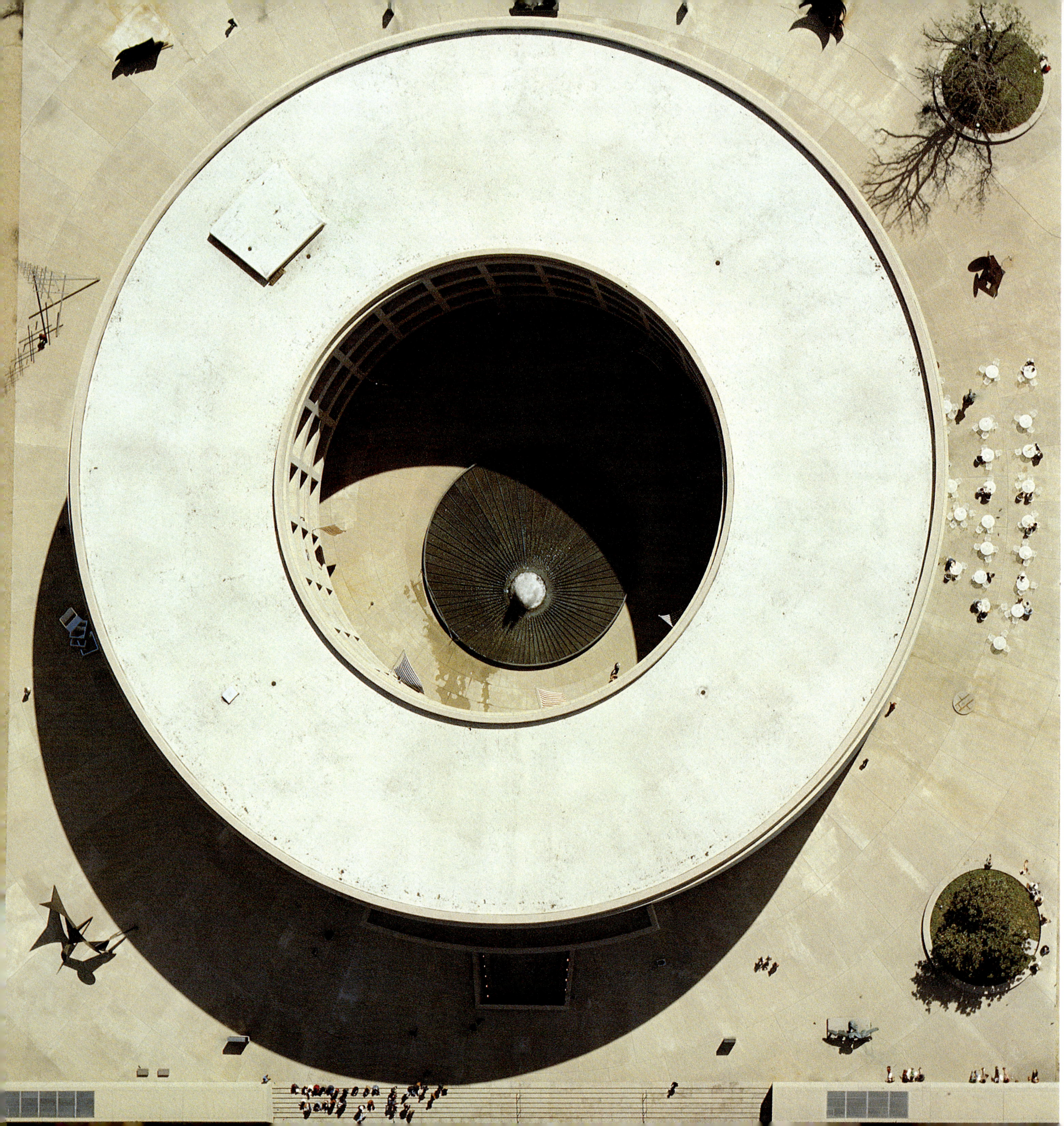

The Hirshhorn Museum celebrates painting and sculpture of the last 125 years, with works by Rodin, Picasso, Magritte as well as modern pop art. It was designed by Gordon Bunshaft. The lack of windows outside means more wall space inside for paintings and their protection from sunlight. An absolute circular design might have been tense. These circles are slightly asymmetrical.

The Jefferson Memorial rests on steel cylinders filled with concrete 82 by 132 feet deep driven to bedrock and countersunk in this site of reclaimed landfill. The portico looks to the Washington Monument and the White House due north. The broad steps and terraces lead down to the Tidal Basin.

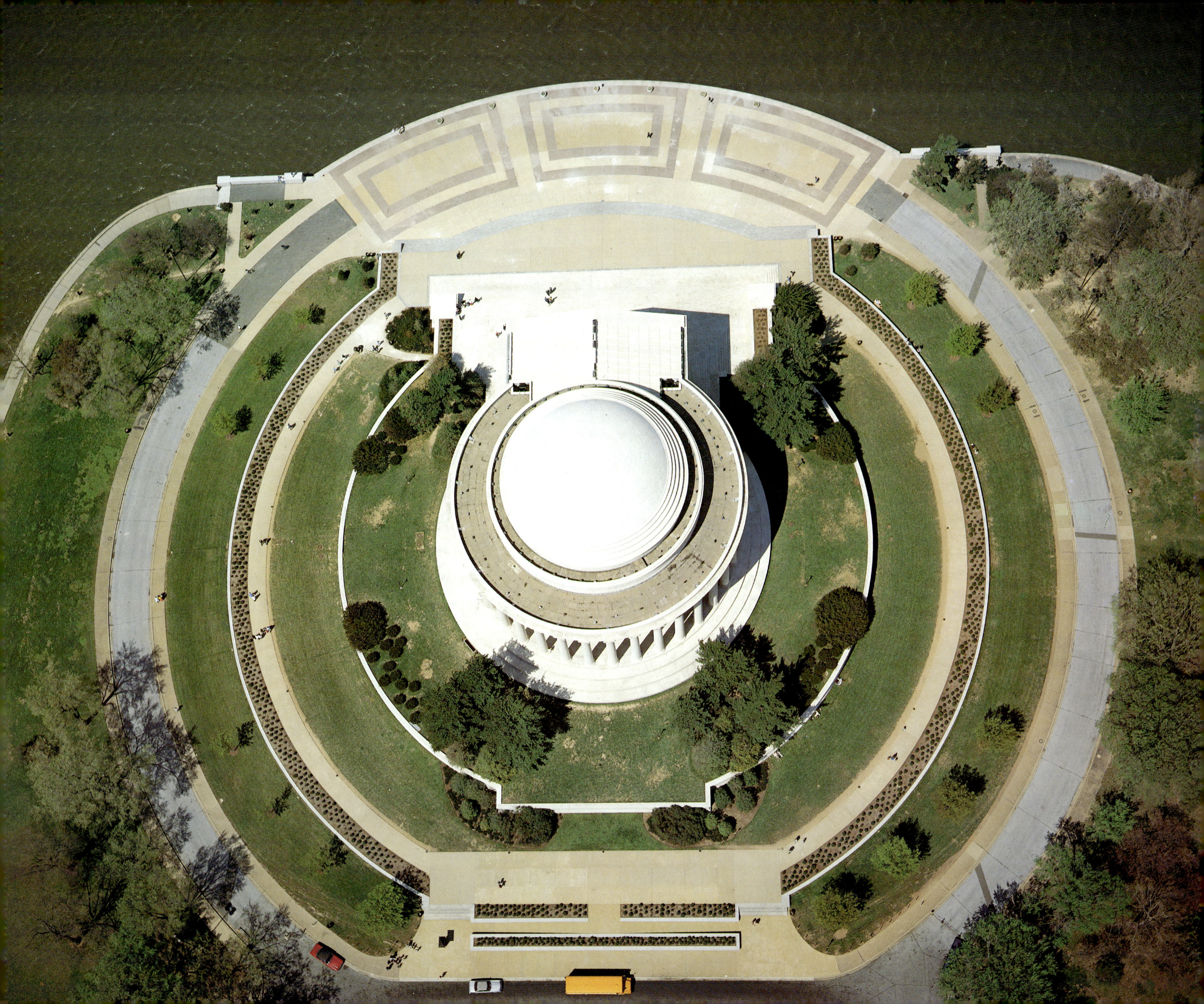

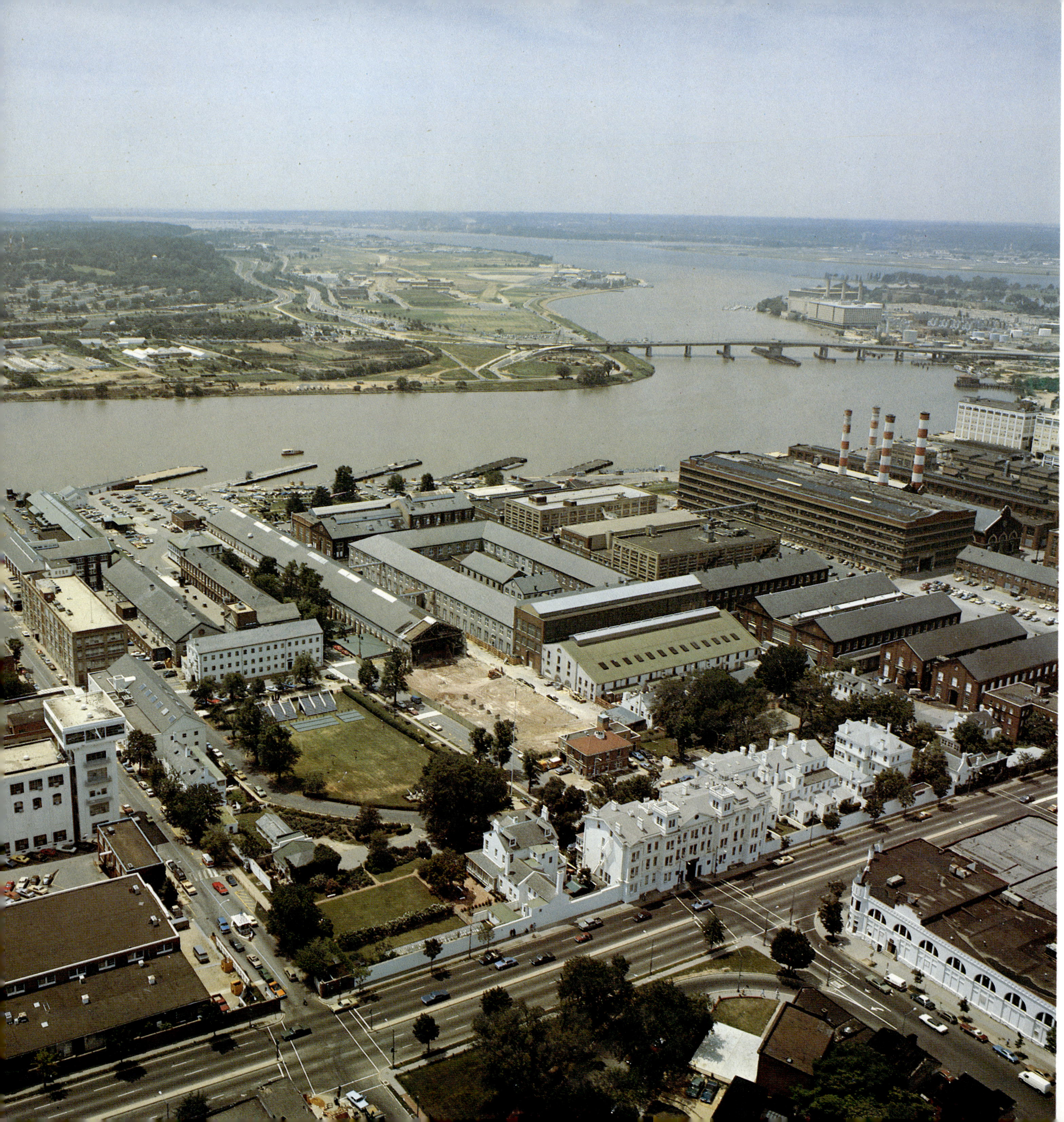

The Navy Yard structures are an evolution from the Tingey House of 1801 in rows of workshops, and then the utilitarian styles of the present. The Yard specializes in the production and testing of naval ordnance. It has its own steel and brass foundries. At the water's edge is the outdoors Weapons Museum, seen in detail on the following page.

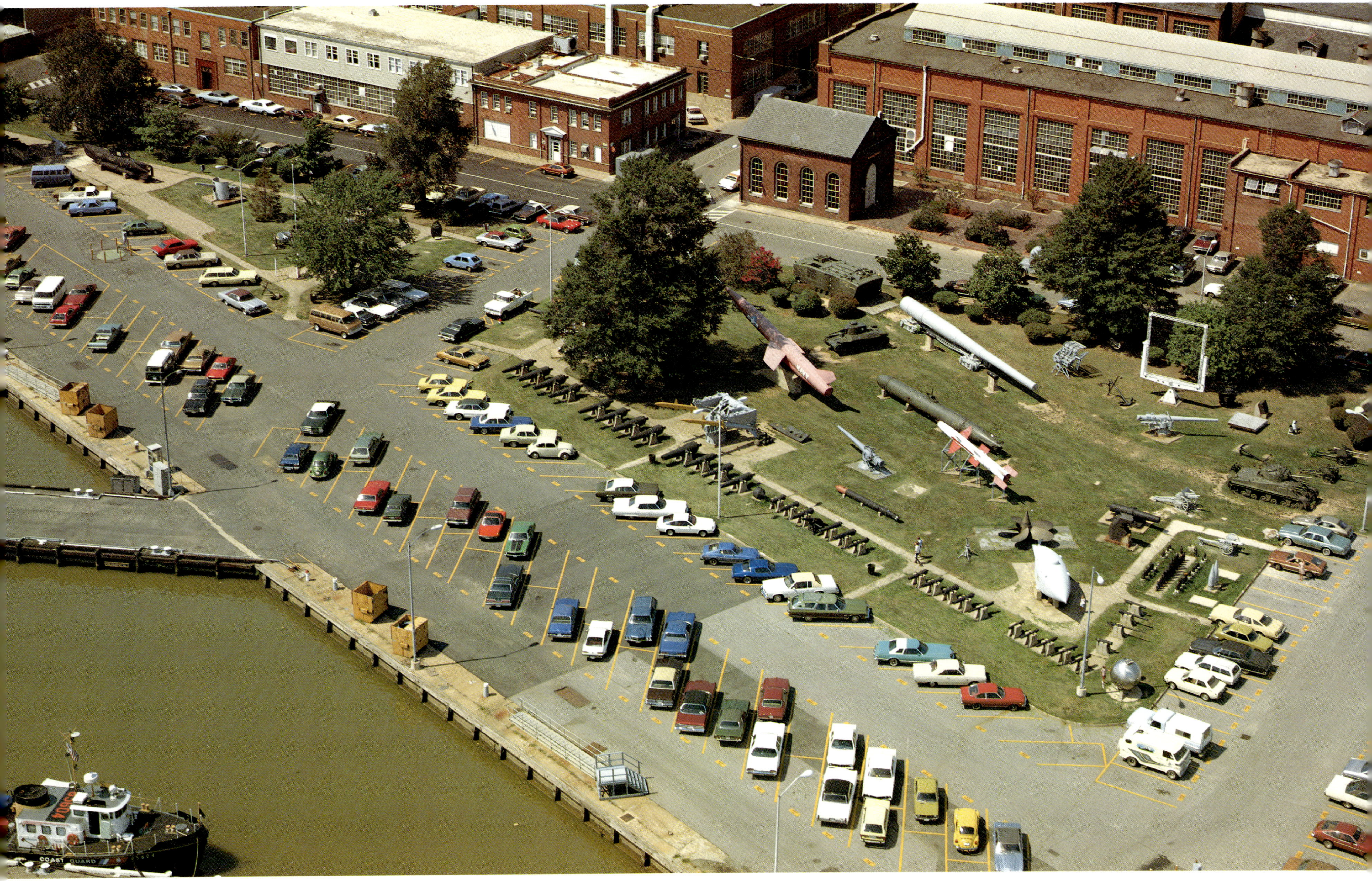
COAST GUARD

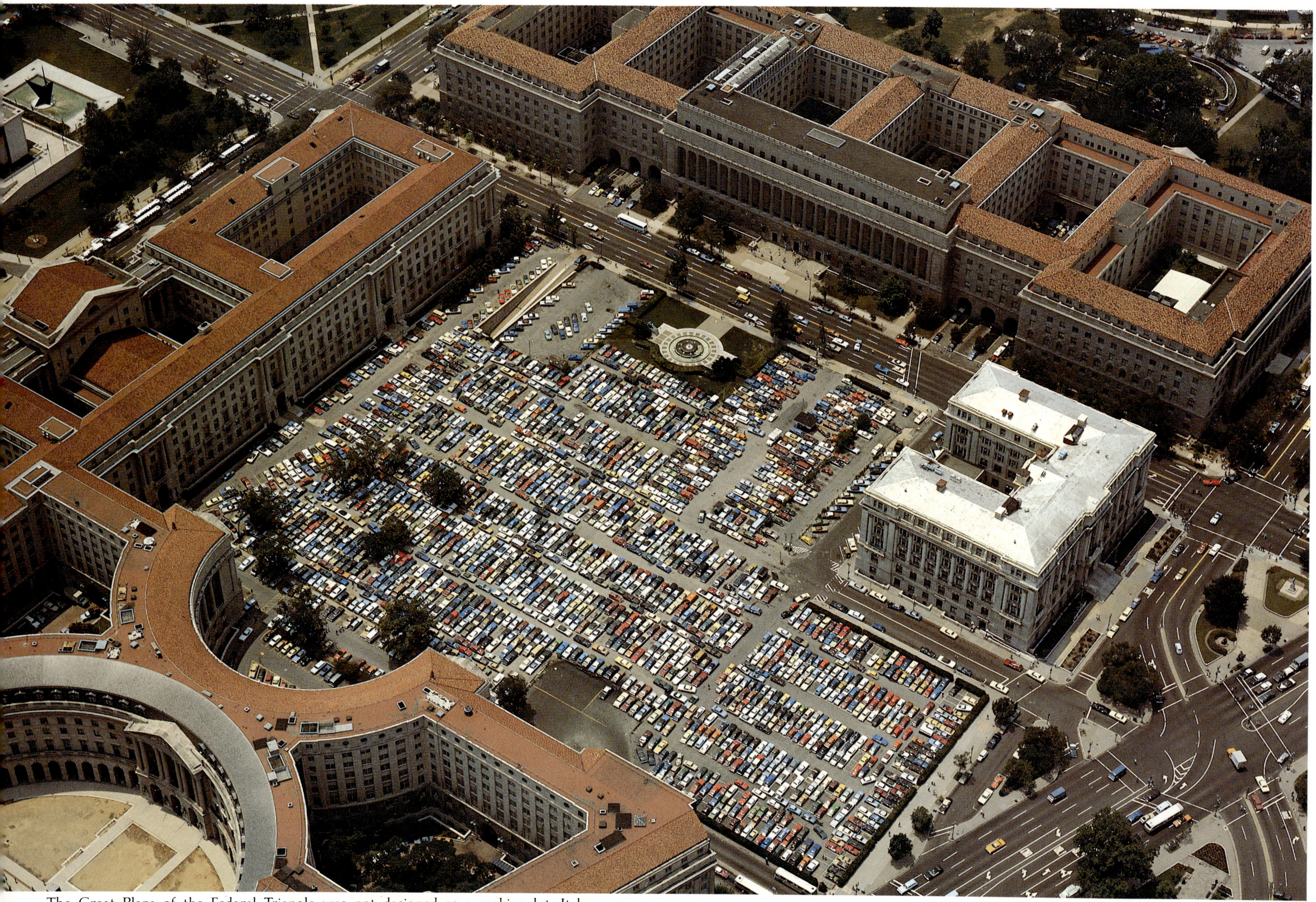

The Great Plaza of the Federal Triangle was not designed as a parking lot. It became one, instead of a great park or plaza, because a parking lot was needed. All the approvals for making it what it was meant to be were established long ago, except the one for funds from Congress. It epitomizes the confrontation of prerequisites and planning, more and more relieved in Washington by the Metro, and underground access and parking.

At Judiciary Square the Pension Building, once called "Meigs' Old Red Barn," is at lower left. It may soon be known as the "Building Building" to house a National Museum of the Building Arts. Like the new HEW Building, across the Mall, the Labor Department Building at center is constructed around 90 foot vertical stacks venting Freeway I-95 which is seen going underground beneath it at far left center. The original Hadfield Old City Hall is at right center.

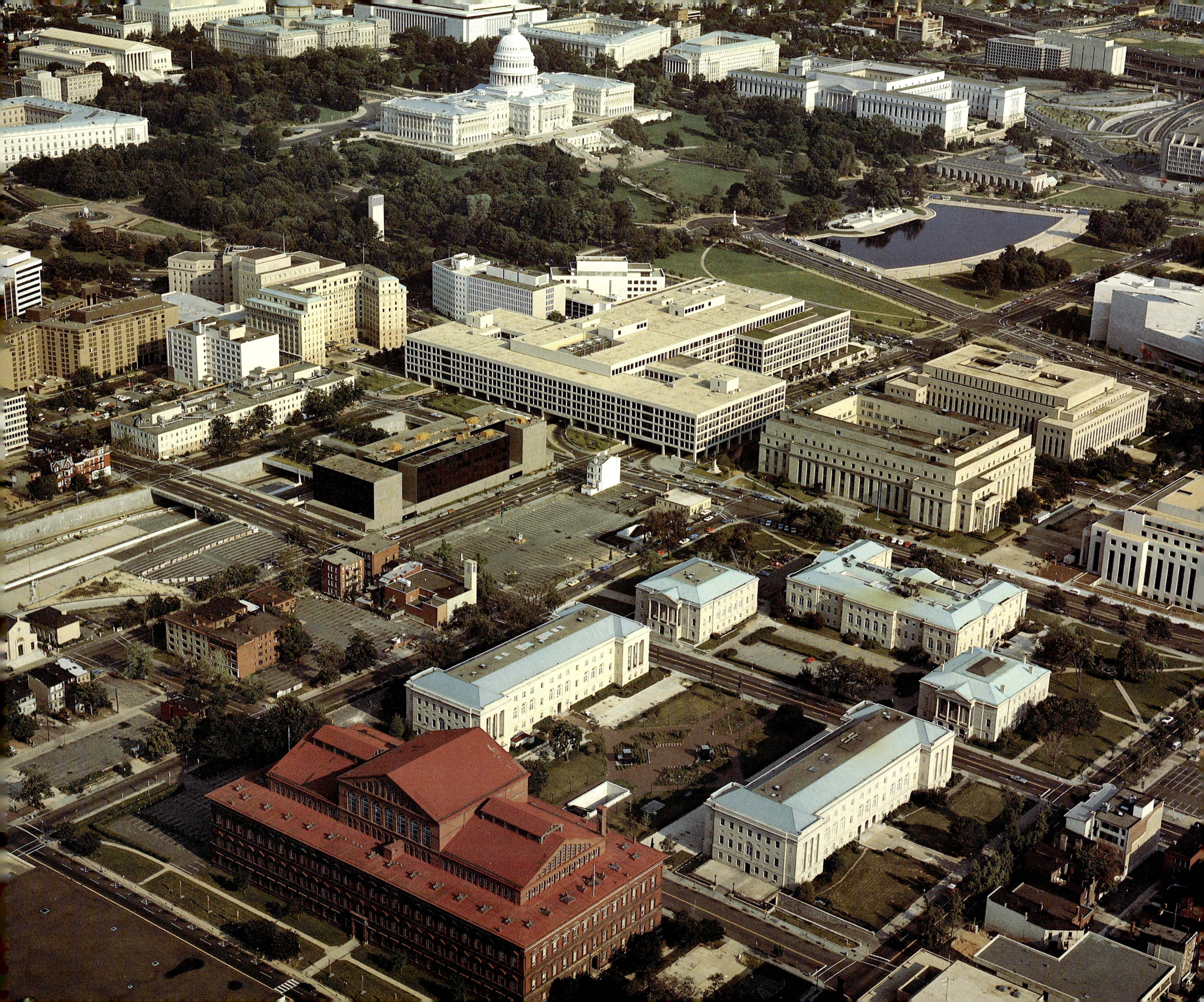

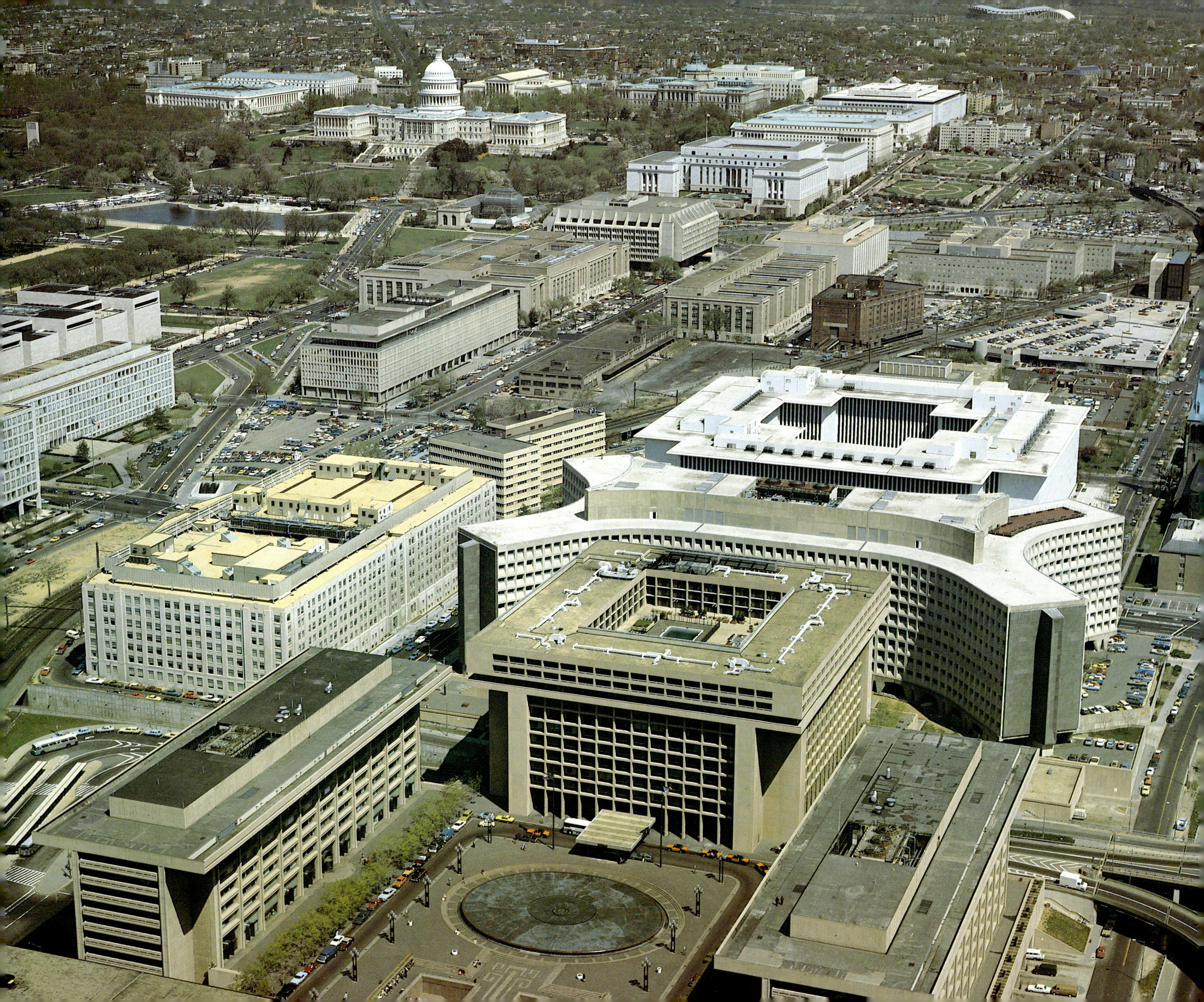

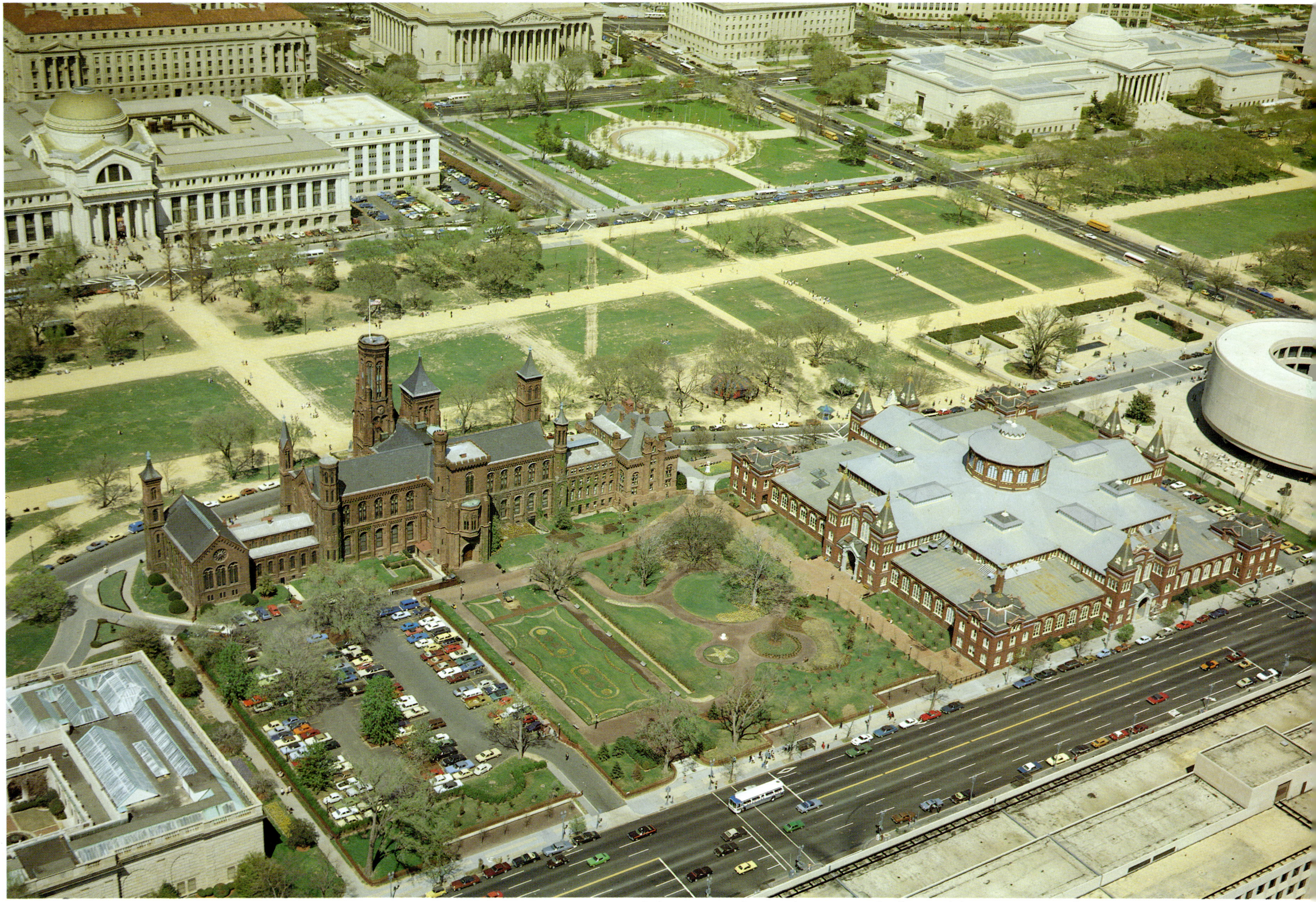

At L'Enfant Plaza the L'Enfant Plaza Hotel is in front of the double-Y Housing and Urban Development Building, beyond which is the privately owned building occupied by the Department of Transportaion. The L'Enfant Plaza complex is the high point of the southwest urban renewal project. At upper right center is the new HEW building, just west of the Rayburn House offices.

In left center is the Smithsonian castle designed by James Renwick. It was completed in 1849, perhaps America's oldest and finest Gothic revival building. Its gorgeous color is from local Seneca red sandstone. The Arts and Industries Building is at right foreground. The sculpture garden of the Hirshhorn Museum, extreme right, is set below mall level to avoid disruption of the greensward. Just below us is the Forrestal Building home of the Department of Energy.

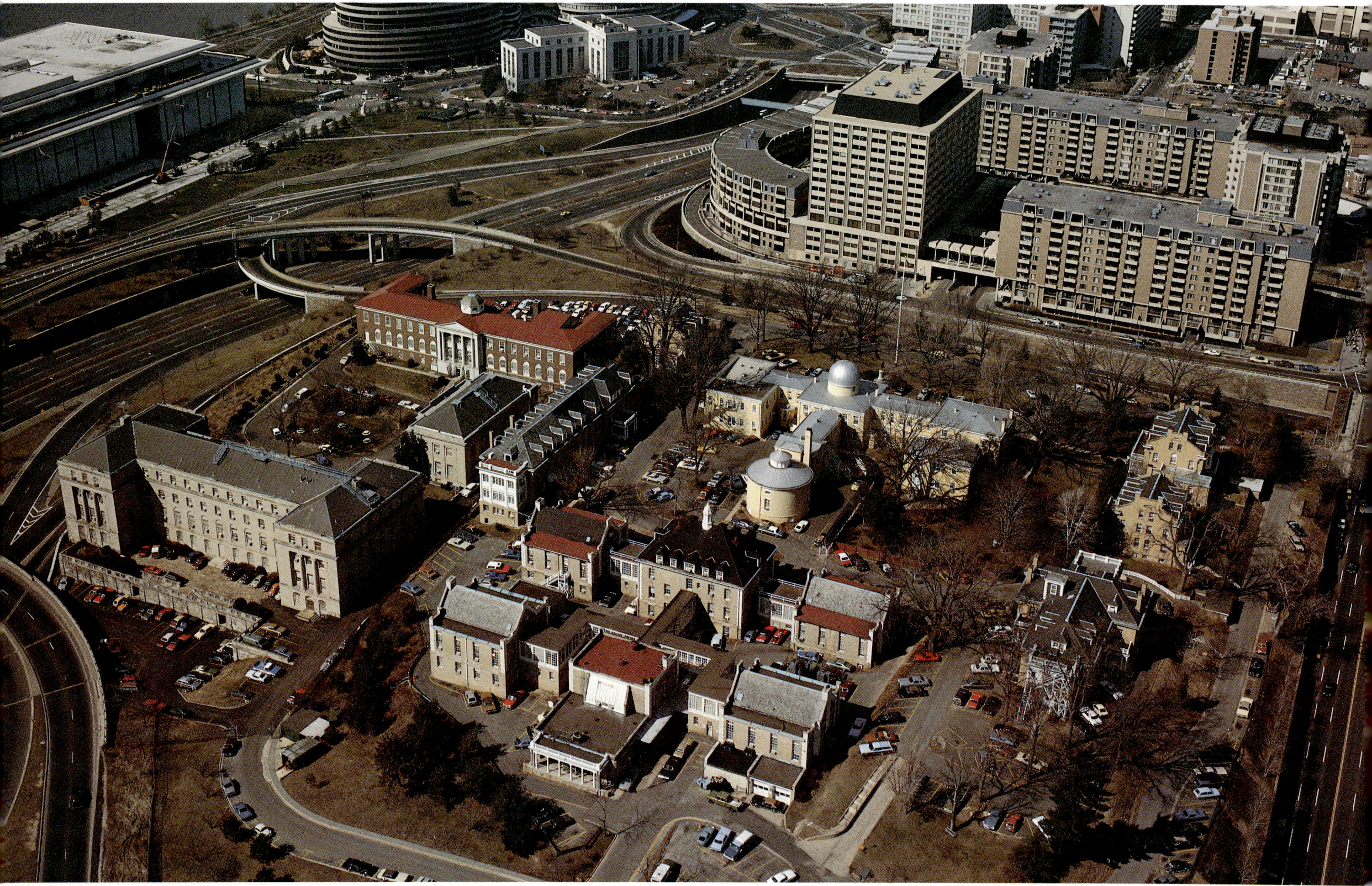

Prior to 1893 the Naval Observatory was at this site. It had taken rank with the Greenwich Observatory in England, and the Russian Observatory in Pulkova, growing out of a naval depot for charts and instruments. The setting is now the Naval Bureau of Medicine and Surgery.

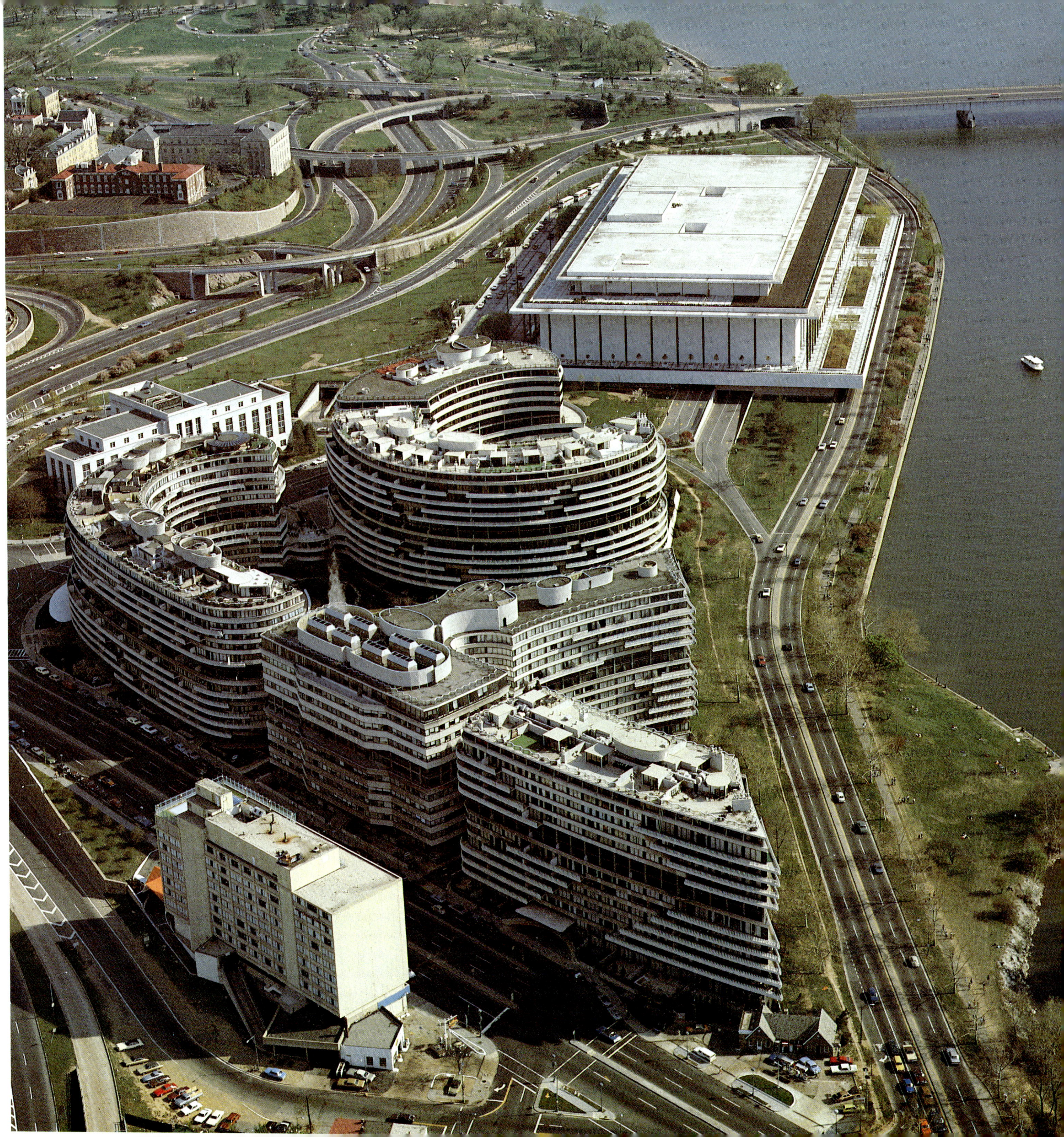

The Watergate complex is made up of cooperative apartments, offices, retail spaces, restaurants and, of course, the hotel which was the scene of the break-in by CREEP, triggering a tragic national scandal. Beyond is the Kennedy Center for the Performing Arts, famous for its facilities for opera, theater and concert. And for the views of the Potomac, from its roofs and terraces.

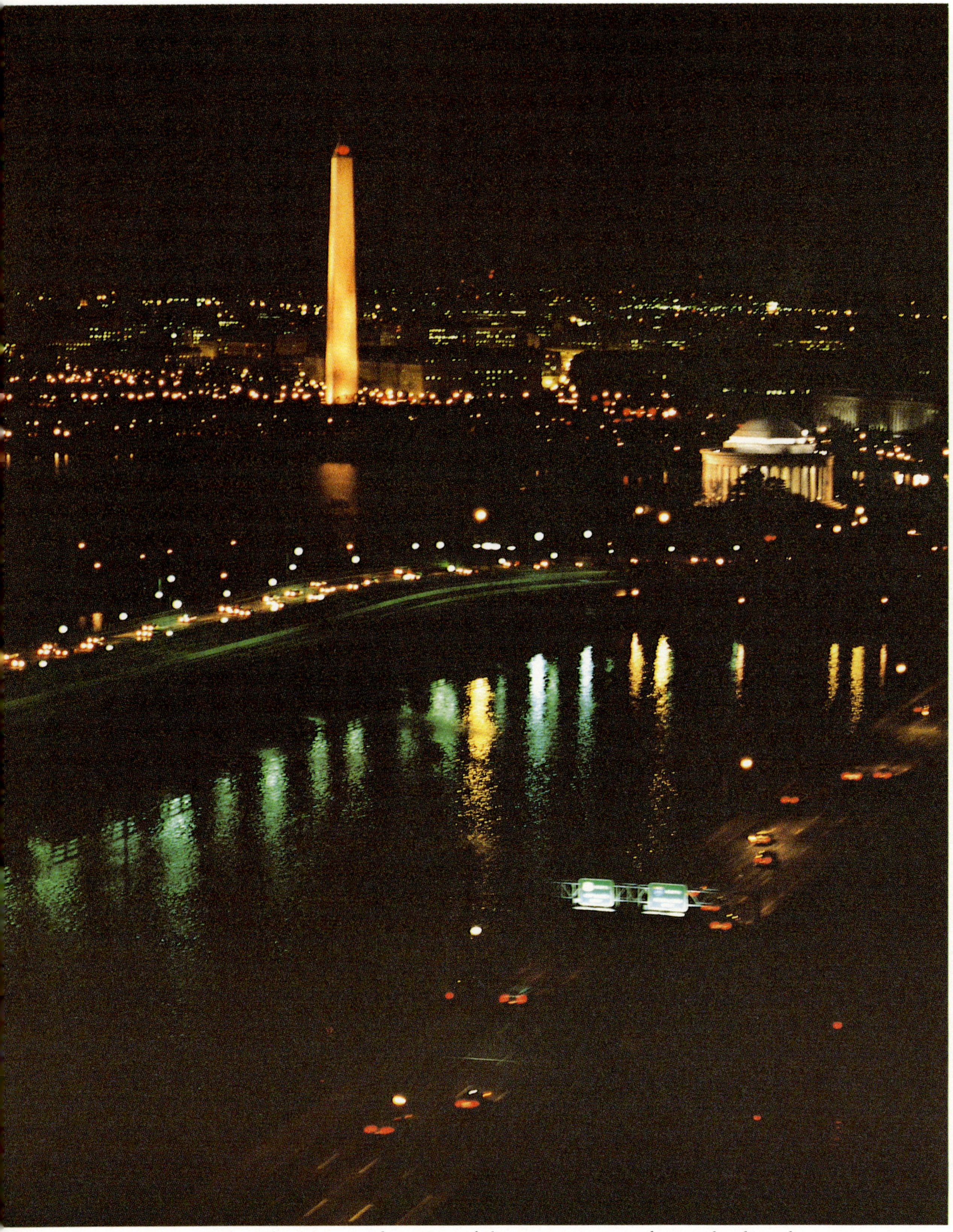

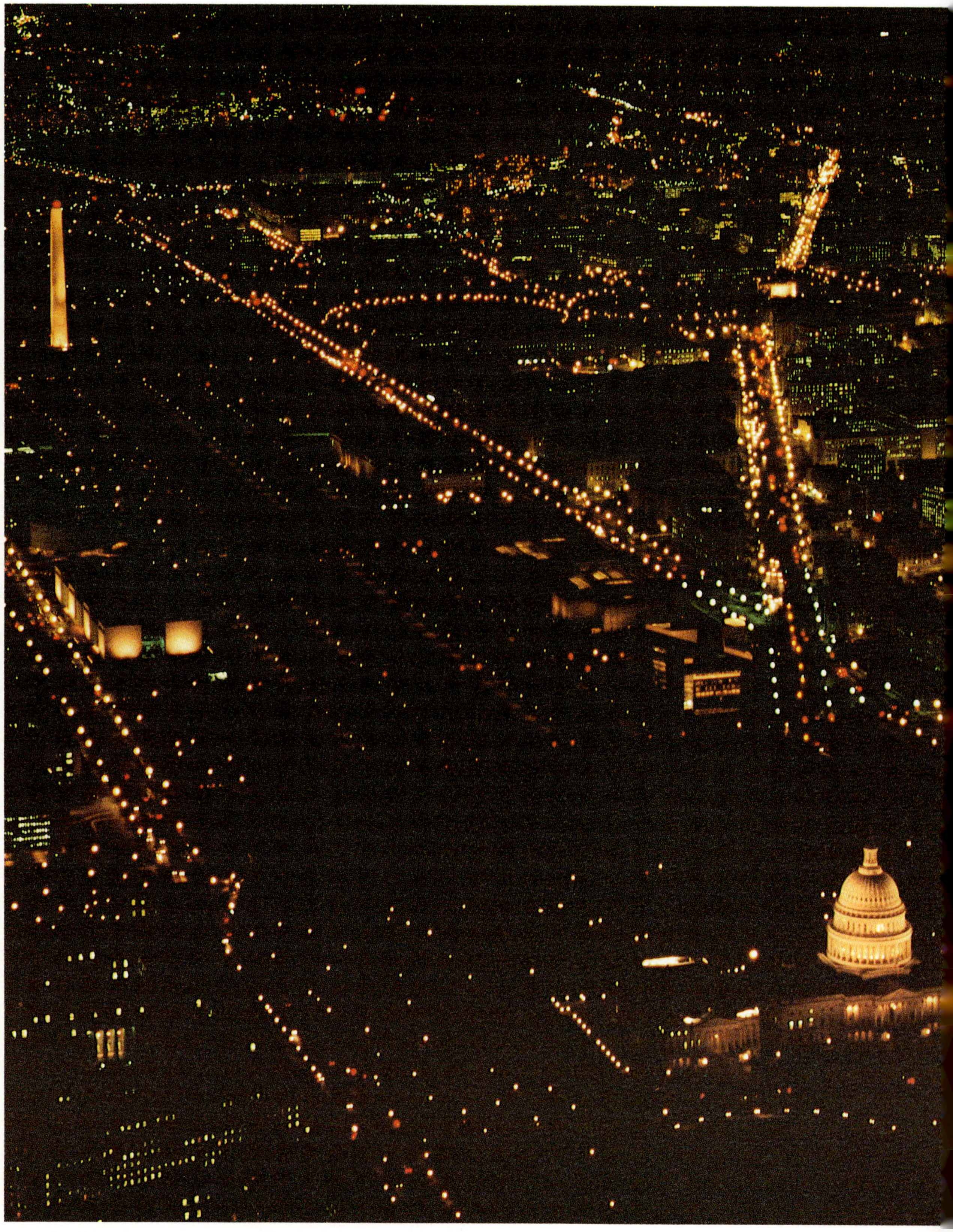

Two night time aerial aspects of the nation's most obvious land mark.

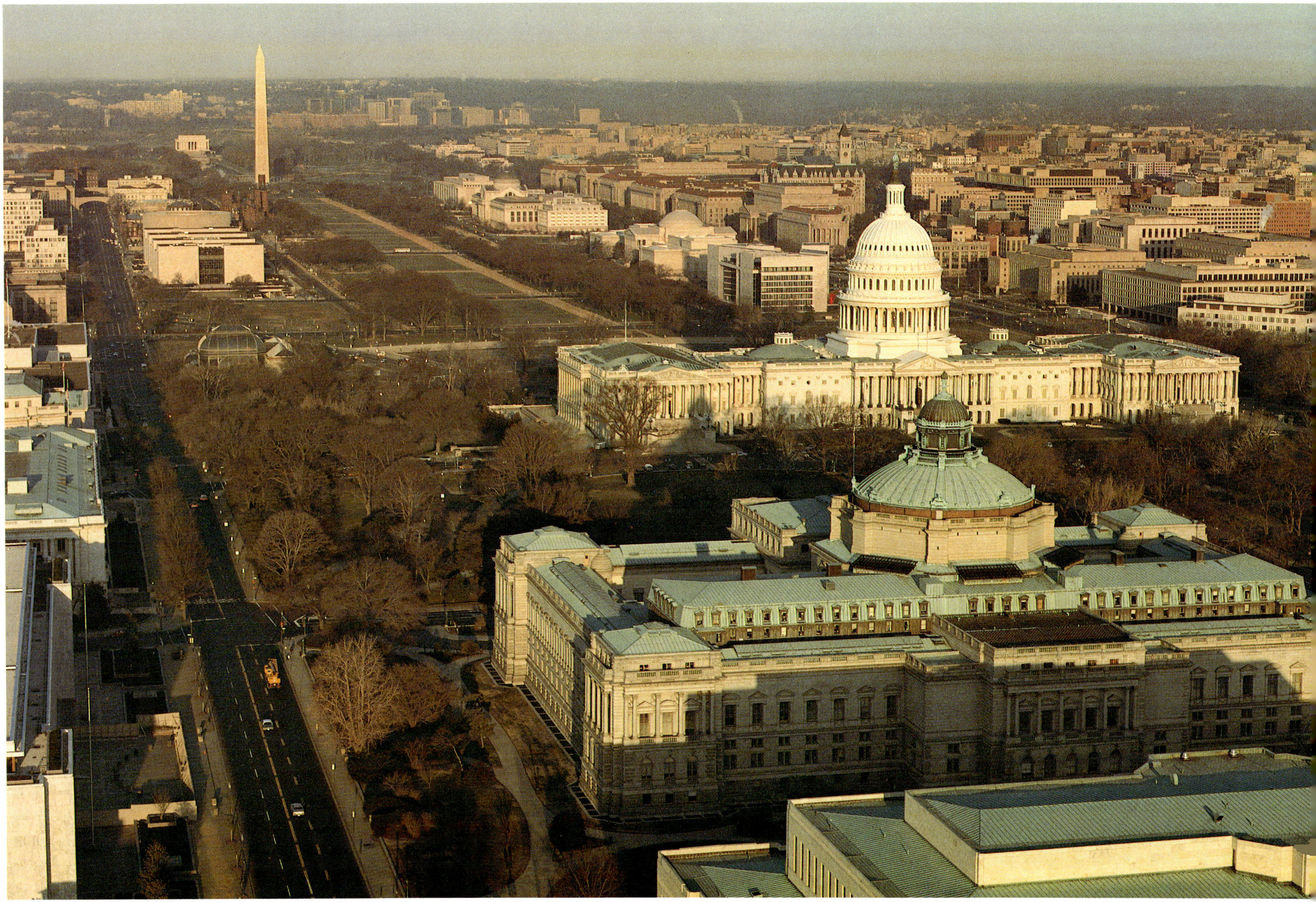

The Library of Congress was built in the Pennsylvania Avenue right-of-way; here the axial relationship of the two domes is most evident, picking up again with the National Gallery and Natural History Museum to the west on the Mall. The National Gallery is also just off of Pennsylvania Avenue at the intersection with Constitution. While all four are very different types of architectural domes, the rhythm is here all the same.

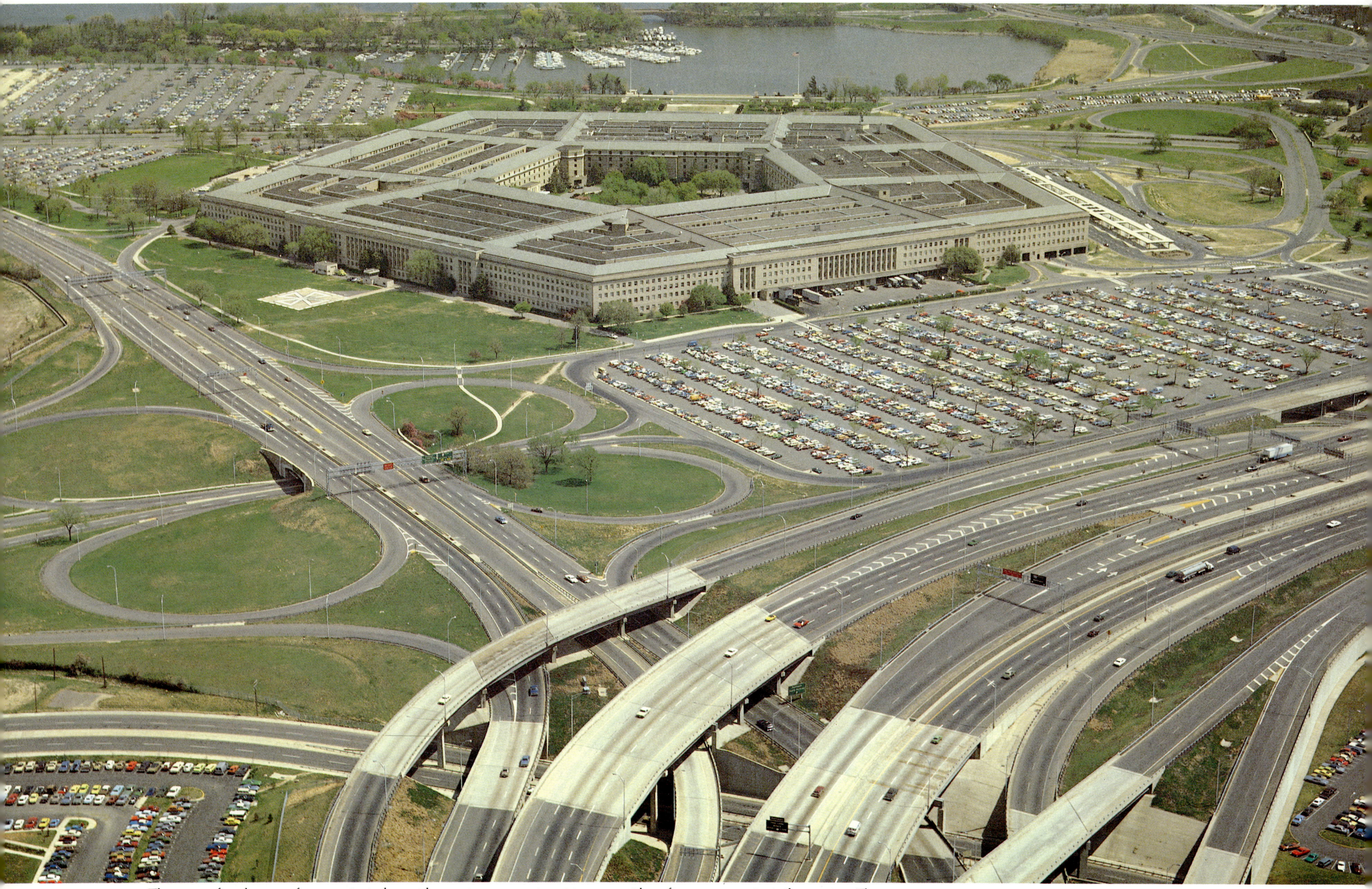

There are five layers of concentrated corridor systems covering 34 acres with a five acre court at the center. The length of the corridors is 17½ miles. The Pentagon has 4,200 clocks, 1,900 toilets and 672 fire hose cabinets. It is said that President Franklin D. Roosevelt insisted on a blank, five-sided shape with opposing windows until he was advised that if the building were bombed the windows would blow outward, allowing the masonry to stand. The "Mixing Bowl" is the name popular now for the writhing freeway complex in the foreground.

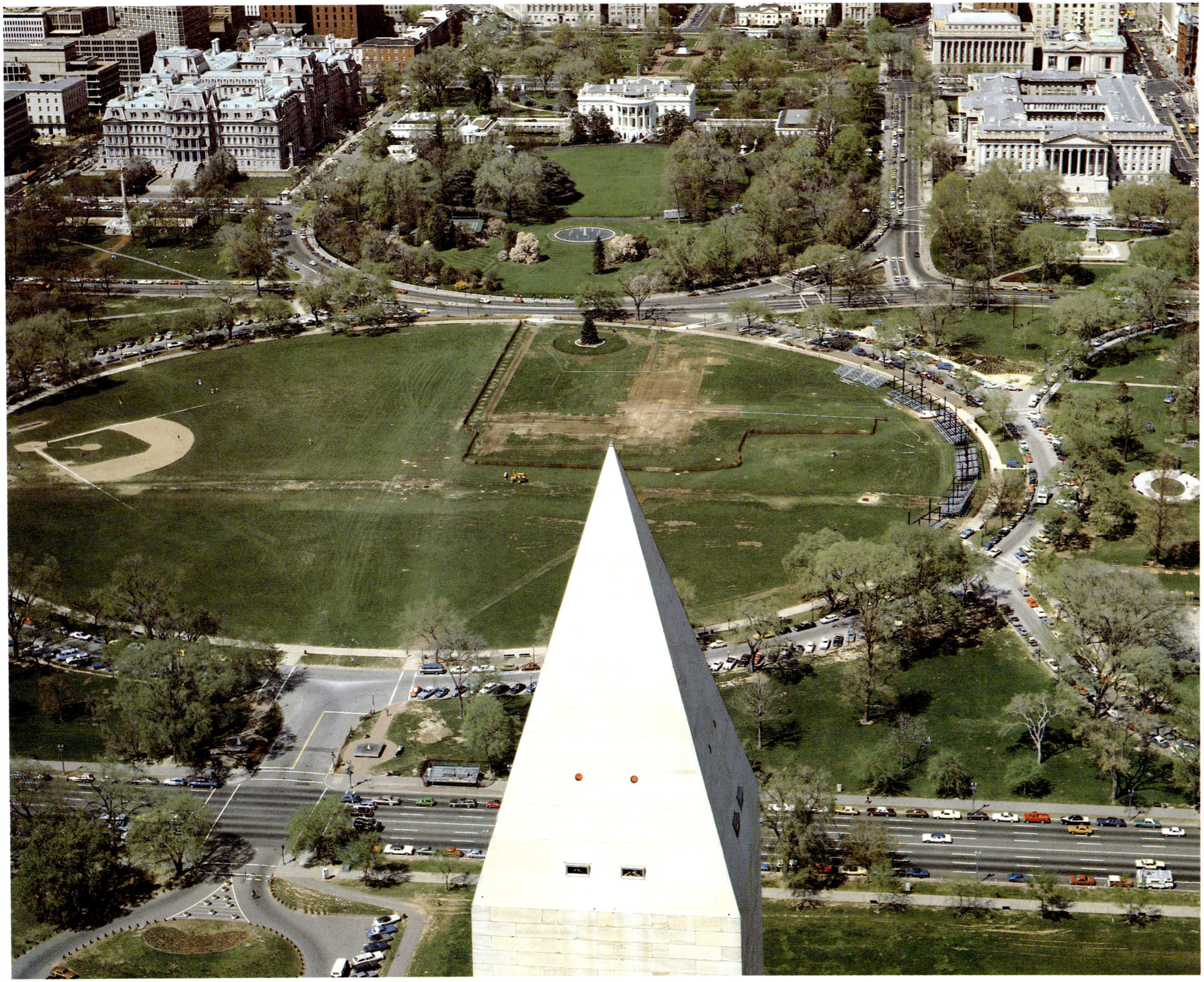

The capstone of the Washington Monument is tipped with a nine inch aluminum pyramid surrounded by 144 platinum lightning conductors. The round openings emit red-light aircraft warnings. The barred windows view the entire District of Columbia. Below is the Ellipse. Spaced from the White House, in the background, are the Greek revival Treasury Building on the right, and the stylistic complexity of the Executive Office Building on the left.

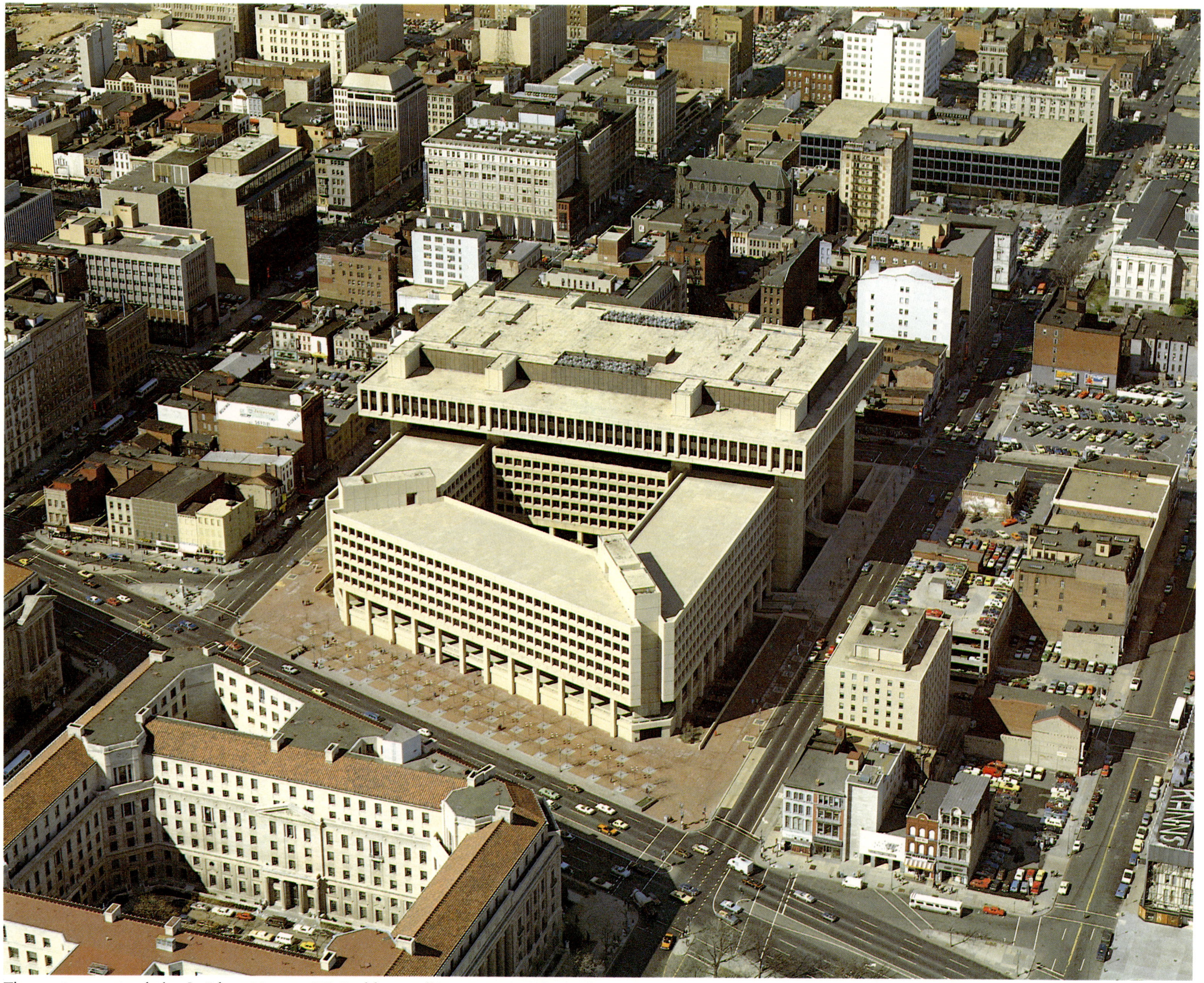

The center court of the J. Edgar Hoover FBI Building will contain a sculptured memorial to Hoover placed there by the Society of Former Special Agents. The design of the building was dictated by Hoover himself. This is the first Federal project on the north side of Pennsylvania Avenue to observe the planned 50 foot setback.

Part of the Naval Observatory and once the Admiral's residence, the marvelous old Victorian house at left center is now the Vice-Presidential Residence. The elaborate security arrangements of the recent past have made the customizing of private homes for vice presidents expensive and difficult. Hence, a central place of residence was selected in 1975.

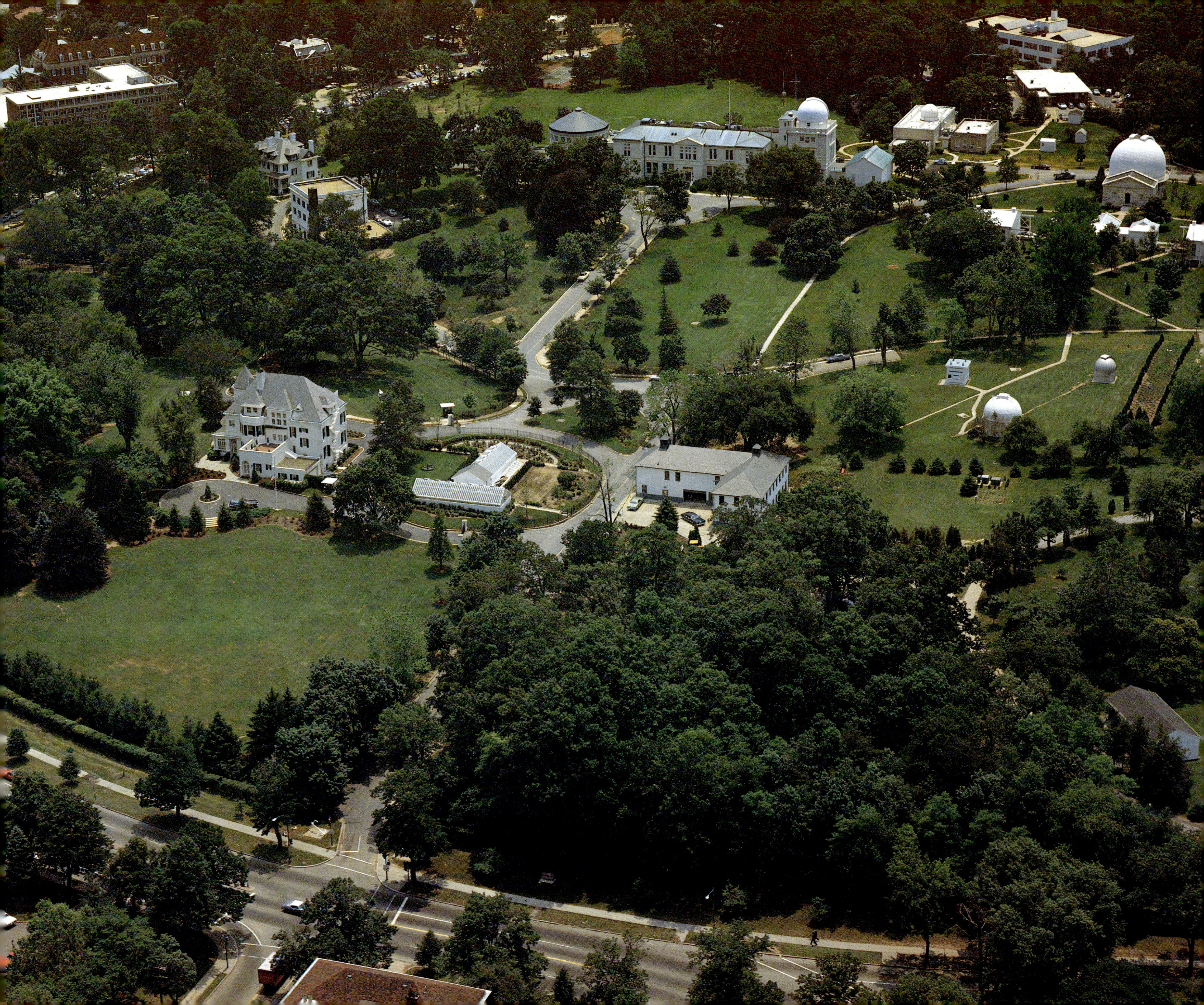

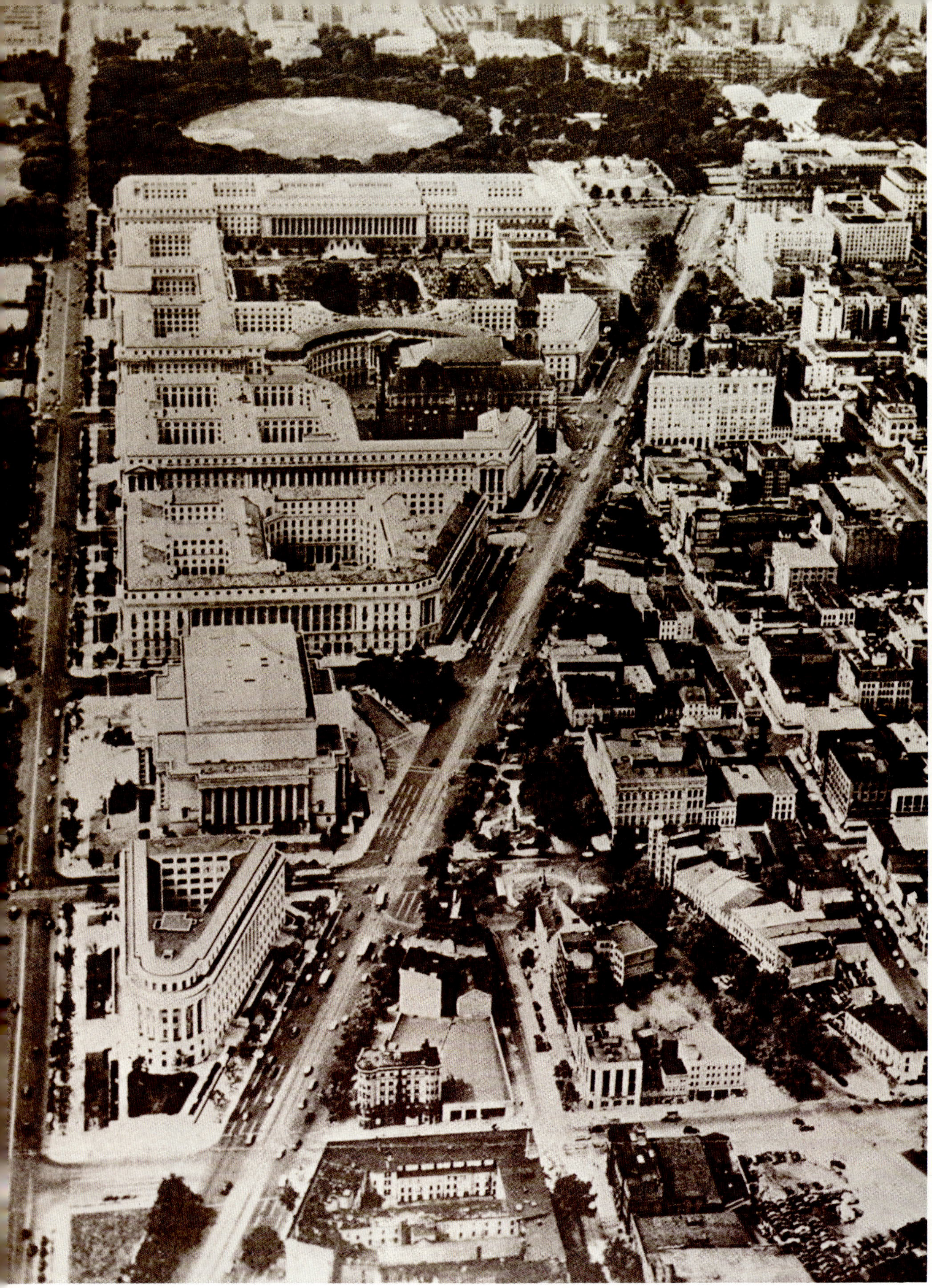

Planned as a single unified development the Federal Triangle project was outgrown by the time it was built and never really "finished." Construction began with the Commerce Building at top and ended with the apex, the Labor Department Building. The Triangle reiterates the geometric relationship of Capitol, Washington Monument and White House.

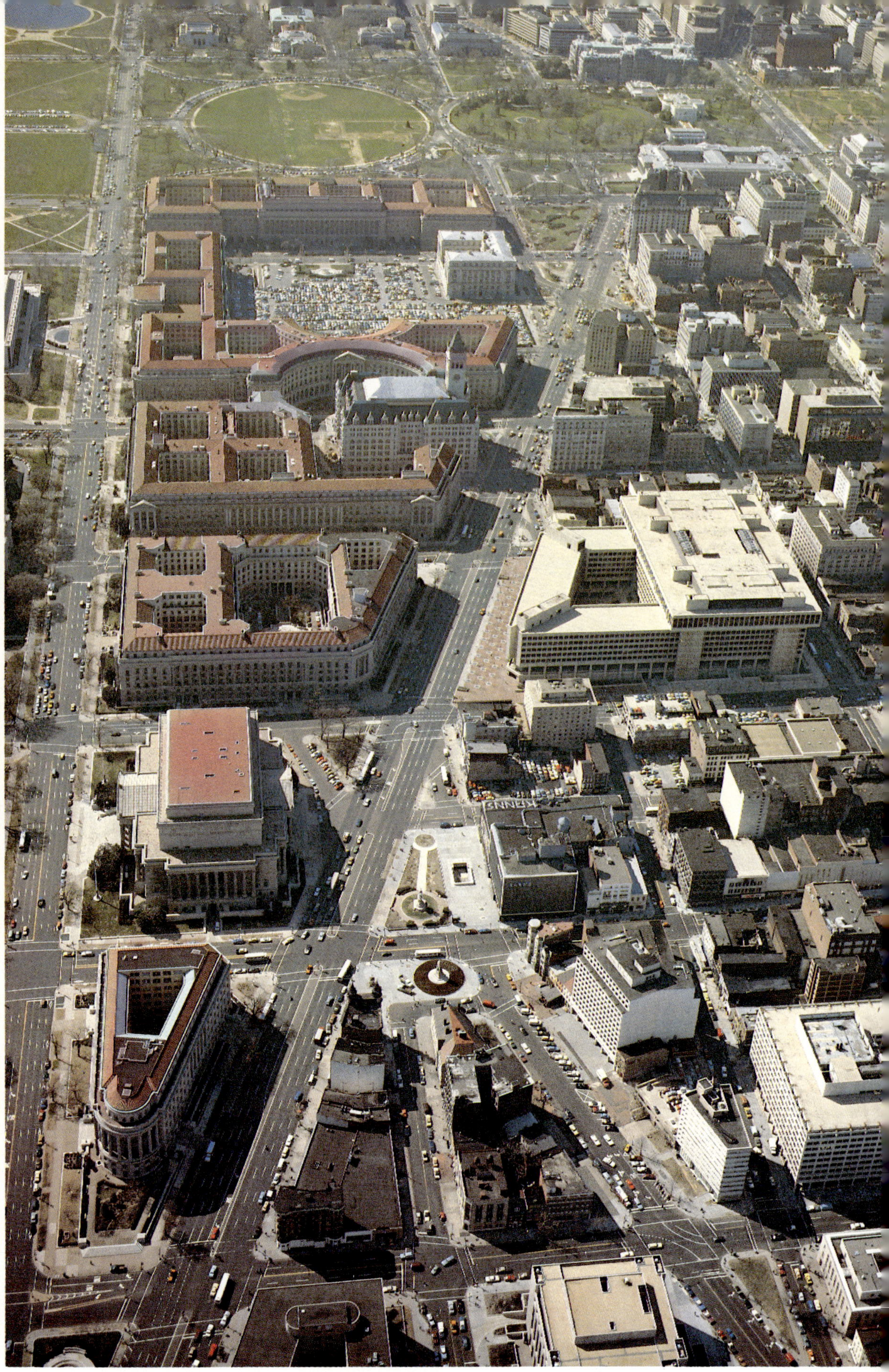

Today from the air the red tile roofs relieve the limestone grays of the horizontal city and contrast with the new white of the J. Edgar Hoover FBI Building. And, from the air, the survival of the old Post Office Building, and the District Building, is perspicuous.

THEN AND NOW

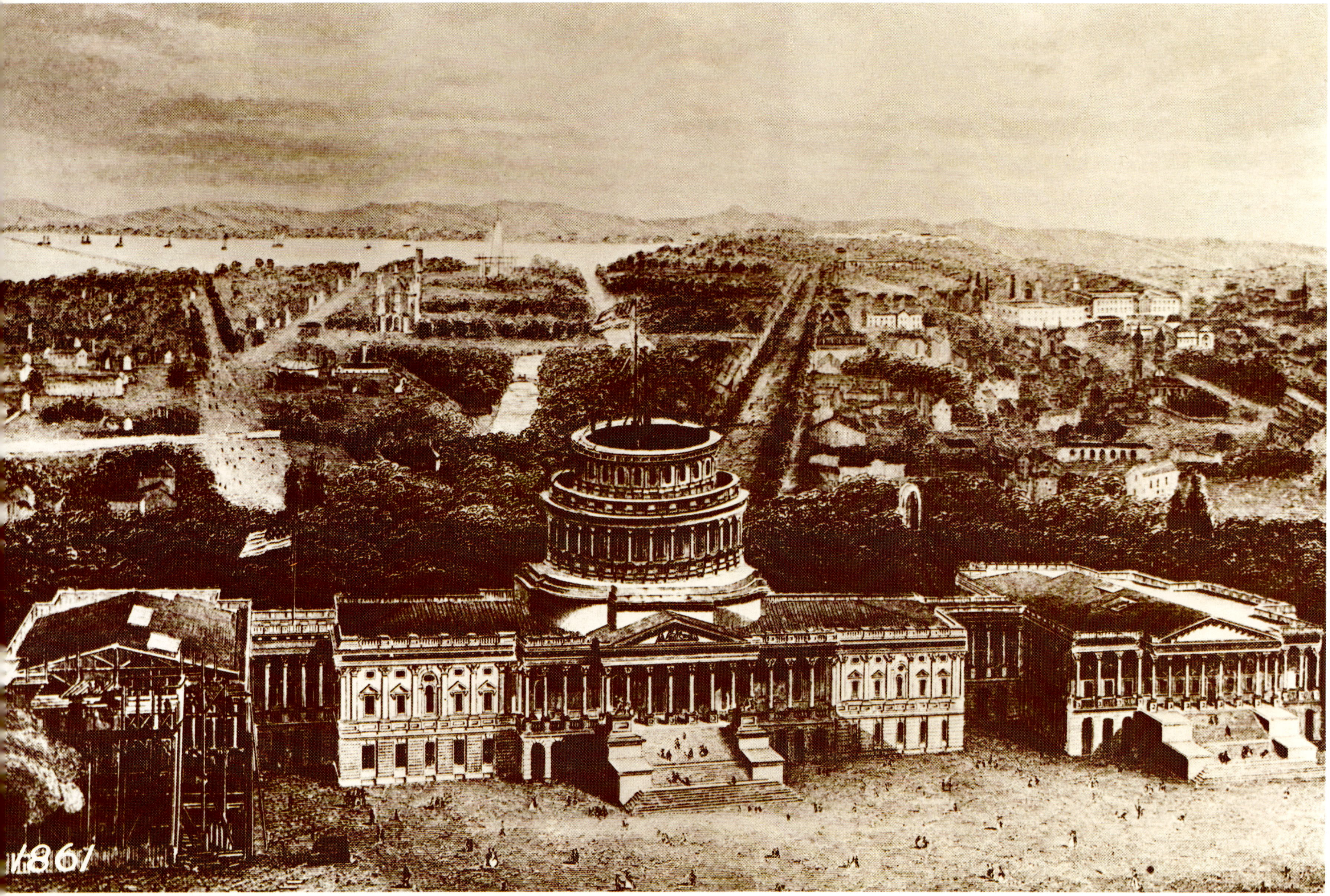

An early sketch of the construction of the Capitol made for Harper's Magazine from a balloon. A train station is at Second Street with tracks across what is now the Mall. The Potomac was closer then; the westward land was not reclaimed and filled. Though the crisis of the Civil War was at hand, construction was carried forward. It was as unthinkable to stop as it would have been to mask the flag.

Peacefully, serene in a completion of much, the nation's capitol's lights are coming on at dusk.

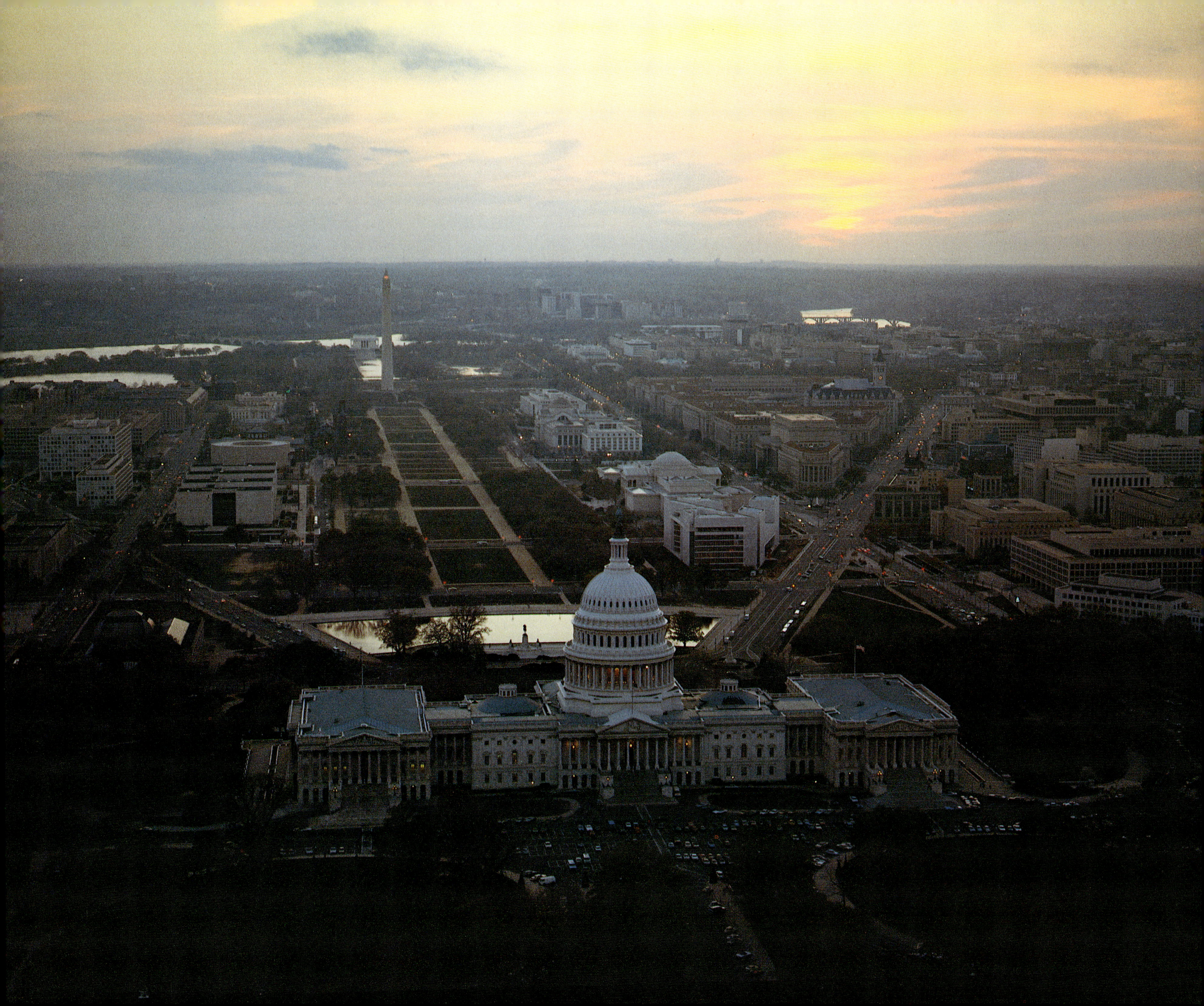

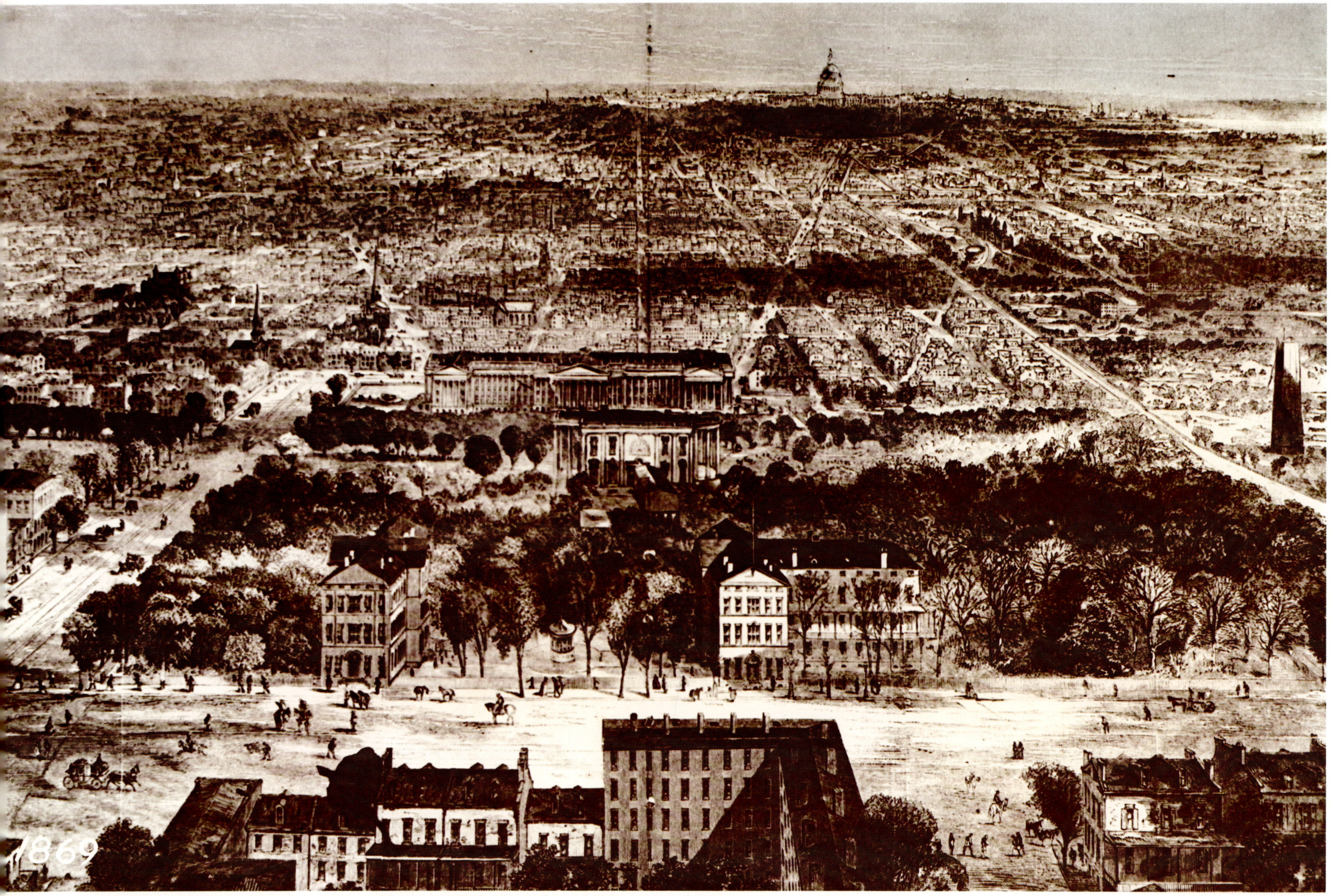

In another ballon view, Seventeenth Street is in the foreground. When the old State War and Navy Building was erected here, it settled the question: the capital would not be moved to St. Louis. The Treasury Building blocks the view from the White House to the Capitol on Pennsylvania Avenue. It is said Andrew Jackson, piqued by the delays of the committee he had appointed to come to a decision, walked out of the White House one morning, examined the grounds, jabbed his cane and said, "Right here is where I want the cornerstone."

Although it is still not possible to look from the White House up Pennsylvania Avenue to the Capitol, the view south has been opened and gardened, and all seems well. The White House is, however, sinking at a rate of a quarter of an inch in thirty years. The Washington Monument, too, is in trouble. Built on what was once a swamp, it might disappear, at the present rate of sinking, in the year 113,053 A.D.

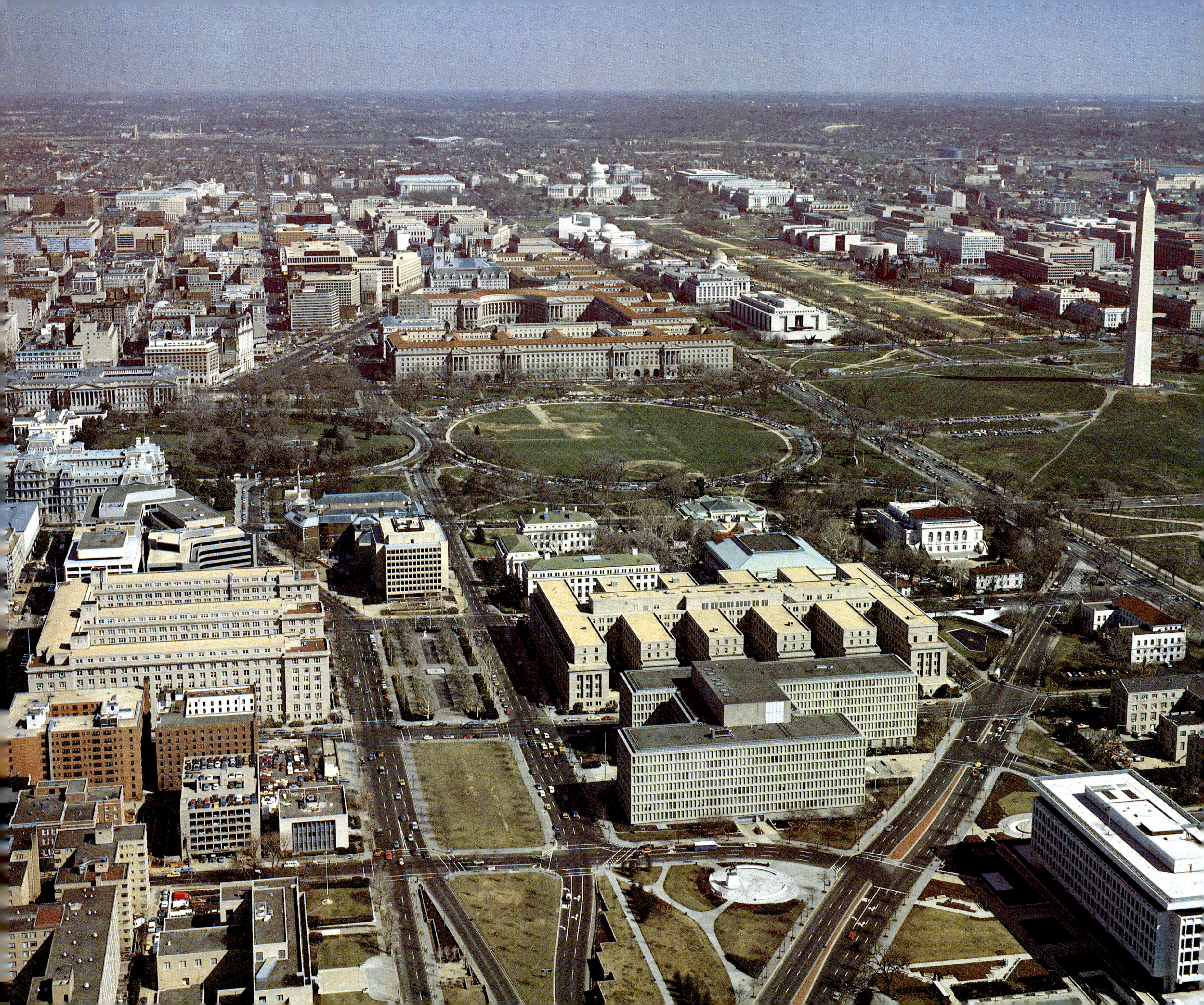

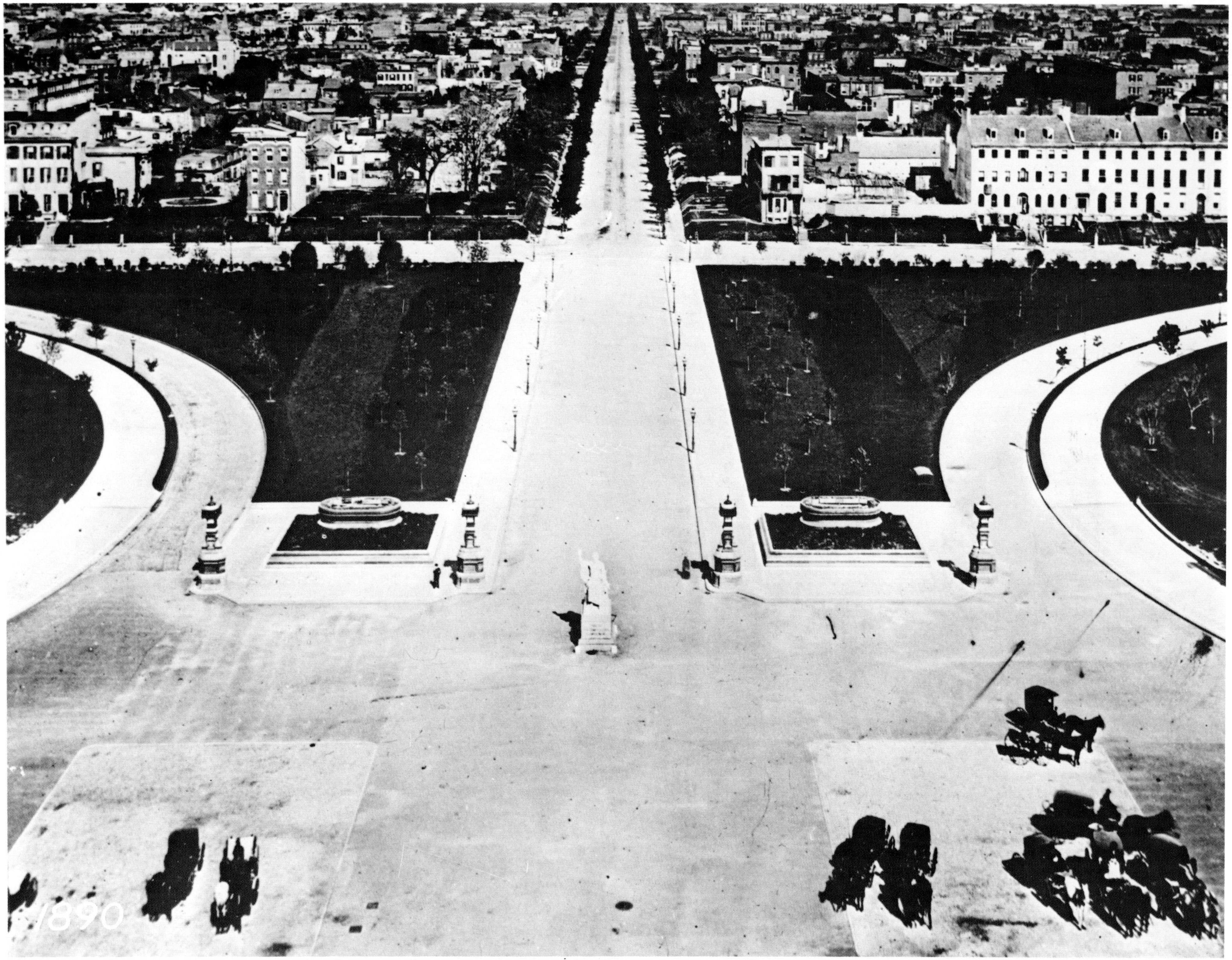

The statue of George Washington in the foreground was commissioned by Congress in 1830. Horatio Greenough sculpted the father of our country classically, bare to the waist in a draped robe. Here we see the statue in its second location. Its nudity had offended a considerable number of congressmen, and it was removed from the rotunda. Soon after, the public was scandalized, viewing it where we see it here. It was moved again. It is now in the Smithsonian History and Technology Museum. In the vicinity beyond First Street the small houses and residential units, some of them rooming houses, were the dwellings of administration and congressional people. When he was a congressman from Illinois, Lincoln was a boarder in this "Carroll Row" vicinity.

In the "Capitol East Area" today, the Olmsted layout and street furniture, lighting standards, trolley waiting stations are unchanged in spite of the East Front Extension of the Capitol in the 1960's. The Supreme Court is center left. The Library of Congress at center right and left of its annex, the Folger Shakespeare Library. But, beyond, how much has Washington changed since 1890?

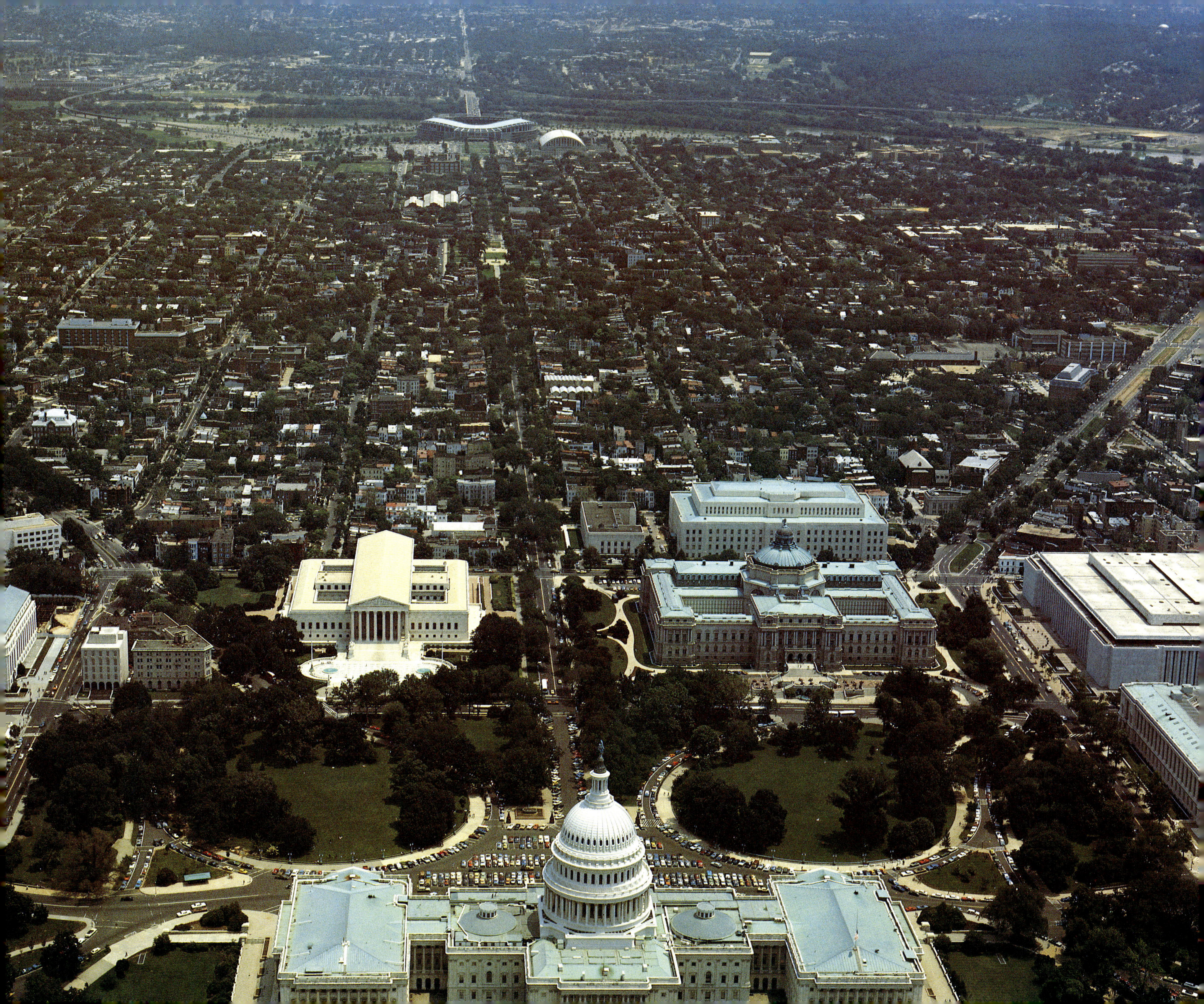

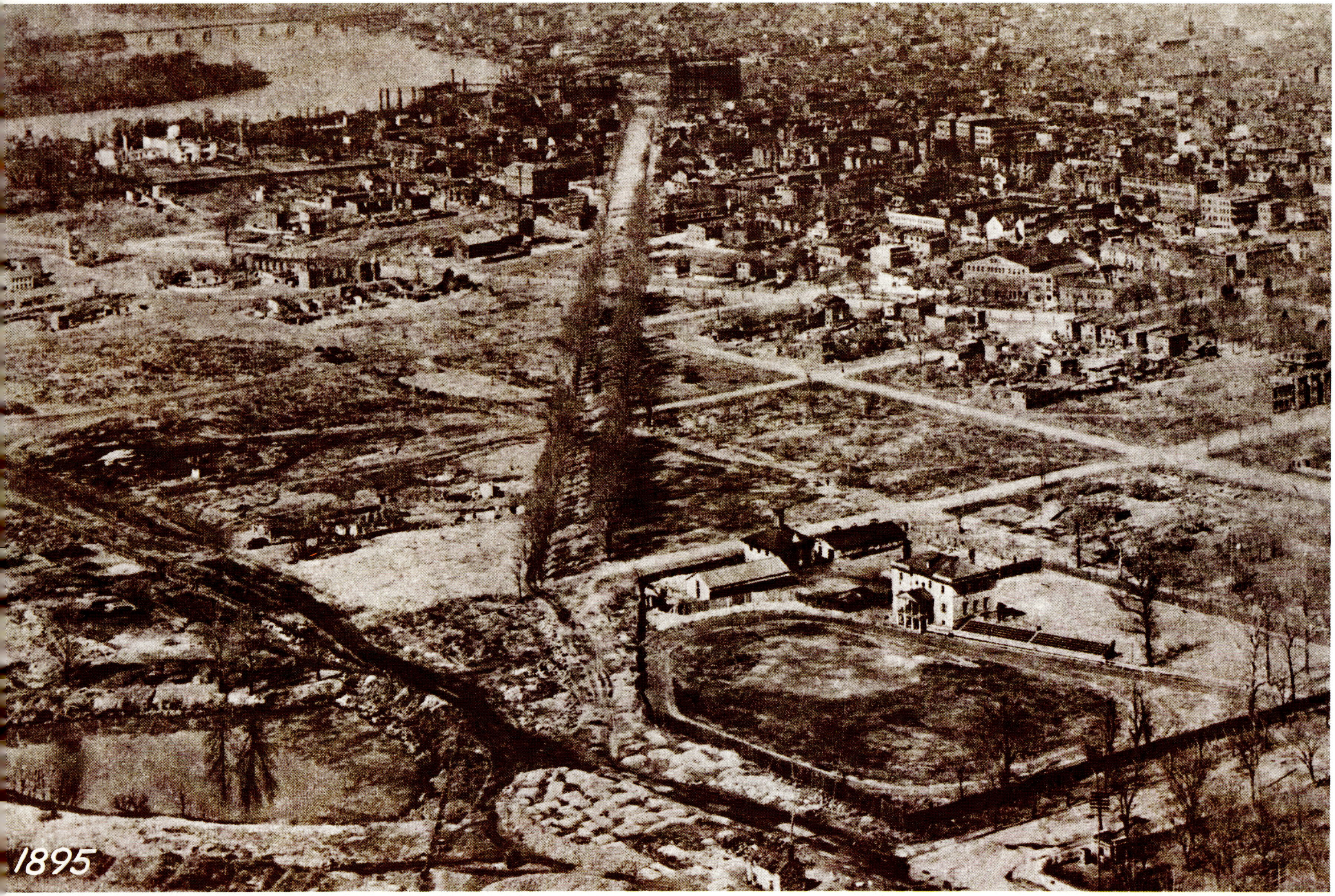

This "aerial" view taken in 1895 was probably made with a long focus lens from the top of the Washington Monument. Its view is northwest along Virginia Avenue. At upper left, crossing the Potomac, is the Aqueduct Bridge which was replaced in 1923 by Francis Scott Key Bridge.

Now, as we look northwest beyond the Pan American Union and the Daughters of the American Revolution right center, we see the Department of the Interior and the Civil Service Commission and then, crossing Virginia Avenue, the Federal Reserve and farther at upper left, the State Department. In the distance at extreme upper left is the John F. Kennedy Center for the Performing Arts. Constitution Gardens, left foreground, was completed for the Bicentennial as a memorial to the founding fathers.

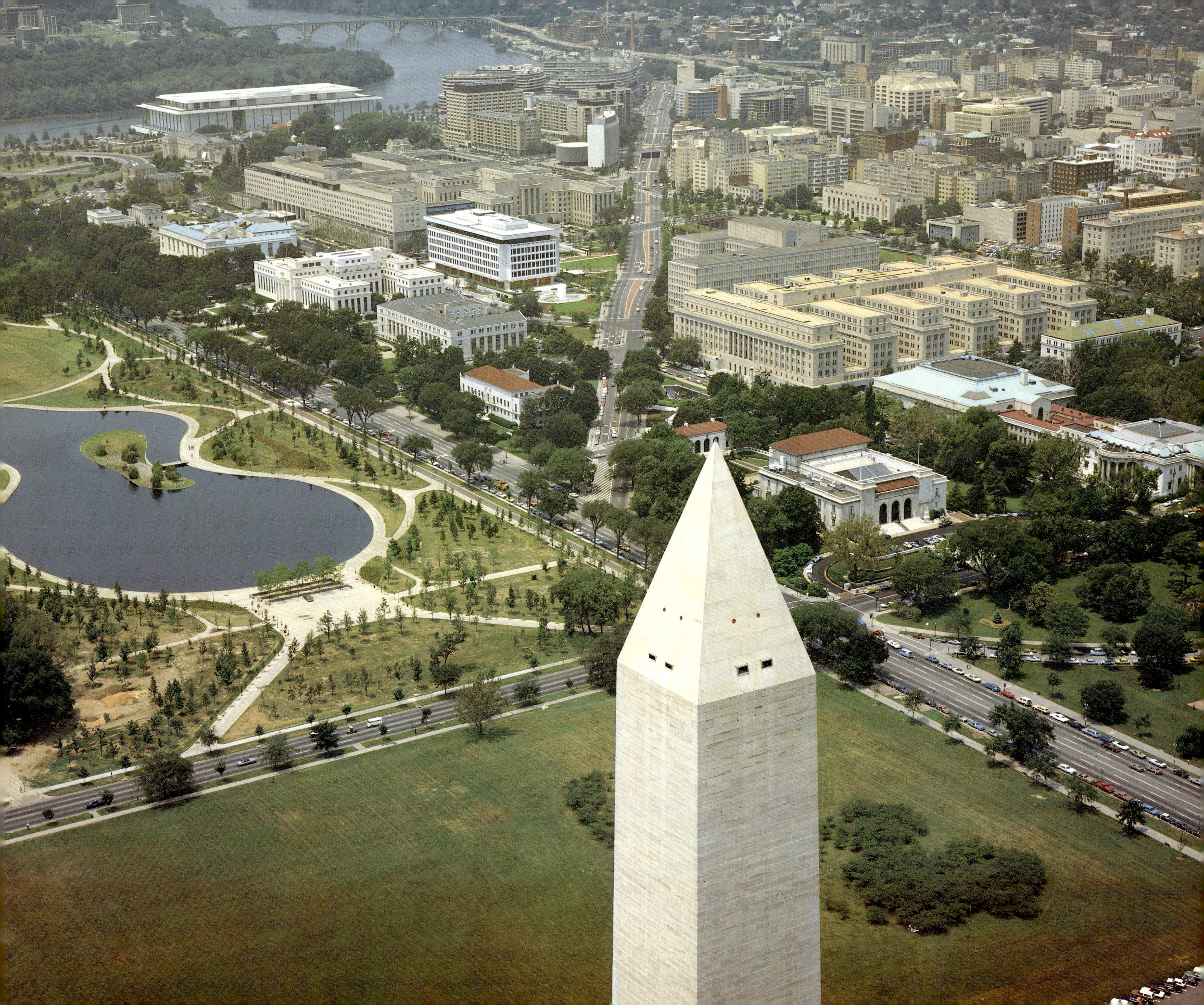

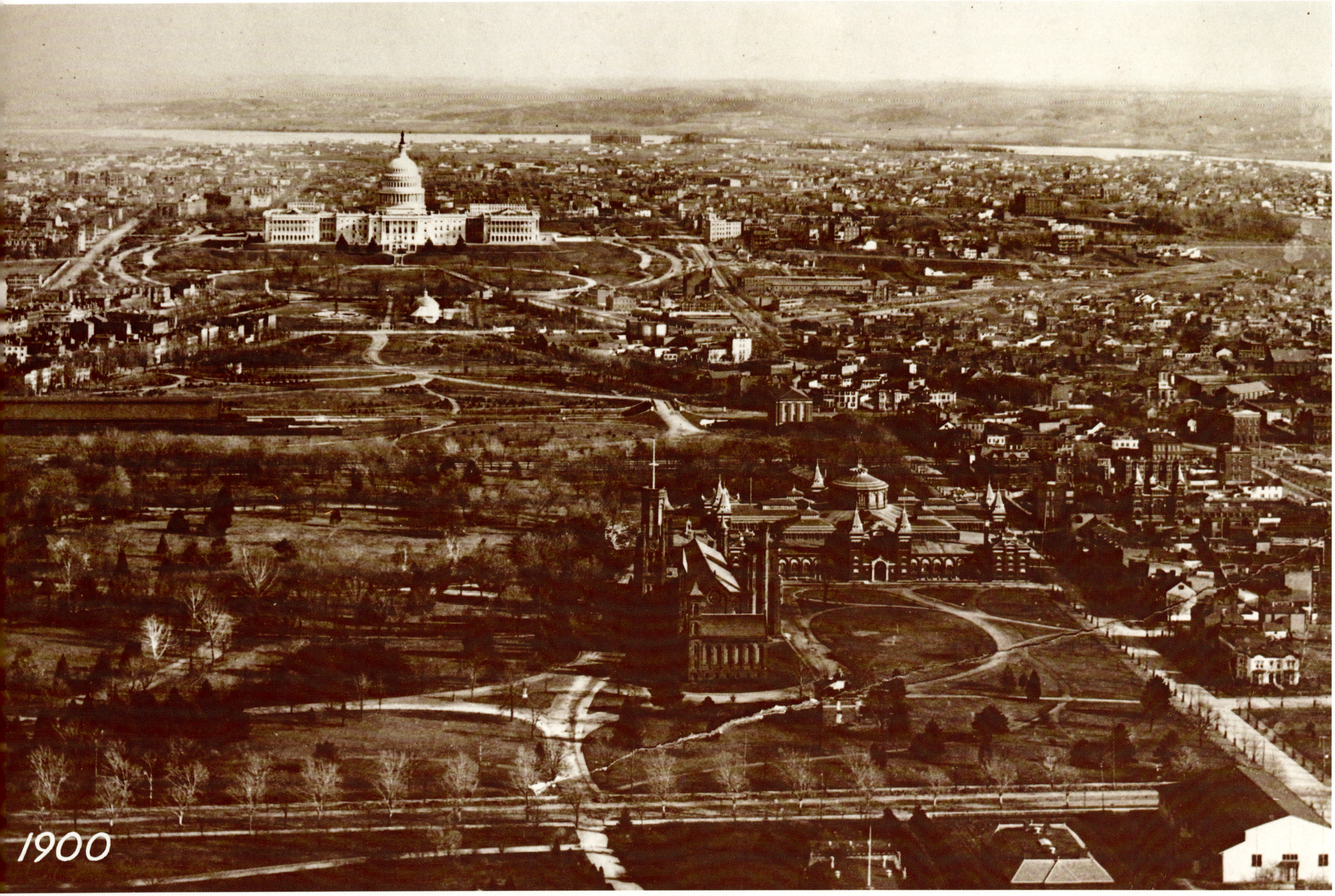

President Fillmore appointed Andrew Jackson Downing to redesign both the Mall and the White House grounds. Little of Downing's plan for the Mall now remains, with the exception of the Ellipse. But, we see in 1900 Downing's romantic winding paths, small gardens, and the evergreens which were to oxygenate the city. Downing wanted large open areas for military reviews and a triumphal arch to the White House grounds. His plans were forgotten after the Civil War. A trainshed has advanced upon the mall, left center, in this photograph.

Now the Mall is a serene and impressive channel of capitol vistas. The Smithsonian's castle bulges non-conformably, but the monumental geometries are ordered in a semblance of L'Enfant's vision of 1790. A story remains that L'Enfant and Washington led their horses up Jenkins Hill together and marked the pleasing eminence for the Capitol building, the apex of L'Enfant's triangular scheme, relating the Capitol, the Washington Monument and the Presidential Residence.

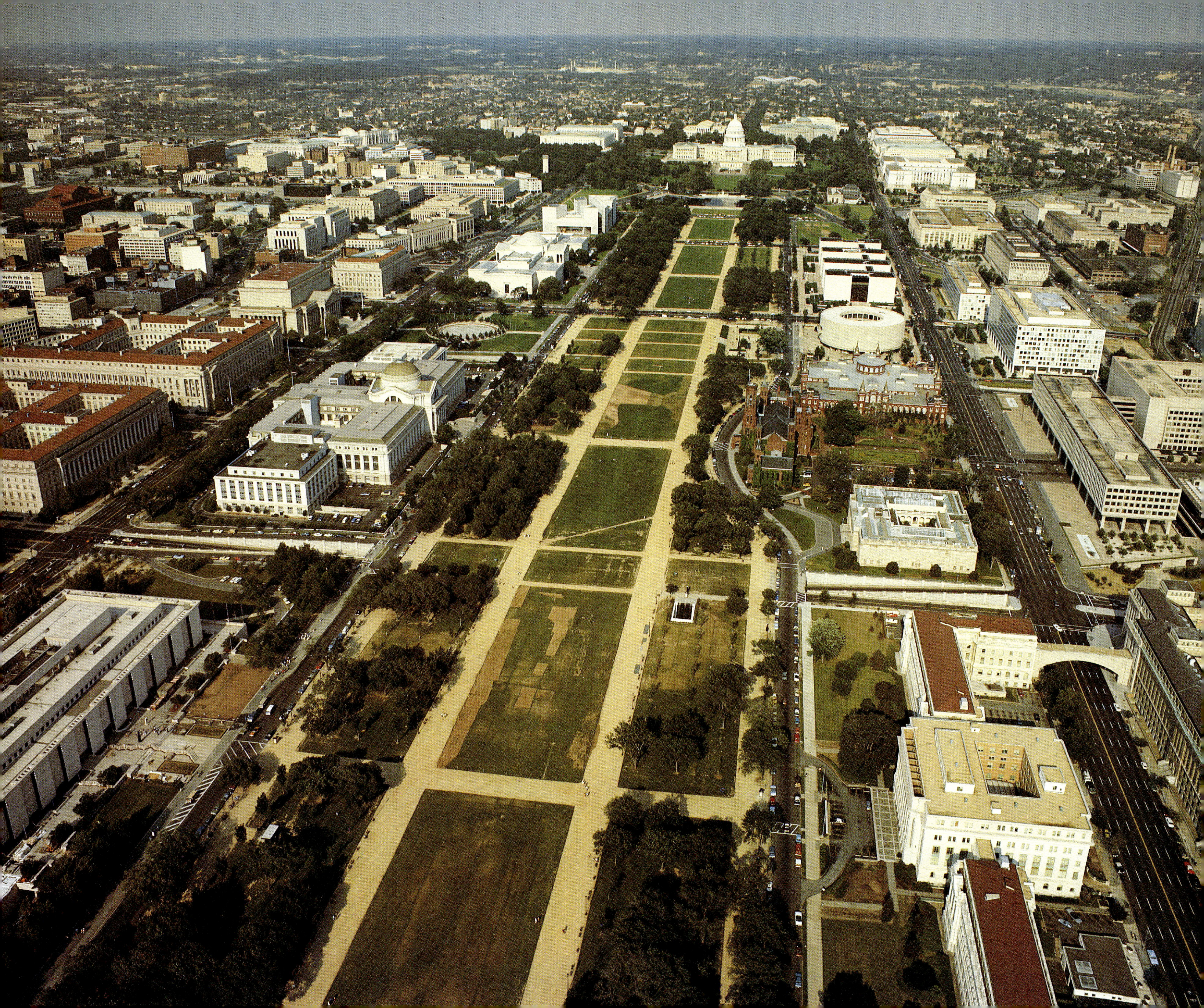

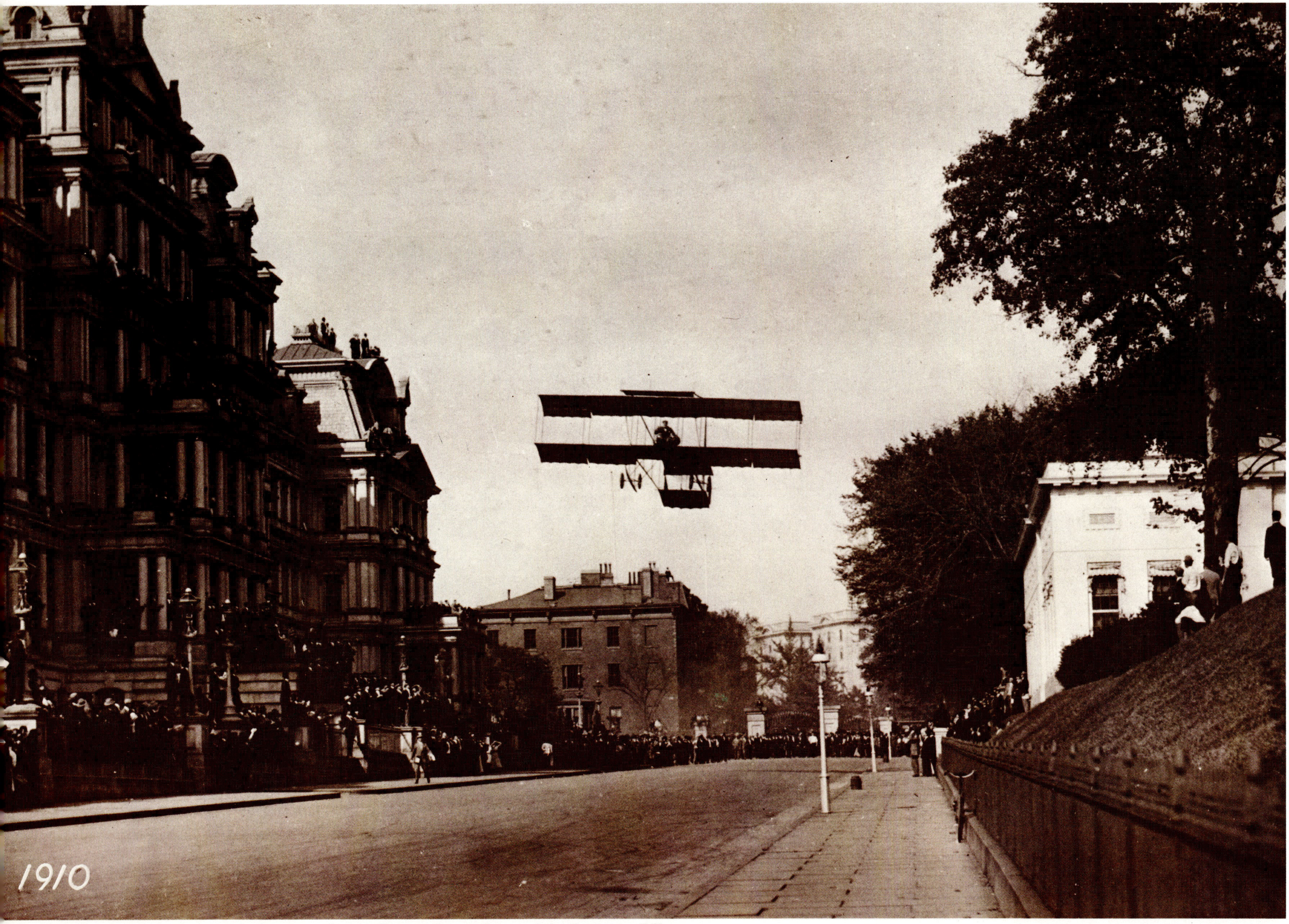

They were expecting him, on the steps, the porches, at the windows, of the Executive Office Building, lining the sidewalks, as he landed, next to the White House and took off, on 17th Street.

Here we have participants, not spectators. Their protest has taken them into the street. They pass the Executive Office Building, the portico of the White House, and they are turning the Treasury Building corner, toward Pennsylvania Avenue.

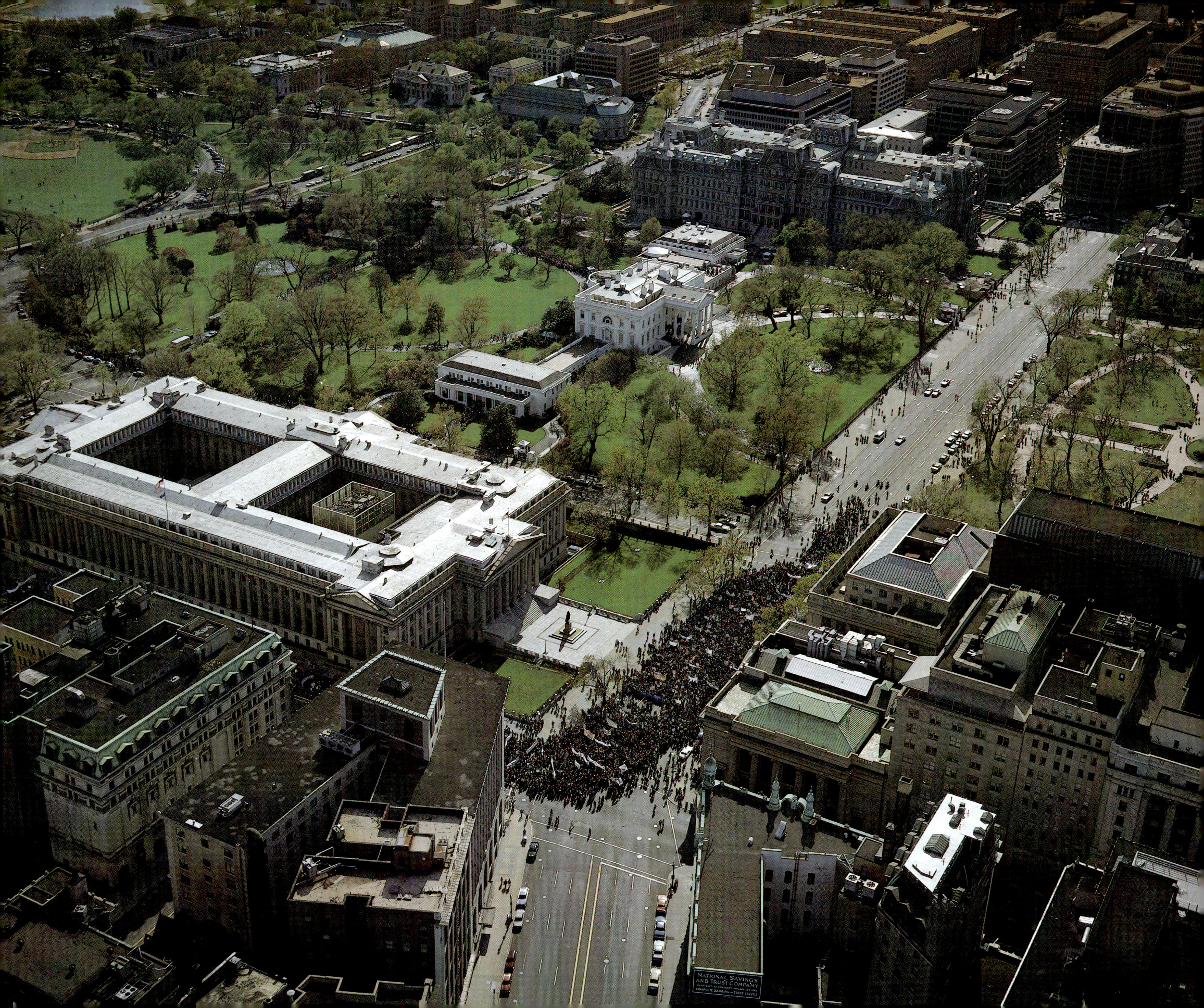
NATIONAL SAVINGS
AND TRUST COMPANY
COMPLETE BANKING — TRUST SERVICE

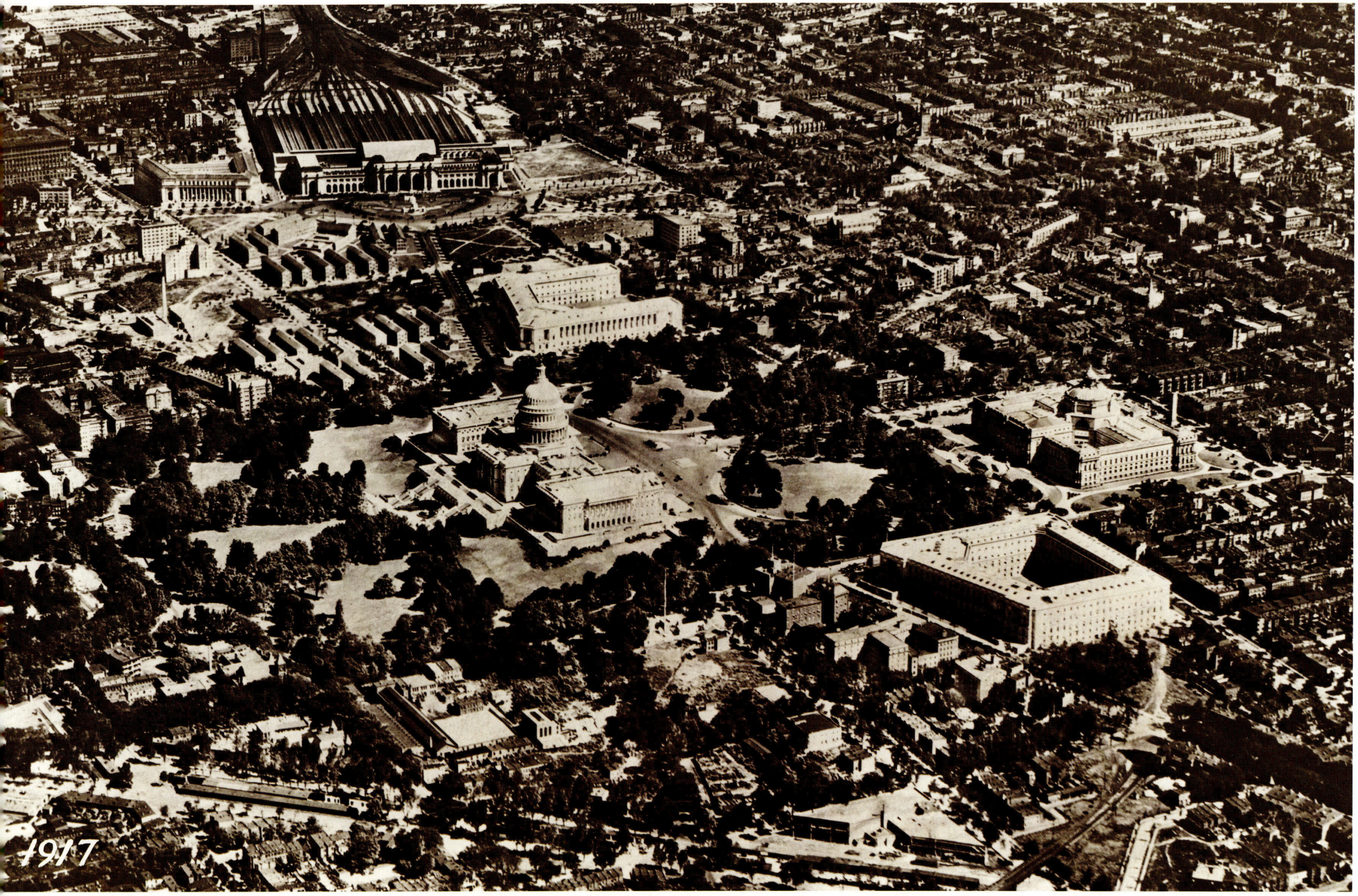

At the Capitol's centennial in 1900 the American Institute of Architects held a symposium on the aesthetic condition of the city. Something ought to be done. Senator James McMillan sponsored a resolution authorizing a committee of experts. Appointed, among others, was Daniel H. Burnham. The Union Station, upper left, by Burnham, was the commission's first fruit. It serves all the city railroads. Previously, they had steamed along the broad avenues, one even having an unsightly station in the present mall. Another member of the commission was the landscape architect, Frederick Law Olmsted, Jr. The beautiful setting which he gave the Capitol in its grounds has protested encroachment and invited extension. The Senate Office Building, upper center, and the Cannon Office Building of the House of Representatives are "unidentical twins." What we see here in 1917 is, generally, response to the three tenets of the McMillan Commission: classical style, uniform cornice height, and concentration of government buildings at the Capitol, on the Mall, and at the White House.

Since the 1917 photograph, the House of Representatives has expanded its offices in the foreground. But the massive cluster of powerful government is still disciplined by the landscaping originated by Olmsted.

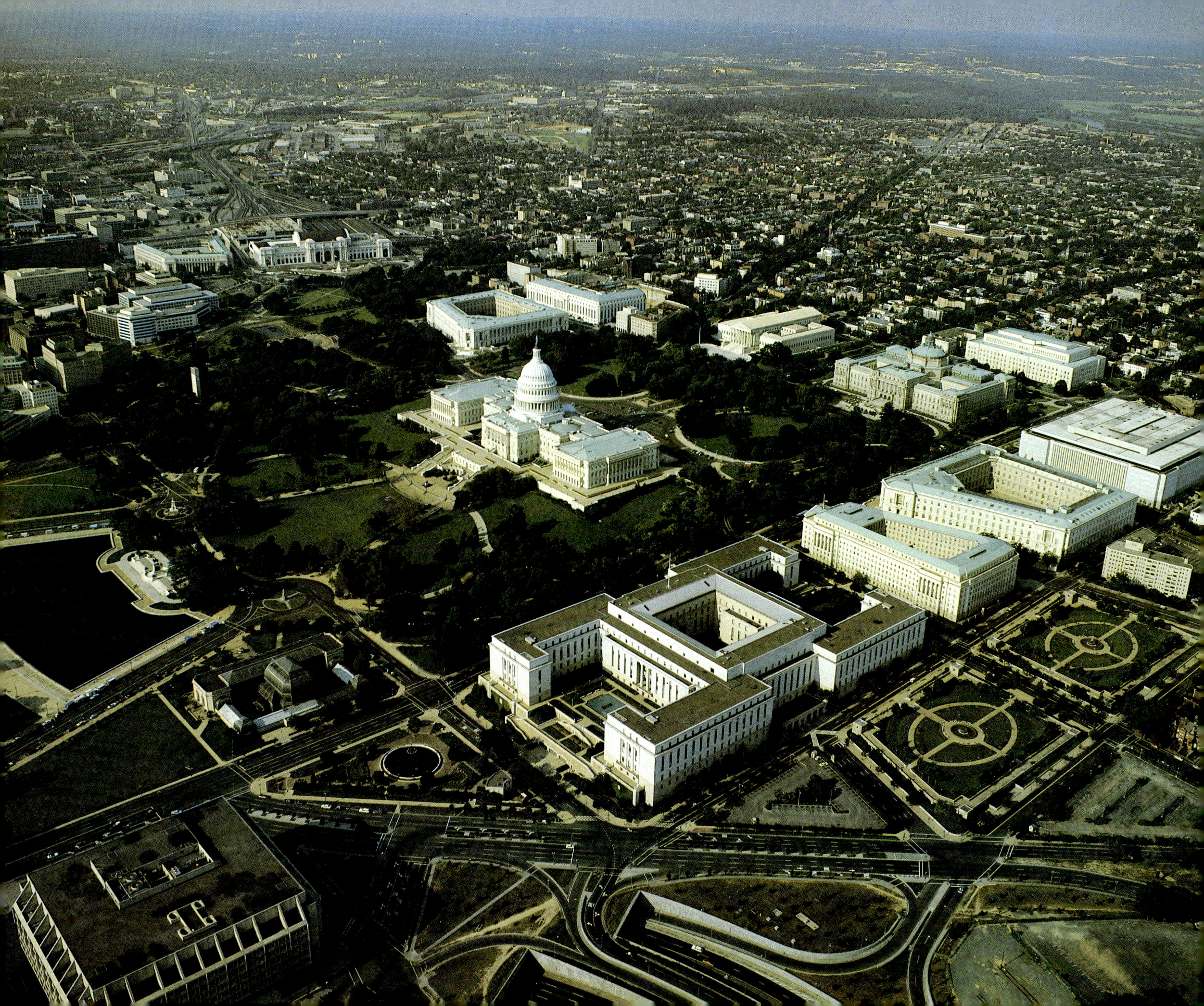

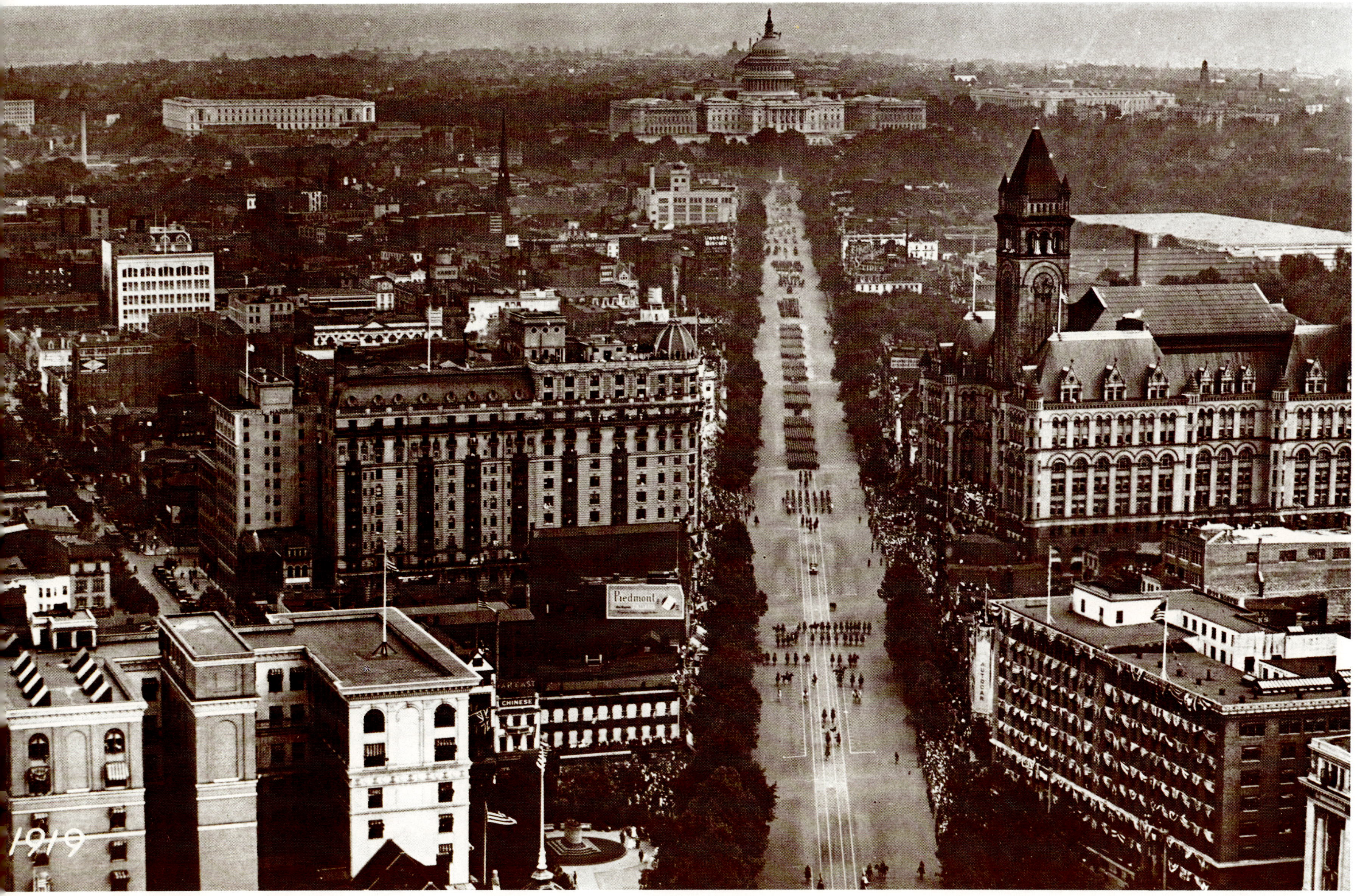

The 1919 Pershing Parade comes up Pennsylvania Avenue from the Capitol toward the White House. The Avenue seems vacant without the Federal Triangle. The Old Post Office, here only 10 years old, is a Romanesque exception to Washington's dominant classicism. Schemes have been hatched to get this building torn down, but it is still with us, though not without a struggle. It is a symbol of an awakened energy in Washington that insists on values from a time when government was less occluded by obdurate bureaucracy. Immediately across the Avenue, razed in 1964 to make way for an office building, is the Raleigh Hotel, designed by New York architect Henry J. Hardenburgh, and built in 1898.

Pennsylvania Avenue has changed and will. The mid-twentieth century agglomeration of the north side has beginnings of a setback. If the President inaugurated in 1981 walks, as Jimmy Carter did, from the Capitol to the White House, he will see a Western Plaza between 13th and 14th Streets, and a Pershing Memorial at the Commerce Building. The Willard Hotel, sister to the late Raleigh, by the same architect and completed in 1901, lately threatened by a plan which called for its demolition, will remain as part of an exciting new development of the western end of this ceremonial route. The Pennsylvania Avenue Development Corporation has completed much planning for public improvements at both ends of "America's Main Street."

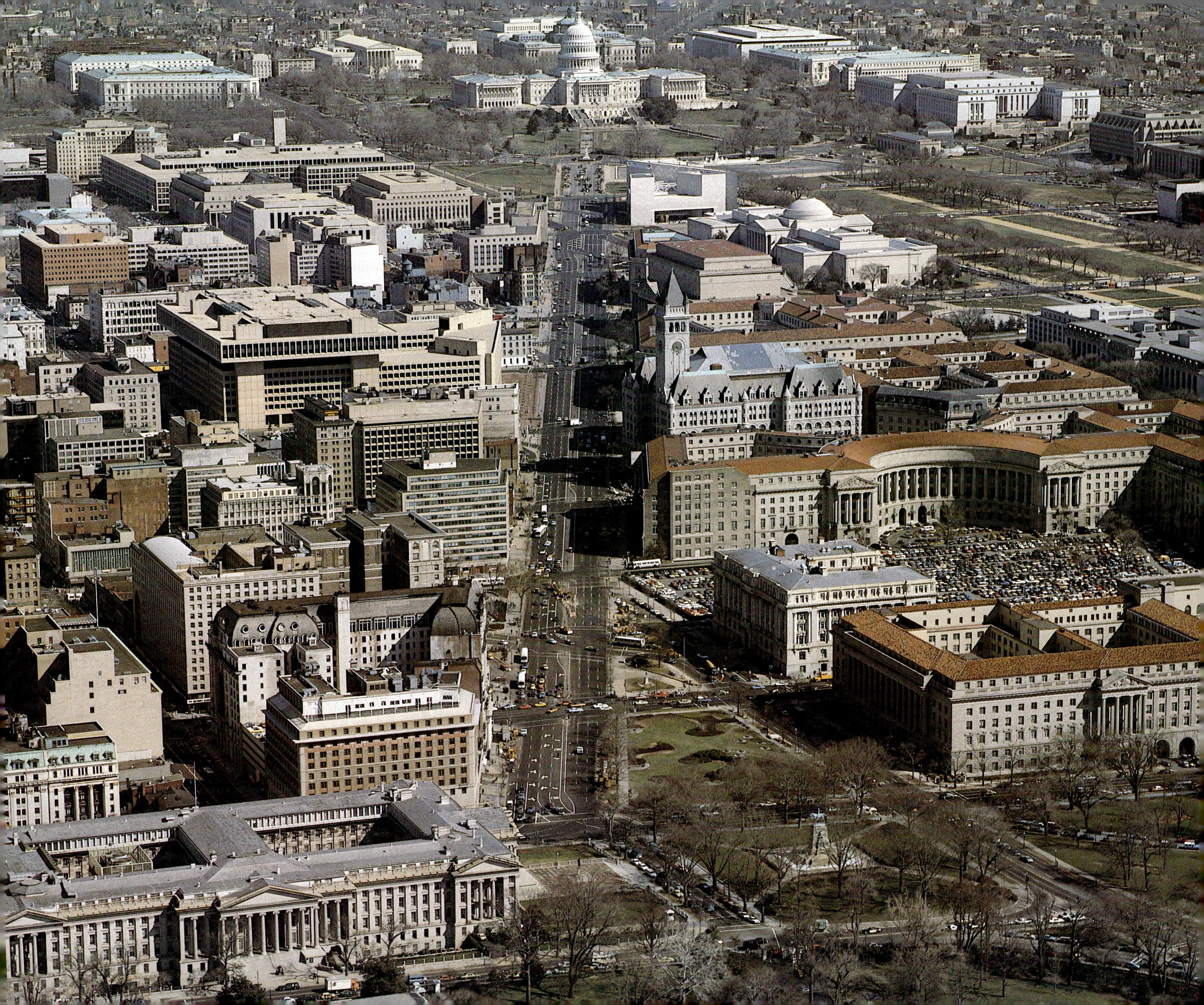

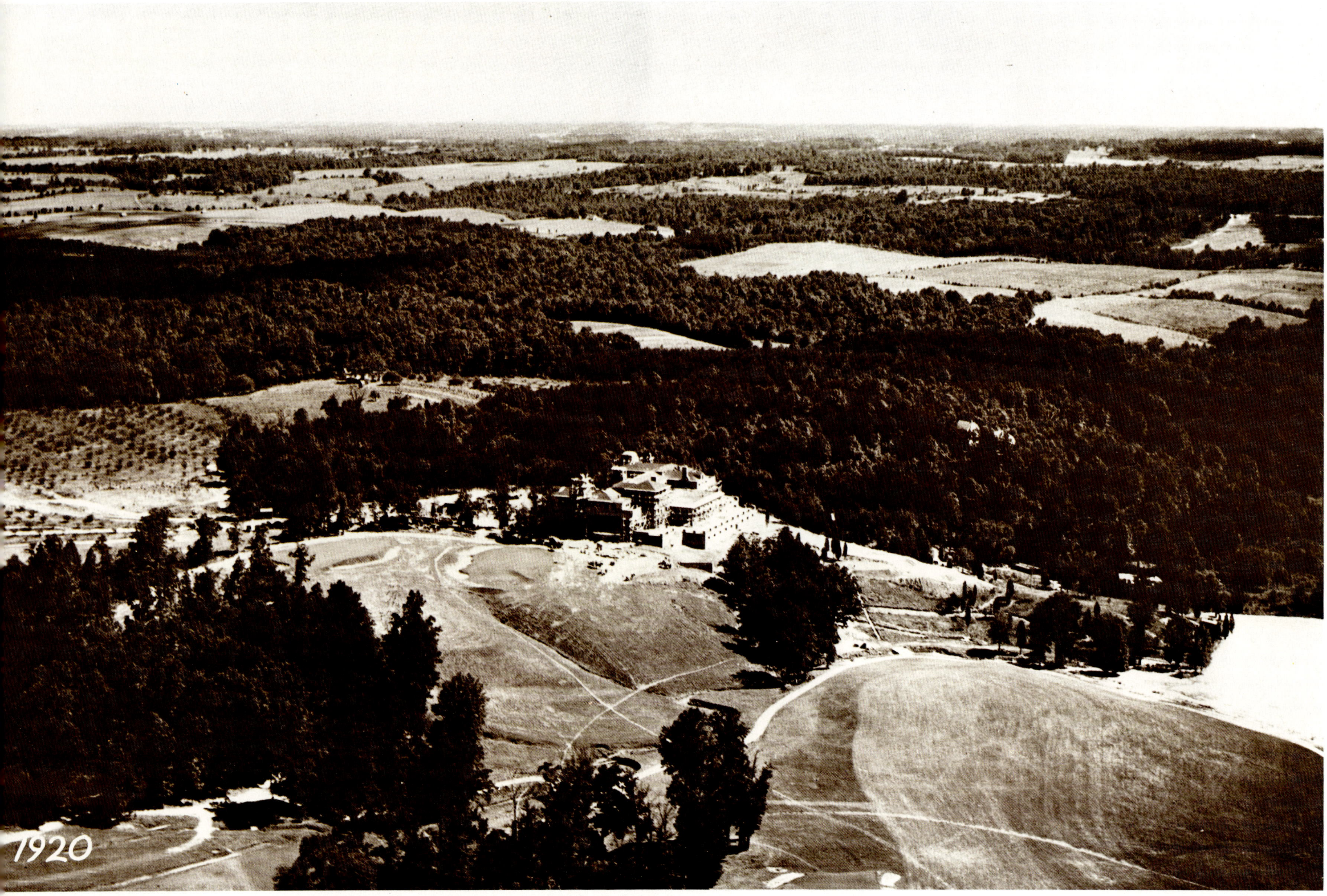

In 1920 the Congressional Country Club grew to completion in a largely rural area.

Today the fullness of its trees and swards give it visual insulation as development spreads all around and above it.

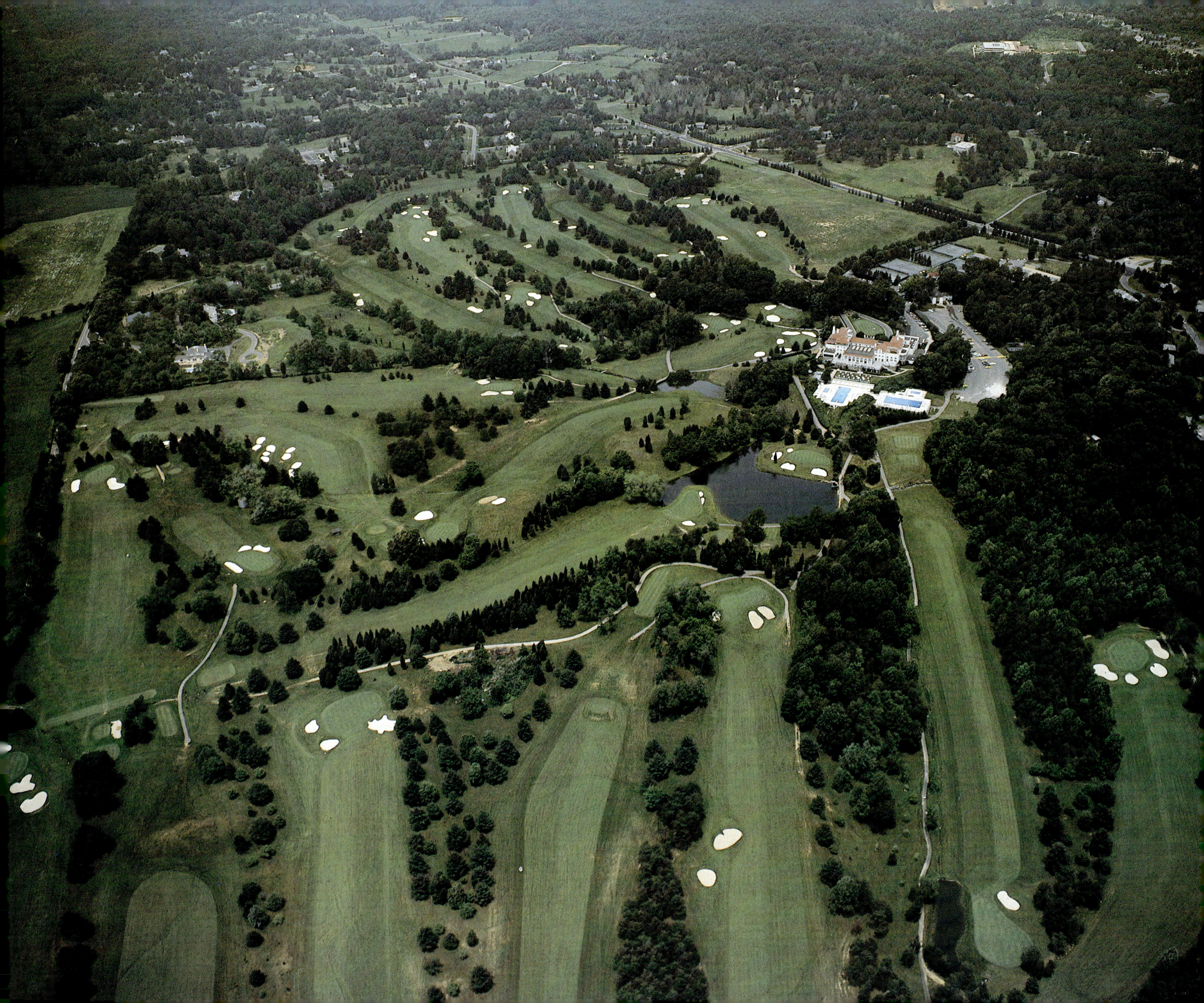

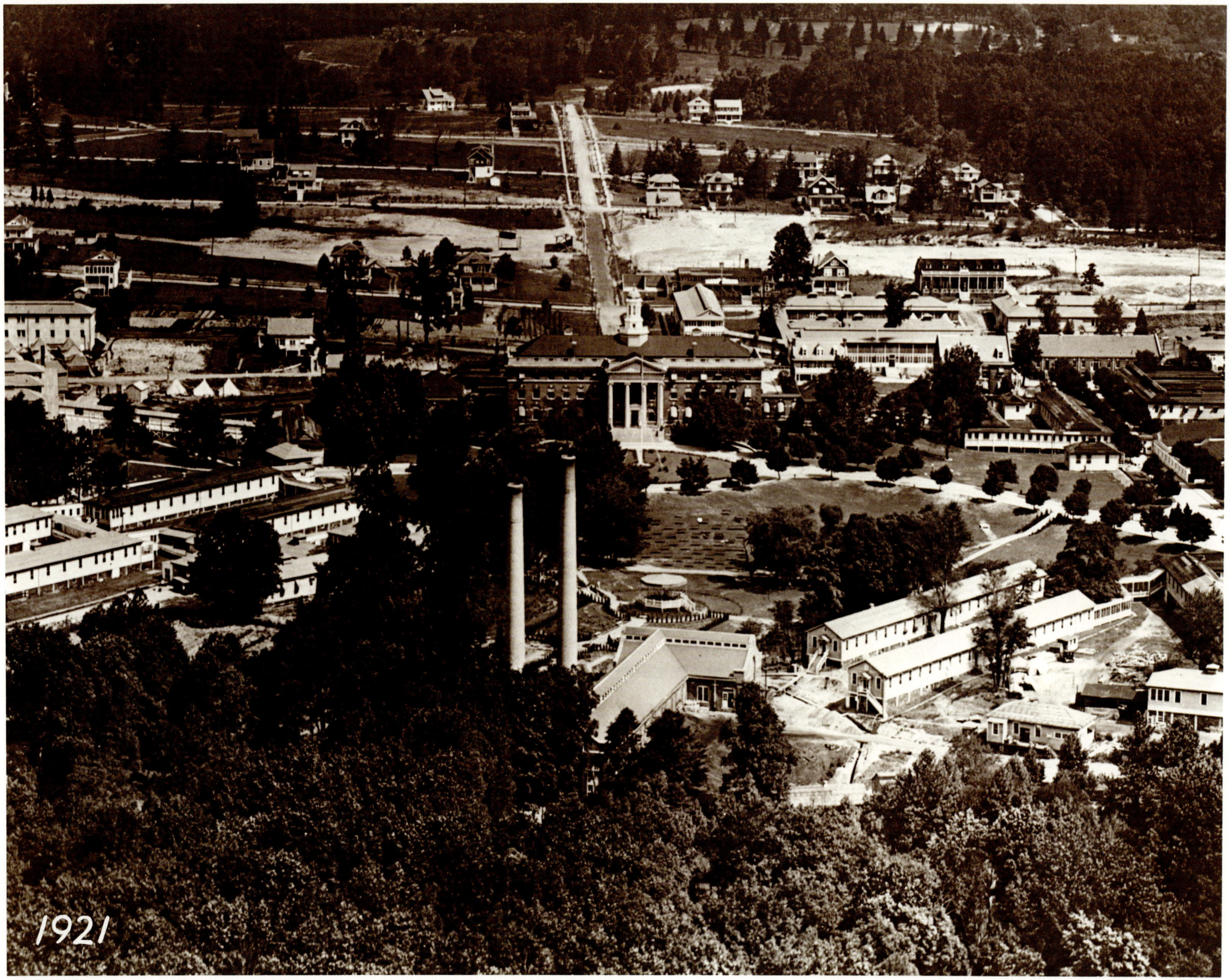

At Walter Reed Hospital the Georgian building at center was erected in 1908. It signalized the 1896 plan to group scattered military medical facilities. It was named for the surgeon whose death was hastened by his great research in yellow fever. In this 1921 photograph the enormous expansions of 1917 and 1918 have raised the number of beds to 2,500 from the original 60.

Today the hospital dominates the Shepherd Park neighborhood. The quadrangular facility at right center, completed for the bicentennial, backs older structures with the new Armed Forces Institute of Pathology, upper left. It presents modern and major deviation from the Georgian initiative, perhaps comparing what can be done today in healing with what was possible in ruder times.

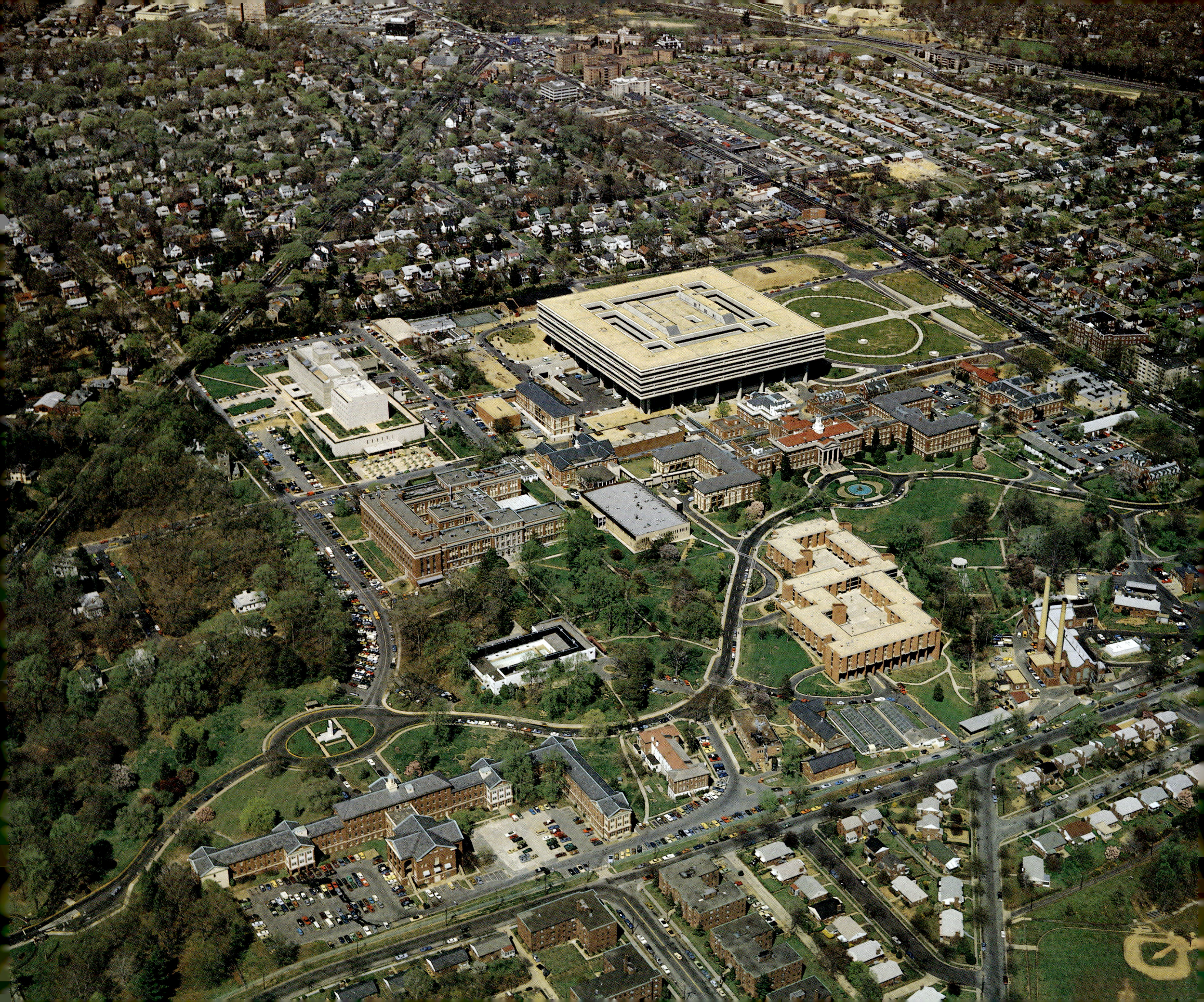

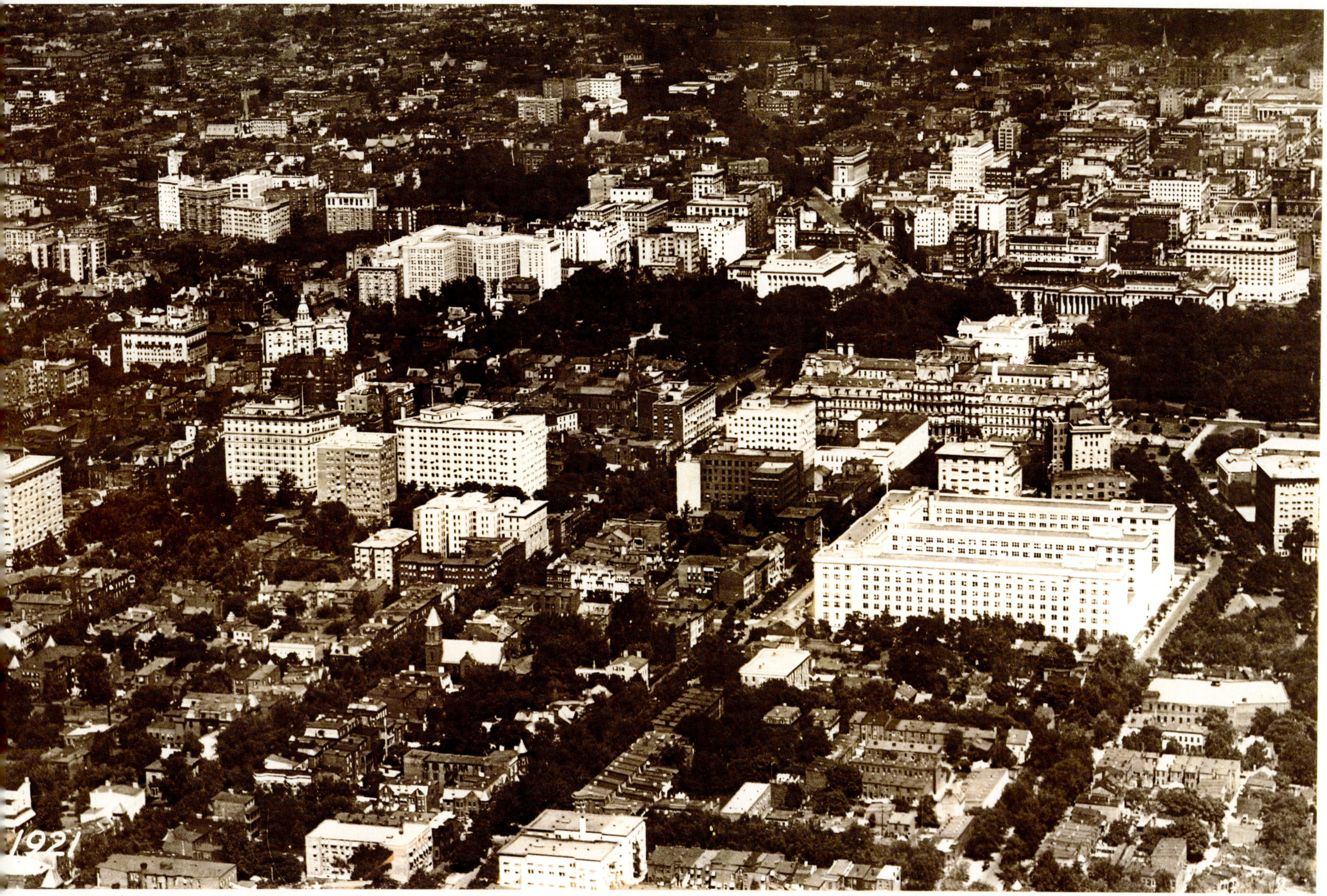

In 1921 Lafayette Square's aspect was low-scale residential. Across from St. John's Episcopal Church, above left center, were the houses of Henry Adams and John Hay. They and the square were urbane, genteel. Guests were H. H. Richardson who designed the houses, the sculptor St. Gaudens, the painter John LaFarge. Here Adams, son and Secretary to the Minister to England, grandson to the sixth president and great-grandson of the second, wrote the autobiography which intimately relates the great Massachusetts family of his name, to a Washington it knew so well in the first 100 years.

Now the North, West and East edge hugely toward the White House. They're held off by the old square in a scheme for which much of the credit must go to John Fitzgerald Kennedy, who mobilized the effort, and to his friend, the architect, John Carl Warnecke.

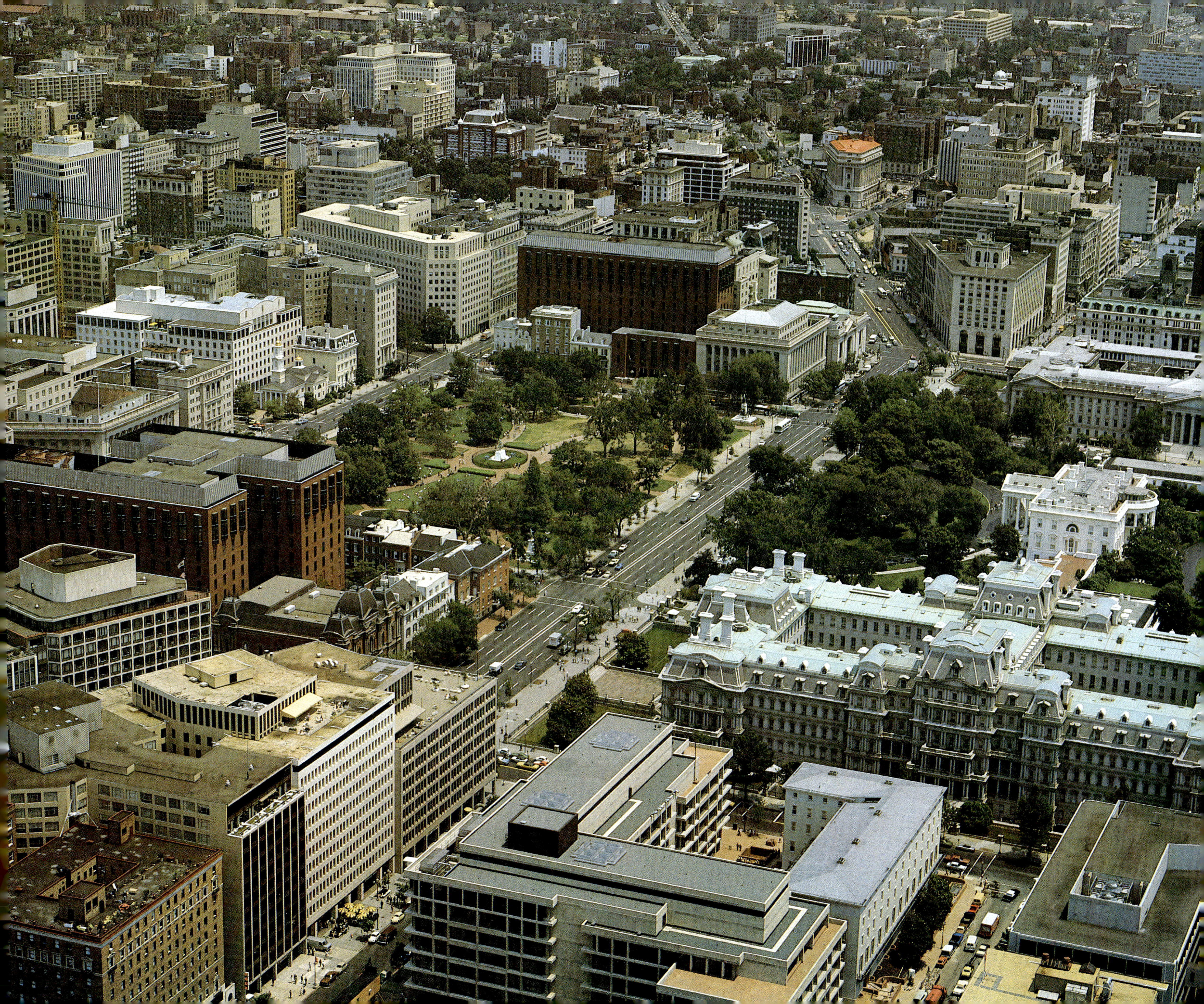

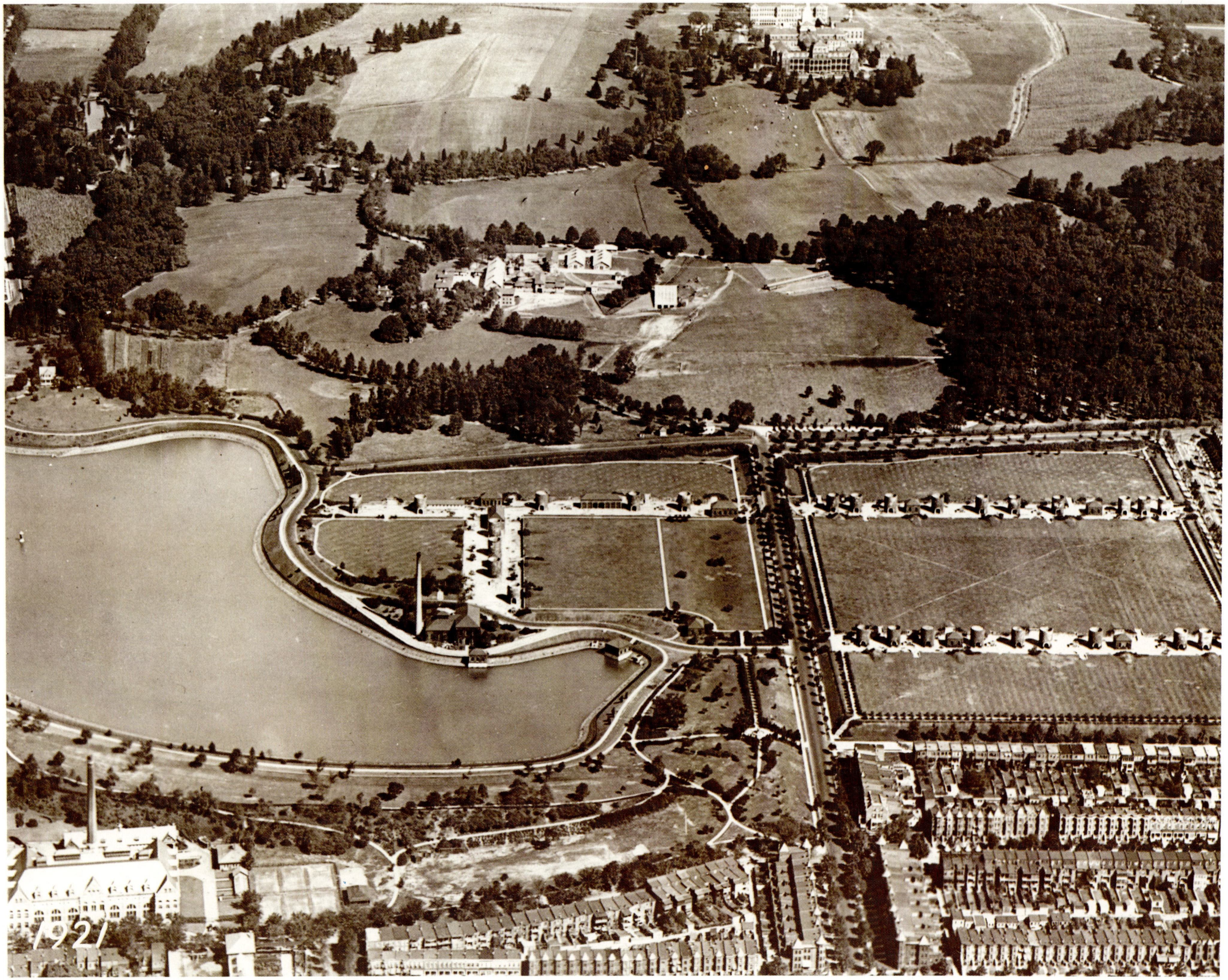

The Soldiers Home was founded by an act of Congress in 1851, at the insistence of General Winfield Scott, an act influentially supported by Senator Jefferson Davis of Mississippi. In 1921 upper right center, there was pasture, grazing. The center right structures were a filtration system for the McMillan Reservoir, water supply to downtown Washington. They are still in place.

Today the green area at left is the Soldiers Home. The Veteran's Hospital was developed on Soldiers Home land. The hospital complex was expanded with the completion in 1976 of the New Children's Hospital National Medical Center.

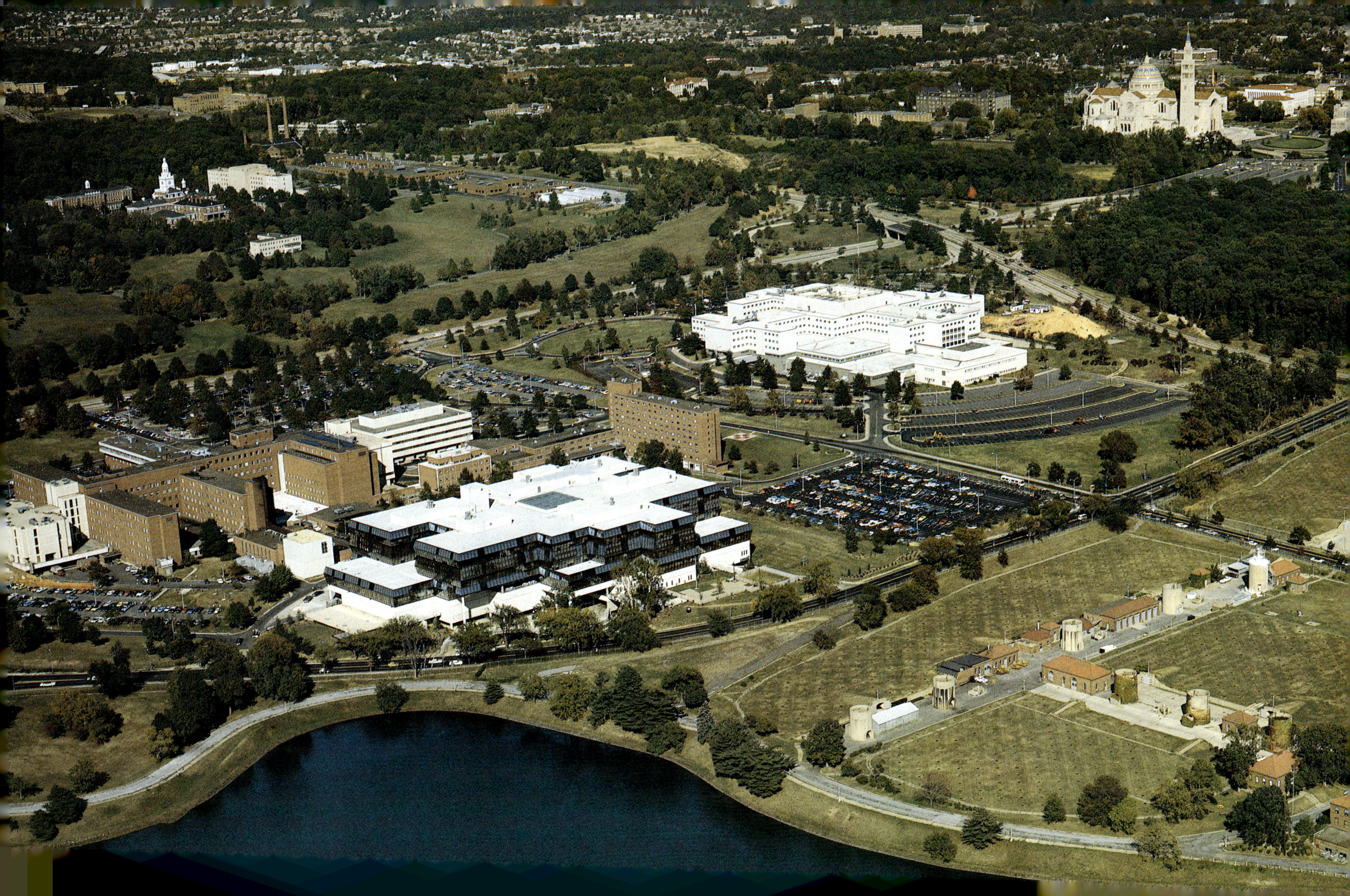

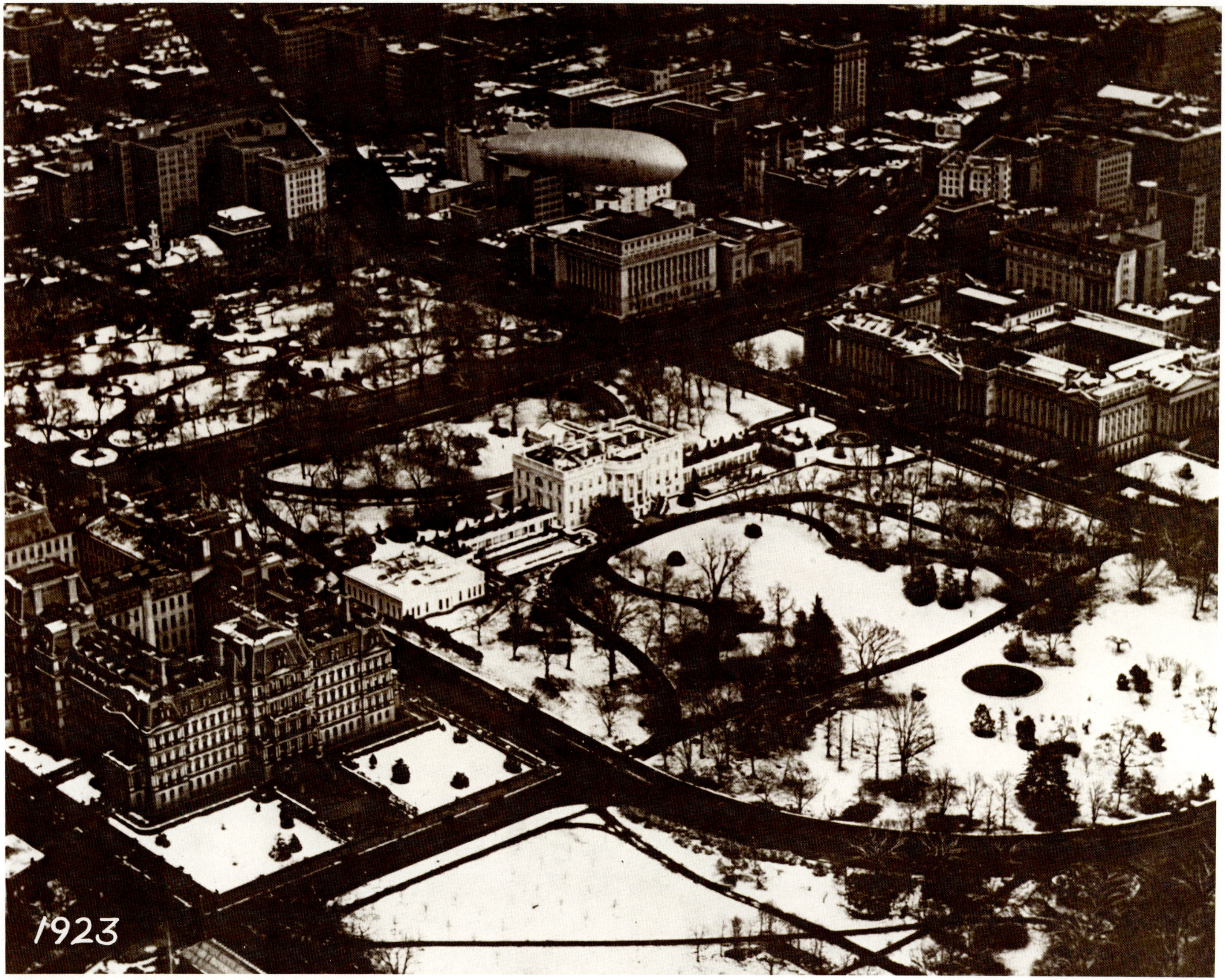

Blimp over snowy White House, circa 1923.

Helicopter on White House lawn, 1979.

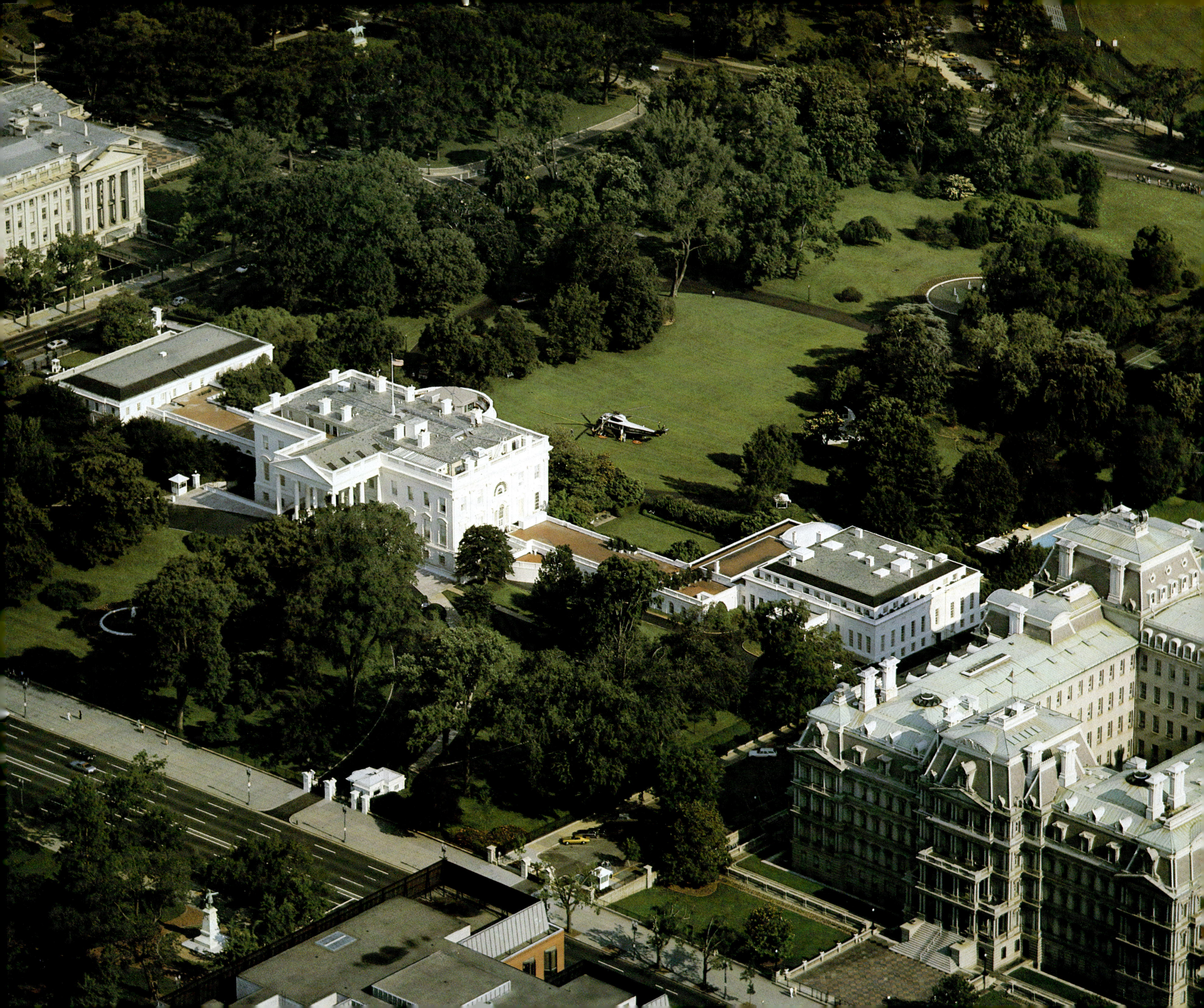

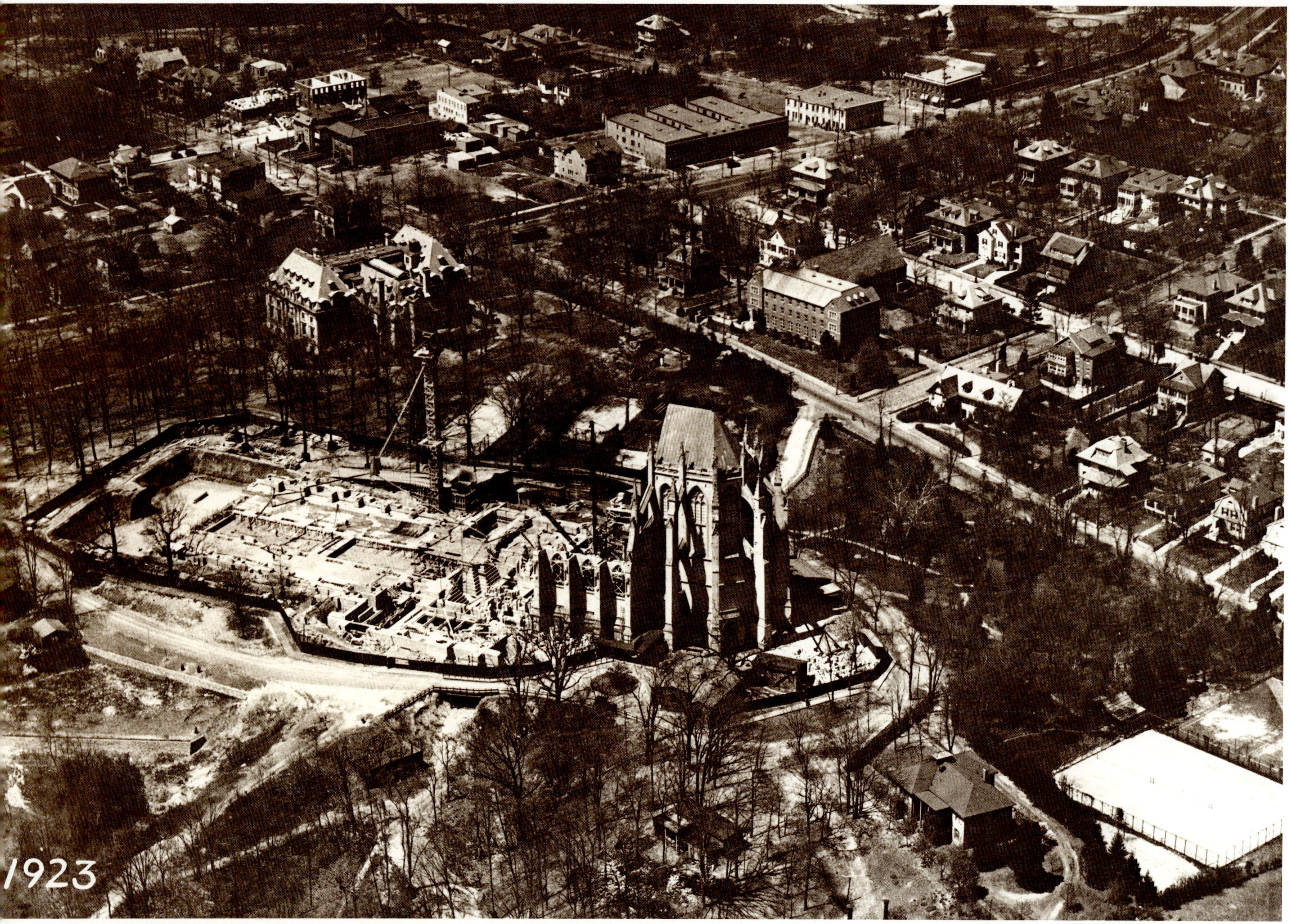

In the National Cathedral the precepts of fourteenth century Gothic architecture are dicta of time. Two stonemasons who worked on the structure as we see it here in the 1920's are still living, and it is still unfinished.

The cathedral of Sts. Peter and Paul, known as the Washington Cathedral, commands an unrivalled view from Mount St. Alban's. The central tower rises three hundred feet with a carillon of 53 bells. The south transept entrance is approached by the pilgrims steps. The square towers of the west face will be 232 feet high. The stones for their completion lie in front of them. The cathedral has no membership of its own. By the 1893 charter to the Episcopal Church from Congress it is "a house of prayer for all people."

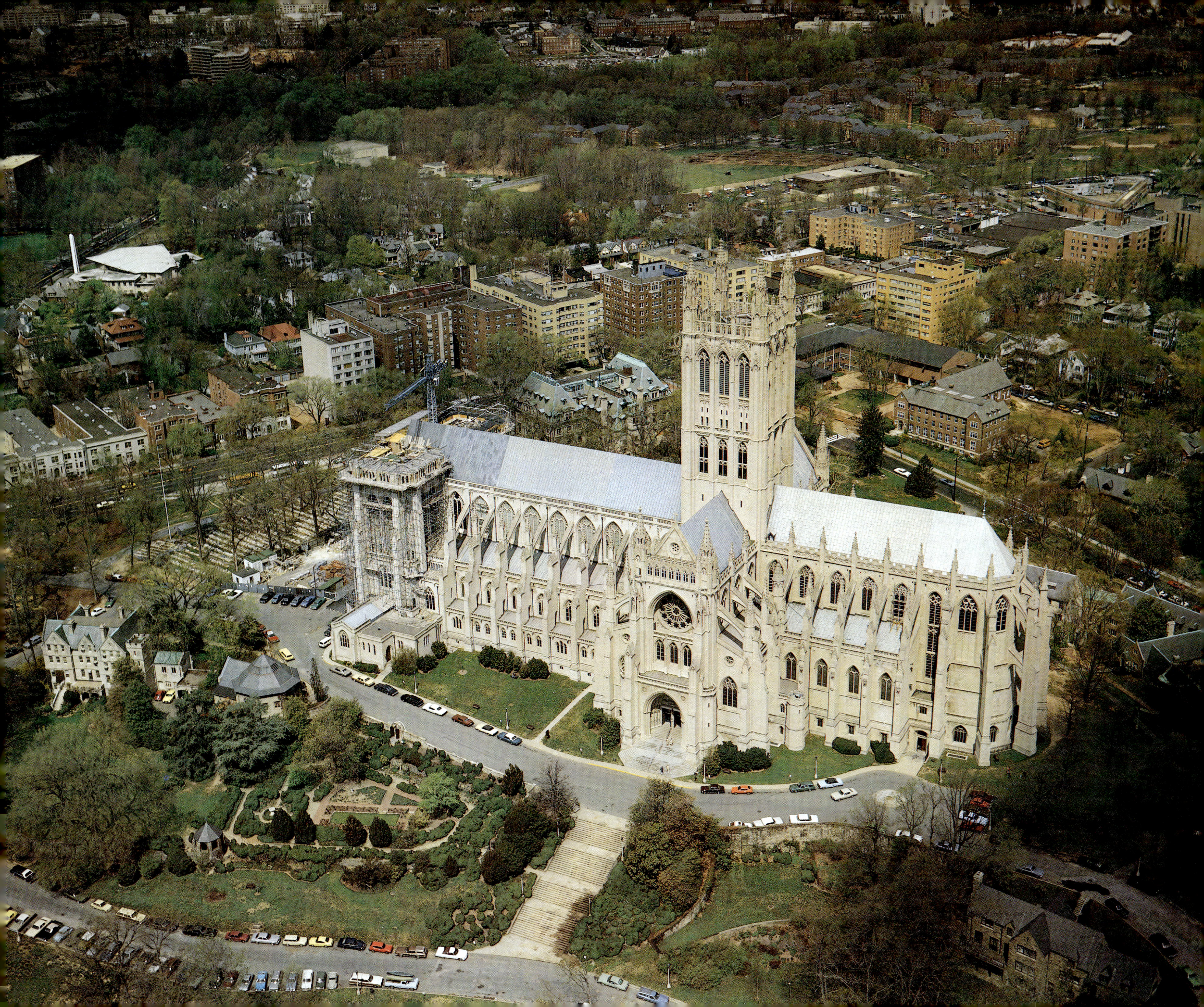

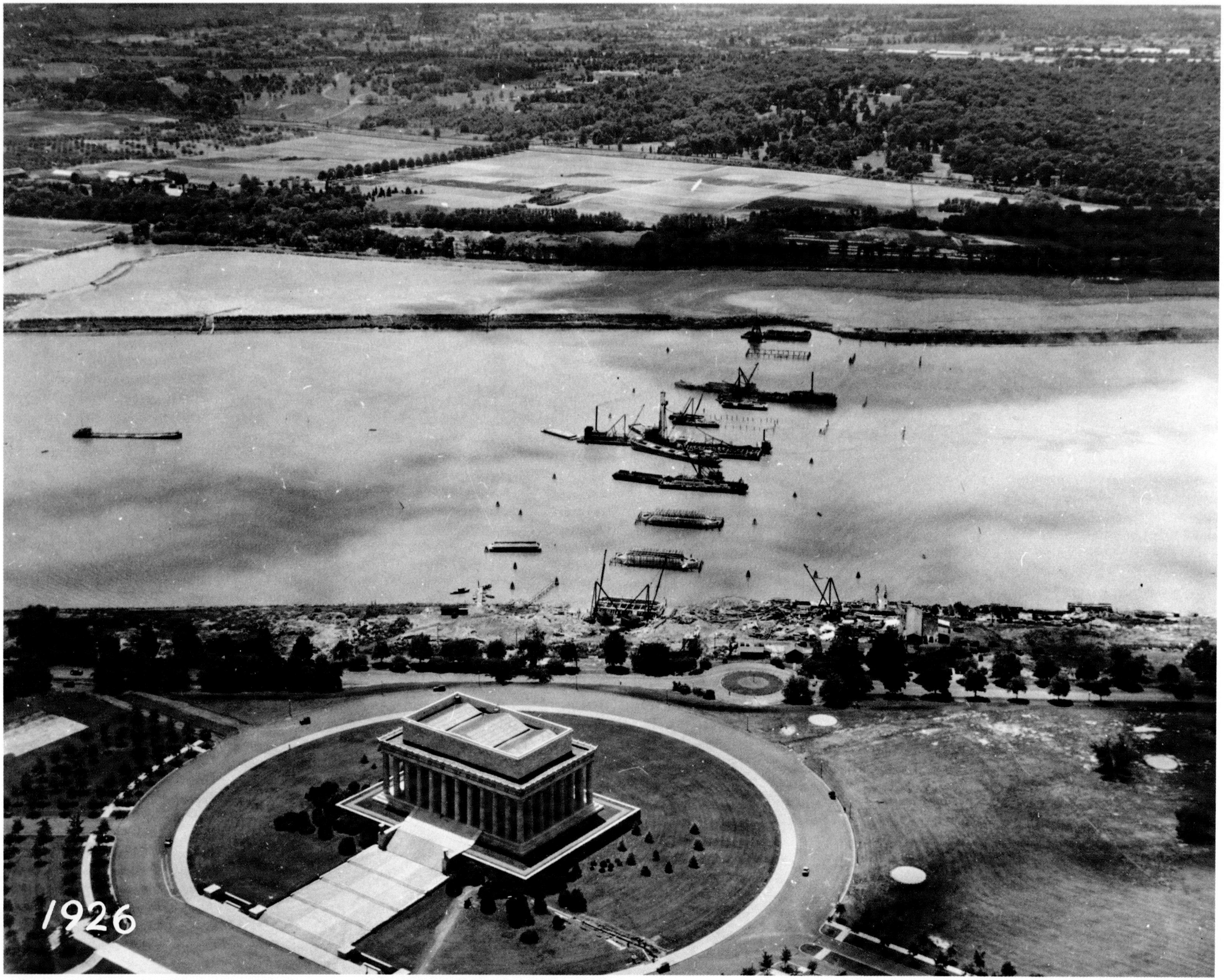

Arlington Memorial Bridge construction began in 1926. The piers seen here are from 32 to 41 feet in thickness and rest on rock 35 feet below the water. The need for a bridge had recurred strongly to President McKinley, accompanied by the McMillan Commission, when they were delayed by traffic jams trying to reach Arlington on Memorial Day in 1901. The cemetery, in the distance, was then still spacious. Now the burial sites are almost wholly occupied.

The bridge is now a formal compositional link between Arlington Cemetery and the monumental area of the District of Columbia. It was not intended as a commuter access, and is now somewhat overused. The watergate in the right foreground was planned as a formal entrance for dignitaries arriving in the city by water.

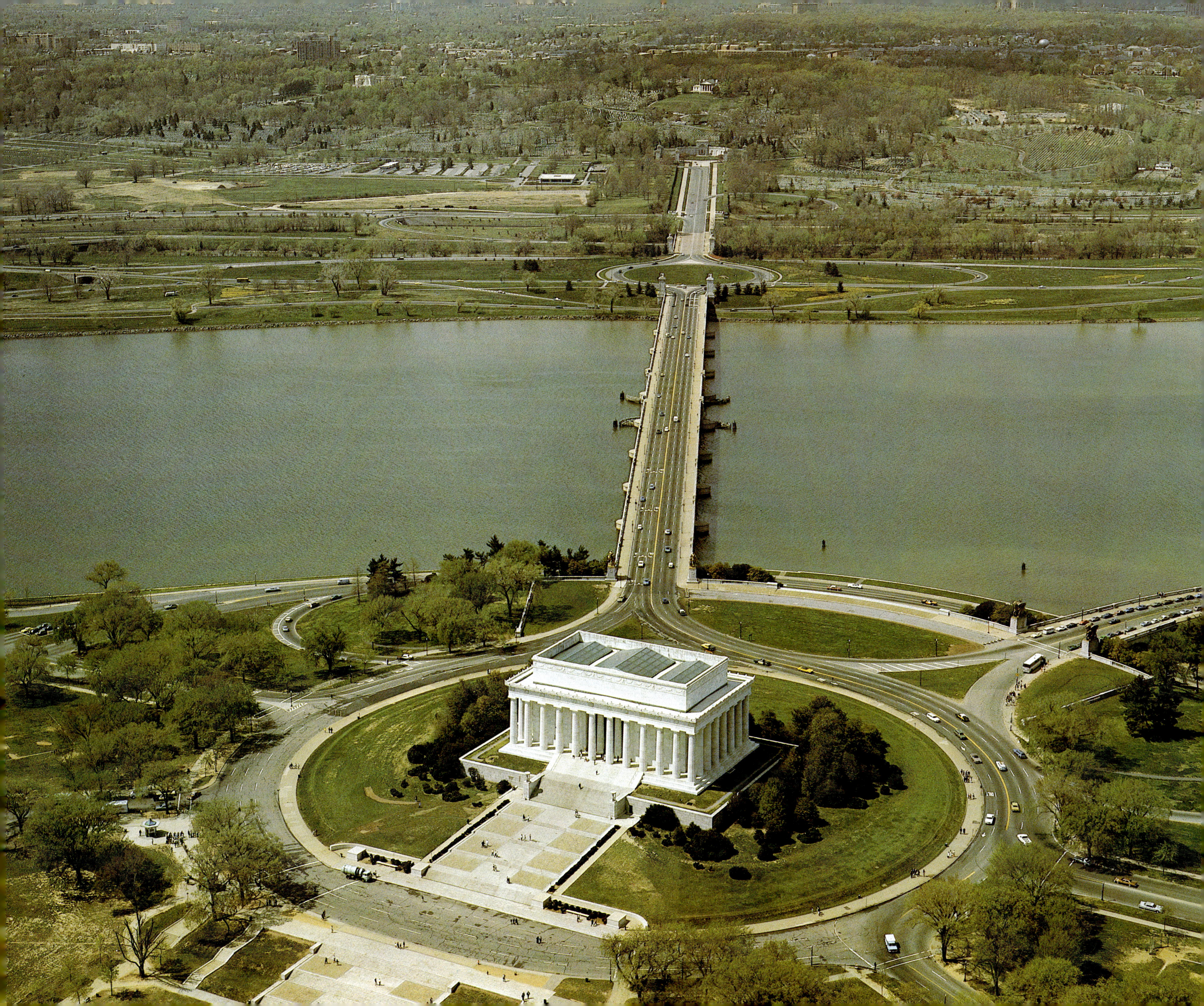

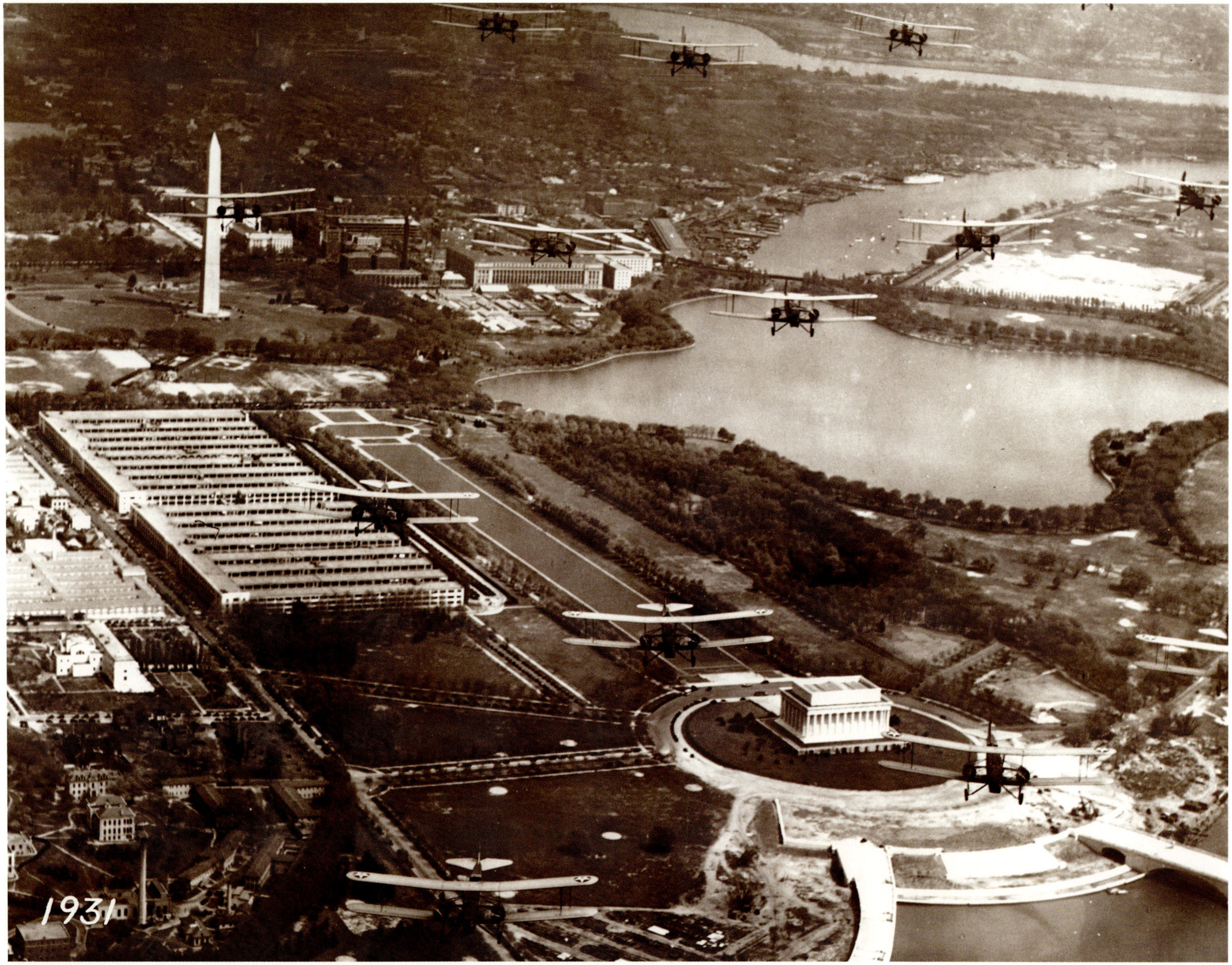

The Army Air Force 2nd Bombardment Group in a flyby above the Washington and Lincoln Monuments in 1931. Constitution Gardens have replaced the structures at left center. The Bureau of Engraving and Printing, at center, under the number two bomber of the right echelon of five, is still the greatest money-making plant in the world.

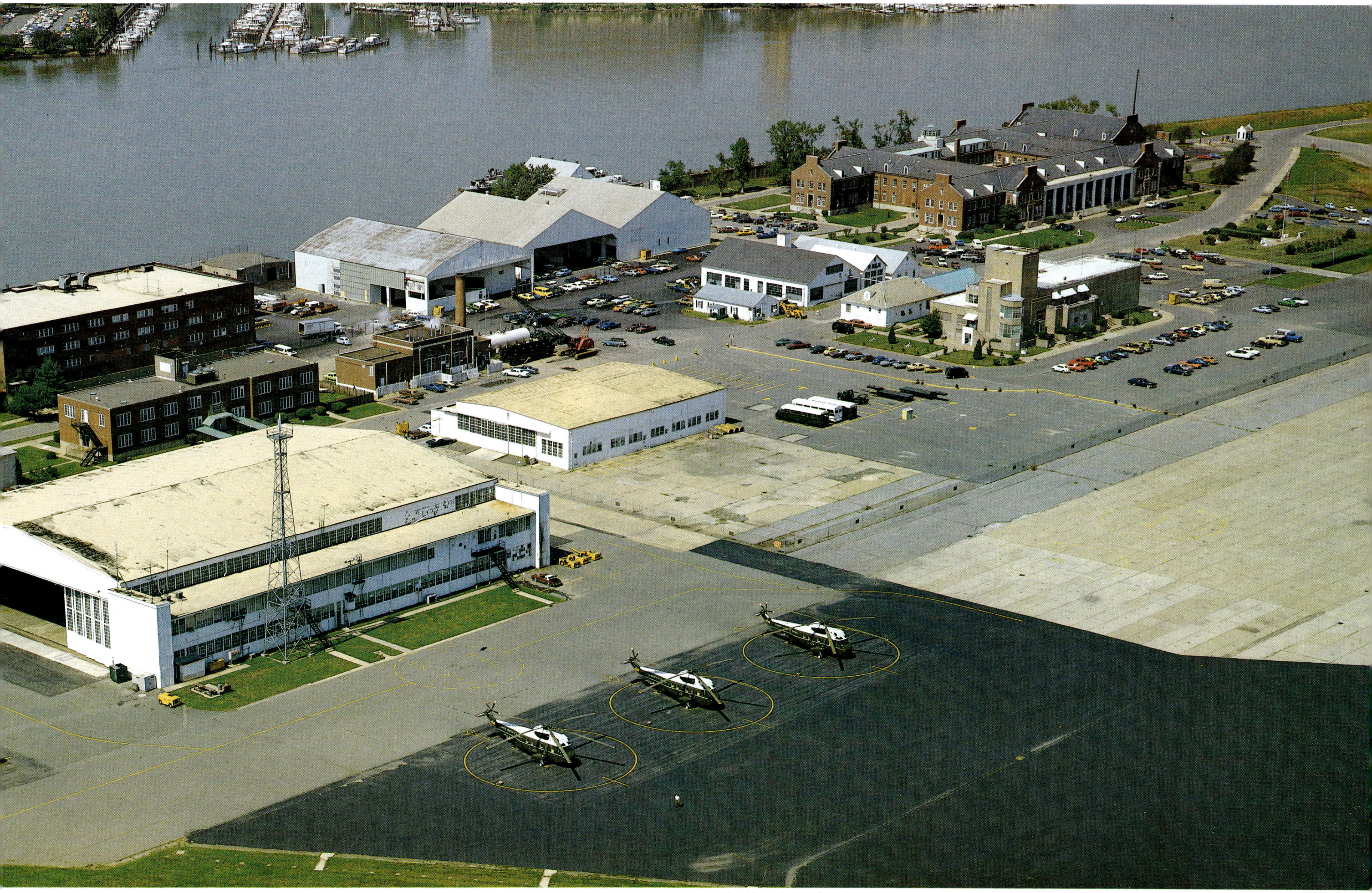

The Presidential Helicopter Flight Detachment is always at the ready. These helicopters transport the President and his family in the frequencies of local travel, from the White House to Camp David, to Air Force One, from Camp David home again. If more than one is in flight, that one occupied by the President is Marine One.

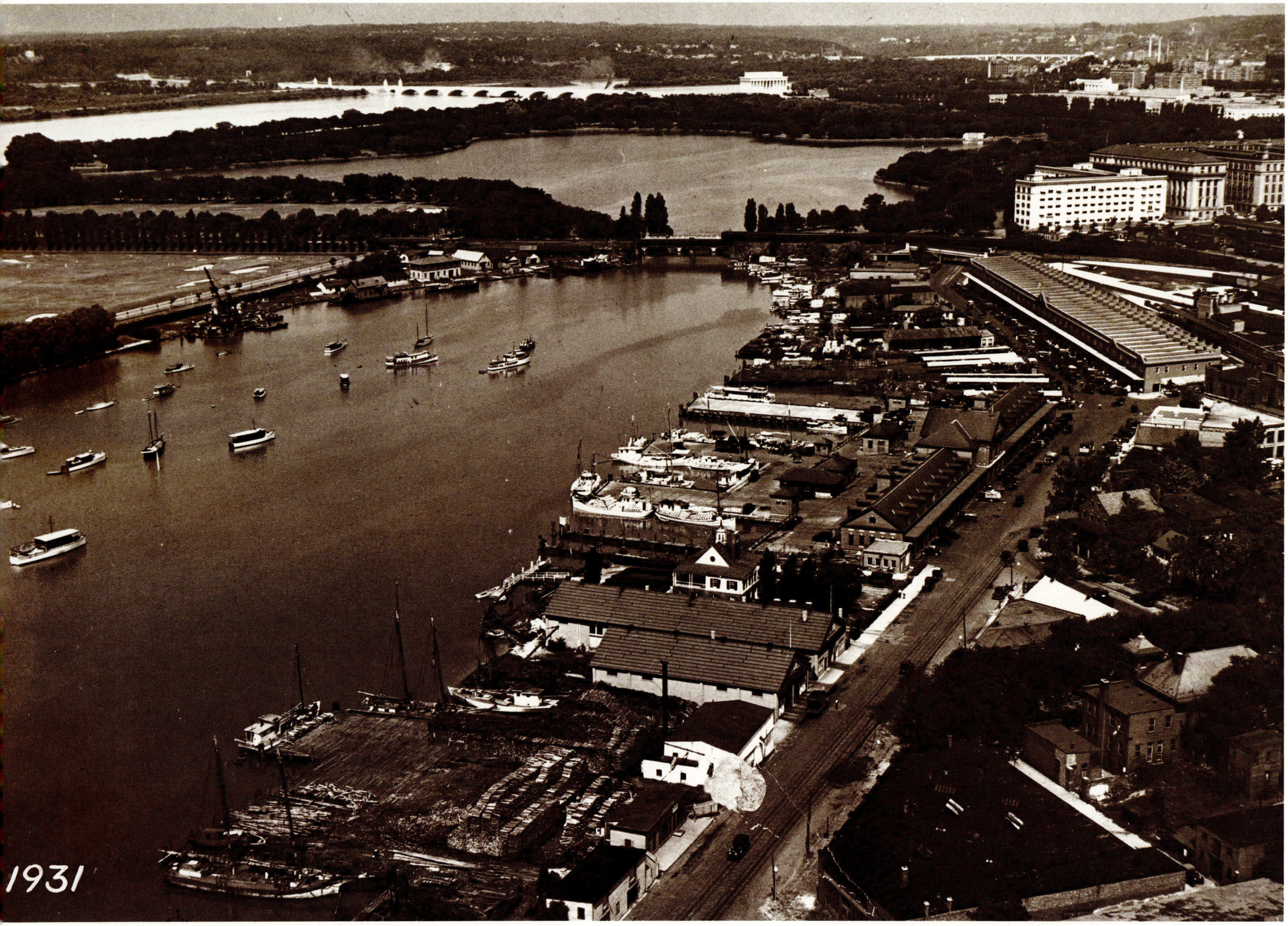

In 1931, it was a fishmarket and an active, cluttered, boating, low-scale waterfront, a contrast to the impounded elegance of the city's parks and the monumentality of the Mall. The 14th Street Railway Bridge was there and the Arlington Memorial Bridge newly completed.

Today the Southwest Freeway dominates the area with 1960's urban renewal all about on every hand. At right midground is the Bannecker overlook, southern terminus of L'Enfant Plaza. Benjamin Bannecker, a Black mathematician, served by George Washington's appointment on L'Enfant's commission for surveying and laying out the city. Pleasure craft, marinas, restaurants and hotels now line the river's edge. At left center we see the Metro Tunnel construction now in progress.

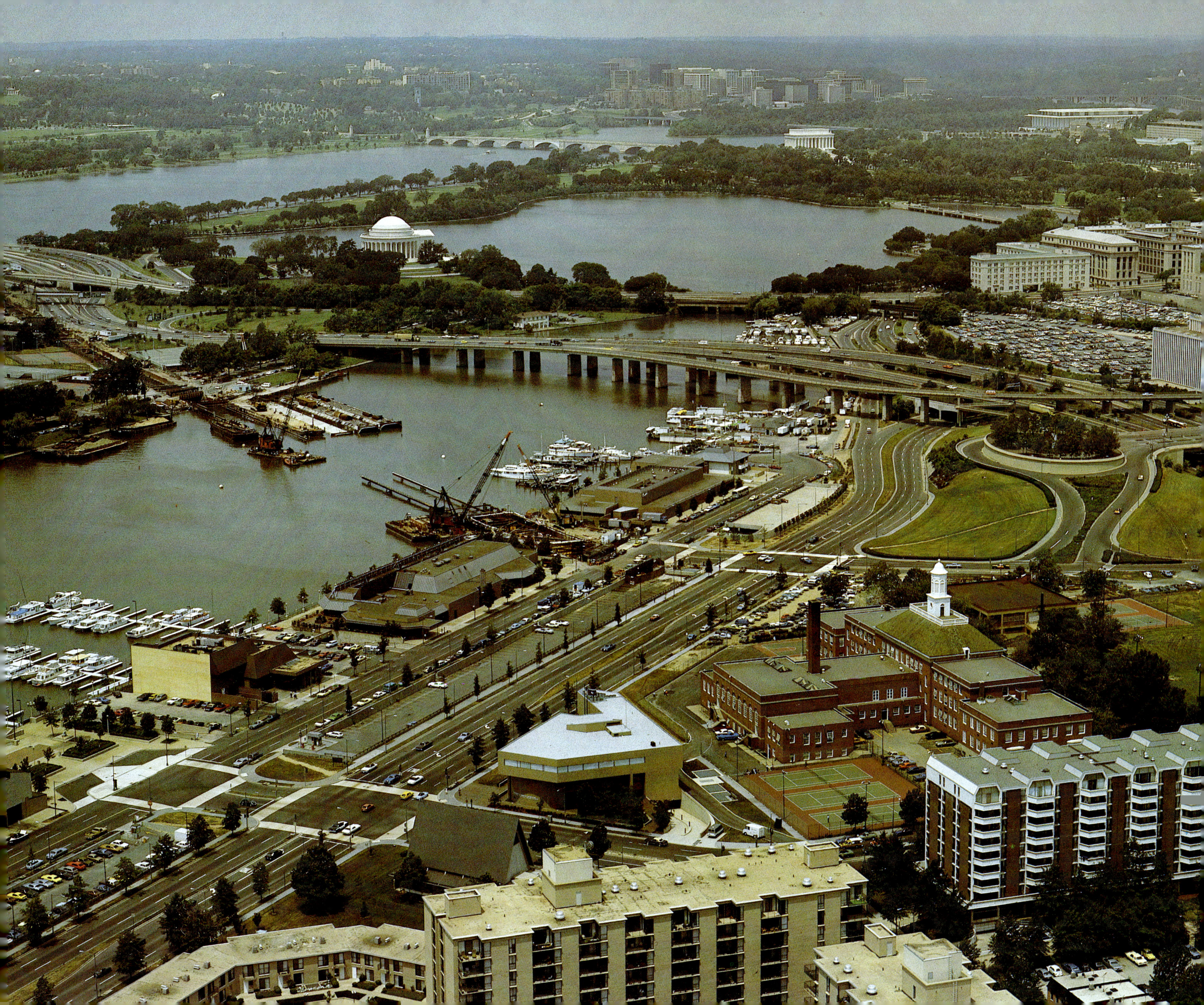

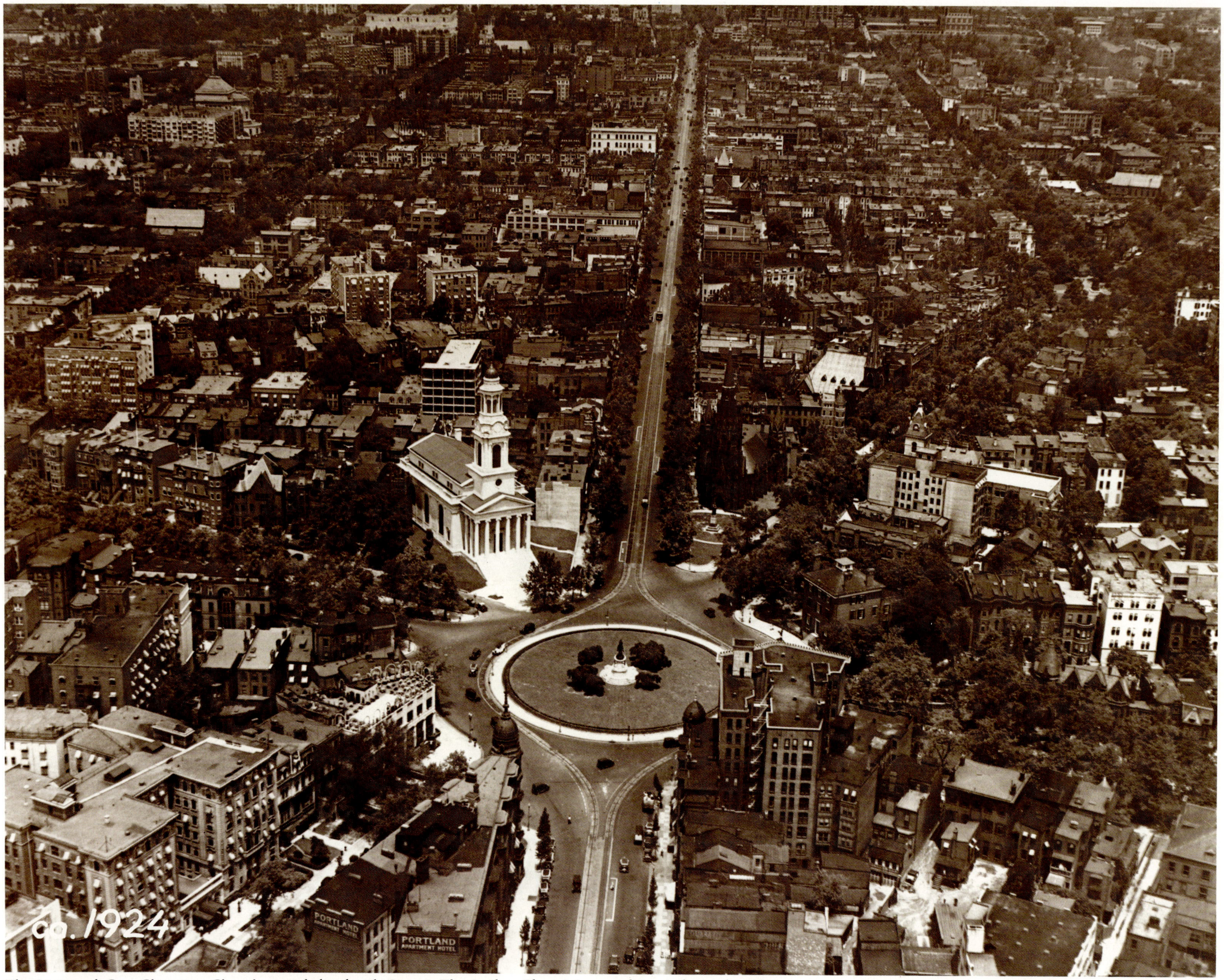

The National City Christian Church is at left of 14th Street. The Luther Place Memorial is at the right. The box-like house on the circle at right, demolished in 1947, was the home of Andrew Wiley, one of the judges responsible for the conviction and hanging of the conspirators in Lincoln's assassination. The great horse chestnuts extending from Logan Circle at upper right are long gone. Many other splended varieties of trees in an older Washington are victims of blight, neglect and pollution.

Today Massachussetts Avenue passes under Thomas Circle. Downtown pressures have surrounded the circle with high rise office, apartment and hotel buildings. The Burlington Hotel, above the circle at center, is in the process of demolition.

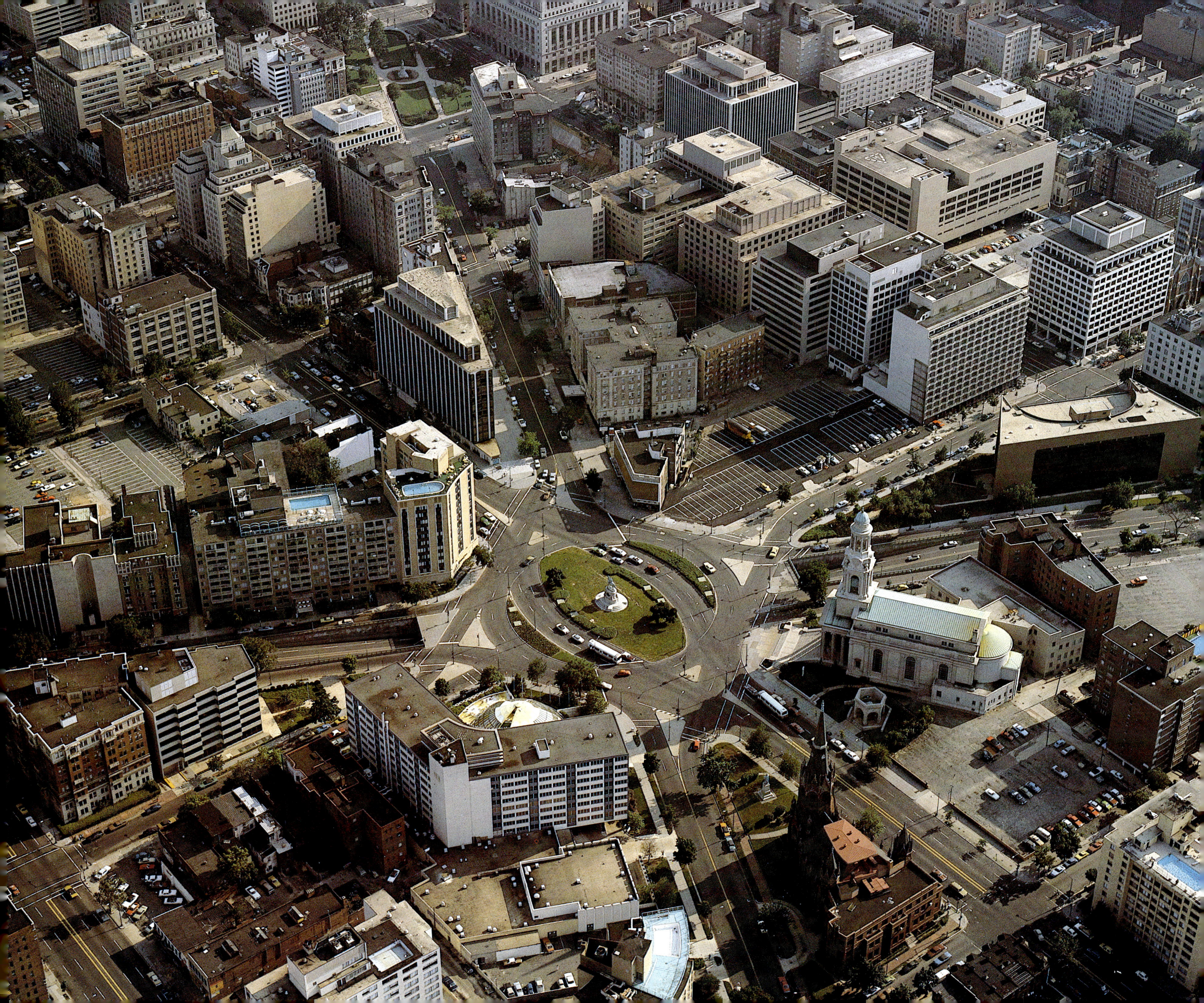

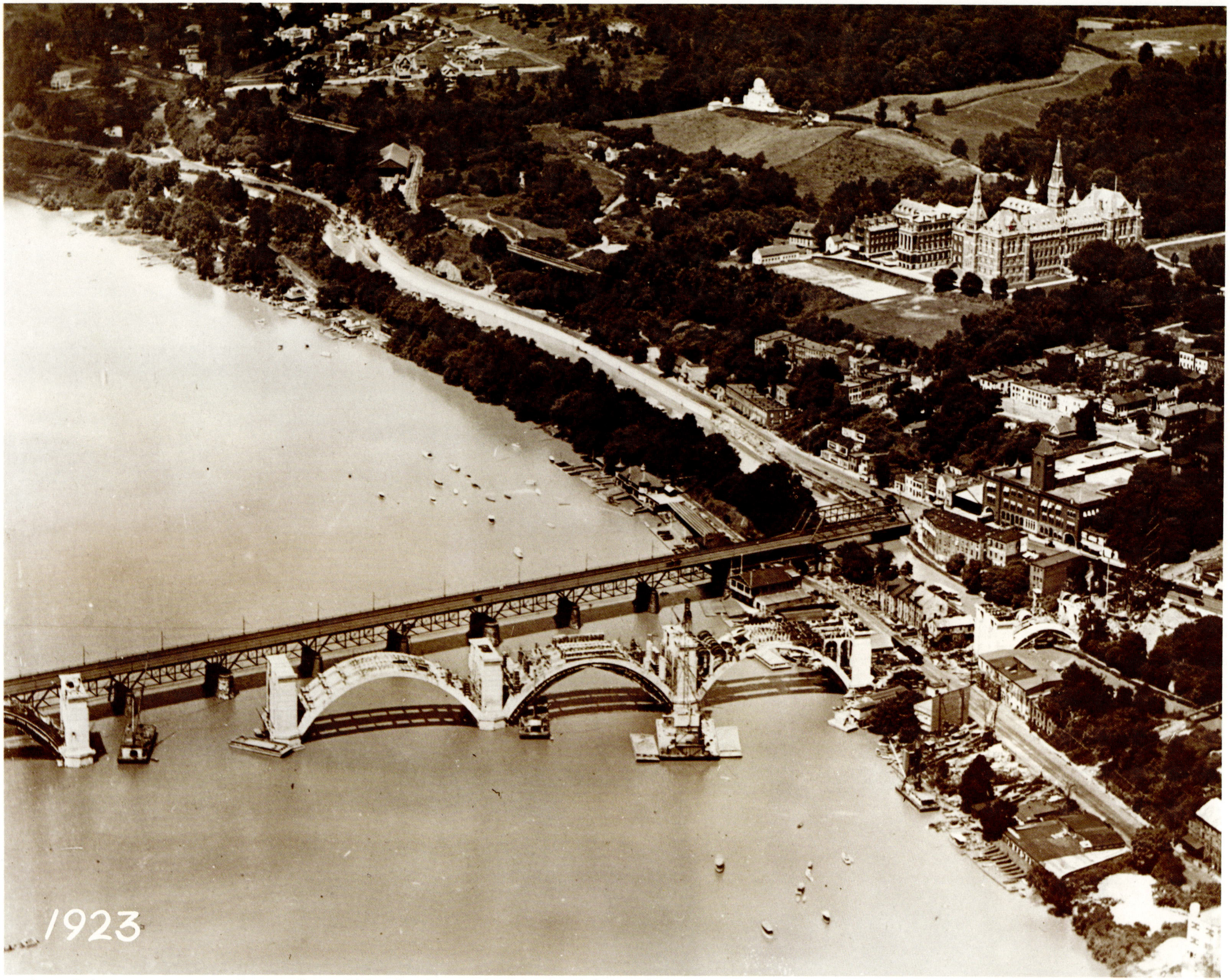

Healy Hall from 1879, upper right, was designed by the same architects who did the Library of Congress. Old North, at the north side of the square formed by this building group, is the oldest campus building, a gem of the Georgian-Federal style, from 1793-1795. Georgetown is the oldest Catholic college in the U.S. The Observatory was built in 1843. The Aqueduct Bridge will make way for the Key Bridge.

Today the Key Bridge-Whitehurst Freeway is in the foreground, beyond them the old car barn. The university buildings are expanding, encroaching on the surrounding community. But to the right of the car barn "Hessian Hill" is still cobblestoned from what was ballast in Hessian ships of the revolutionary times.

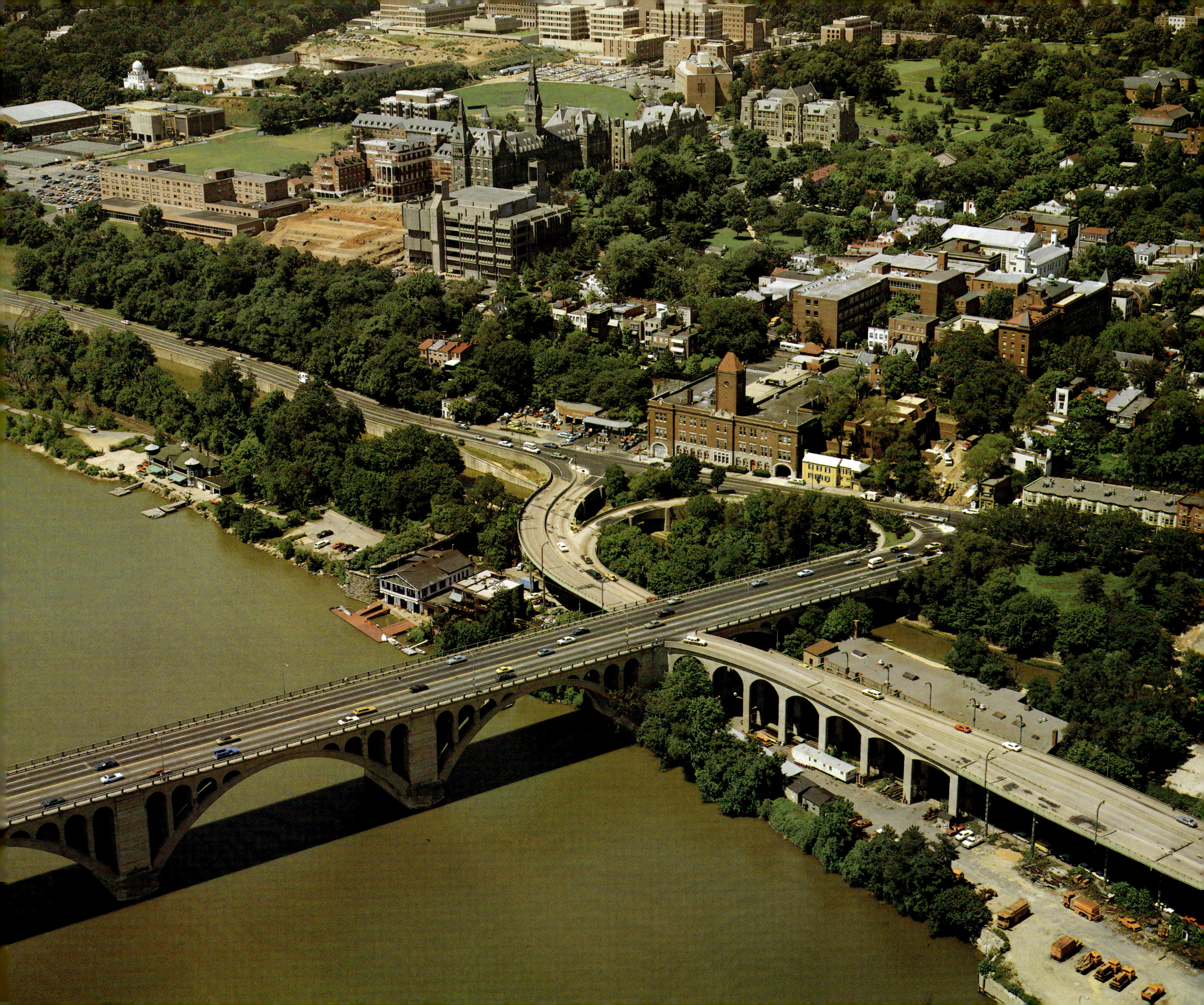

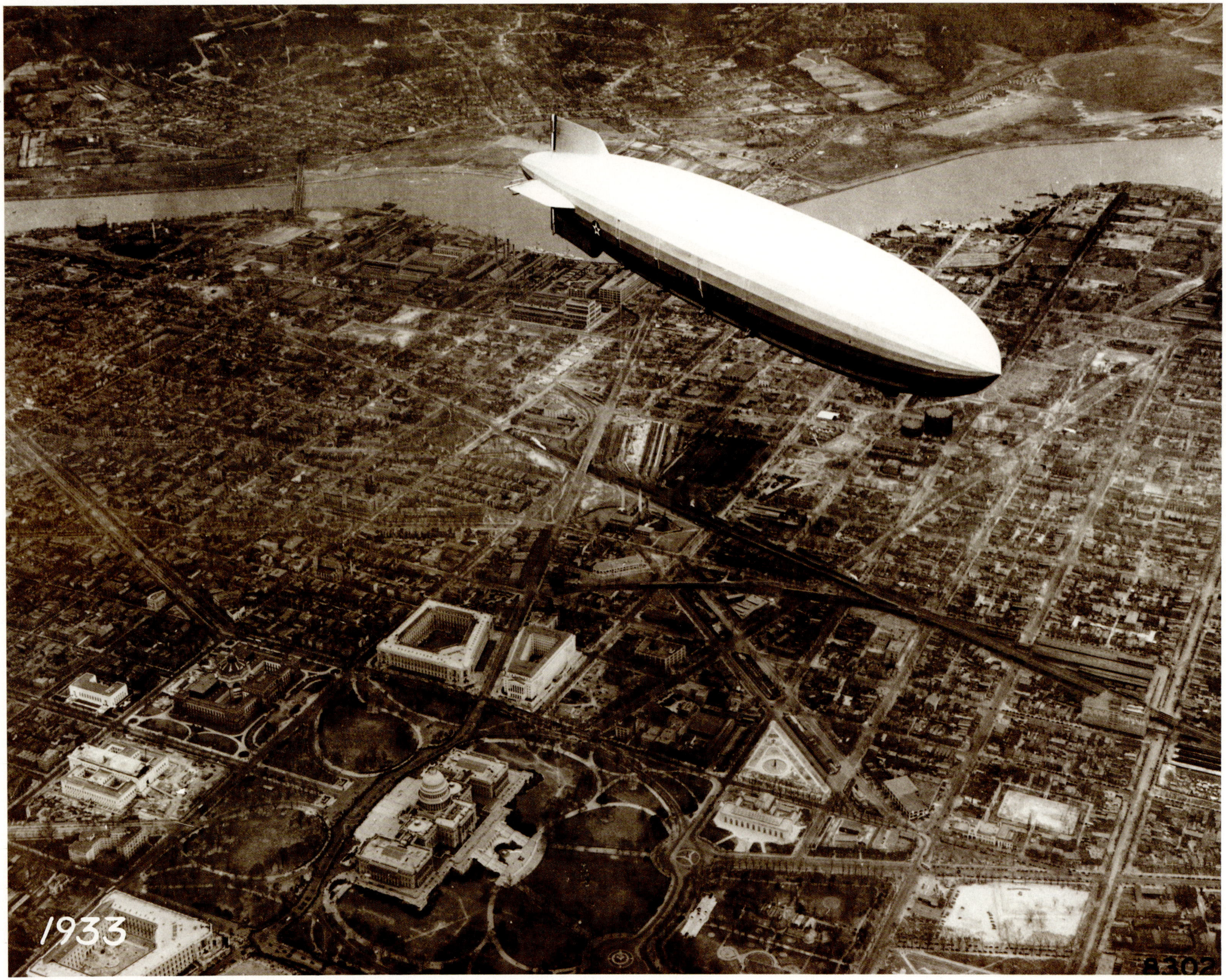

The dirigible "Akron" is over the Capitol on March 4, 1933, the day of the inauguration of Franklin Delano Roosevelt. There is a bareness, vacancy, as we involuntarily compare what we see here with what we know has come; an apprehension in the gray of the picture, that remembers the Nation's anxiety on that date.

A bright day shines upon a more hopeful present. The remarkable I.M. Pei East Wing of the National Gallery, 1978, at low center, is perhaps a signal of imagination for the times to come.

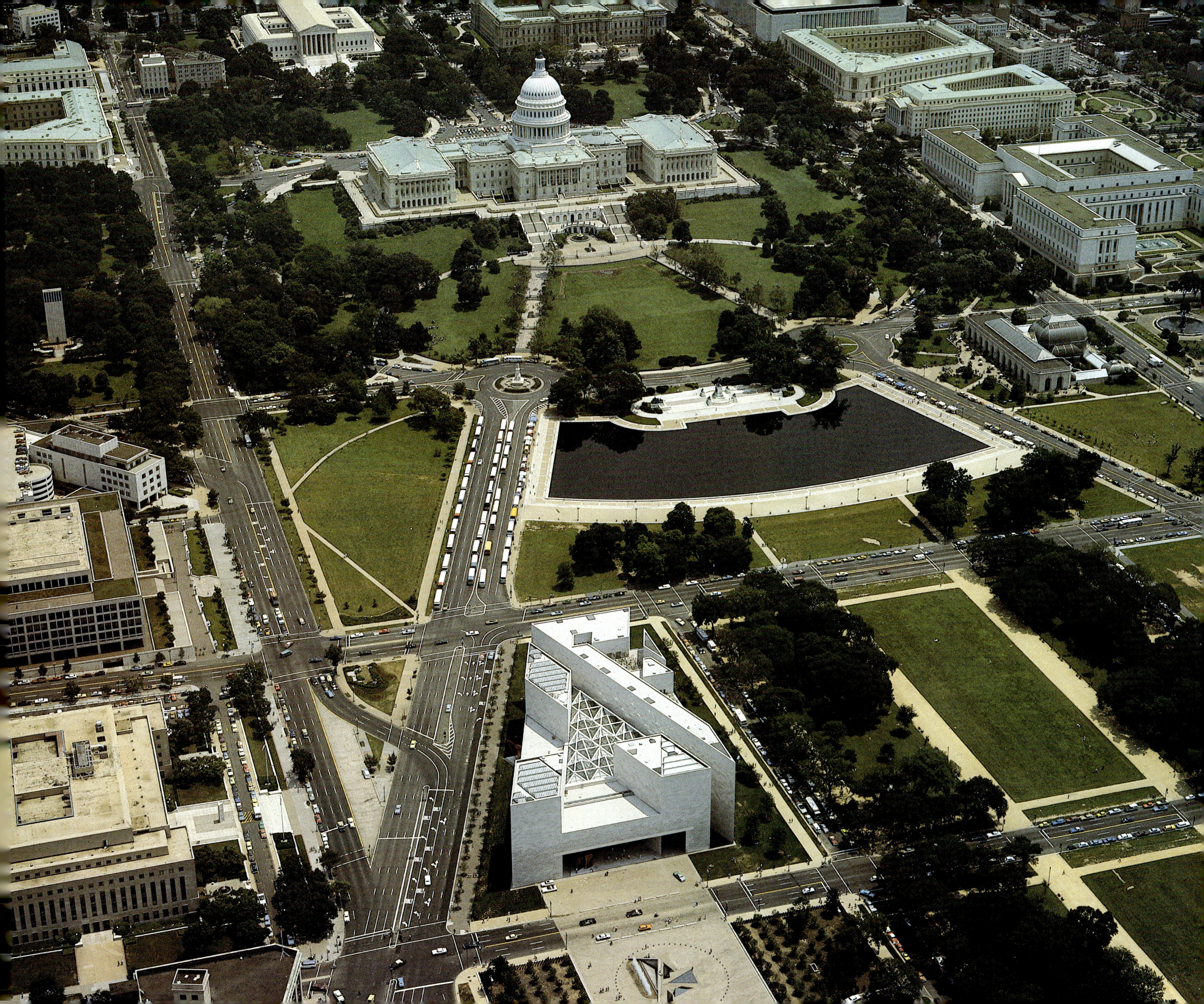

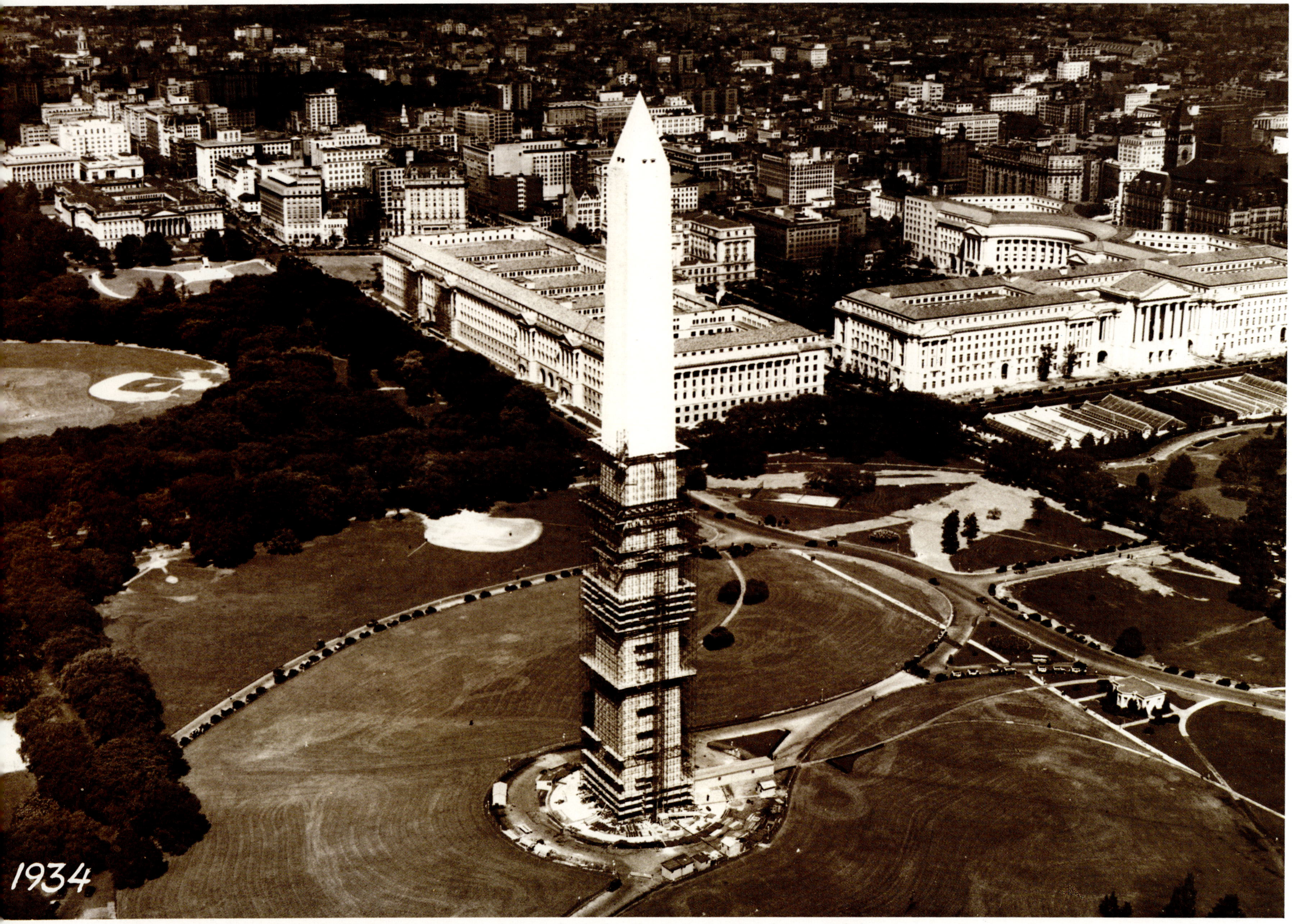

It took some 80 years to build the Washington Monument. It was finished in the 1880's. By 1934 when it needed refurbishing, the ideas of the McMillan Commission of 1901 were reaching an aggrandized fulfillment in the Federal Triangle. The Commerce Department Building is at center, on its right the Labor Department and then the Post Office Department, beyond which, indestructibly, remains the old Post Office Building, with its clock tower.

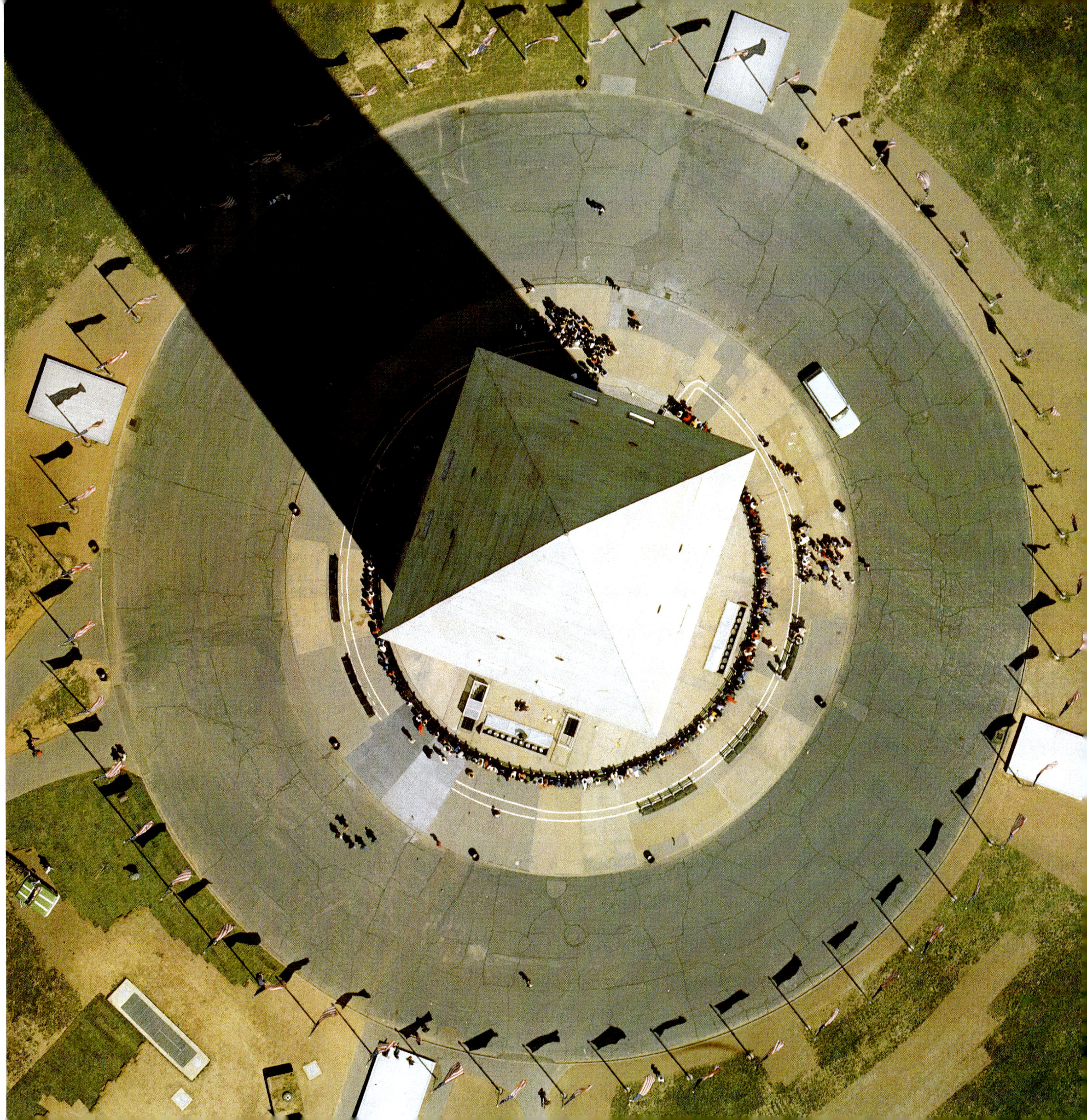

The Washington Monument is ringed by a flag for each state of the union. When Army engineers, with Federal financing, resumed the work which had been interrupted by the Civil War, the substructure was found inadequate. The monument had tilted. With a new base it was conformed to the traditional proportions of an obelisk. The squat cap of the original design was replaced by the steeply inclined pyramidion we look down to here. Straight down.

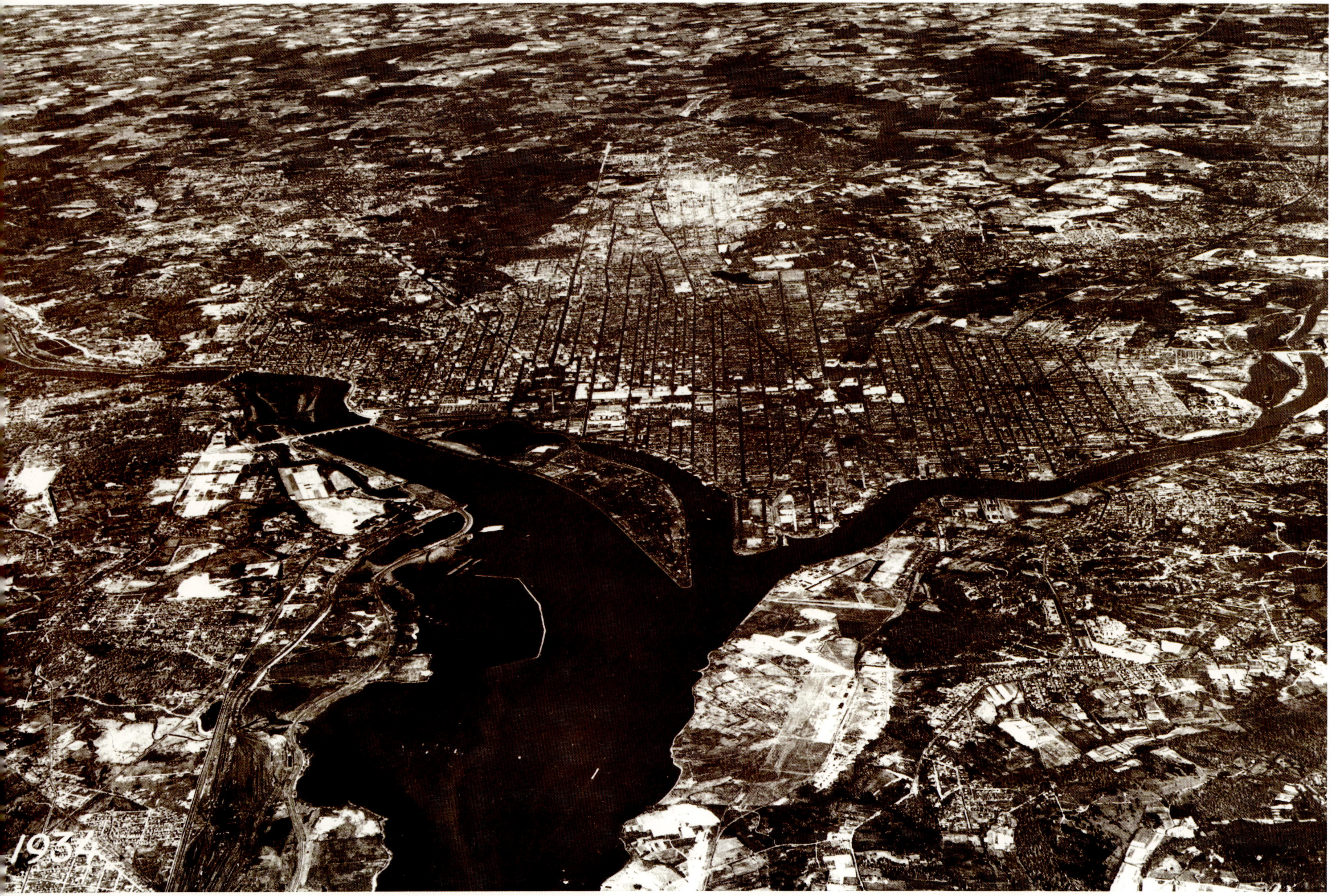

At lower left is the construction site for the Washington National Airport. At this great height we see the Y formed by the Potomac and the Anacostia in the fork of which the city is shaped. 16th Street is visible to the D.C. line. In the V formed by 16th Street and Connecticut Avenue, Rock Creek Park stretches into Maryland. Building along Connecticut Avenue was excited, at the turn of the century, by the development of Chevy Chase and its trolley line. But we see that beyond Florida Avenue, as late as 1934, the densities of the present were still to come. Certainly not the plan, but some of the concepts of L'Enfant lie before us. The layout called for square and rectangular grids of streets and broad radial avenues branching from park-like hubs and plazas.

Today's high aerial brings many realized features of the McMillan plan into compass. Relationships of the Capitol, the Washington Monument and the White House, to the Lincoln and Jefferson Memorials have been resolved. A low scale is generally preserved. In the Federal Triangle the principle of the uniform cornice has been apotheosized. The McMillan Commission's success stimulated Congress. We now have the Fine Arts Commission, founded in 1910, and the Capital Park and Planning Commission, in 1924. All have influenced a constantly amending and amended Washington.

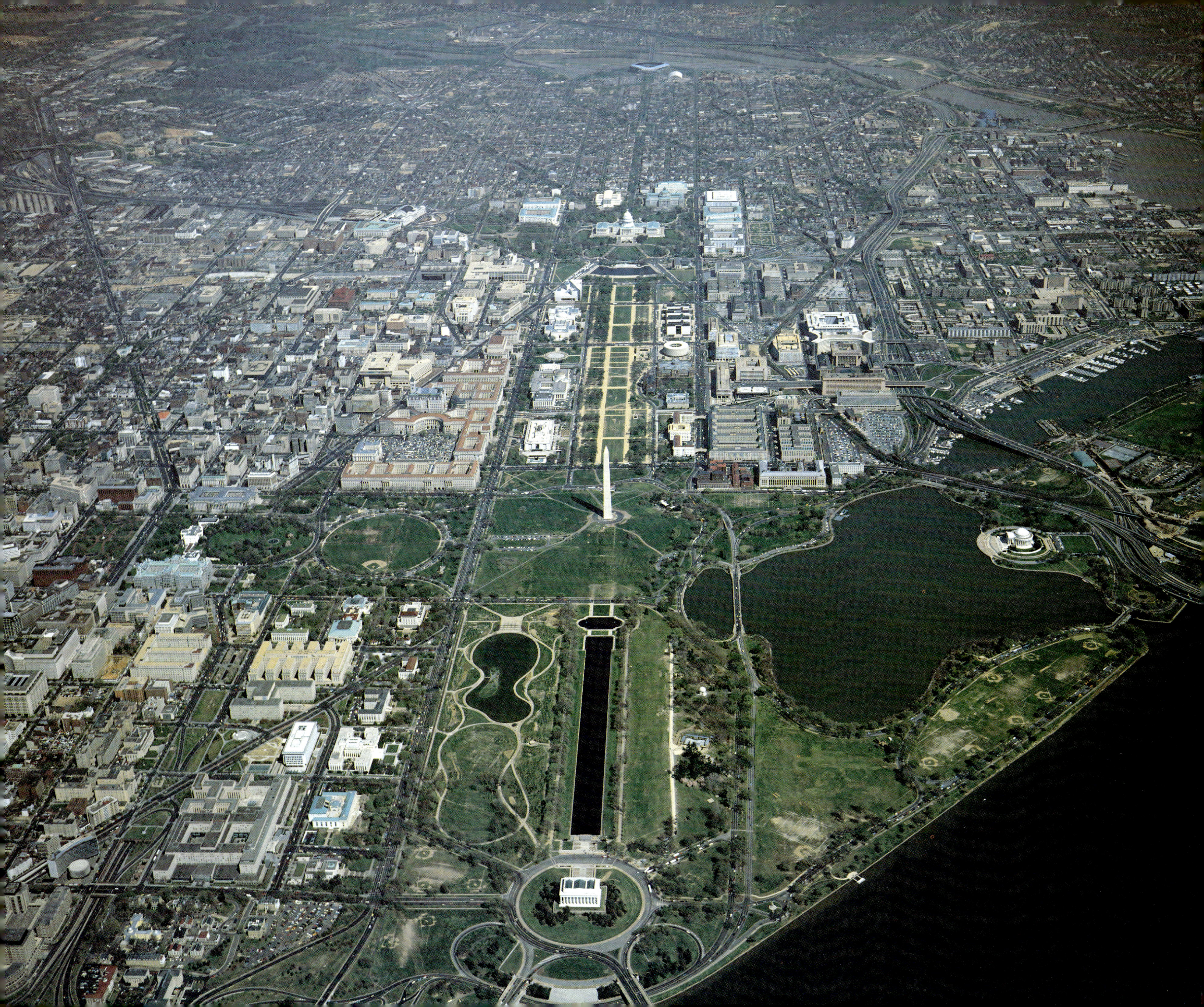

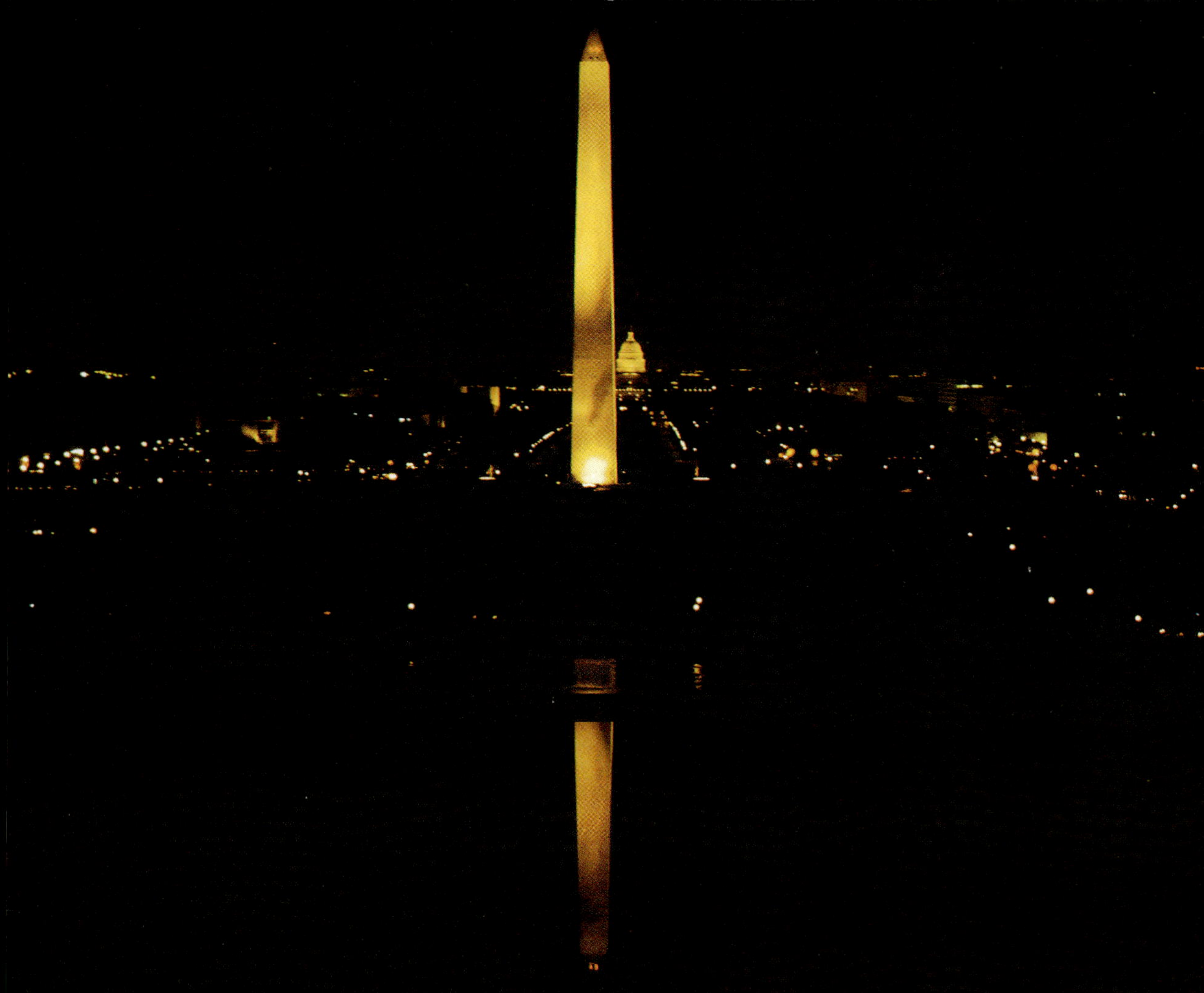
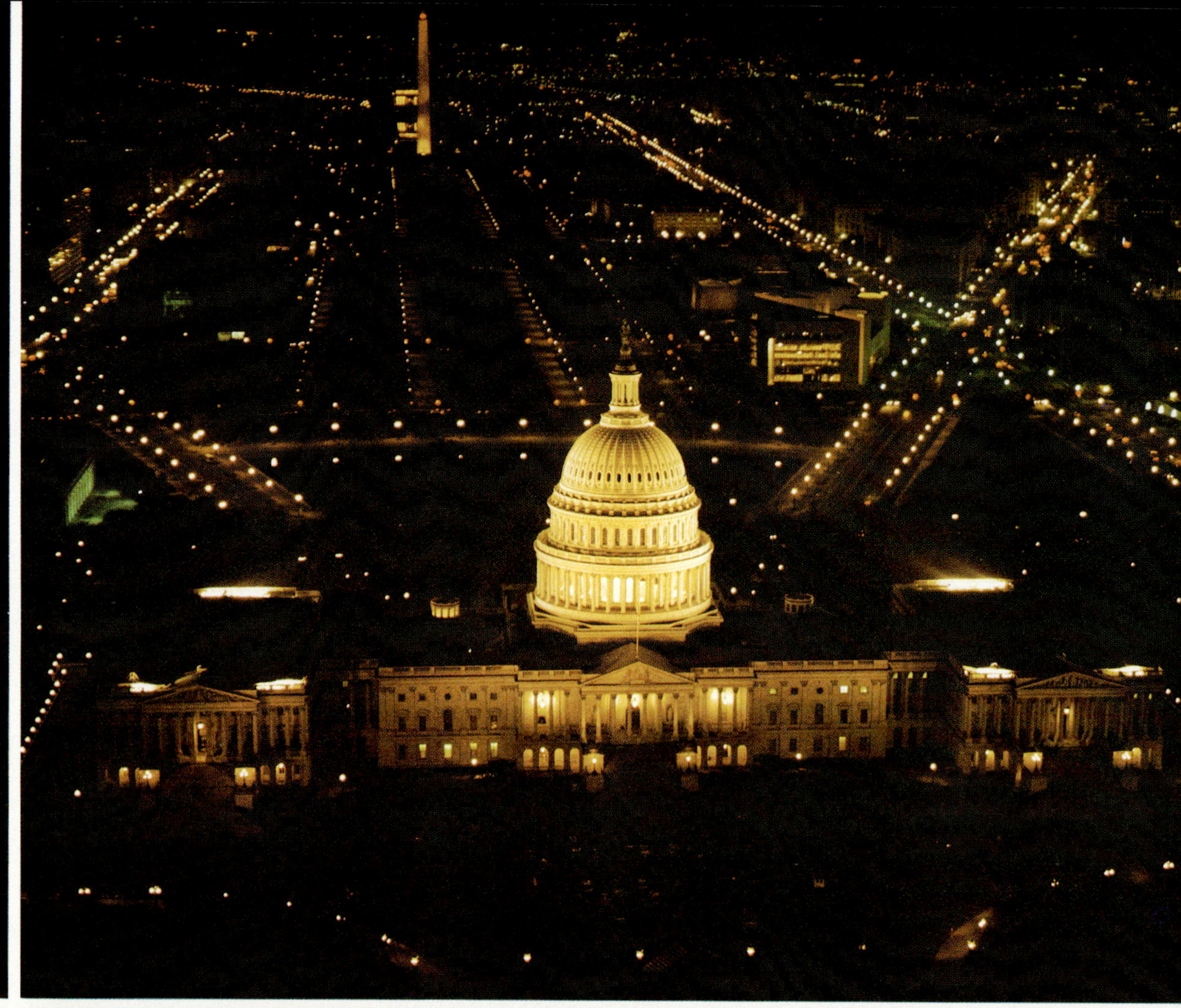
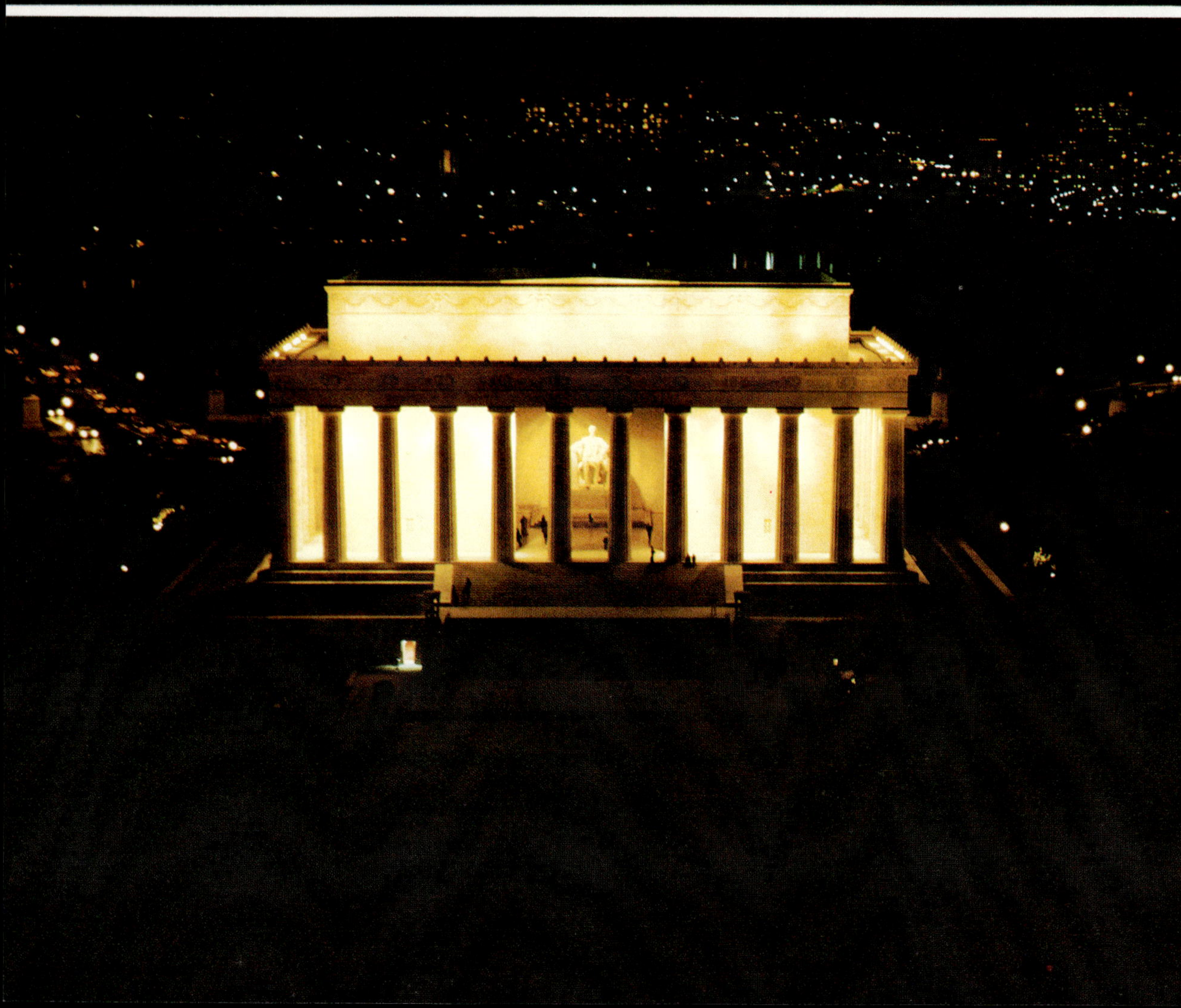
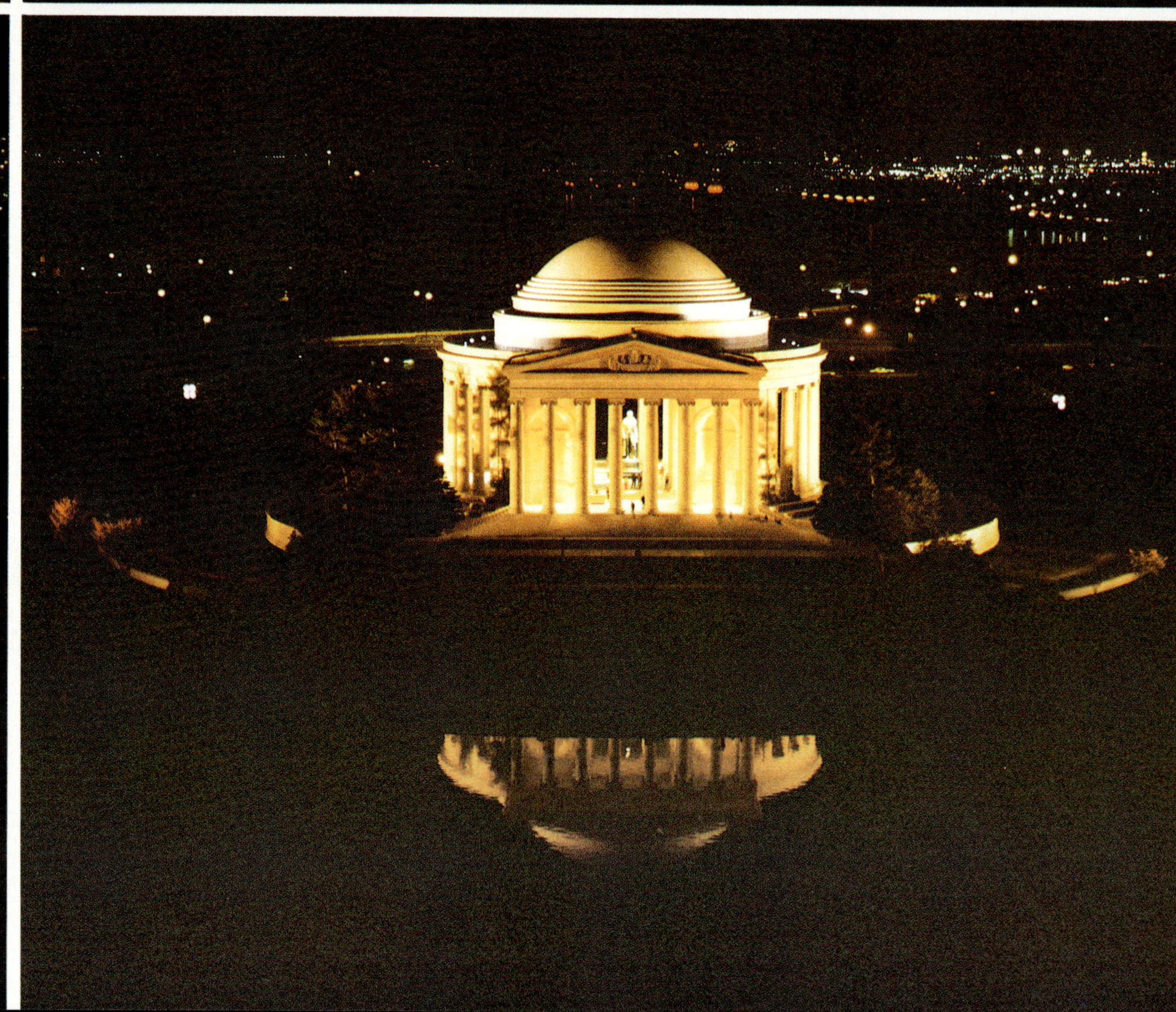

DISTRICT OF COLUMBIA

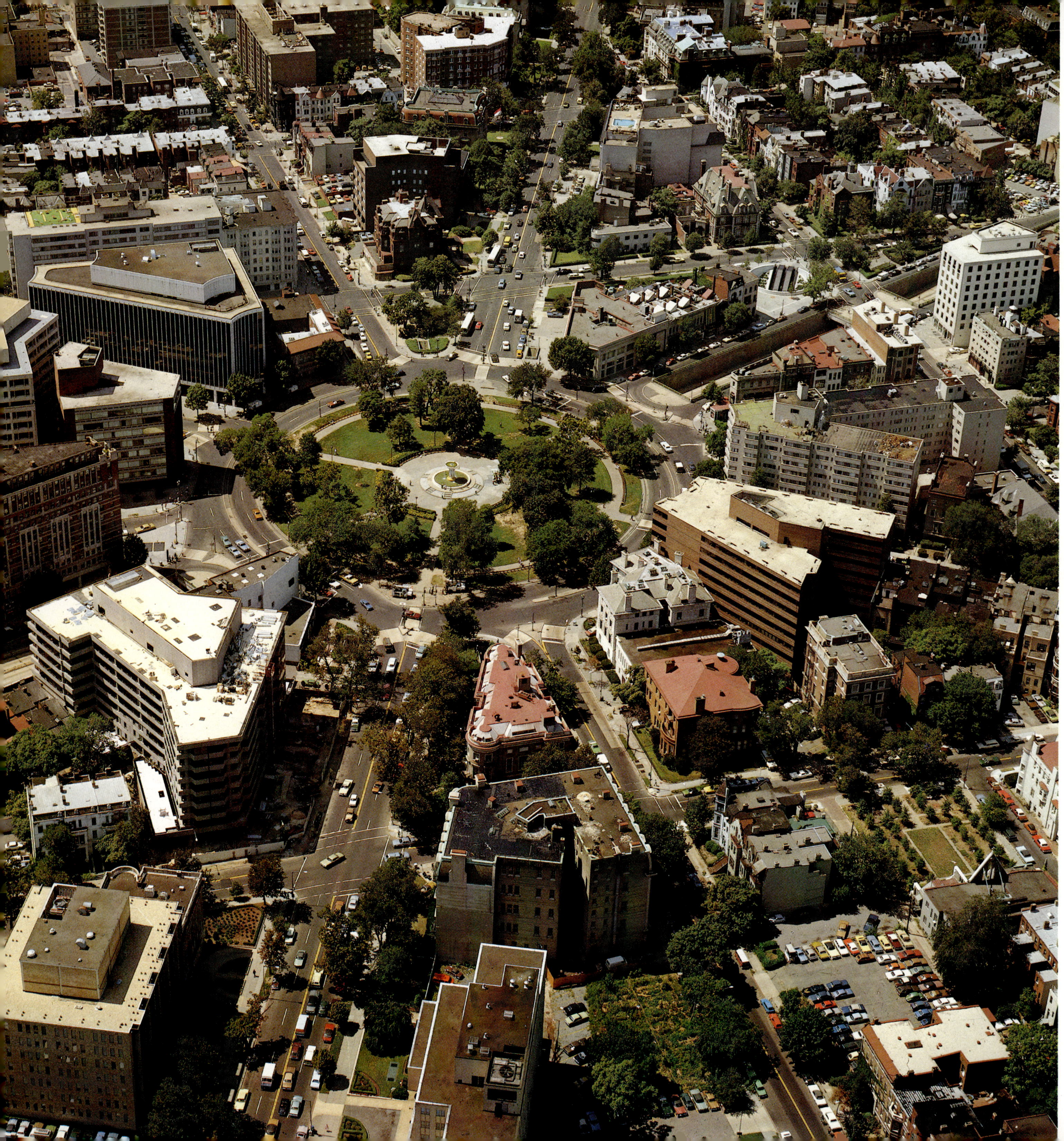

Dupont Circle is another of Washington's circles named for a Civil War hero; it became a prestigious neighborhood, home to the railroad-rich at the turn of the century. Some of these great houses remain in the gathering commercial development of this active, beautiful area.

In the western terminus of Pennsylvania Avenue, Washington Circle has the Equestrian statue L'Enfant intended for the site of the Washington Monument. The George Washington University Hospital is in right foreground, and beyond it lies Foggy Bottom. To the left of the circle is the West End, becoming now a desirable residential and office area. Midtown is beyond, running into Downtown near the White House.

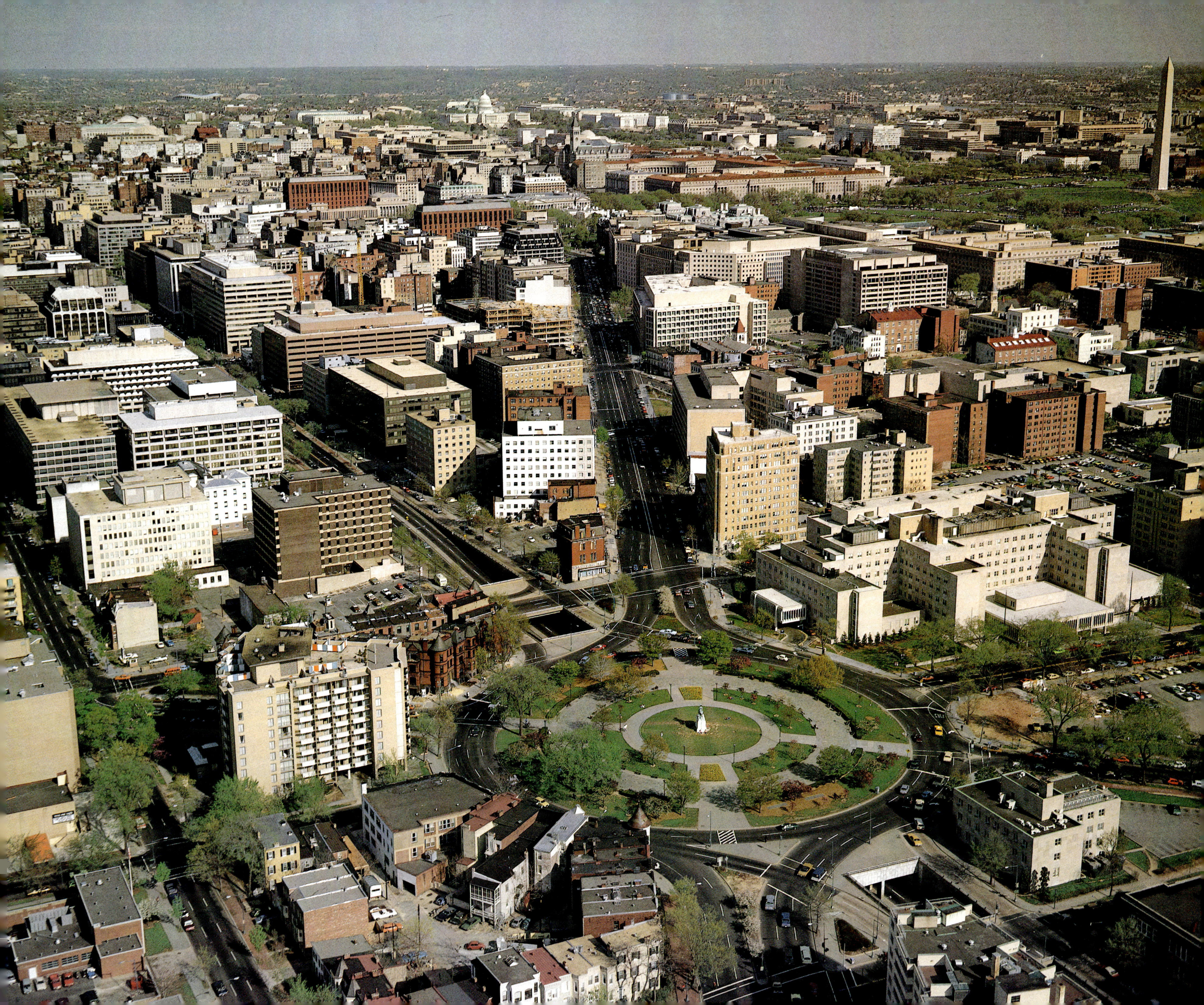

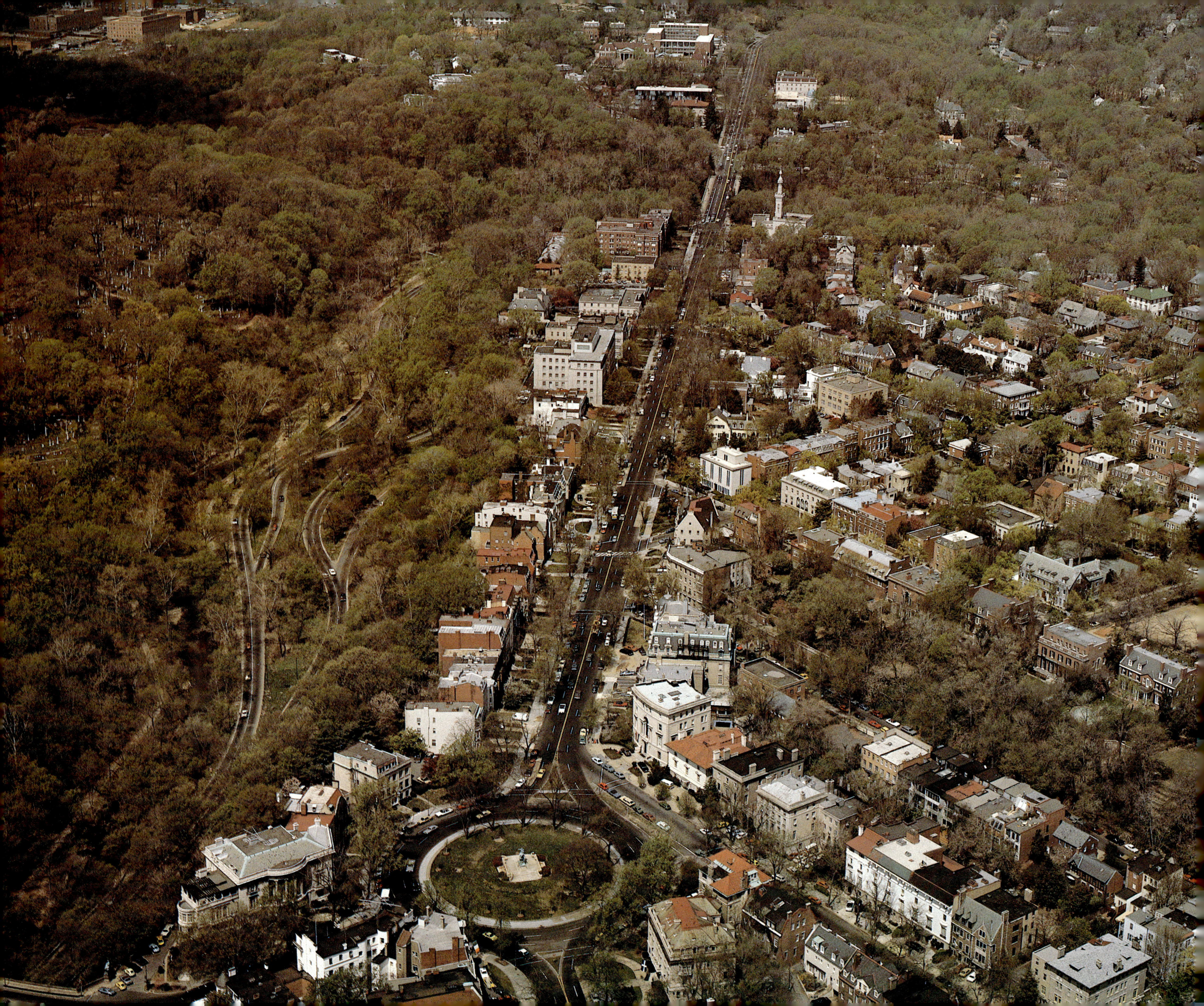

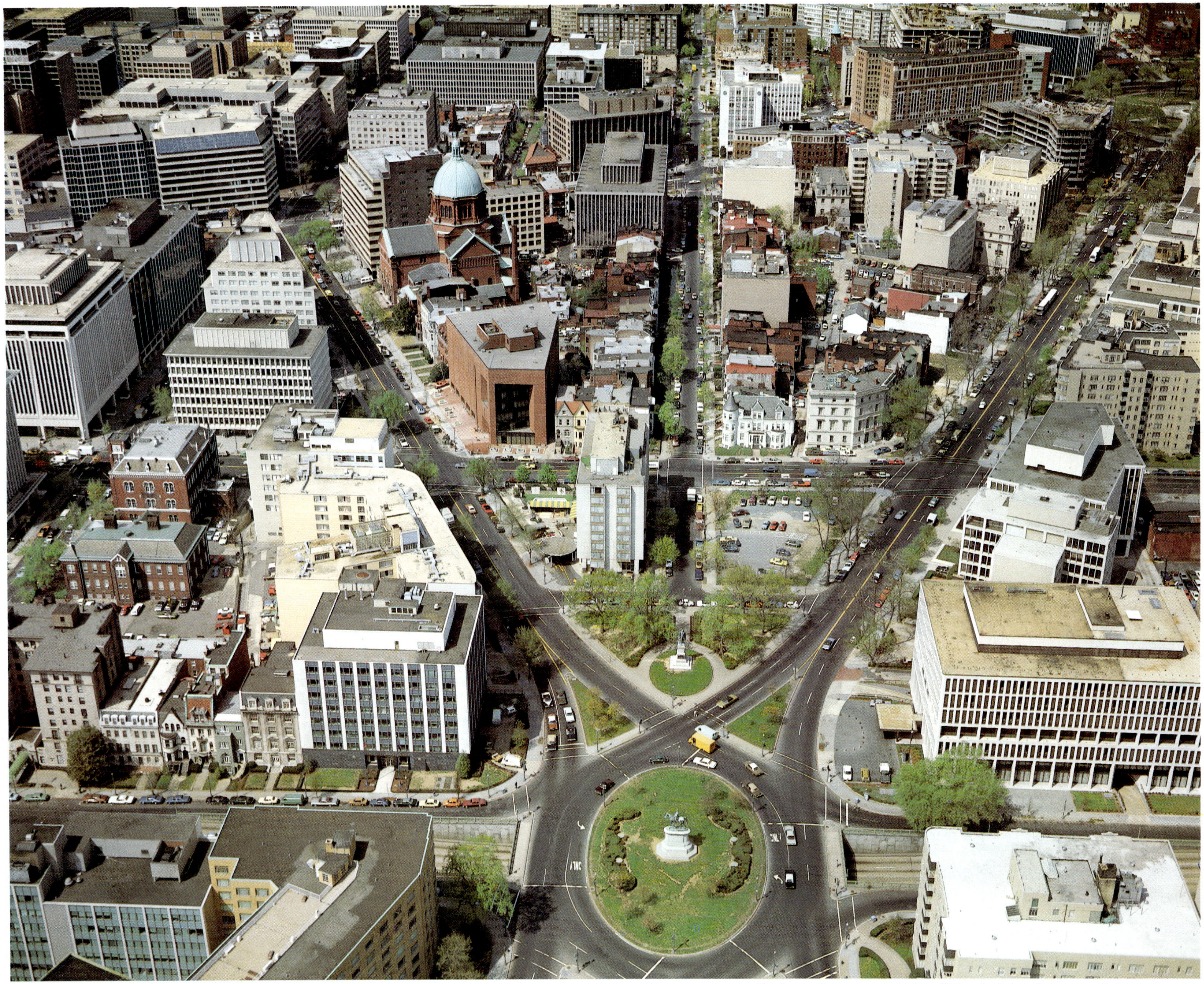

Scott Circle at the intersection of Rhode Island Avenue, Massachusetts Avenue, N. Street, 16th Street and St. Matthews Cathedral.

Sheridan Circle is named for the Union Cavalry leader. The statue is by Gutzon Borglum. The area exhibits the spacious living of the old city limits bordering Rock Creek Park. Many of these homes are now in Embassy use. General Sheridan is encircled by a ring of Norway maples. The Kalorama neighborhood is to the right of Massachusetts Avenue.

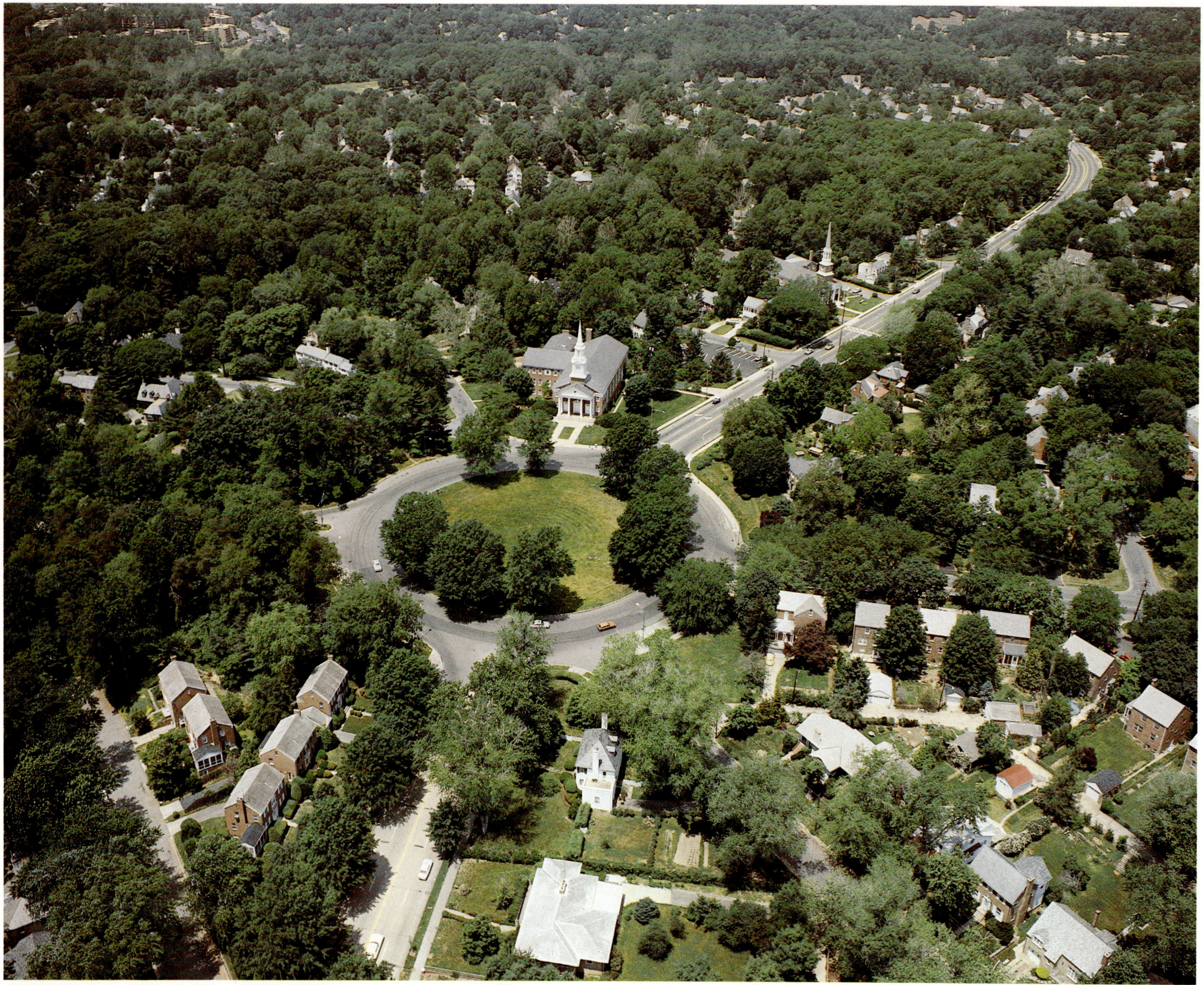

Churches are prominent in the setting at Westmoreland Circle, giving it some of the aspect of a New England village, a park-like residential area. This is the last of the necklace of circles as Massachusetts Avenue crosses the Maryland border.

The nearer circle is Sherman Circle, beyond it on Illinois Avenue, Grant Circle. Beyond them is the Soldiers Home, for whose development Jefferson Davis was primarily responsible. In the distance upper left is the McMillan reservoir.

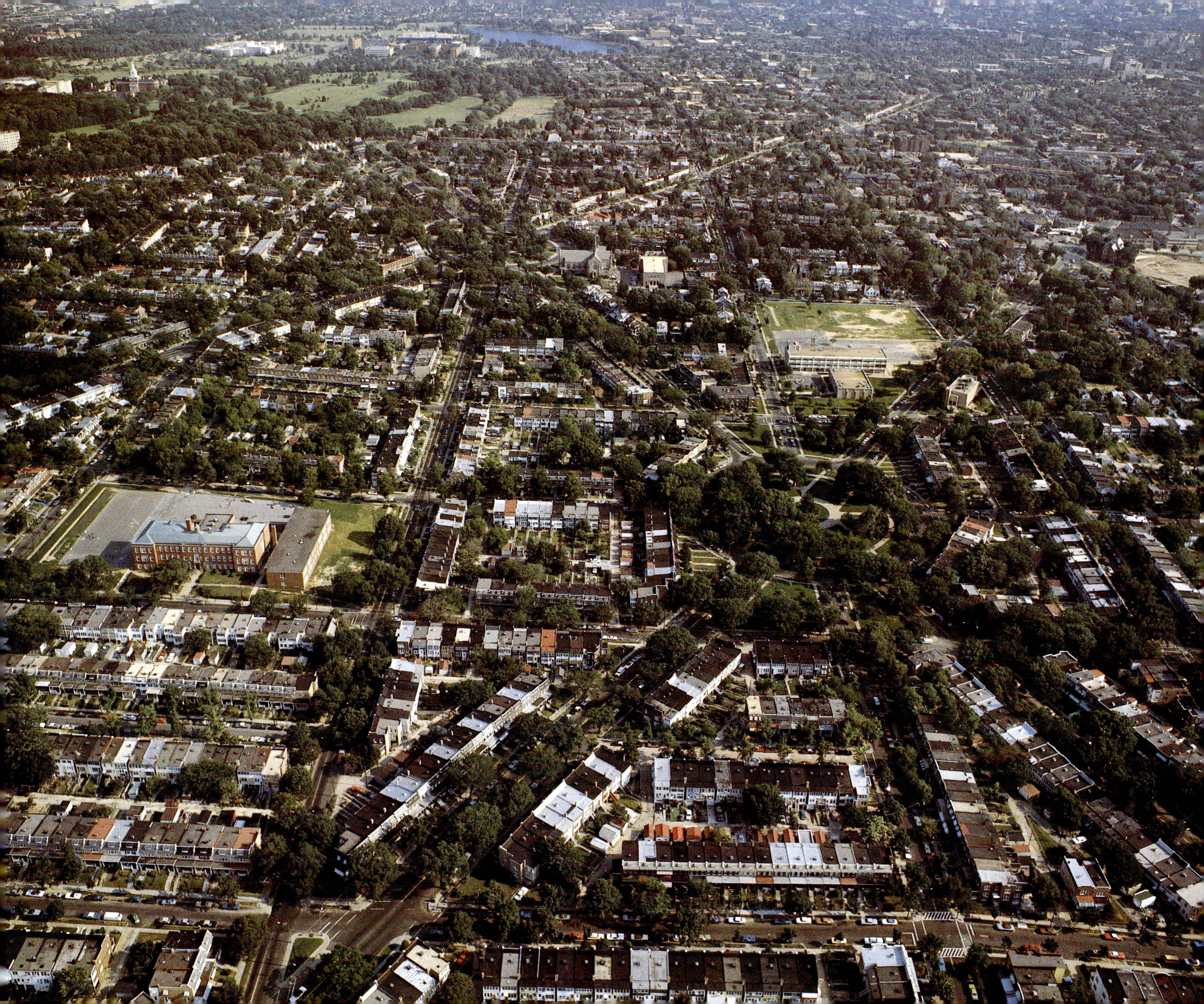

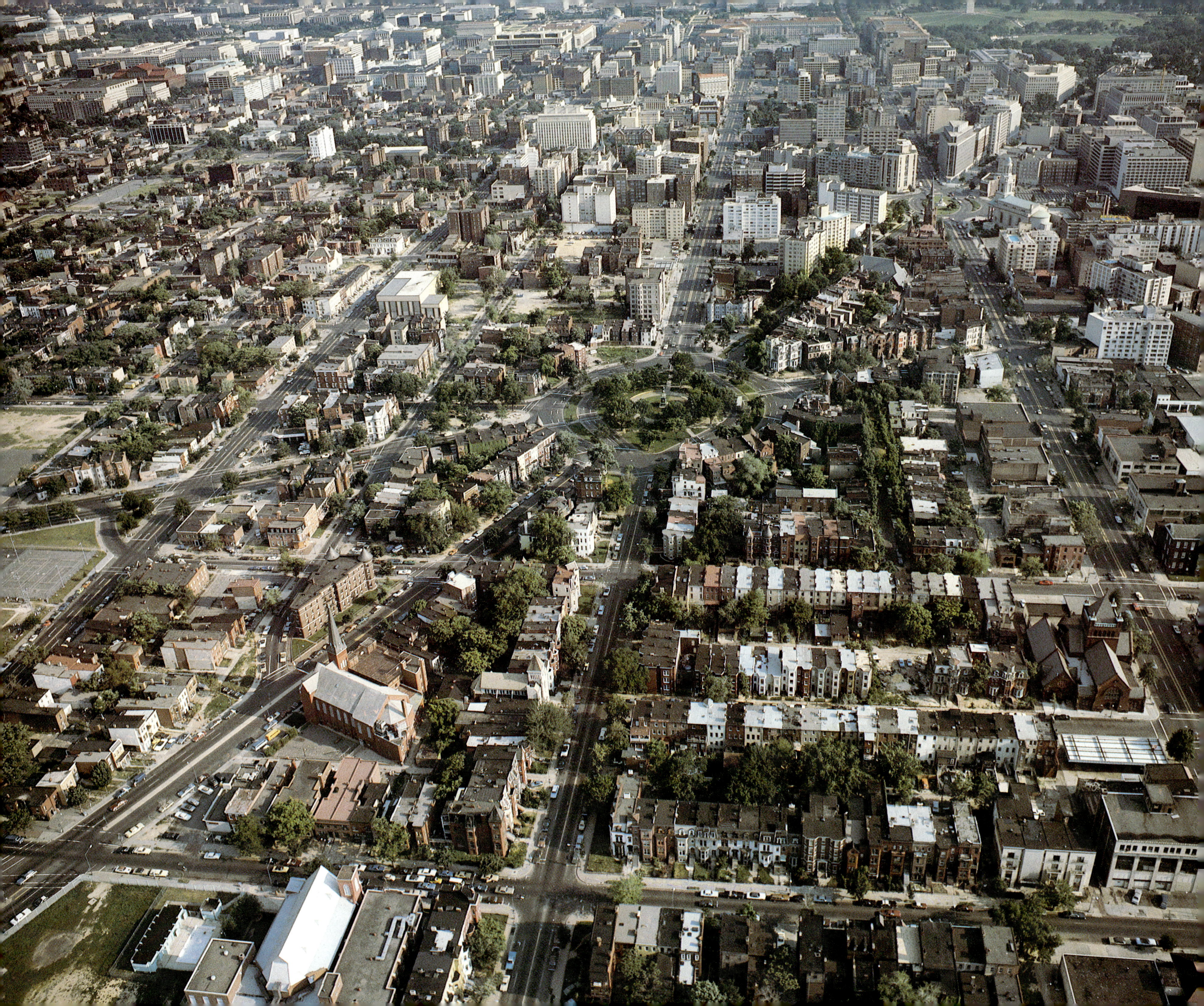

The circles are everywhere given the names of the military heroes of the Civil War. There vicinities were reached and watered and made desirable by the schemes of "Boss" Shepherd in Grant's administration. Shepherd, commissioned to develop in debt proportions of $10,000,000, quickly reached $20,000,000, and was only then halted by a national depression. Logan Circle's downtown location is now a hub of very active restoration and rehabilitation. It must be made clear that despite disparagement in the title "Boss", a Congressional investigation of his impetuous spending found Alexander Shepherd innocent of personal dishonesty. "Boss", then, may have been the meaningful word for the man who "Openly, courageously, and with dictatorial abandon" embarked upon a tremendous task of civic improvement.

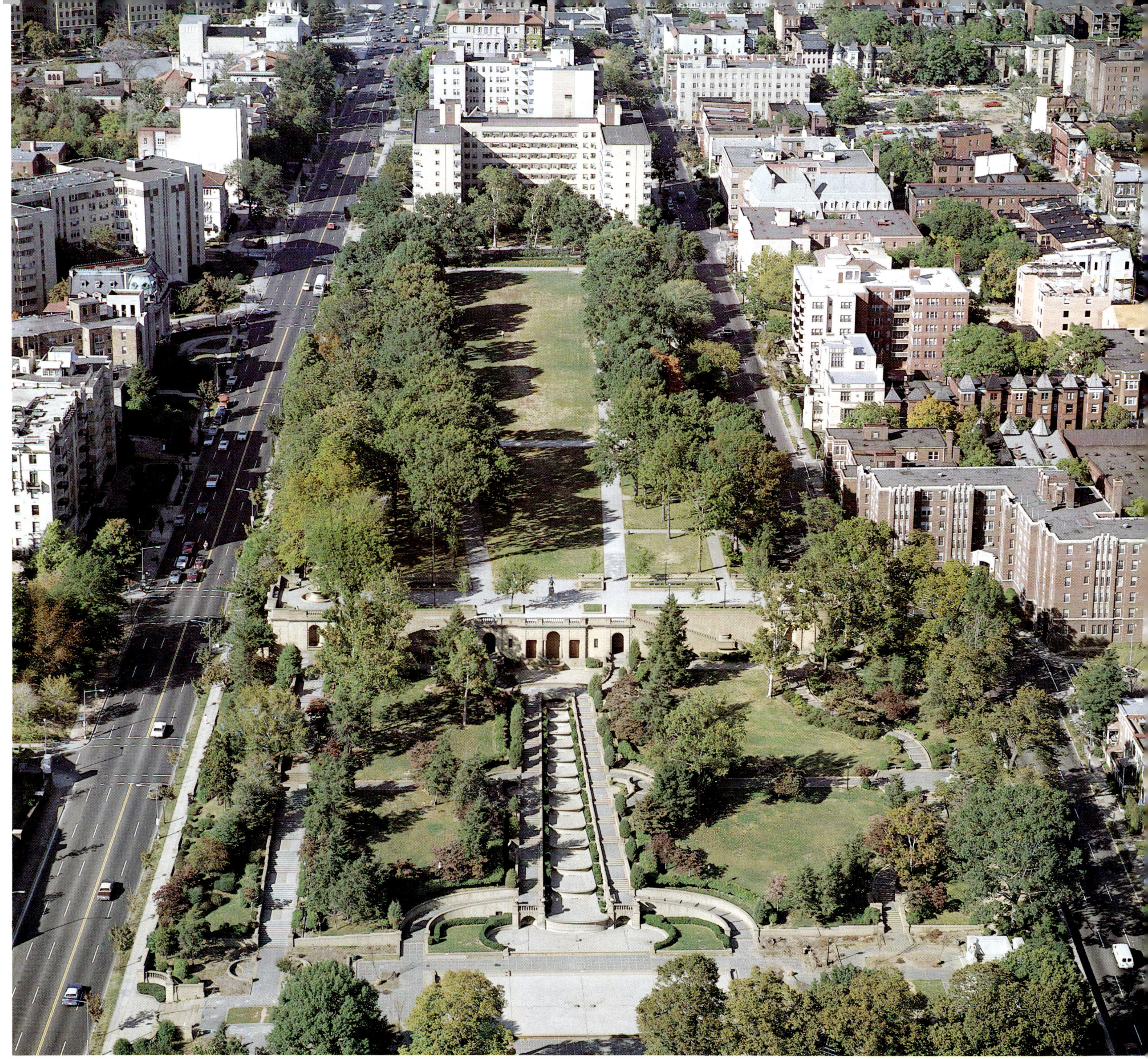

From 1880 through 1920 Mrs. John B. Henderson worked for a grandeur in this area appropriate to her vision of a new White House or presidential palace. 16th Street was to become the Avenue of Presidents. In the foreground Meridian Hill Park's cascade with thirteen falls of graduated size are of Italianate inspiration. A statue of Dante is to be seen. Beyond the equestrian statue of Joan of Arc stretches a formal greensward in the French tradition.

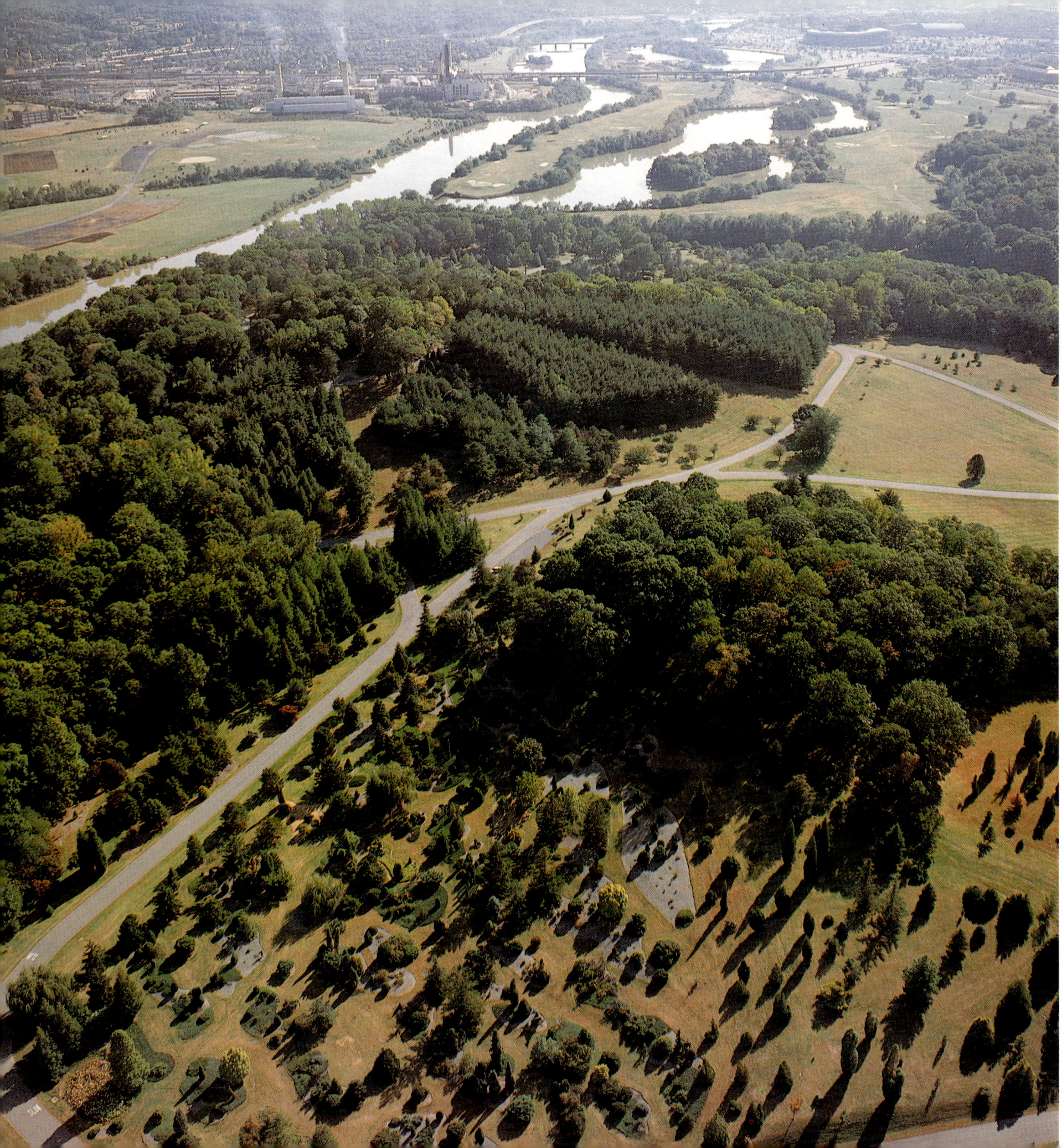

The National Arboretum in Northeast Washington, along the Anacostia River, recommended in 1899 by Secretary of Agriculture Wilson, was purchased by the government in 1927, "furnishing complete material for the investigations of the Department of Agriculture and so managed as to be a perennial feast of botanical education." Thirty-two distinct types of soils make for a wealth of experimentation.

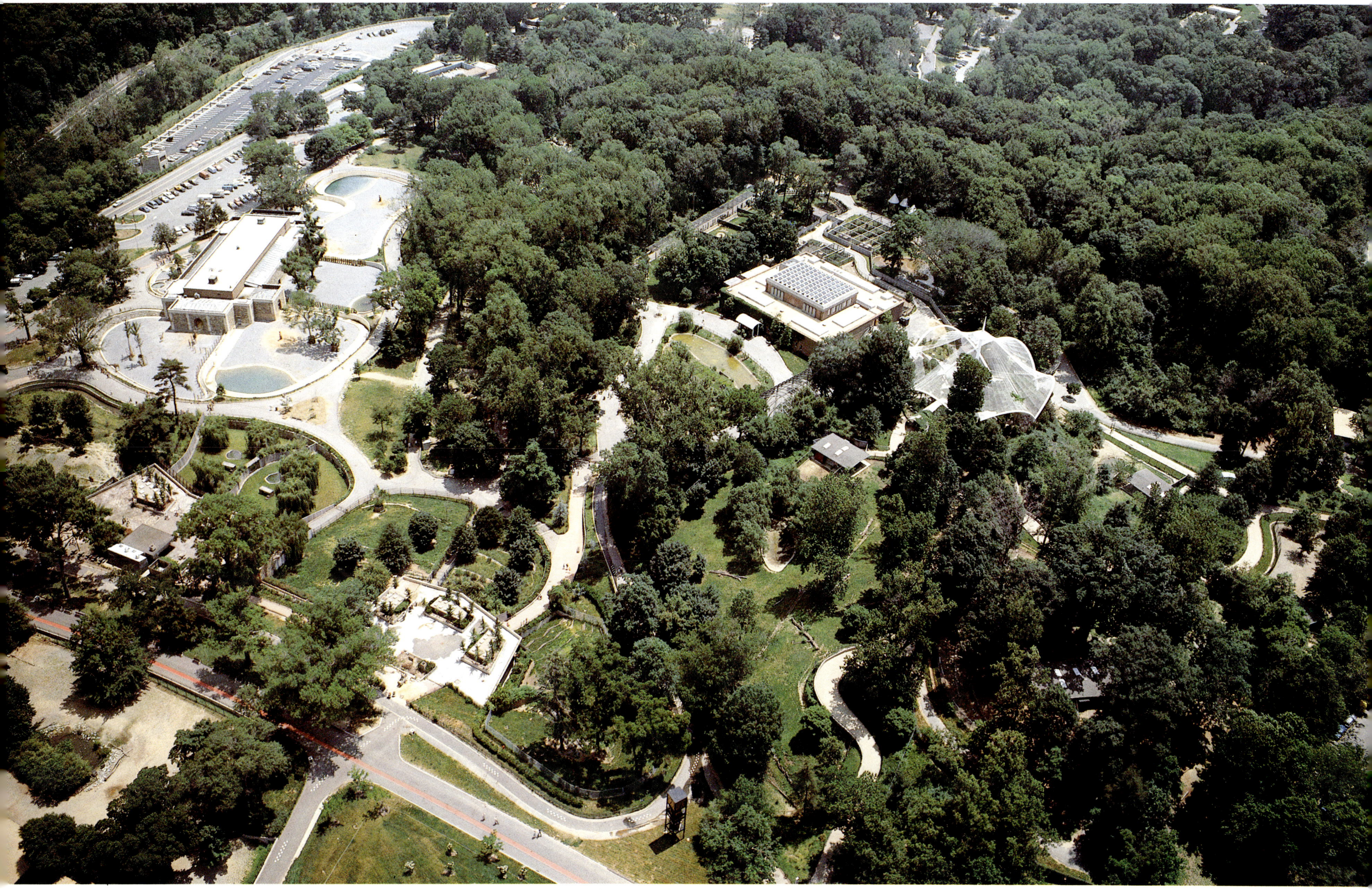

The National Zoological Park, still part of the Smithsonian Institution, was moved from the Mall in 1890. It houses in its present location 2,600 specimens, more than 900 species, including Hsing Hsing and Ling Ling, giant pandas, a gift from the Peoples' Republic of China. Notable is the bird house and flight cage, the webby structure at right center.

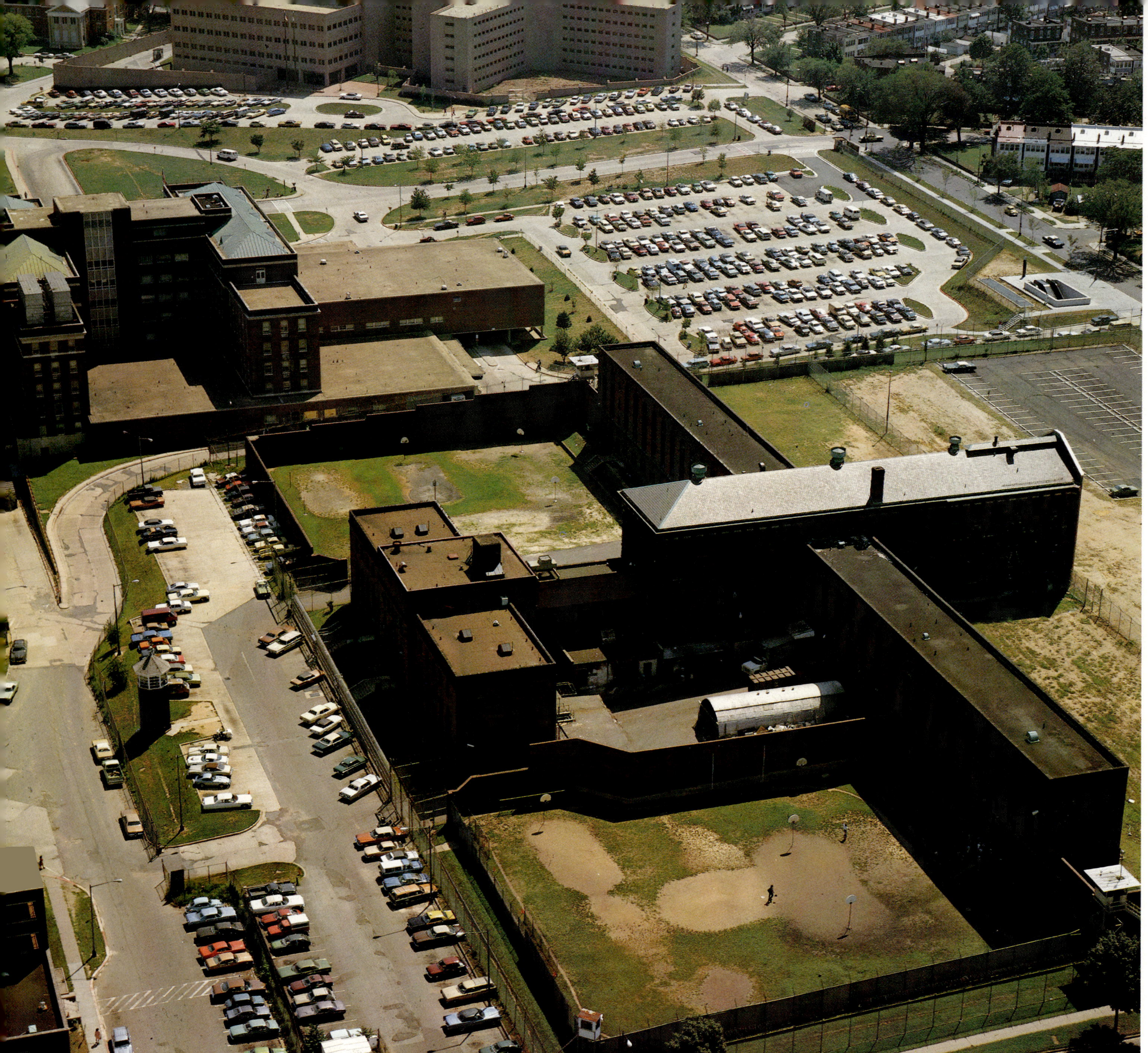

The old District of Columbia prison in the foreground is overcrowded and dangerous. Security for the new one, at the top, is dependent on the limited access intrinsic to its plan and such devices as internal television scanning.

Founded in 1852 and formerly called Government Hospital for the Insane, St. Elizabeth's occupies 320 acres of an old royal grant. Red bricks of the Center Building, the only building remaining, were made on the site from clay deposits there. Woodwork was made from trees of the surrounding forests. It served also as a Civil War rehabilitation hospital. Ezra Pound received visits from T. S. Eliot here. Pound had been brutally confined to a cage when arrested in Italy in 1945. He was at St. Elizabeth's when the Fellows of the Library of Congress voted him the Bollingen Prize for poetry in 1949.

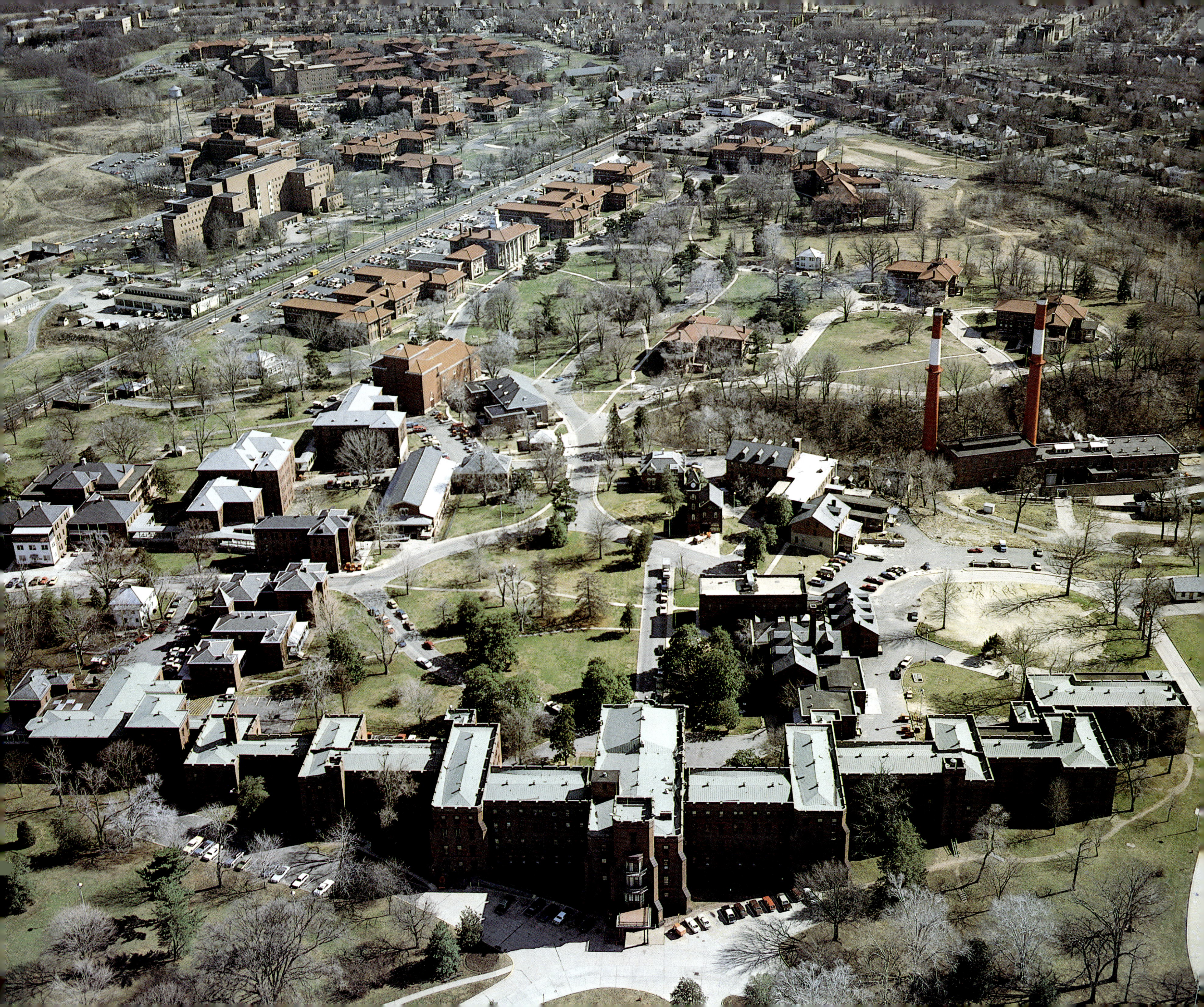

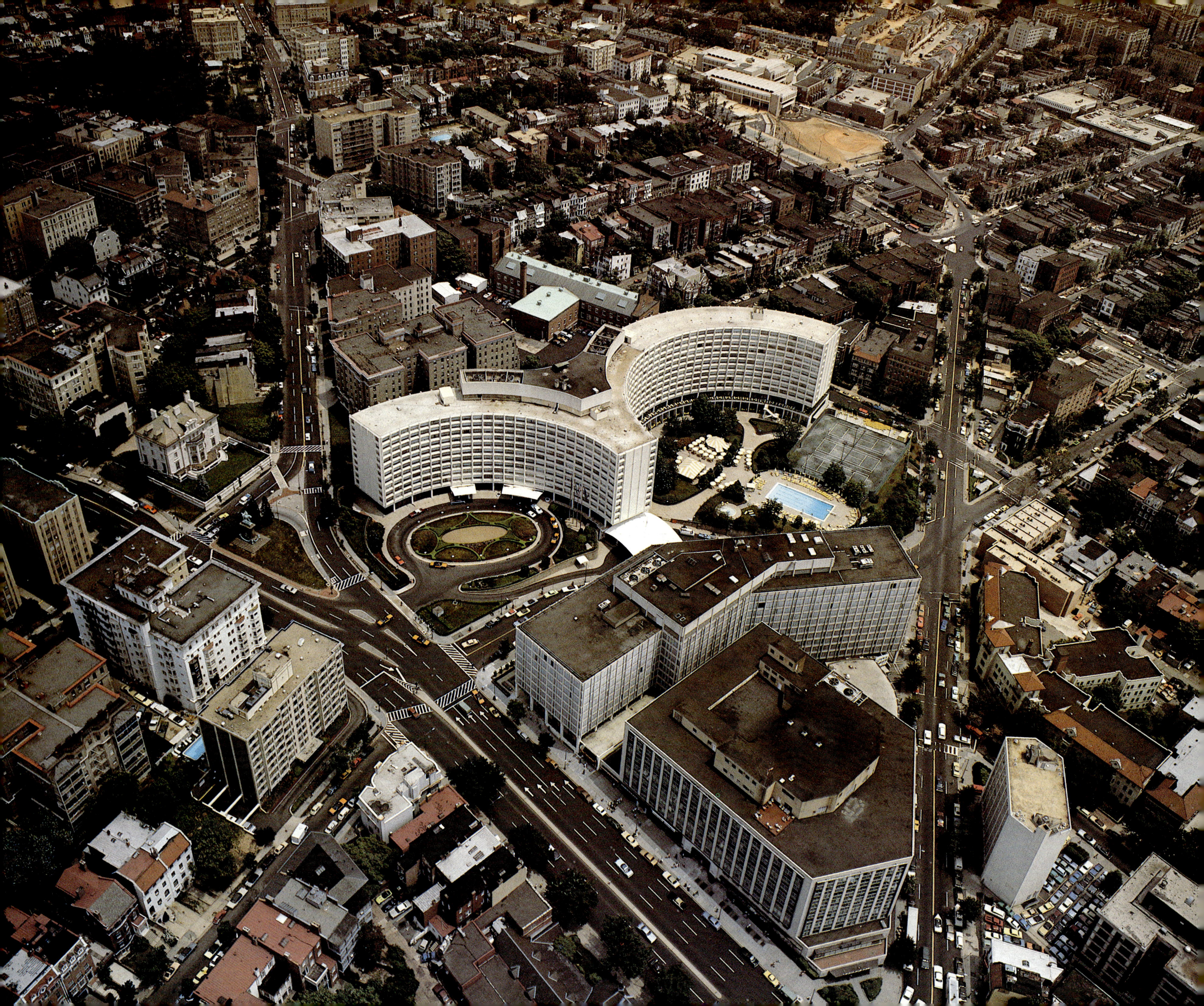

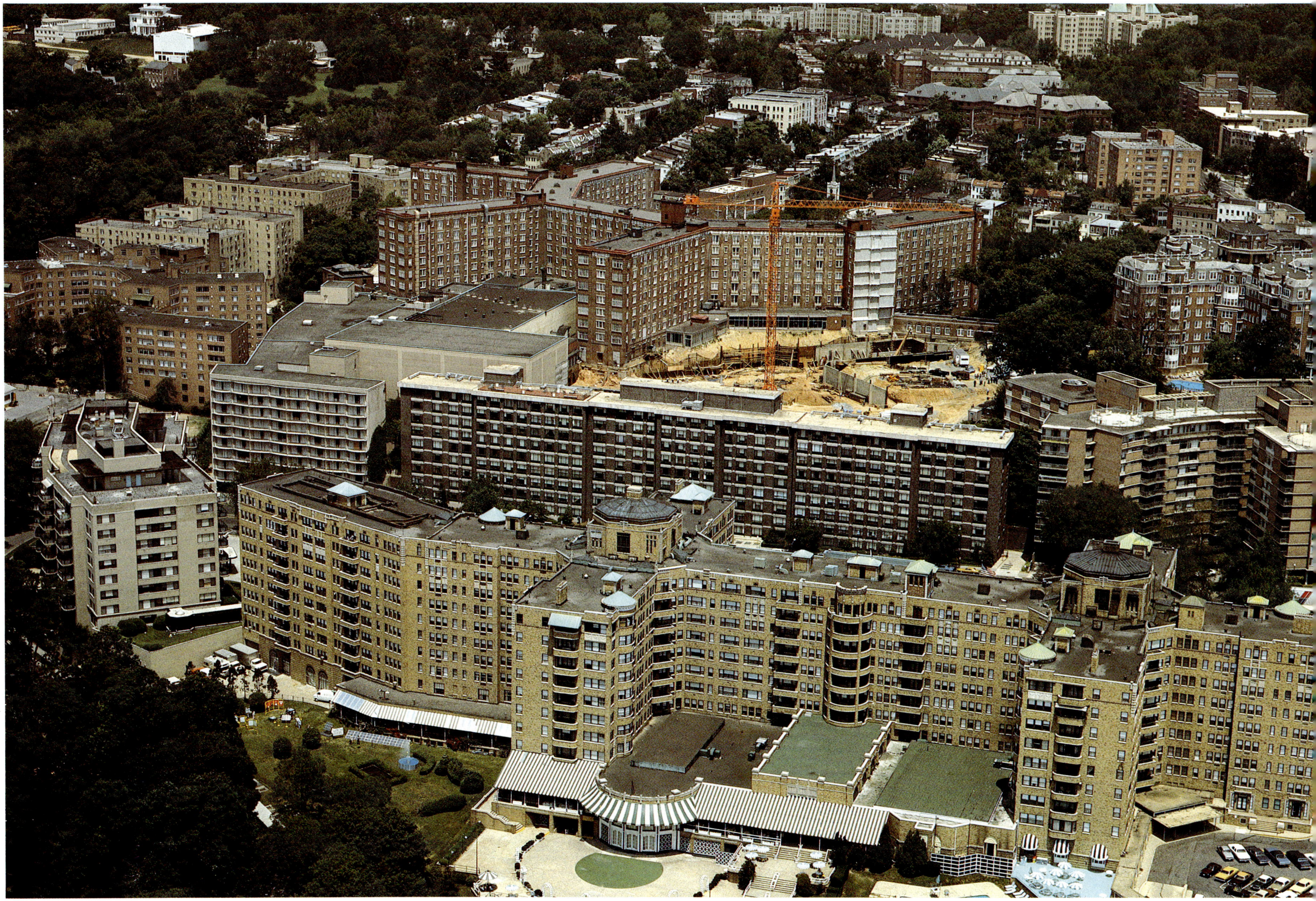

In the Kalorama Triangle neighborhood, the Washington Hilton commands a magnificent view of the city. The Lothrop House at the corner of Connecticut Avenue and California Street is the Italianate mansion at left center, now a part of the embassy complex of the USSR, perhaps the more appreciated by its tenants for the reservedness implied in its grounds.

The Shoreham Hotel, and beyond it the Sheraton Park, are prominent in the area just north of Rock Creek Park which has become hotel and convention center for DC. At upper far left is the Woodley Mansion, which was a summer home for four 19th century presidents: Van Buren, Tyler, Buchanan and Cleveland. Except for the original Wardman Tower, the Sheraton Park is being demolished so that facilities can be enlarged and improved.

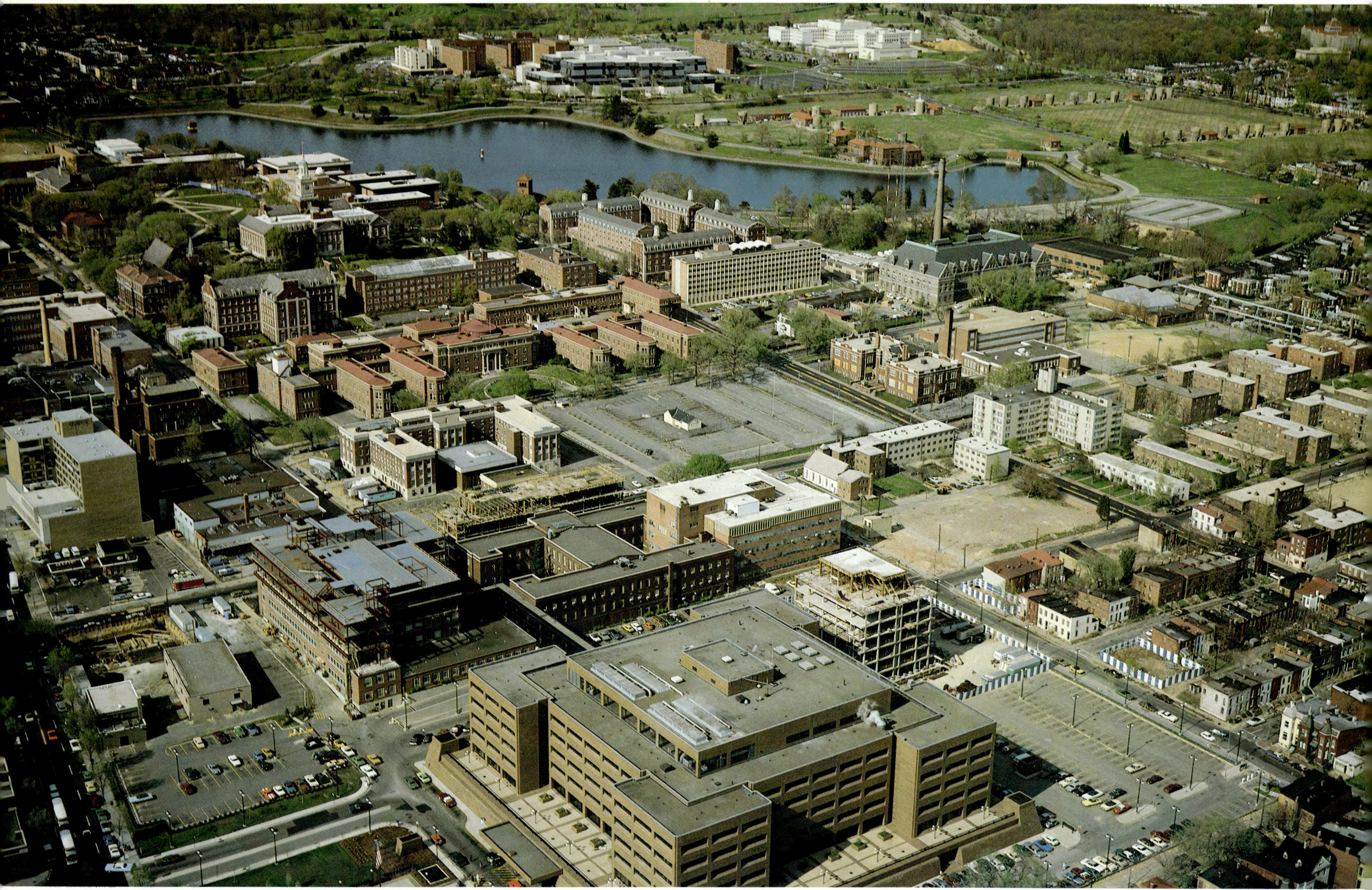

Howard University's first classes were held in 1867 in Howard Hall, the Georgian building with the spire at upper left. This is the largest, oldest, and most diverse Black university in the US. Its scope and influence are now international, in its schools of medicine, architecture, religion, law, music and science.

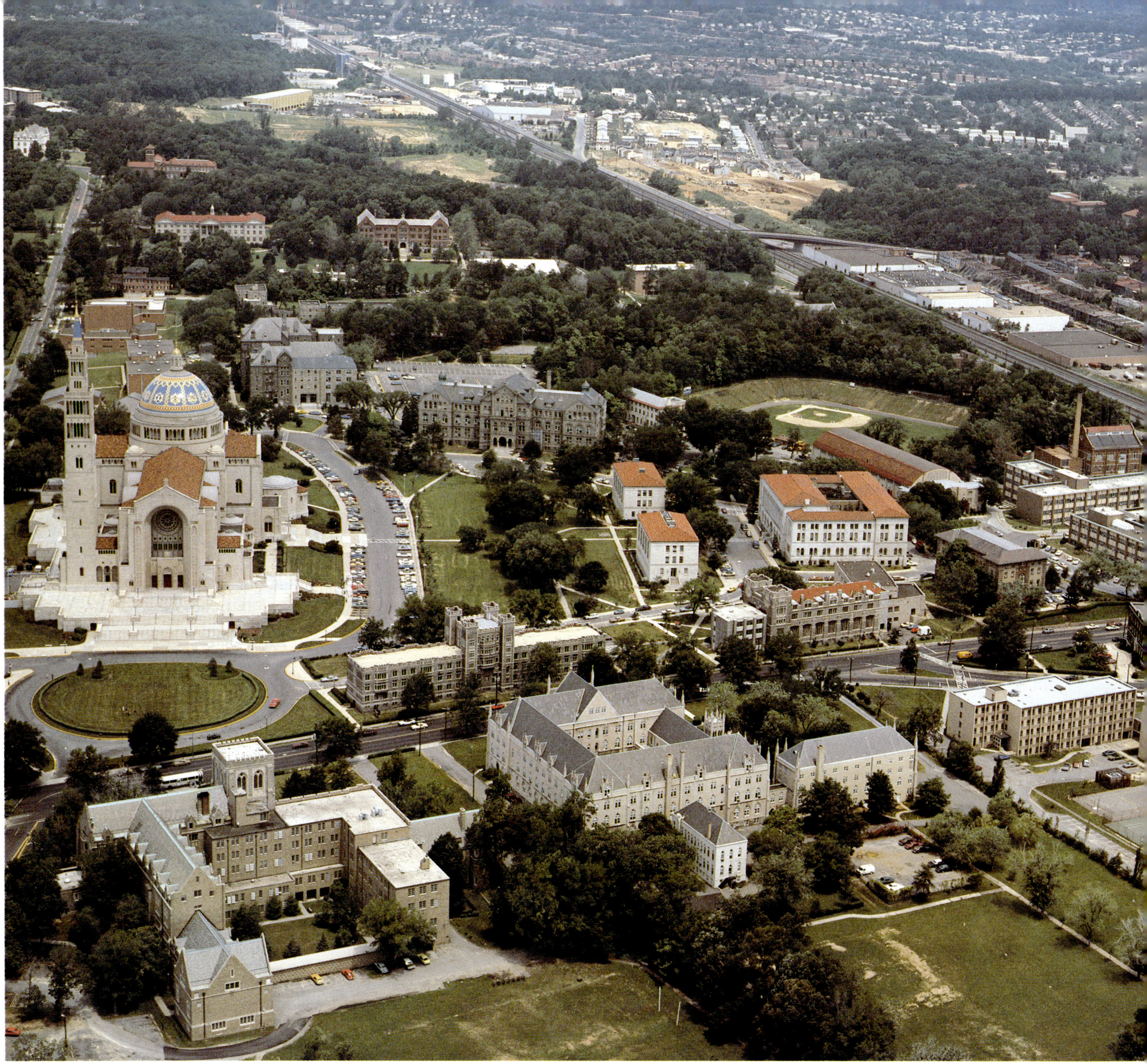

Established 1889, located in the highest part of Northeast DC, this is the only Catholic academic center in the country that receives the direct patronage of the Pope and the Catholic hierarchy. Originally a school of theology, it is now open to Catholics and non-Catholics alike. Associated with the university are autonomous houses of study. The Byzantine style basilica is the Shrine of the Immaculate Conception.

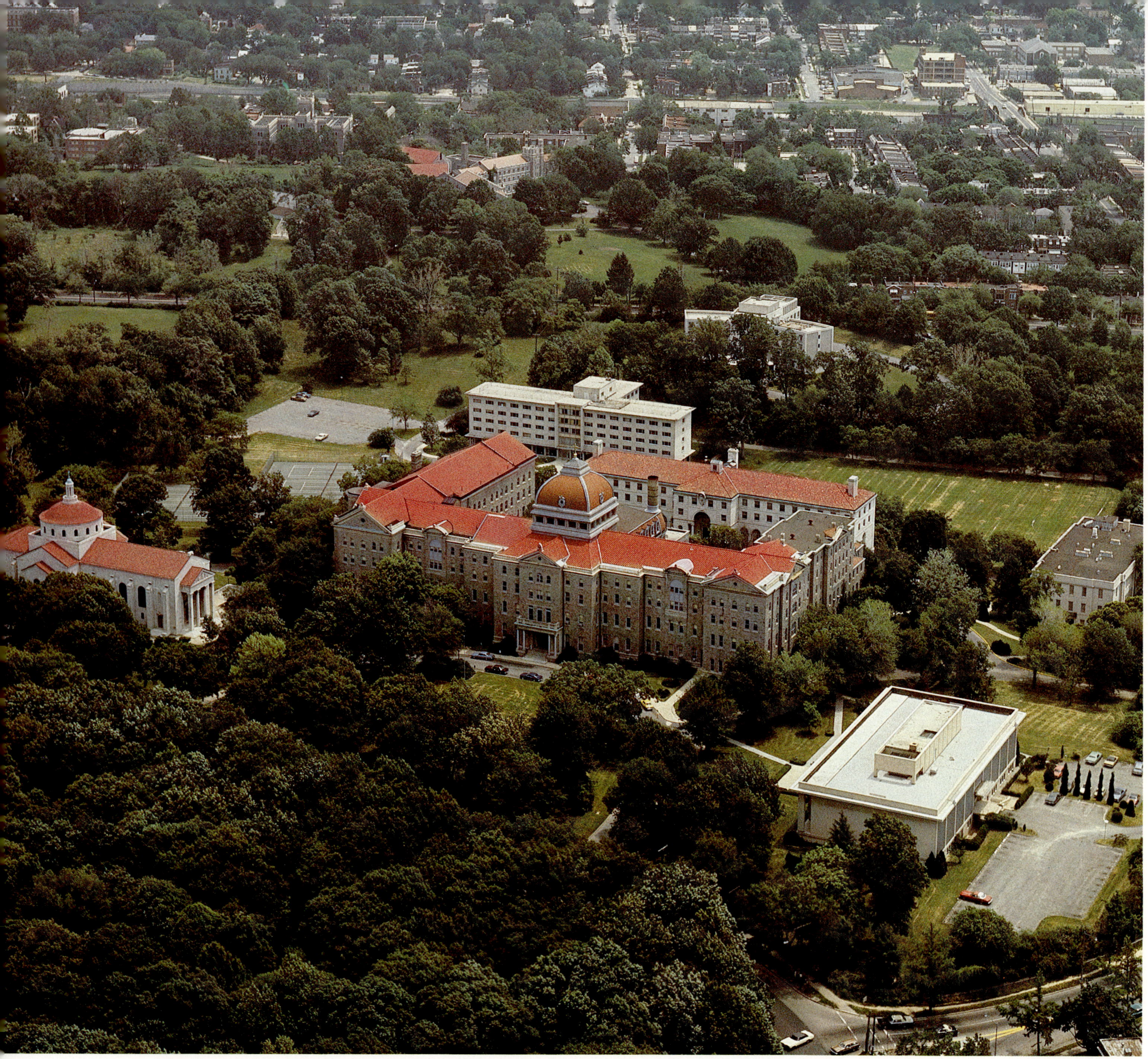

One of Catholic University's affiliates is Trinity College on Michigan Avenue in N.E. Washington. Established in 1897, still managed by the Sisters of Notre Dame de Namur, it is regarded as a fine women's college. The architects for the Chapel of Notre Dame, lower left, Maginnis and Walsh, were awarded the American Institute of Architects' gold medal for general excellence in ecclesiastical design.

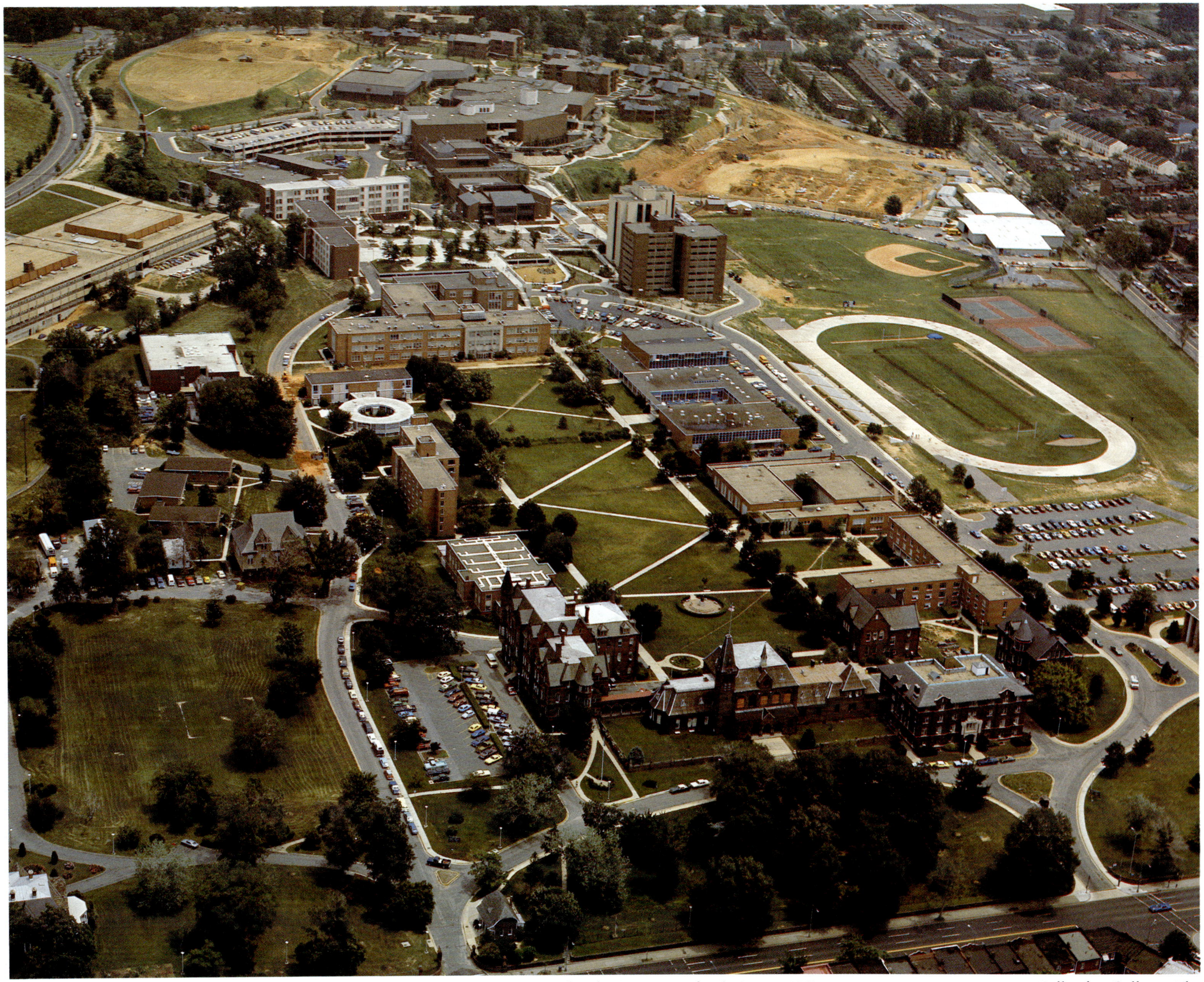

At Florida Avenue and 7th Street, N.E., occupying over 100 acres is Gallaudet College. The College is the only school of higher learning for deaf mutes in existence, attracting students from all over the world. Before Chapel Hall, the main building of the institution, is a bronze memorial by Daniel Chester French of Thomas Hopkins Gallaudet with his first pupil, Alice Cogswell.

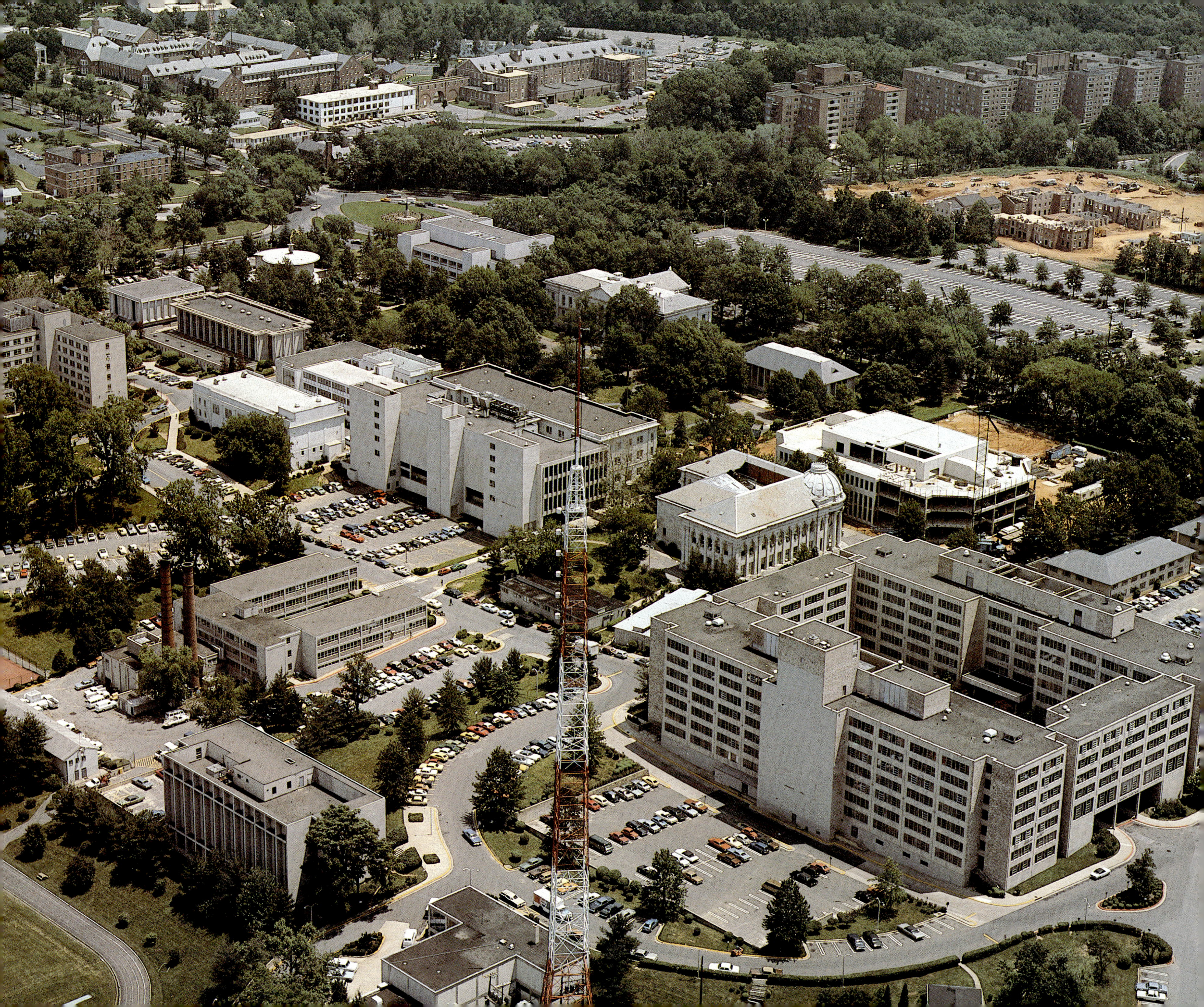

Methodist in affiliation, American University was founded in 1893 by Bishop John Fletcher Hurst, for whom its first building is named. Its campus has, besides the Wesley Theological Seminary, the Colleges of Arts and Sciences and the schools of Government, Public Administration, International Service and Law.

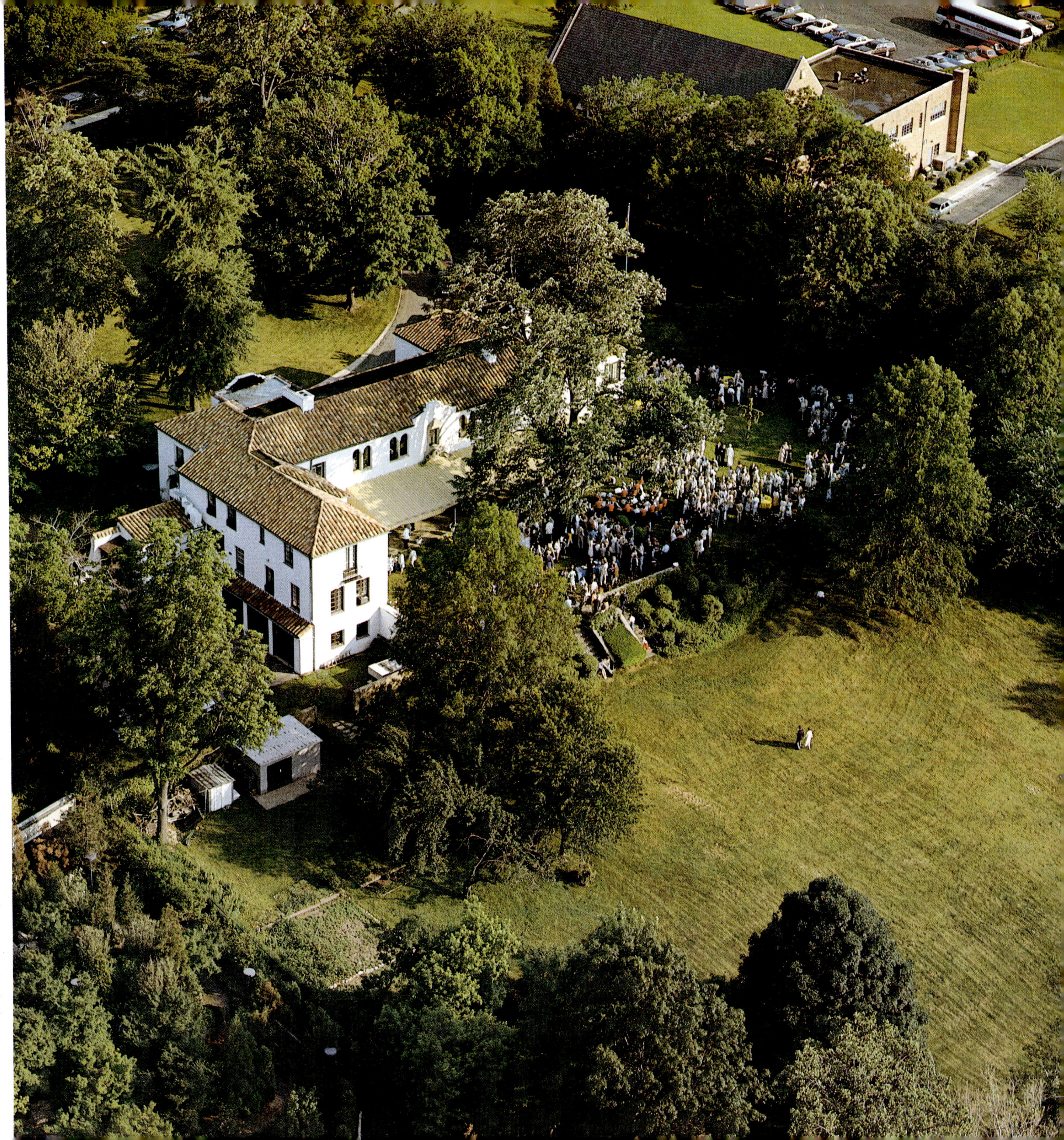

The Midsummer Festival at the Swedish Embassy on Nebraska Avenue, where the Washington-Swedes dance traditional dances 'round the May Pole. The Uniformed orchestra is an import from Sweden.

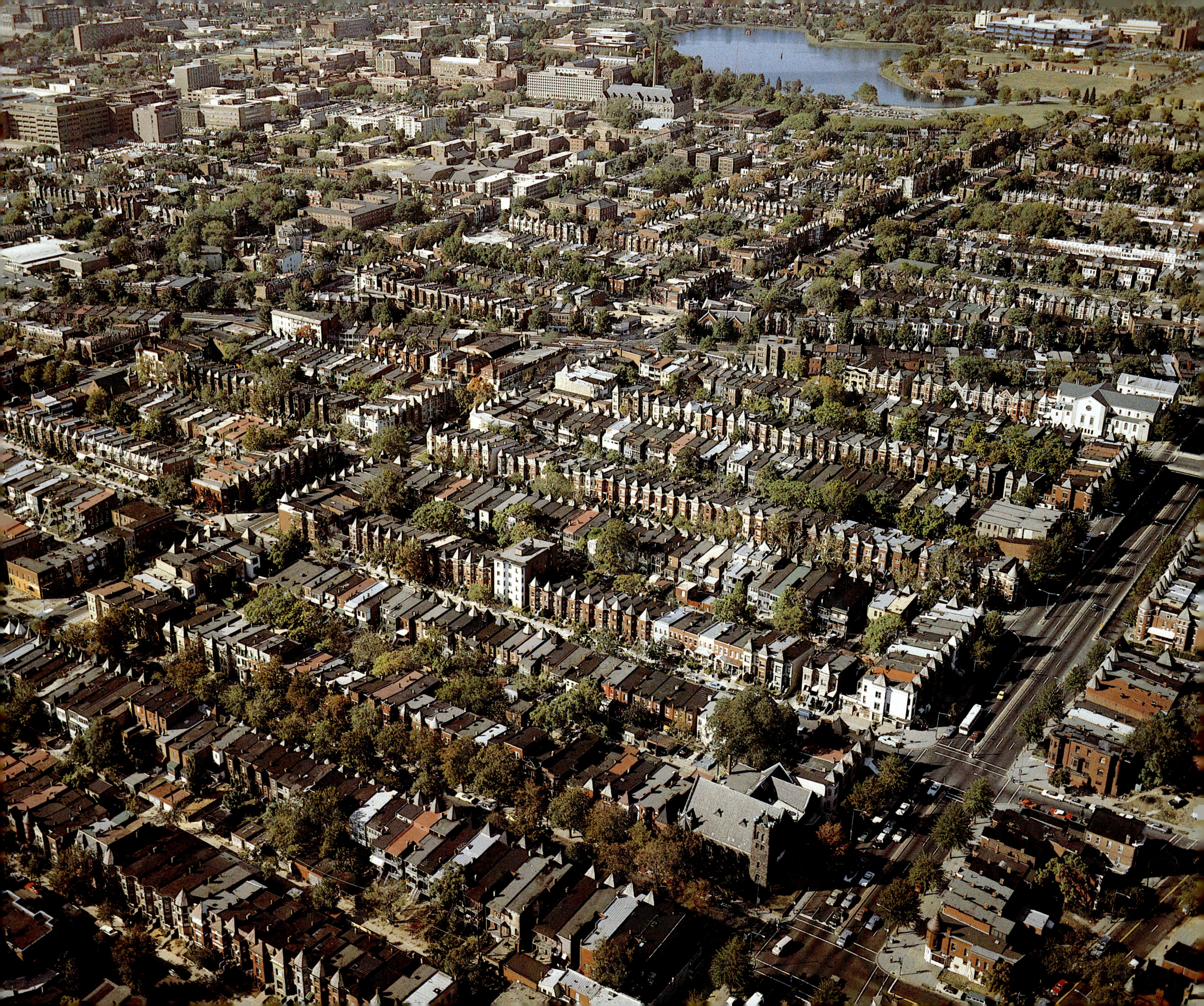

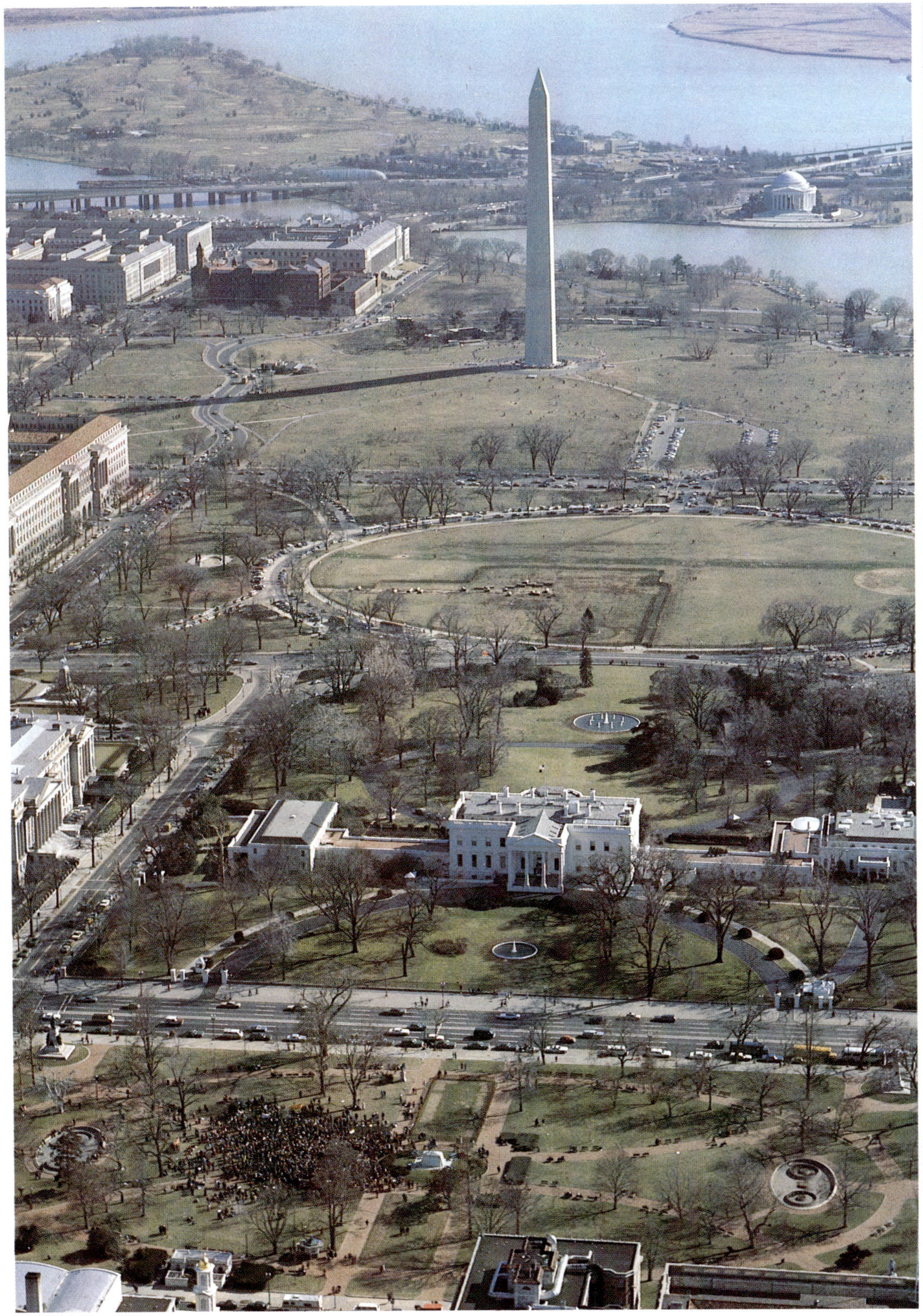

The old monument is sundial to a waning day, as the breadth and sweep of the Potomac move southward to the sea.

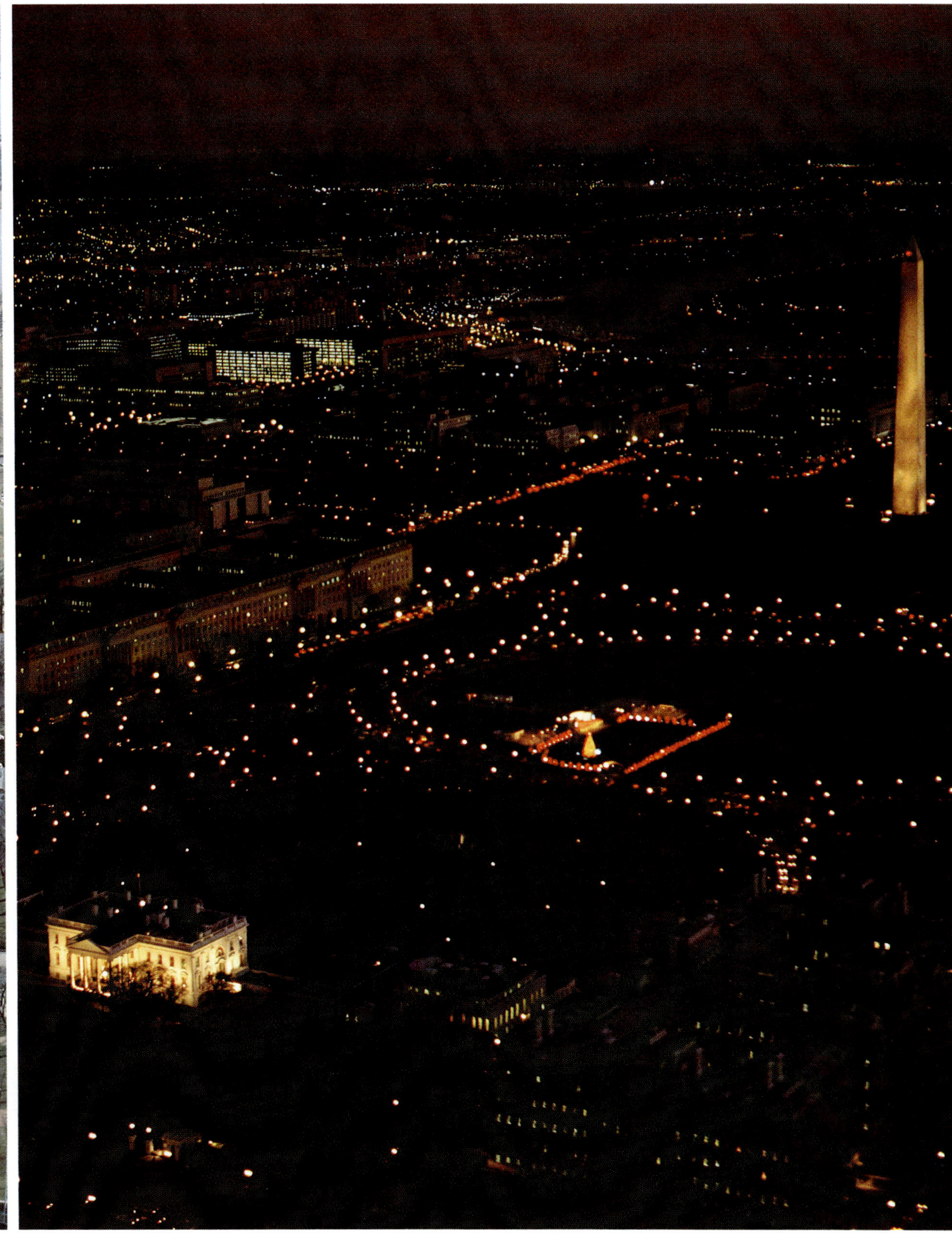

And at night it is Polaris to the electric myriads.

This is the Glenwood area off North Capitol Street. Square miles of these row houses were put up in the 1870's and 1880's, three stories plus a basement, with bay windows, half round, square, or half octagonal, to catch sunlight and afford a view of the street. They are still fairly comfortable, after a hundred years of use.

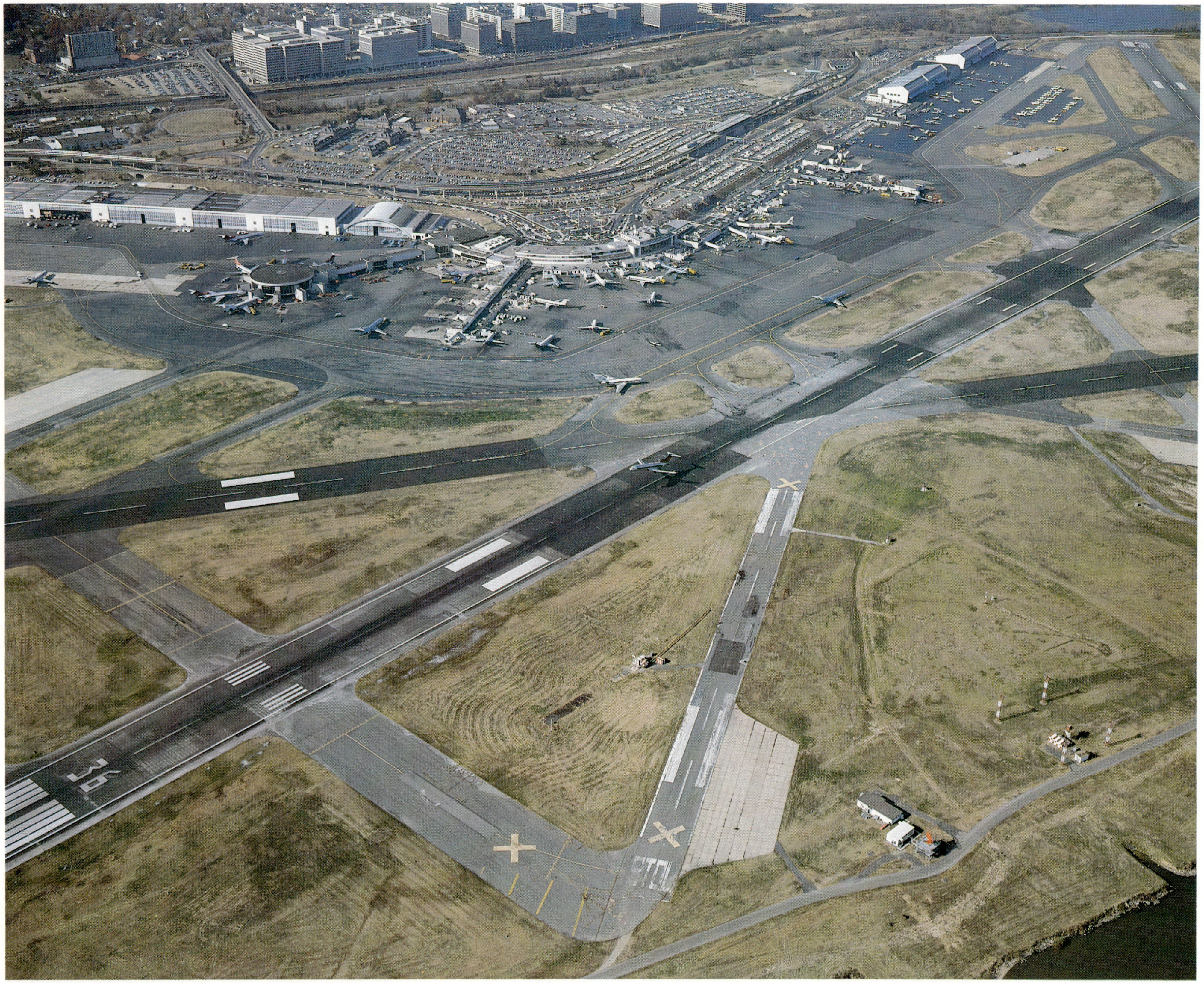

Over-busy Washington National Airport has weathered several attempts to close it to all but commuter-type flights, diverting the rest to Dulles. The subway stop here has made its proximity to downtown Washington even more attractive despite its inconvenience.

The Robert F. Kennedy Stadium-Armory Complex, now called "Starplex", has a highly practical everyday use as well as being the center for sports, trade shows, and summer rock concerts. Its immense parking lots serve as satellite depots for summer tourists waiting for the Tourmobile and for commuters using the Metro stop. It is located on the East Capitol Street axis next to the Anacostia River, where Independence and Constitution Avenues meet. On this fall day the Redskins were beating the Giants.

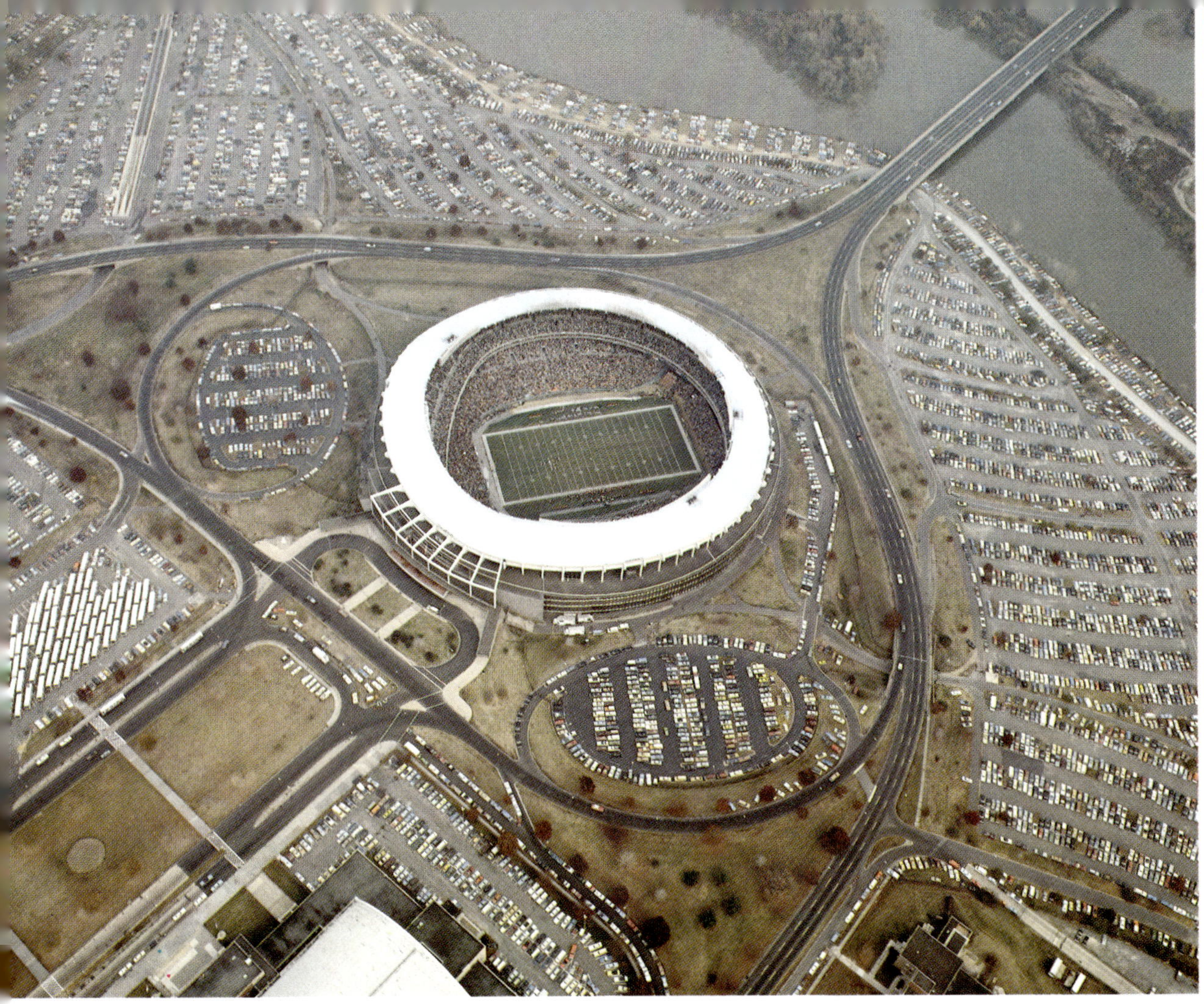
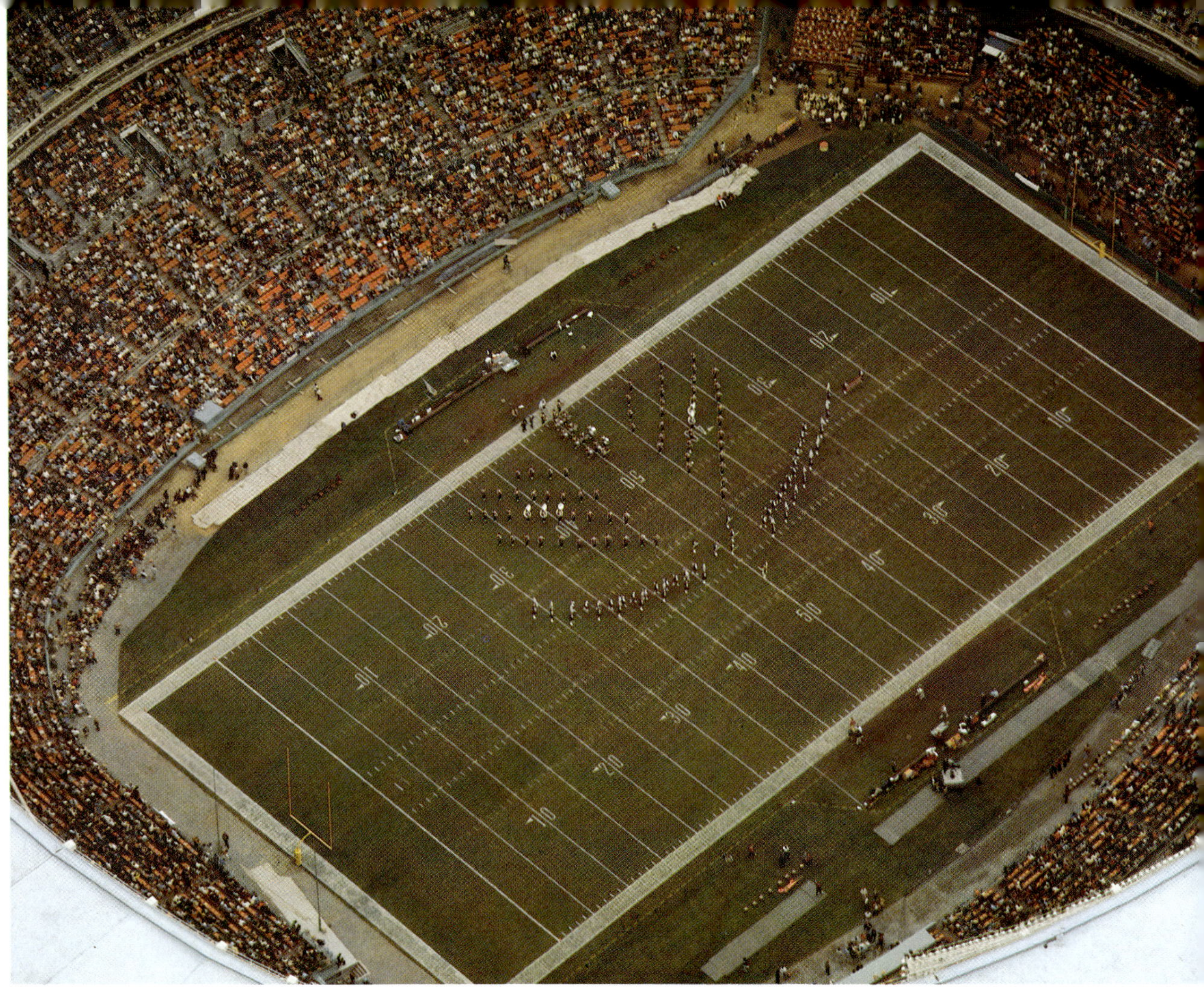
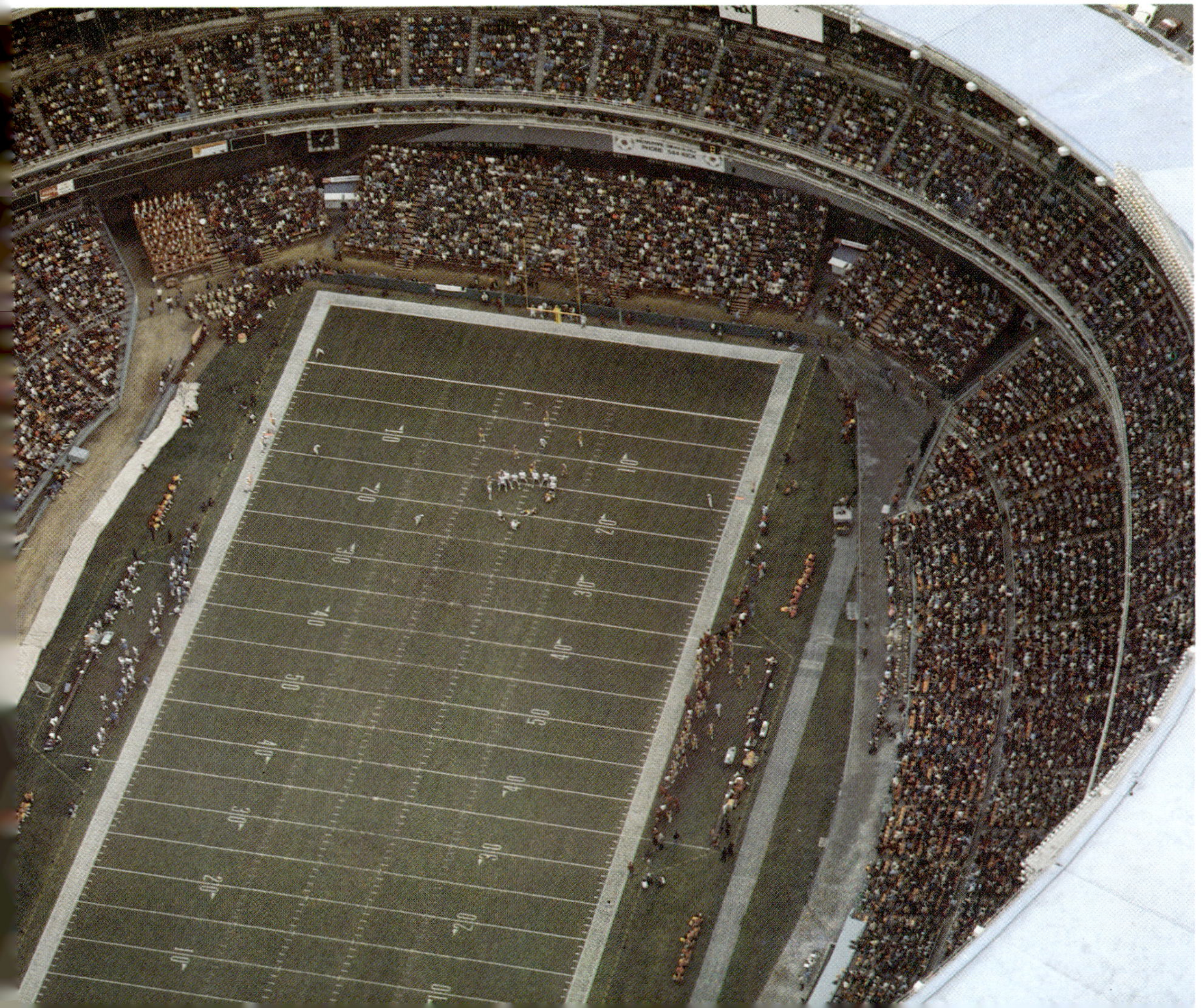
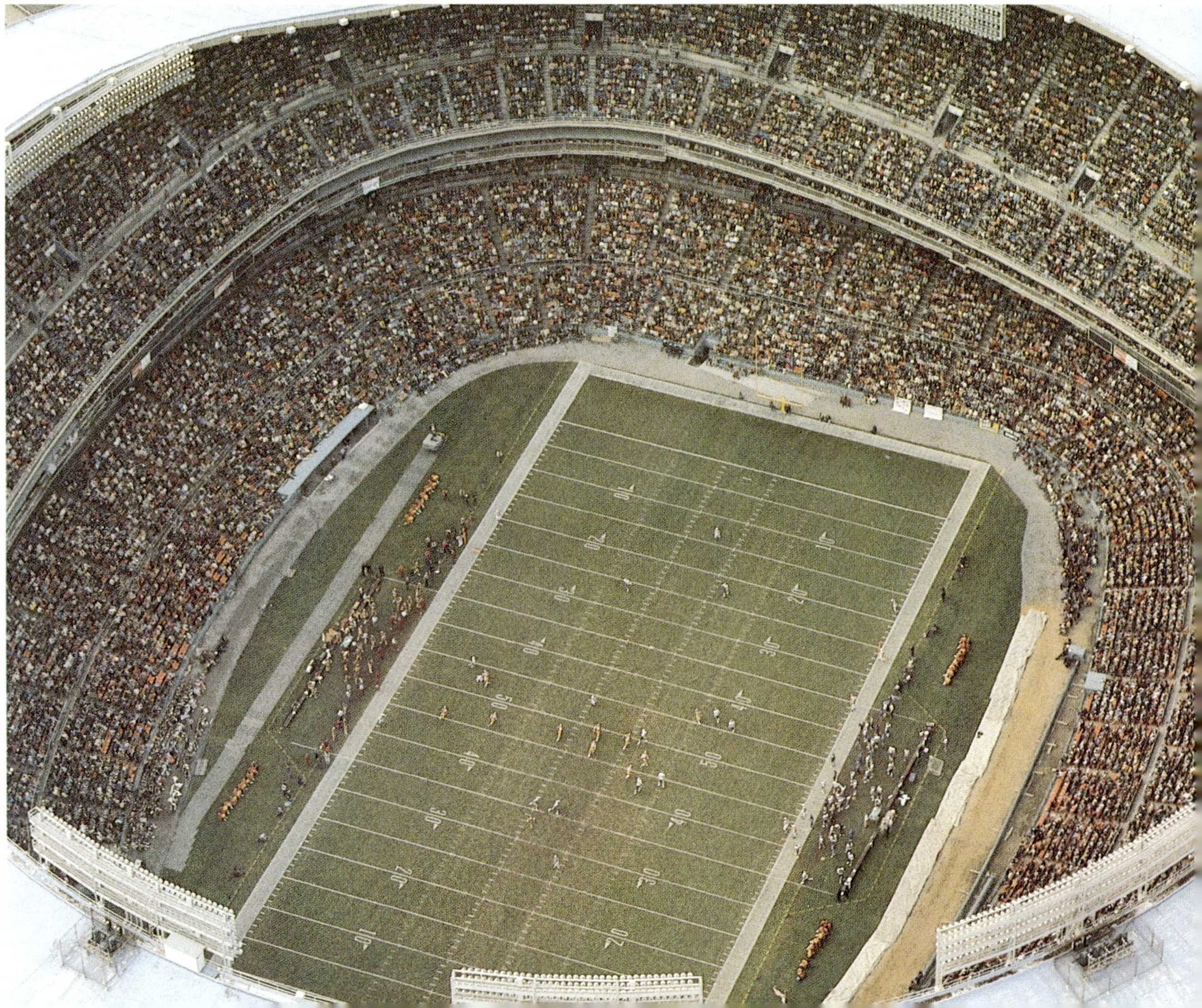

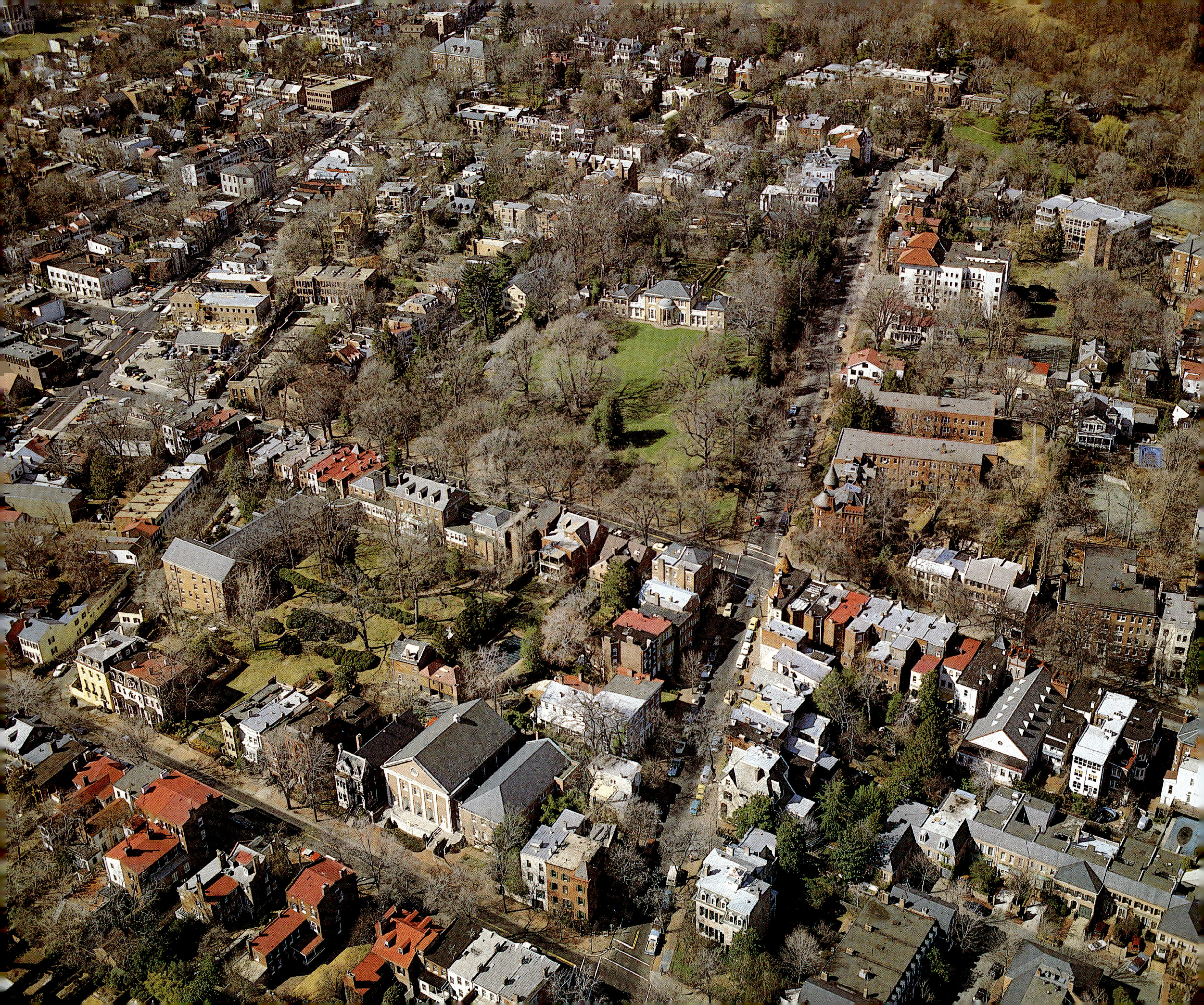

Tudor Place in Georgetown is surely one of the finest early Federal houses in the District, closely associated with the Washington family. It was designed by Dr. William Thornton, the first architect of the Capitol. It was purchased by Martha Parke Custis with money George Washington had left her. Lafayette was entertained here on his last visit to America. Huge brass locks protect, here, Martha Washington's seed-pearl wedding dress and jewelry and the camp trunk General Washington used during the Revolution.

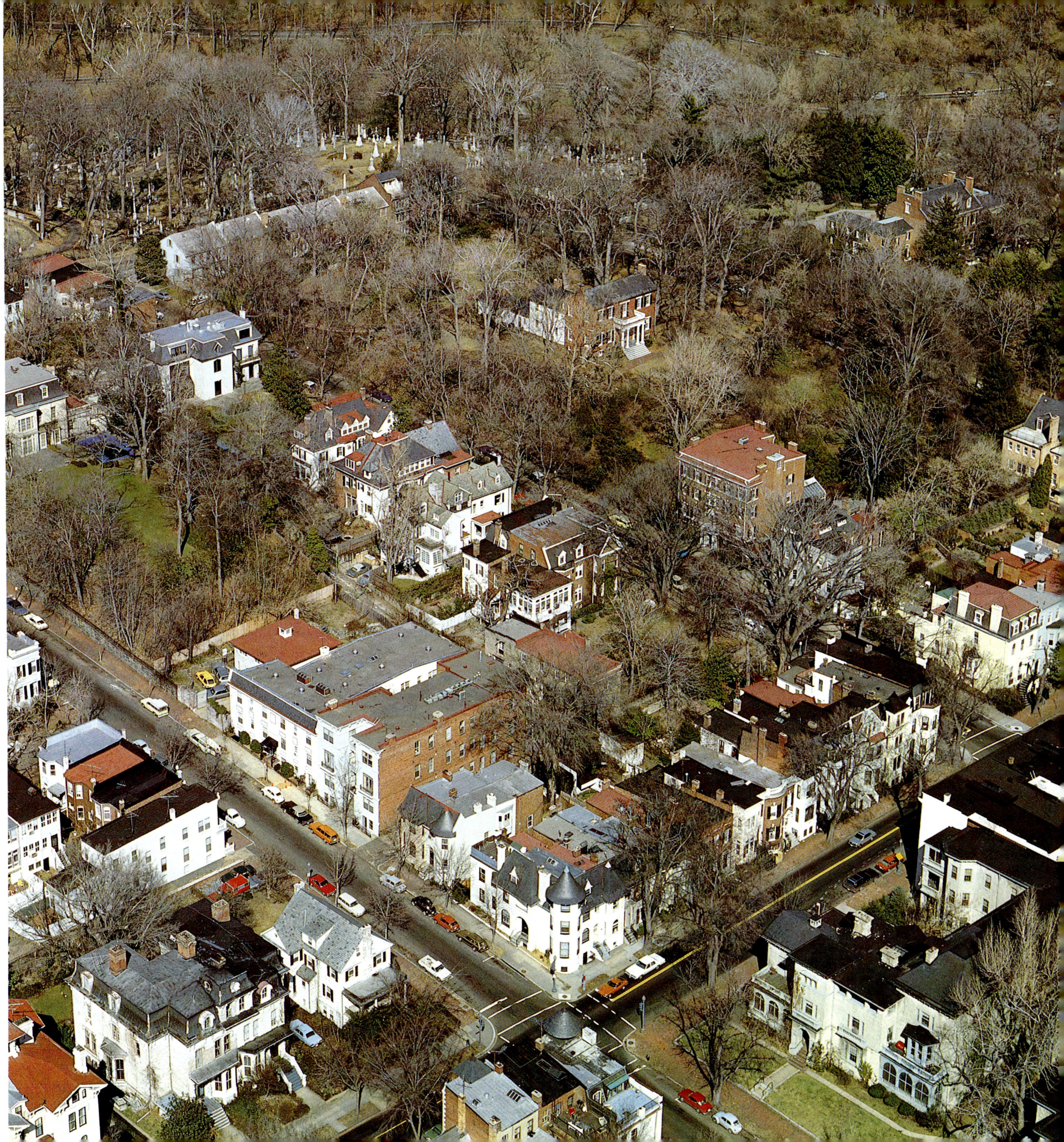

Mackall Square (right center) is also in Georgetown. Behind it is Oak Hill Cemetery going down to the Rock Creek Park Ravine. The north wing of "Evermay" (the house at upper right) may be the oldest structure in Georgetown, believed to have been built about 1717.

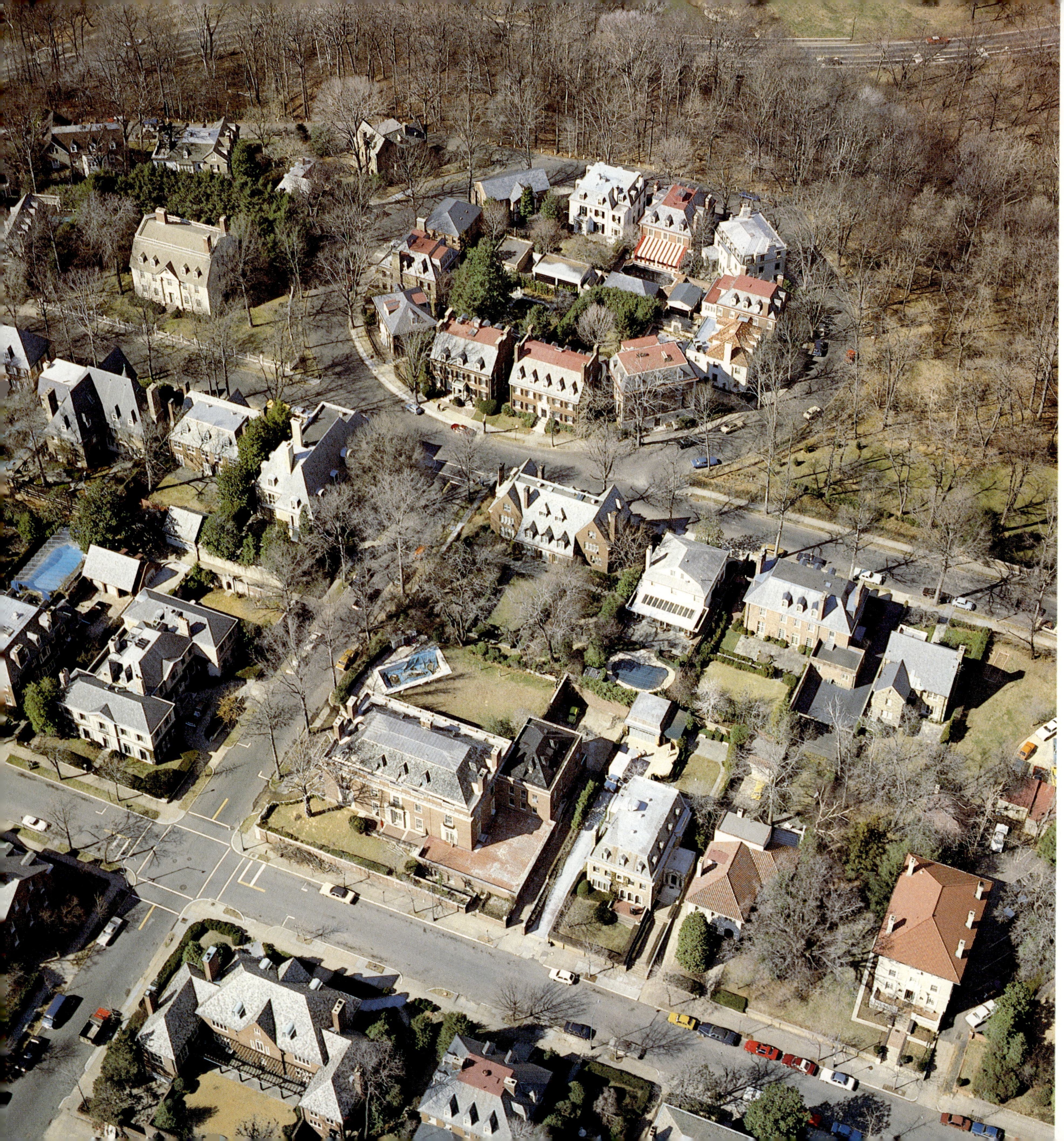

Above Rock Creek Park, with a fine view, the houses here are within, rather than upon the edges of, their circle, the jewel of the exclusive Kalorama neighborhood, north of Georgetown. "The Lindens" at upper left was built in Danvers, Massachusetts in 1754 and, spared from destruction, was moved to Washington in 1936.

A clear demarcation between what seems a separate town, and the demands of a great capital beyond it, is made by Rock Creek Park in the upper part of the photograph. Georgetown reserves its special character.

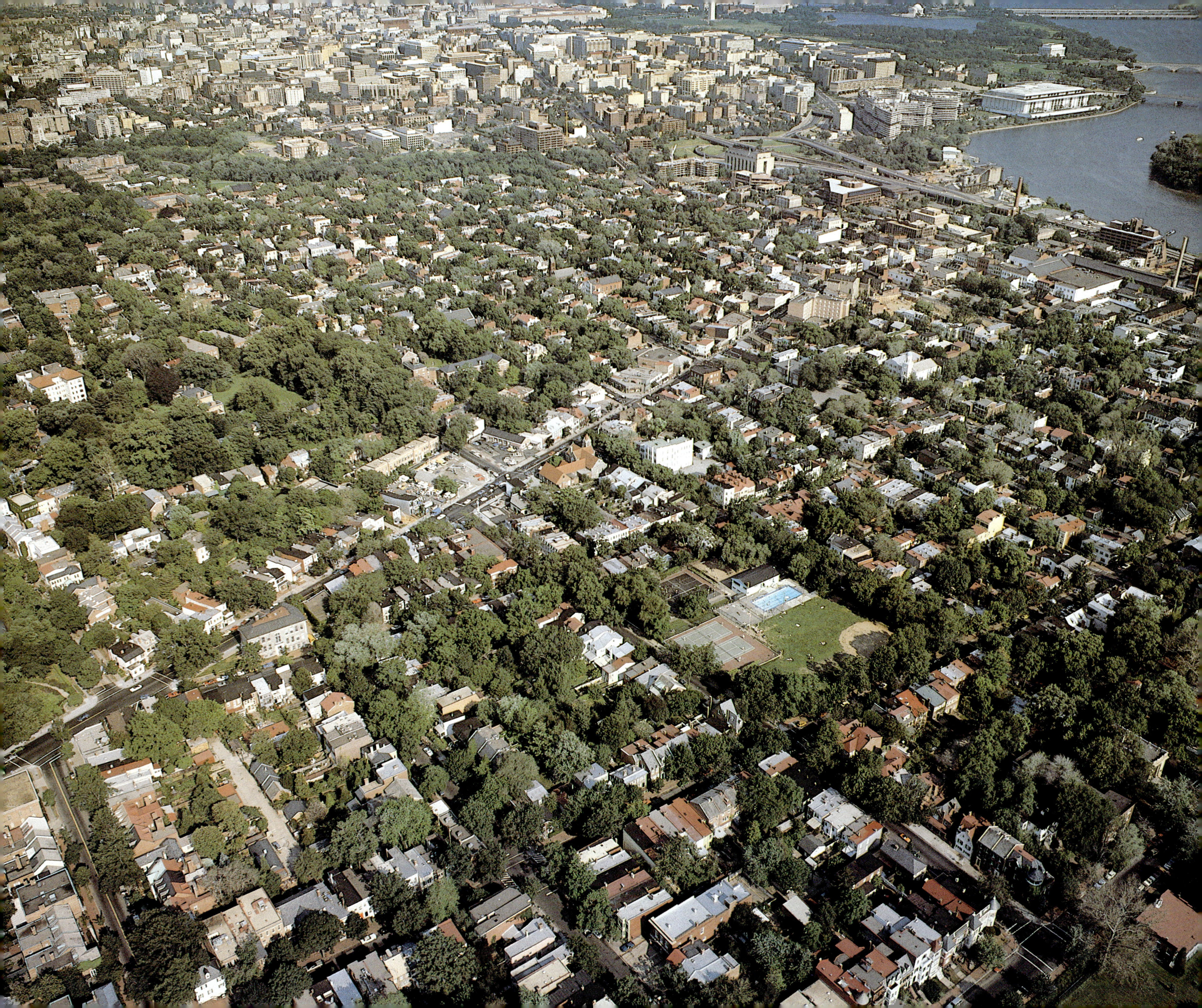

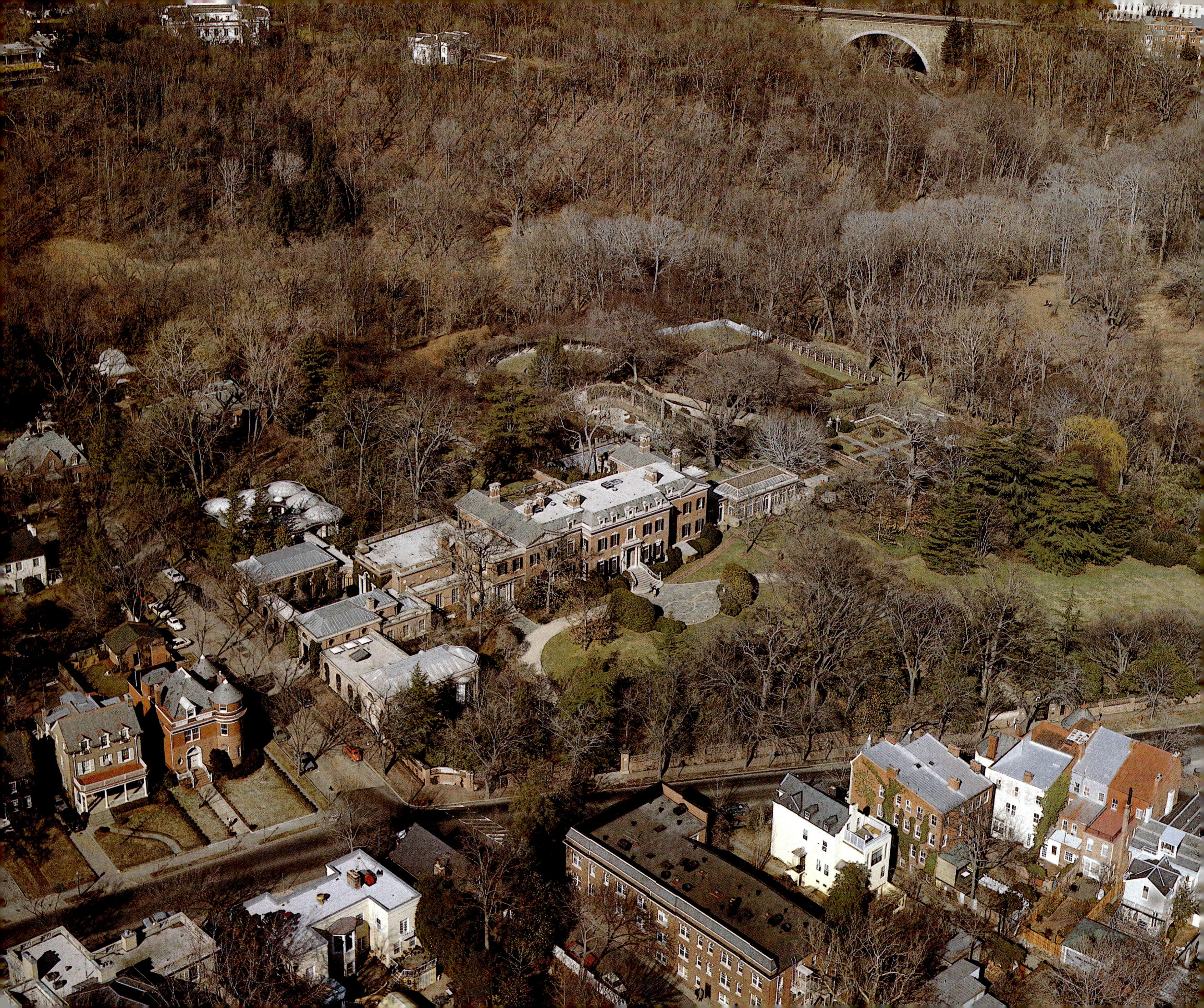

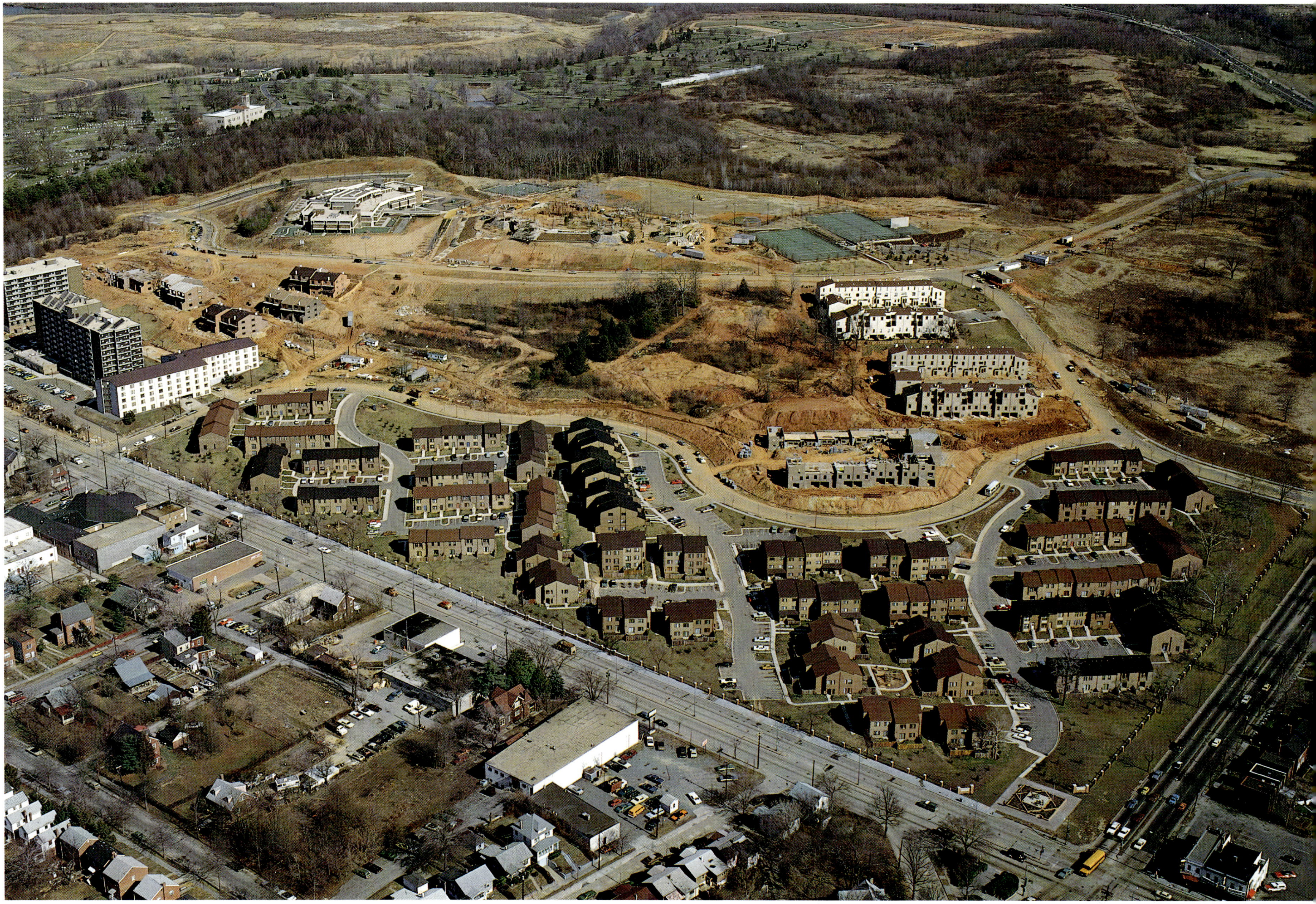

Fort Lincoln is "A New Town in Town." Linked by Metro to downtown Washington, this N.E. Washington community is attracting many of the city's young professionals. Fort Lincoln was one of the forts which ringed the city in the Civil War.

Dumbarton Oaks is the location of the conference that led to the forming of the United Nations Charter. It now houses a magnificent collection of early Christian Byzantine and pre-Columbian art.

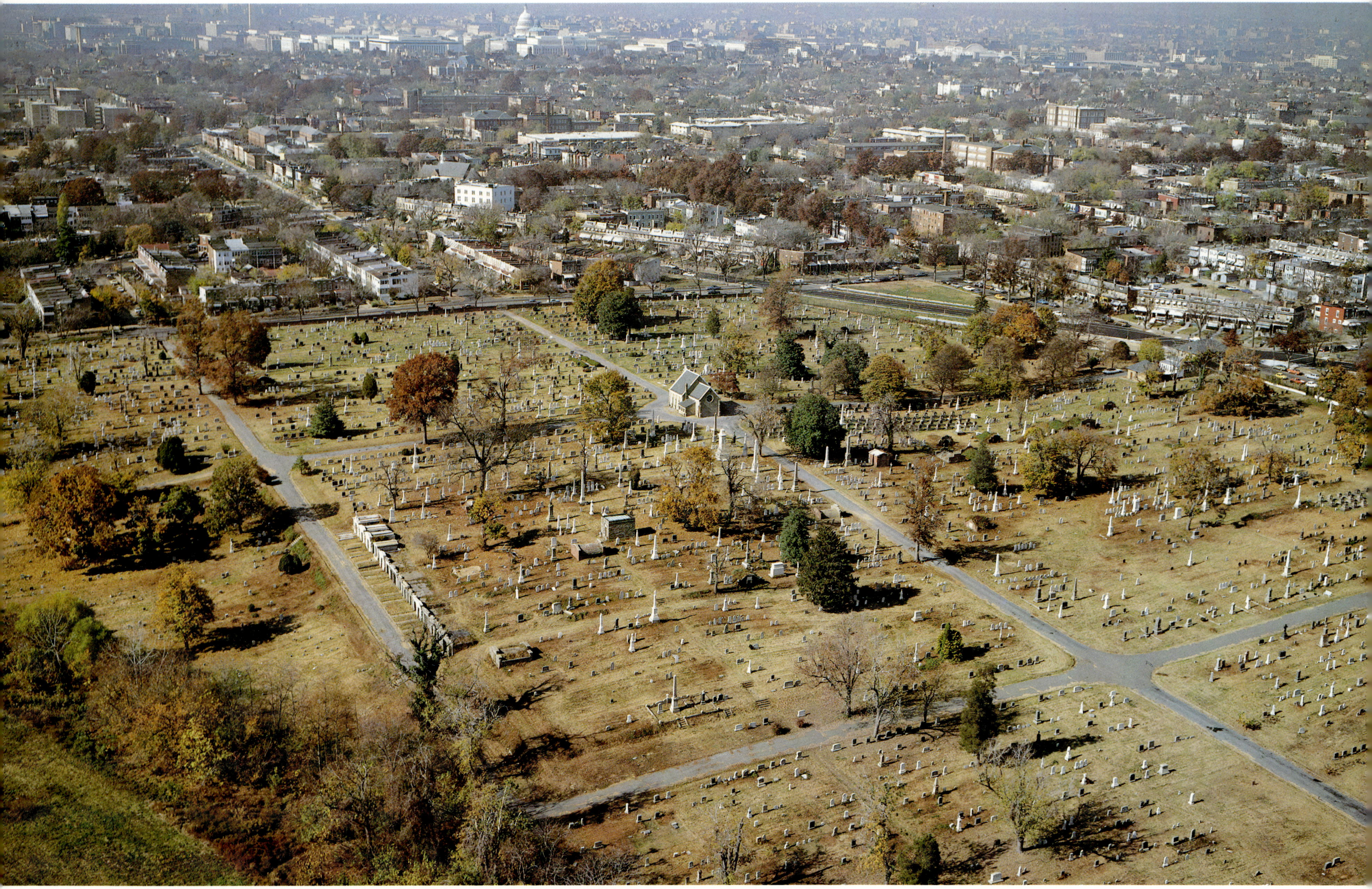

The Congressional Cemetery is at Pennsylvania Avenue where the Sousa Bridge crosses the Anacostia. Congress undertook financial assistance to Christ Church, which established the cemetery, to insure space reservation for government officials. Hence the name. The most famous recent tenant is J. Edgar Hoover. John Philip Sousa is interred here, as are George Clinton, Elbridge Gerry, and many US diplomats, generals, and naval officers. The chapel at center recalls English traditions of the 17th and 18th centuries.

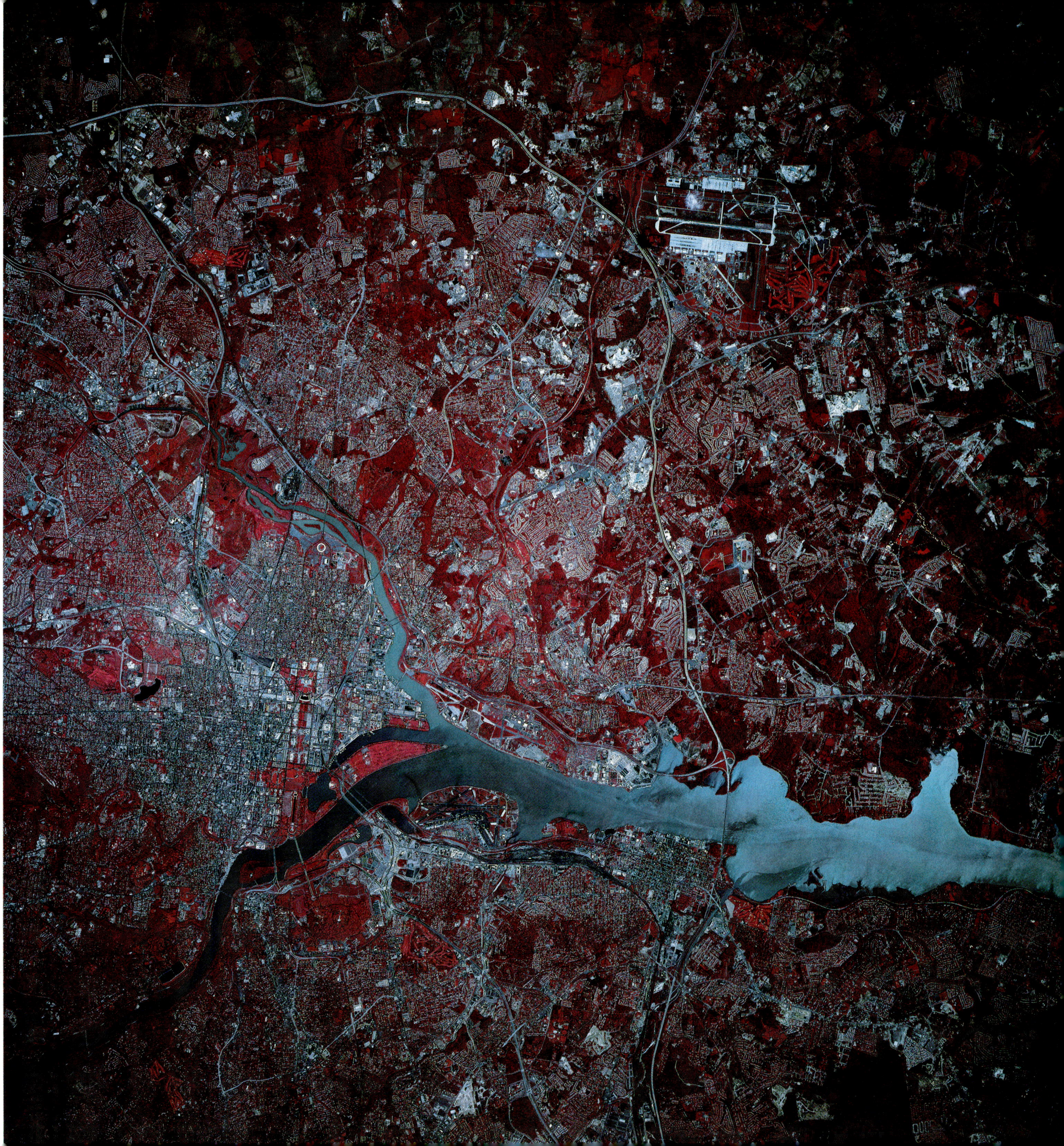

This infrared NASA photograph of Washington demonstrates the ultimate refinement in aerial photography. It was taken from the U-2 aircraft at 65,000 feet. Speed, exposure and all other variables are computer-controlled. The technical "reading" of such pictures as these requires a special kind of sophistication.

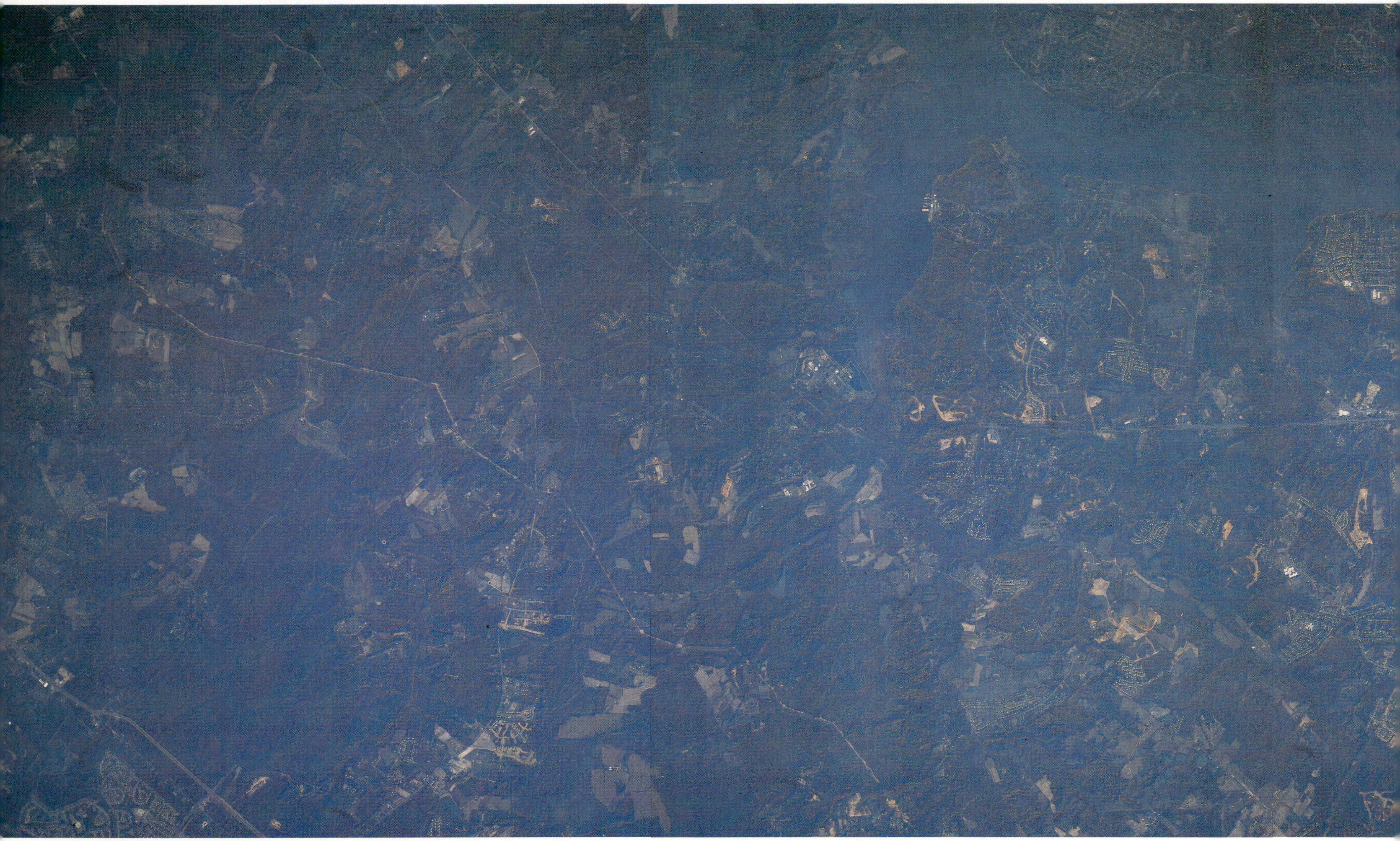

Here is a NASA composite of a flyby using ordinary color film. If it differs in appearance from the infrared, it's because EVERYTHING looks blue from 14 miles up.

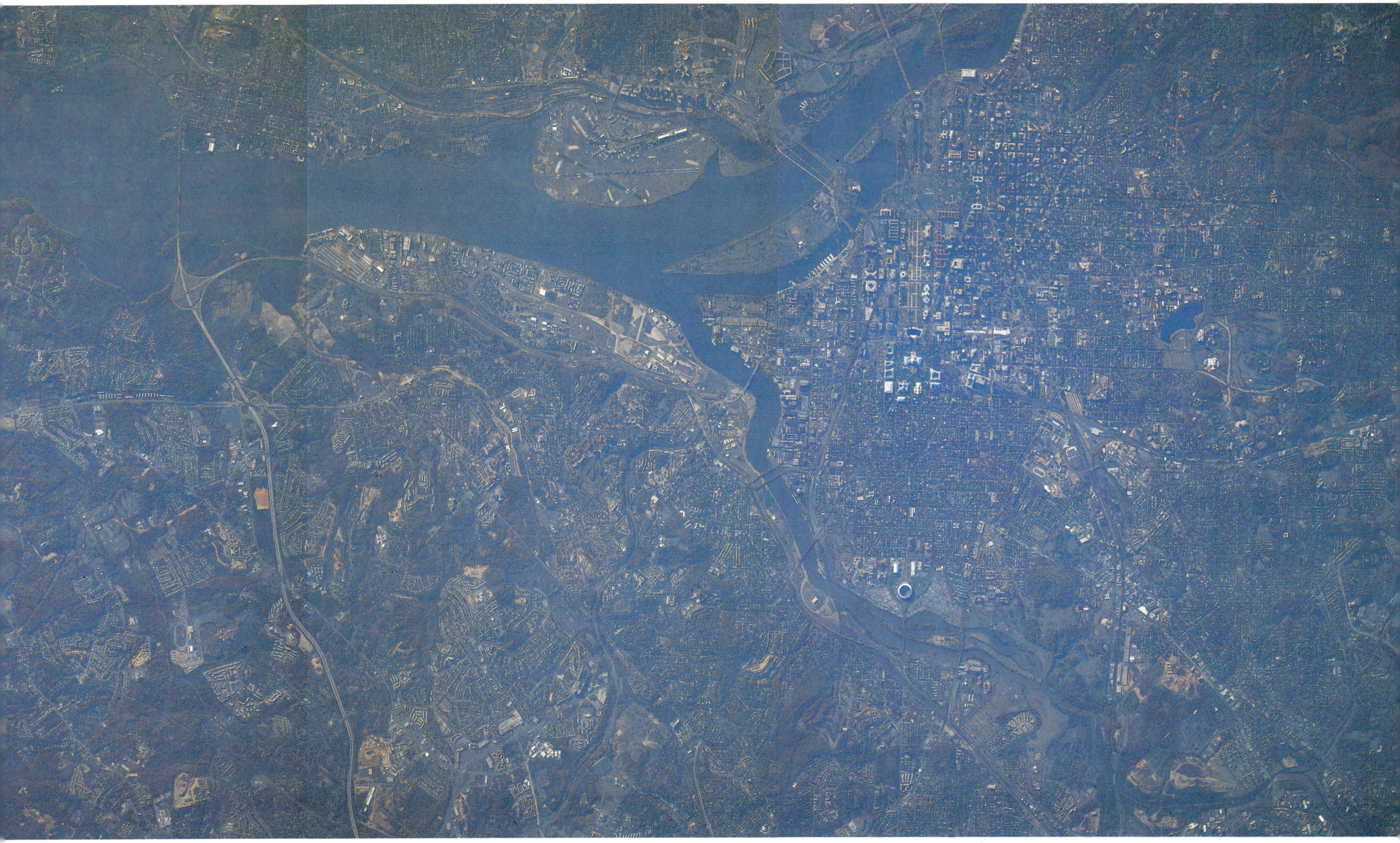

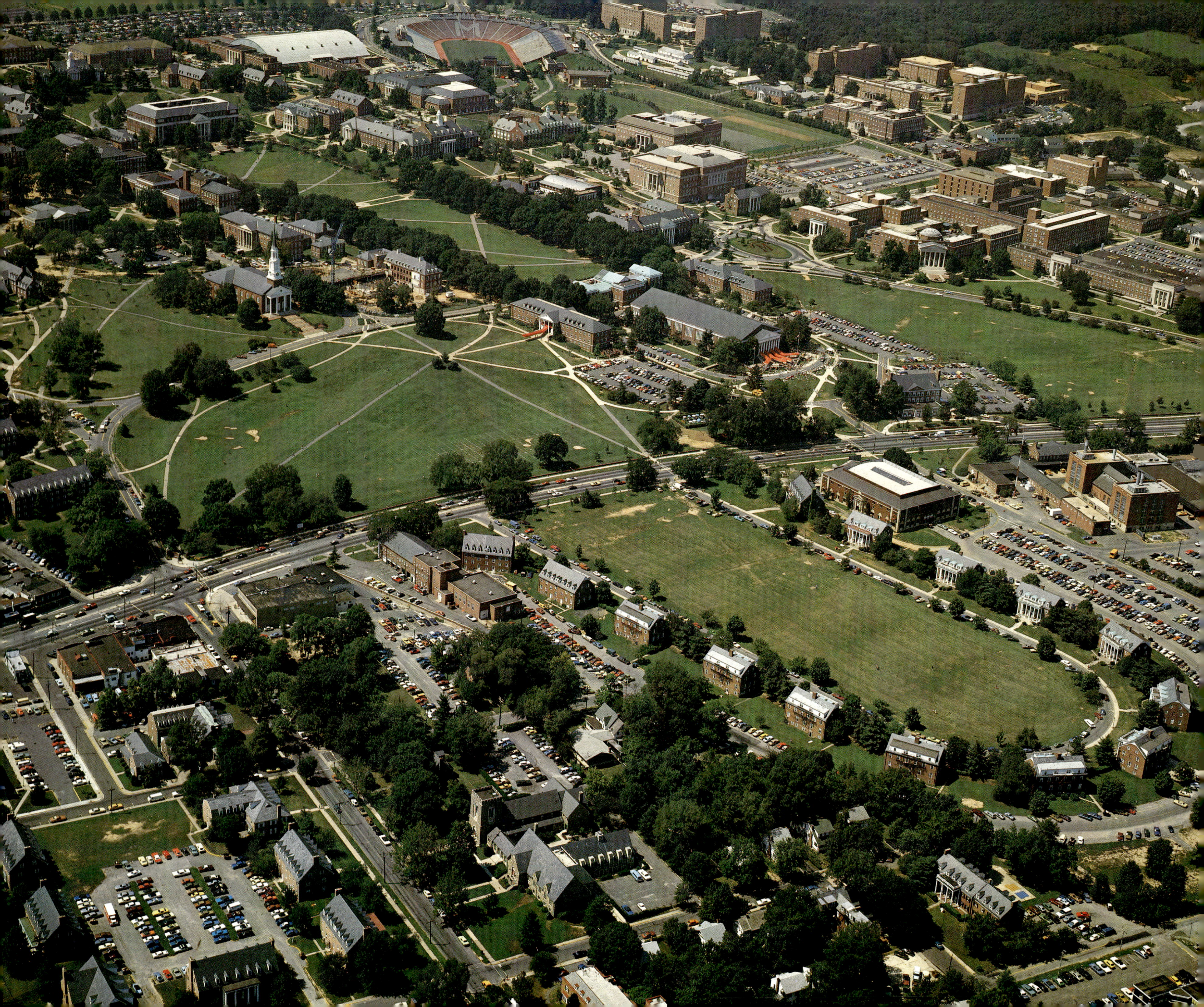

MARYLAND

The University of Maryland, College Park is quartered on broad greenswards with pleasant walkways, student housing attractively related to the university plant. The chapel is upper left, the Byrd Stadium at top center.

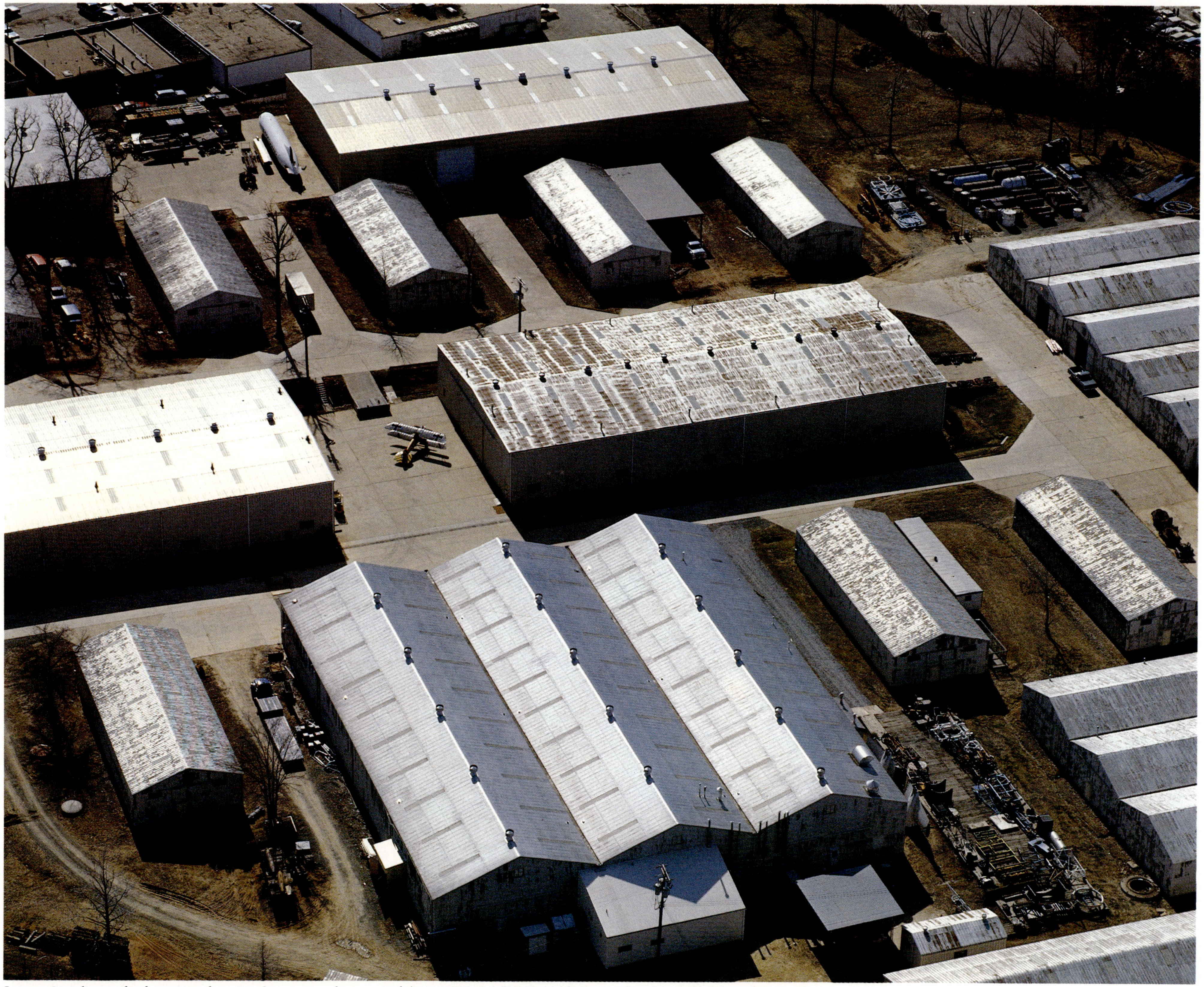

James Smithson died in 1829 leaving his entire fortune of $500,000 to the United States for the diffusion of scientific knowledge. In 1846 Congress took action and founded the Smithsonian Institution. The Castle on the Mall was built in 1849. These pages have shown the Institution's increase and influence, for the capital and for the nation. Its treasures are so extensive that some of them are now warehoused here at Silver Hill, in Suitland. At upper left is a German World War I biplane and beyond it the "Columbine," personal plane of F.D.R.

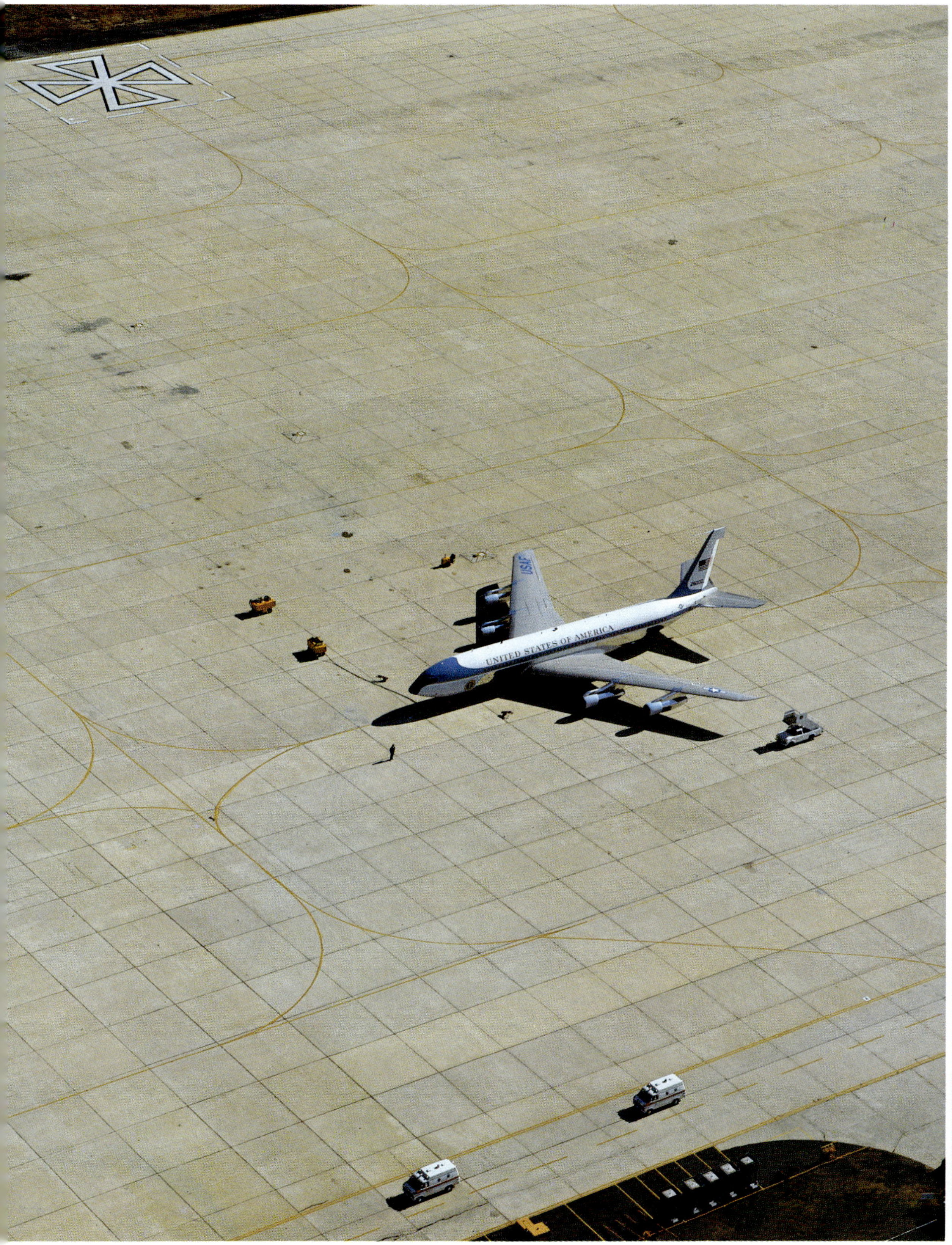

Air Force One is opulently equipped and is the president's personal transportation. It has cabin area and accommodations for other officials and members of the press. At upper left a marker indicates the touchdown for helicopters. Security here is tight at all locations and for all equipment.

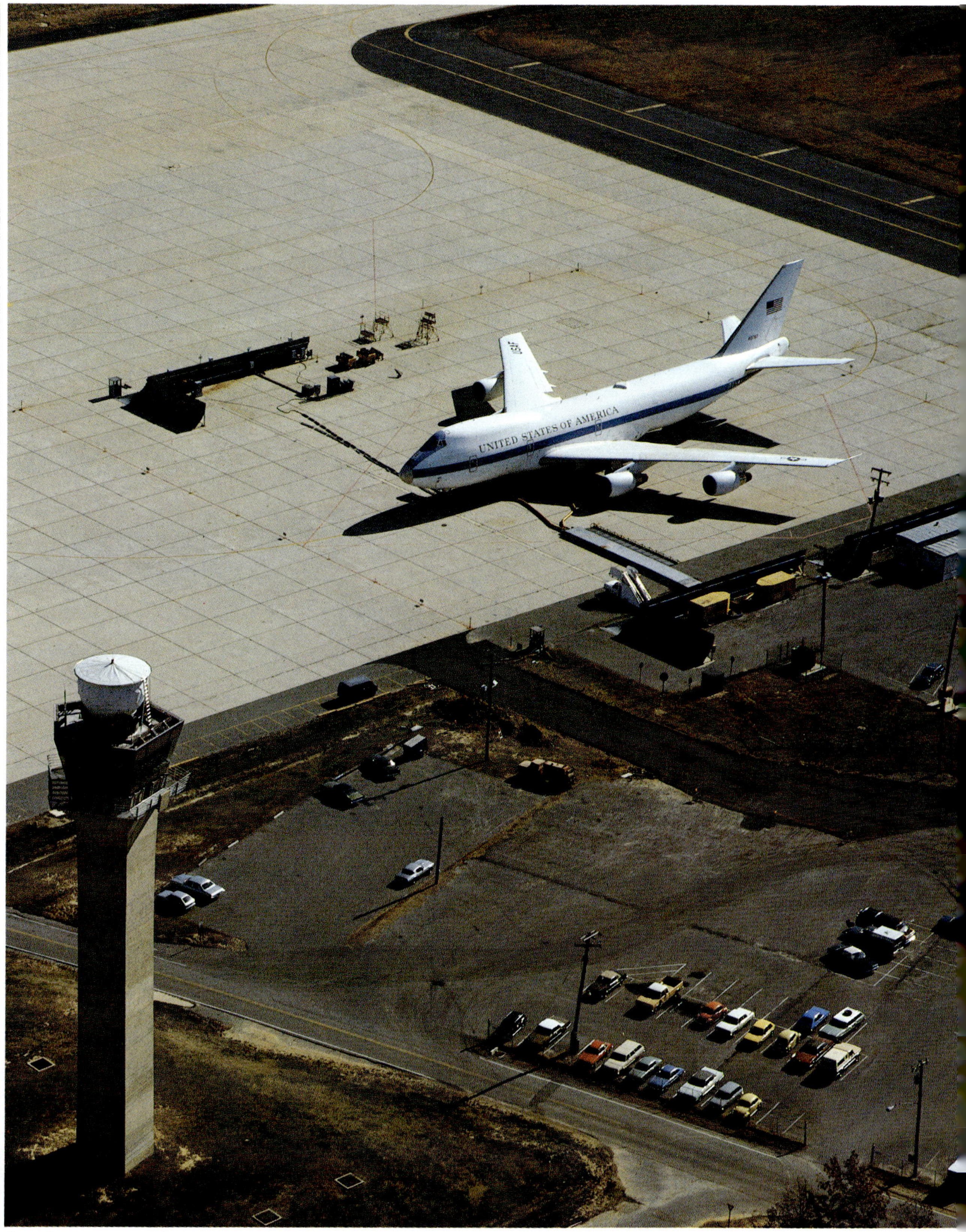

On the same Andrews Air Force Base Airstrip, at the ready, with ultimate communications apparatus, a national emergency command post can fly in this 747. The acronym NECP has the jocular pronunciation "kneecap."

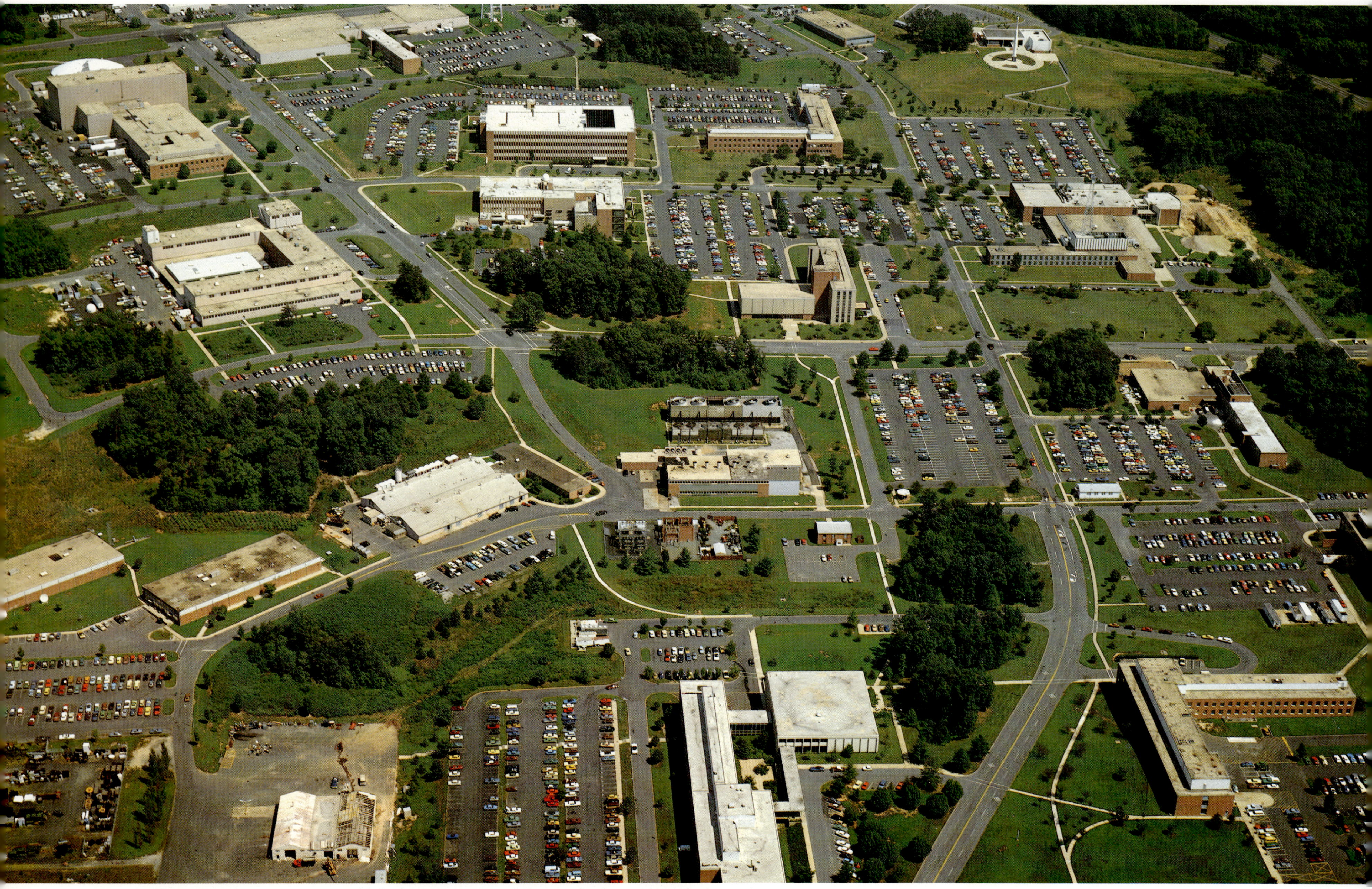

The Goddard Space Center, established in 1959 in Greenbelt, Maryland, is a NASA facility and is primarily in charge of unmanned space flight, tracking all satellites now in orbit. It also launched the Delta Rocket Series, and will be busy in the future with space shuttle activities.

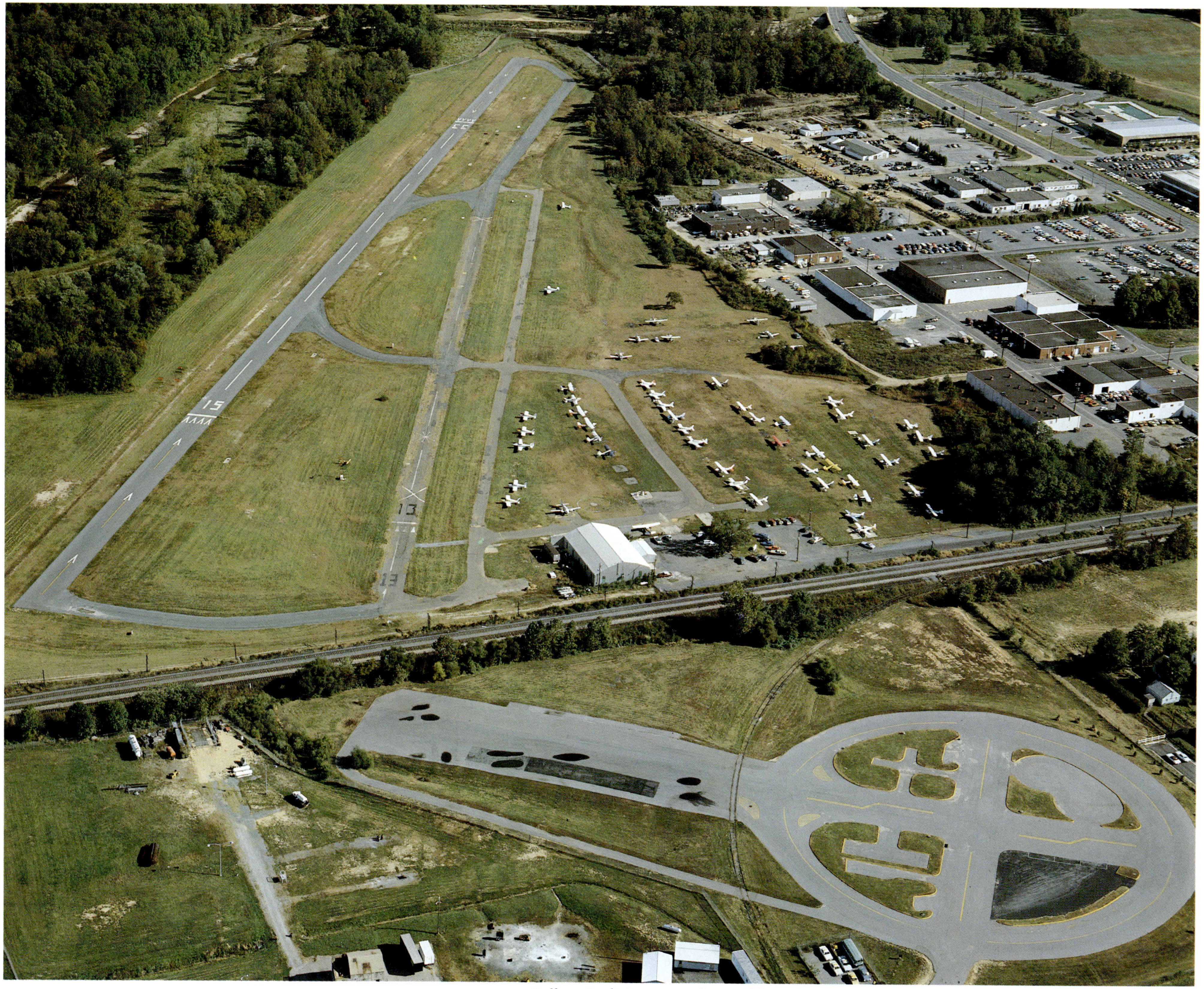

College Park Airport is the world's oldest. The Wright brothers established it in this suburban Maryland location, after their first flights at Kitty Hawk, and after test work at Fort Myer.

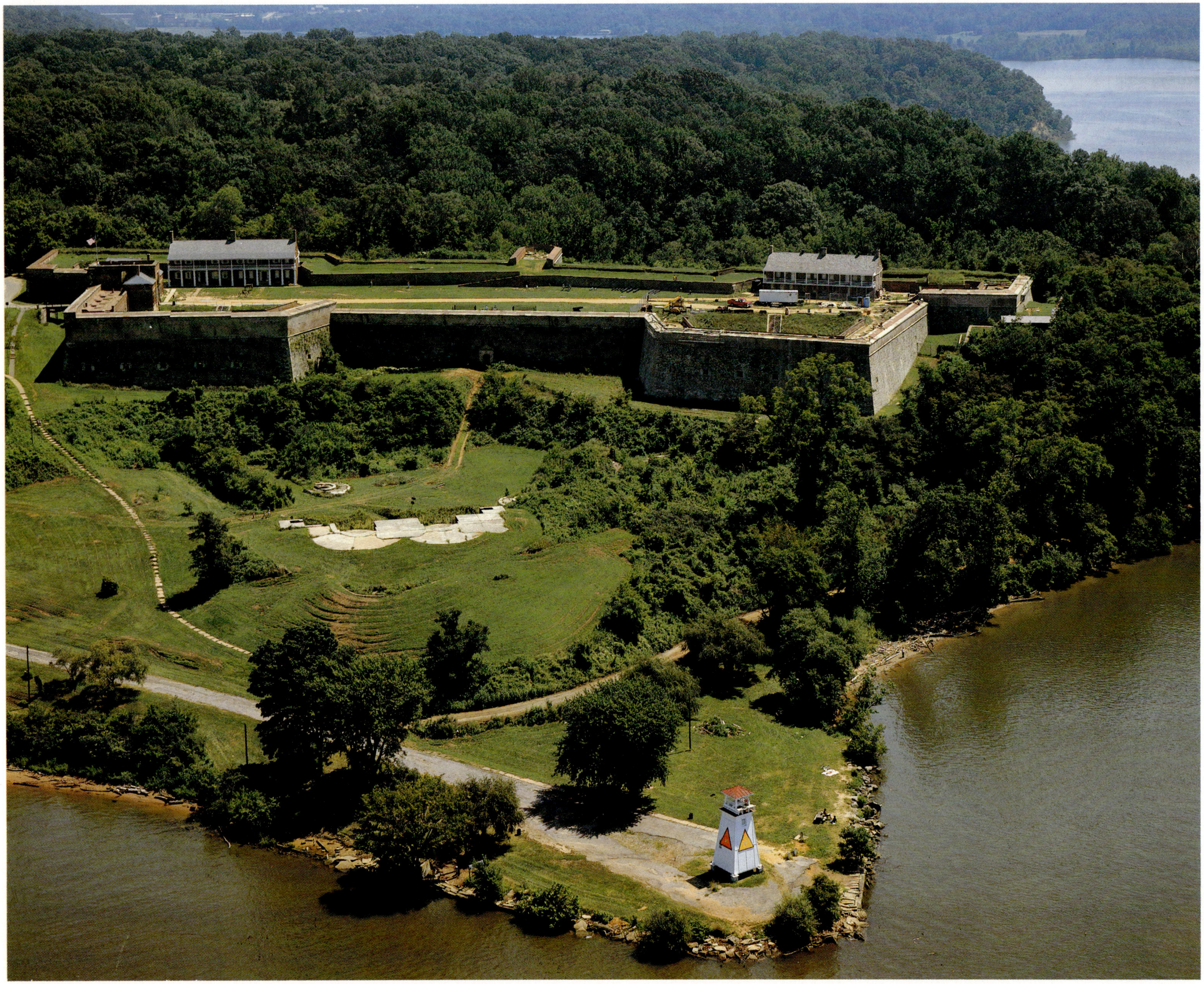

Ft. Washington is south of Washington on the Maryland side of the Potomac. First called Ft. Warburton, it was designed by L'Enfant, who had been a major of engineers in the Revolutionary Army. The Fort's site was strategic for defense of the Capital. We see the structure as it was rebuilt in 1822. The original fort was blown up by its commander in 1814 to prevent its capture by the British.

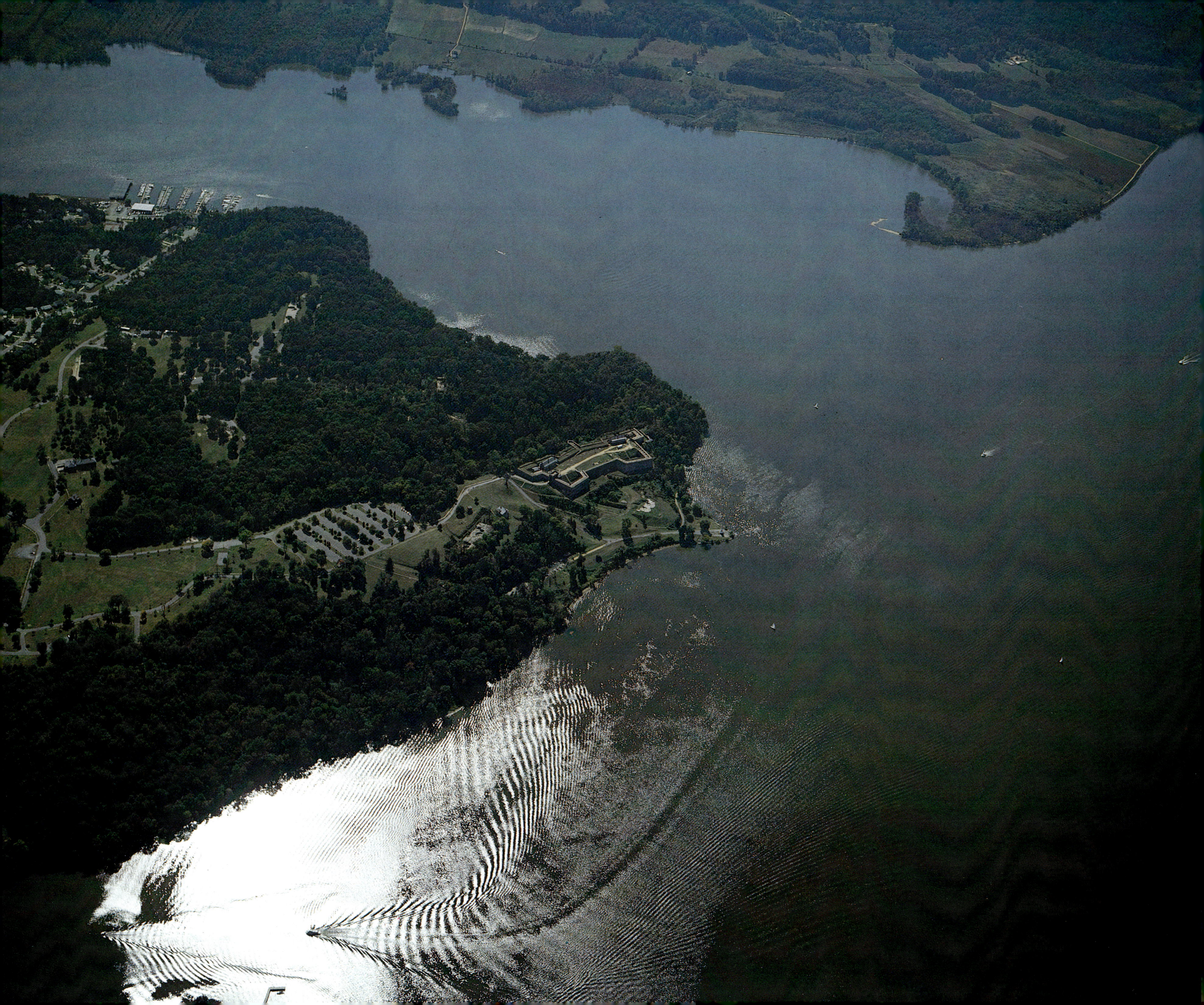

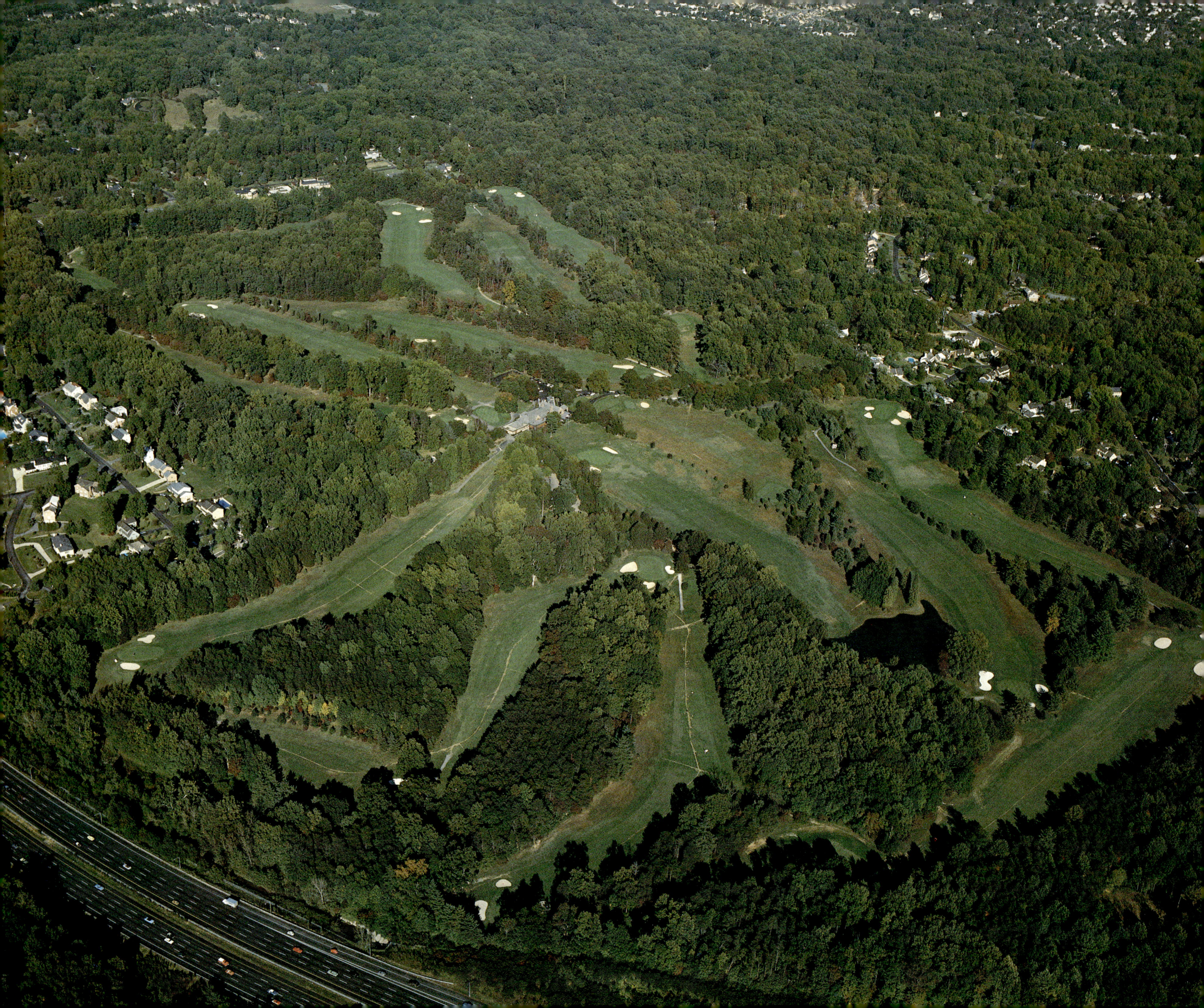

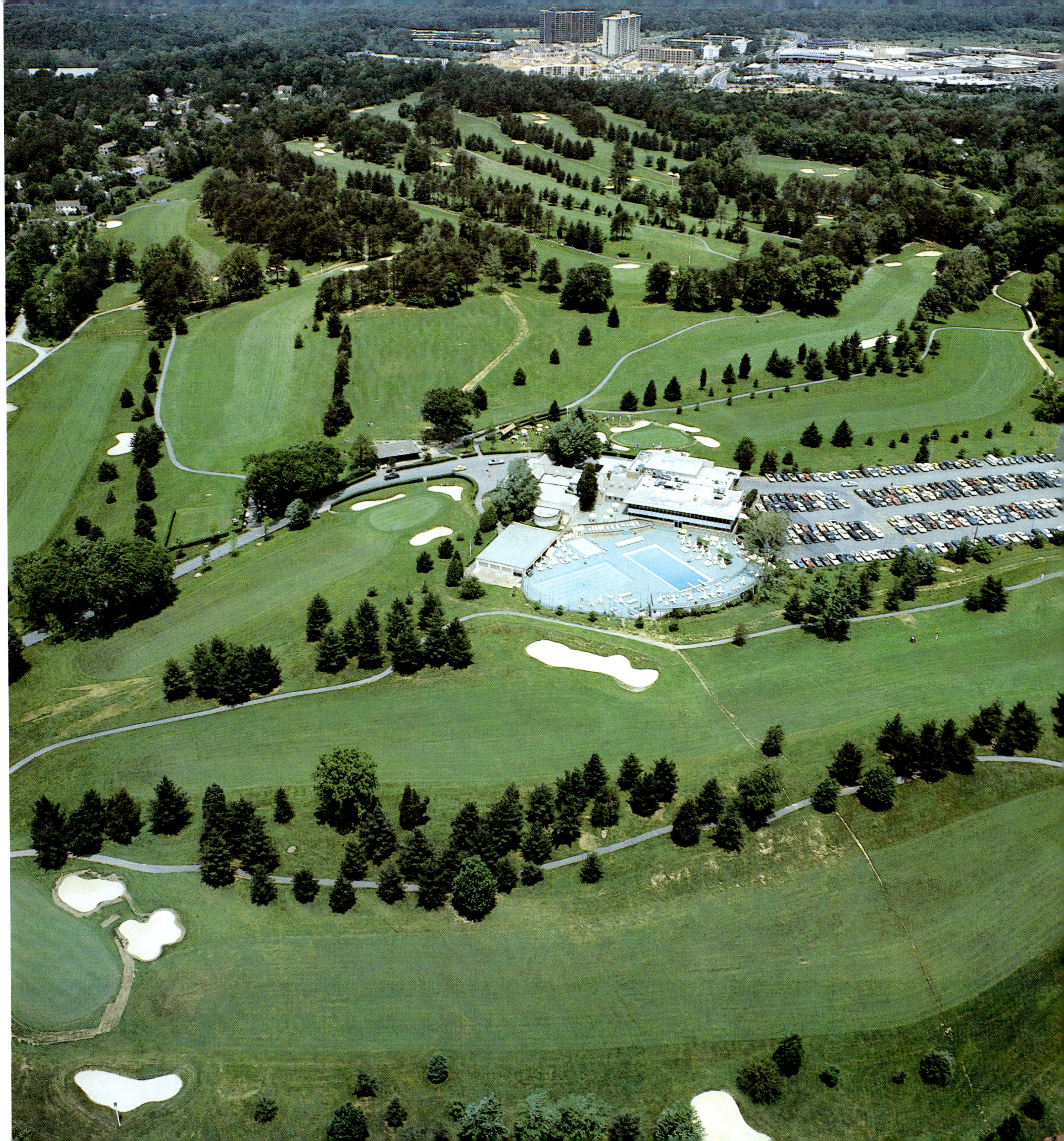

The magnificent verdure of the Burning Tree Country Club defines the layout for golf. Many recent presidents have favored this course, and many national and international luminaries.

Next to the Beltway, between Bradley Boulevard and Democracy Boulevard, the Bethesda Country Club Course, a private facility, expands, from the air, the green of public agencies, Montgomery Country park land in Cabin John Creek area.

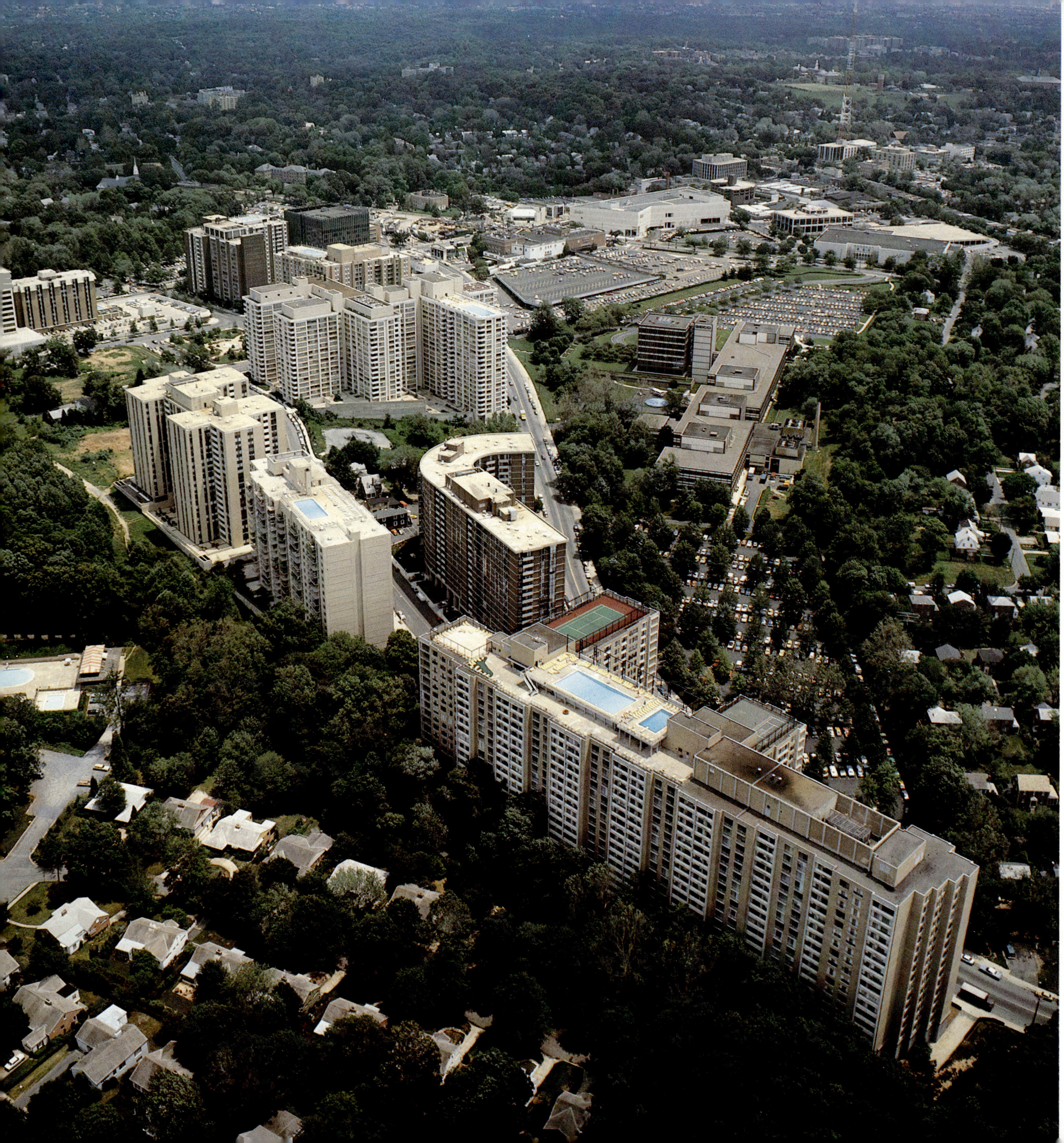

This is Friendship Heights, where Wisconsin Avenue crosses into Maryland, between Bethesda on the west and Chevy Chase, to the east. It is a center of apartment buildings and offices, and an area in which shops and stores make a satellite congregation of the leading names in fashionable and mercantile Washington and New York.

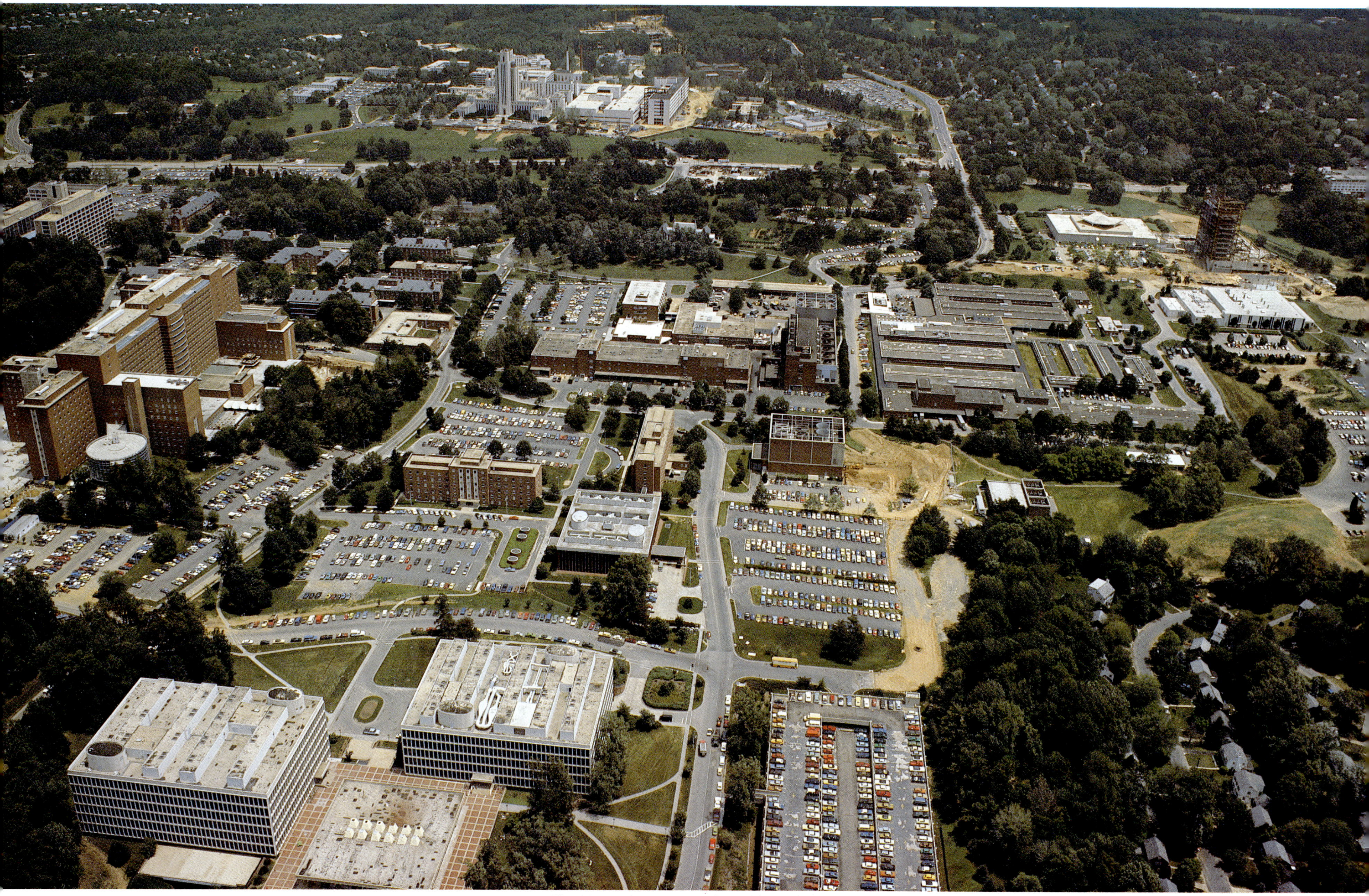

The National Institutes of Health is in the foreground. Bethesda Naval Hospital is above center, with a tower dominating the complex. Bethesda is known for its medical, dental, and hospital facilities; and in suites associated with presidential occupation, for a level of convenience, comfort and solicitude nowhere excelled.

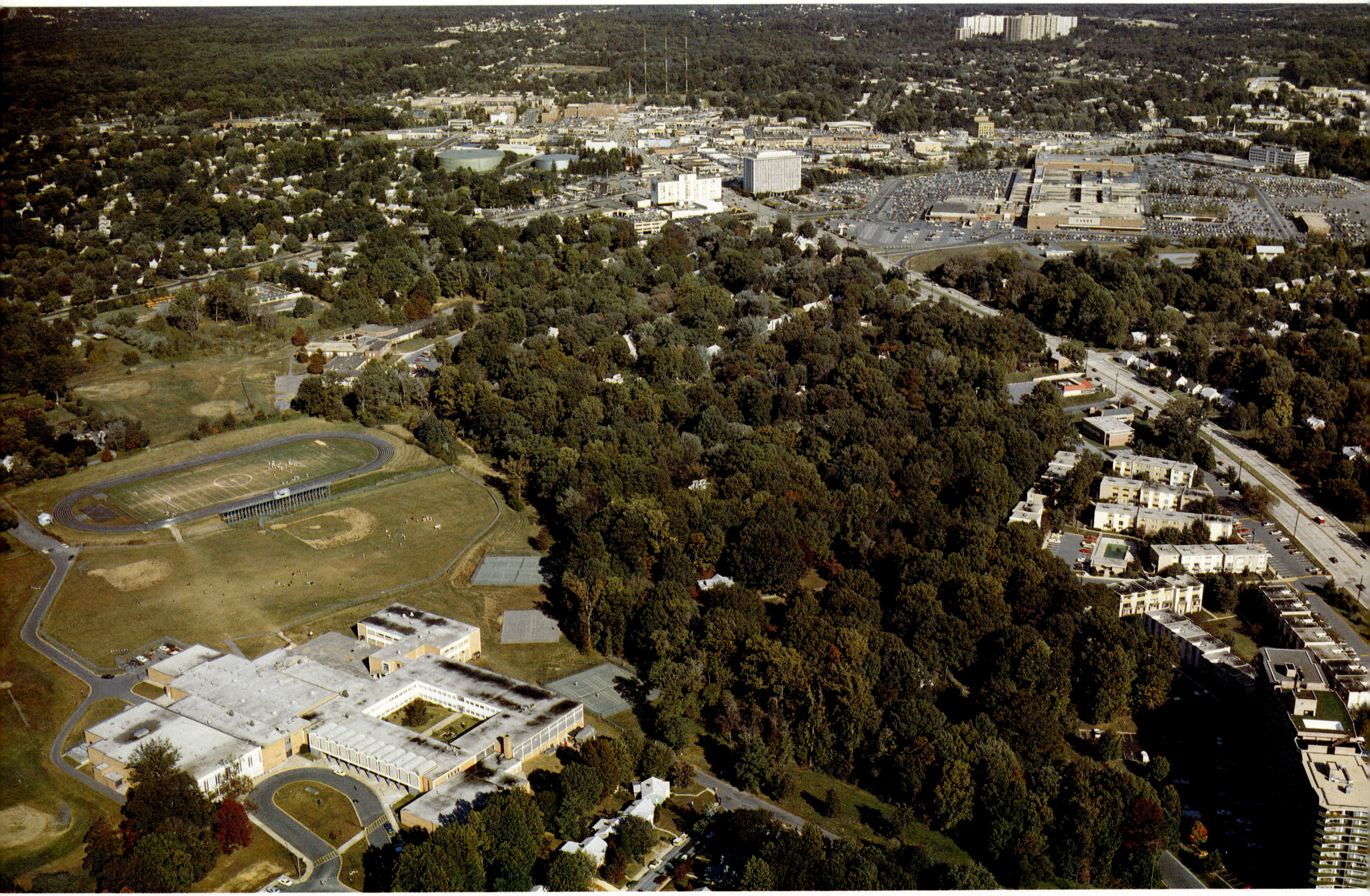

An older suburban community outside the Beltway, Wheaton is directly north of the District of Columbia. Besides recent vertical structures near Wheaton Plaza, and in the distances at upper right, the Albert Einstein High School, lower left, exemplifies current development.

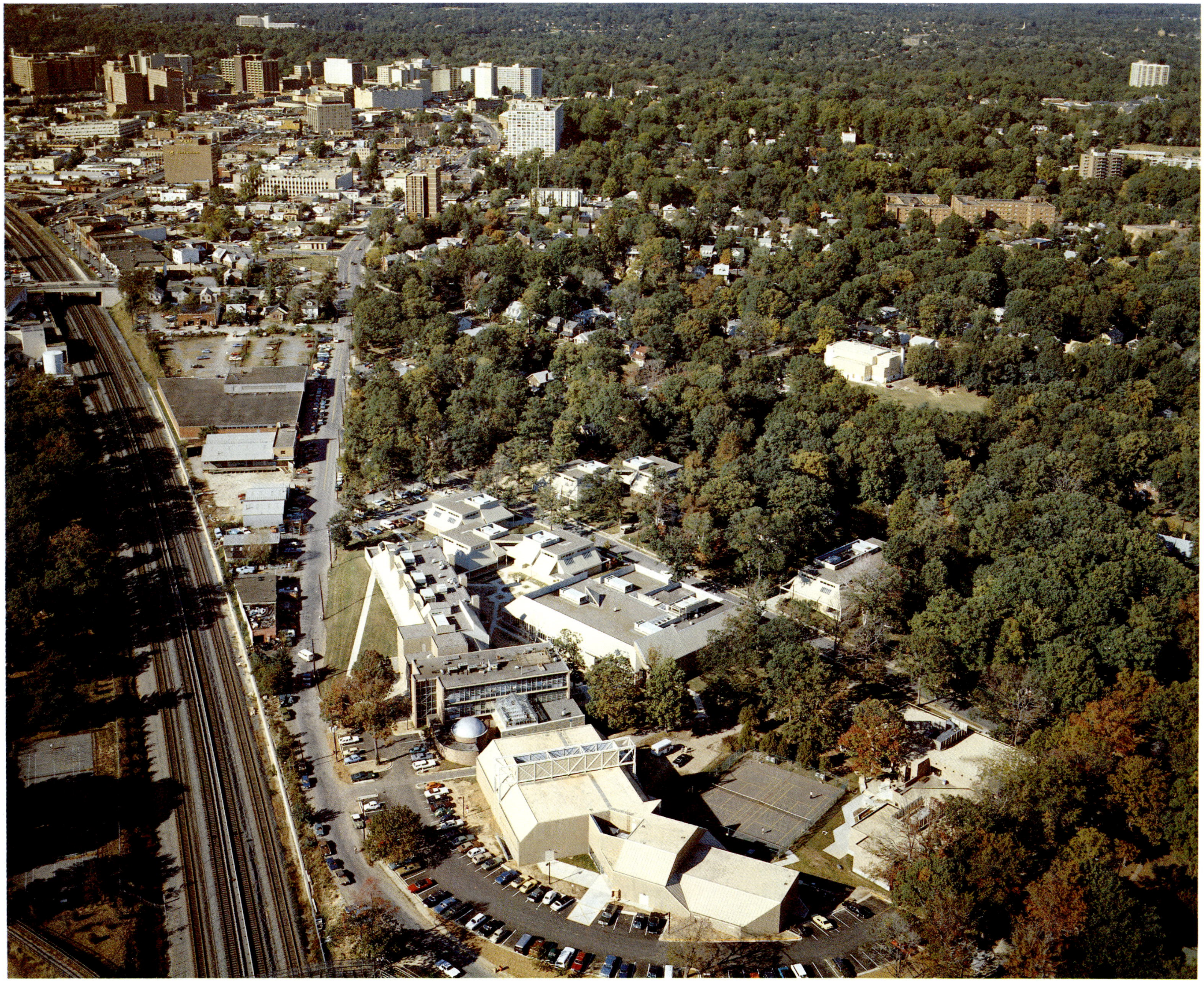

Another early suburban choice, at the DC line, Silver Spring's residential areas retain their trees, and yet concede the cement and stone, and steel rail, which the years have required.

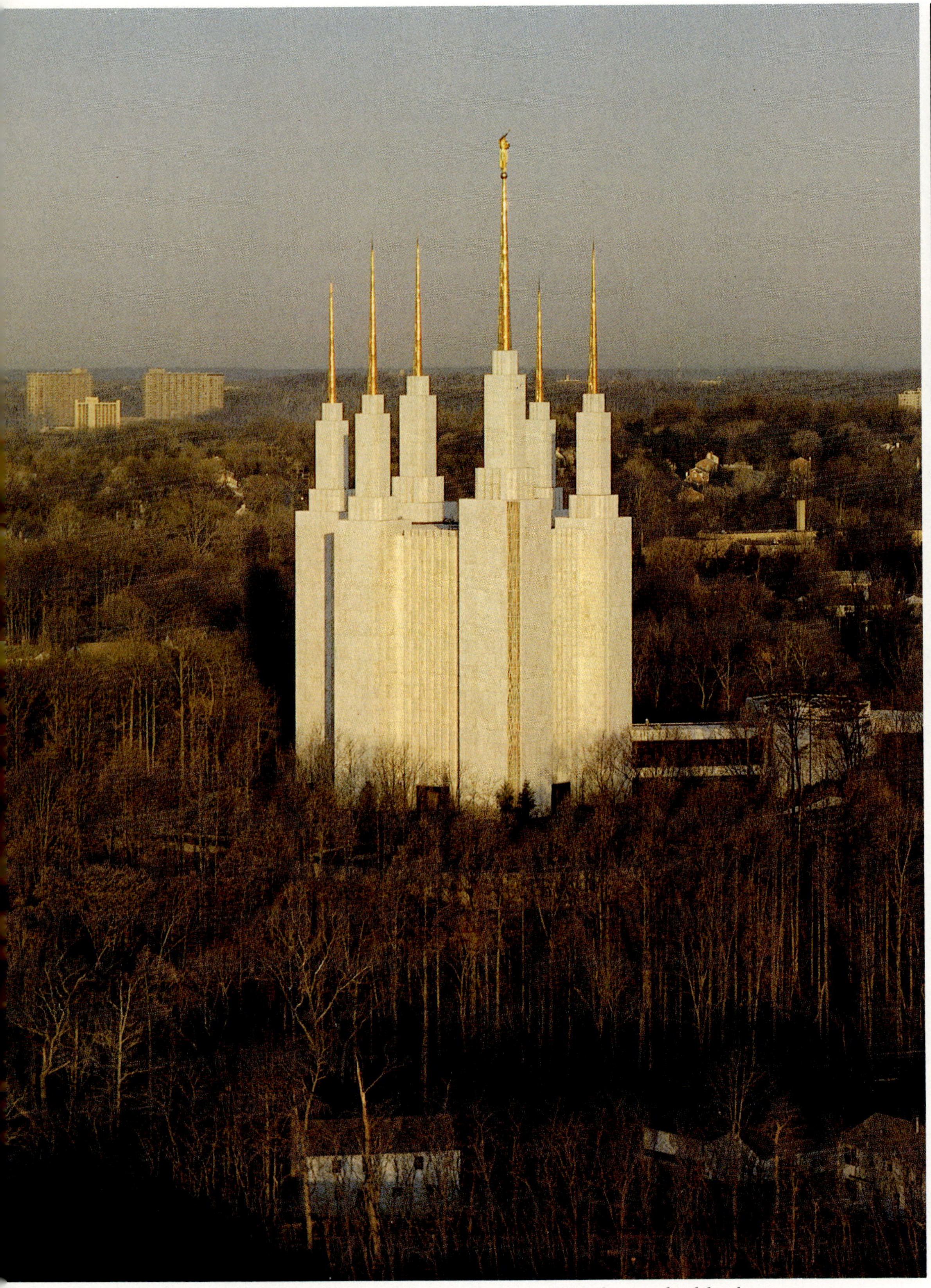

At the beltway in central Maryland the Mormon Temple is a highly dramatic new church facility. At night it glows in the setting of its own lights. The gliding of the spires becomes reflection heightened golden light, at dawn. The Temple was open to public visitation briefly, before its dedication in 1974. It is now limited in access to members of The Church of Jesus Christ of Latter-Day Saints.

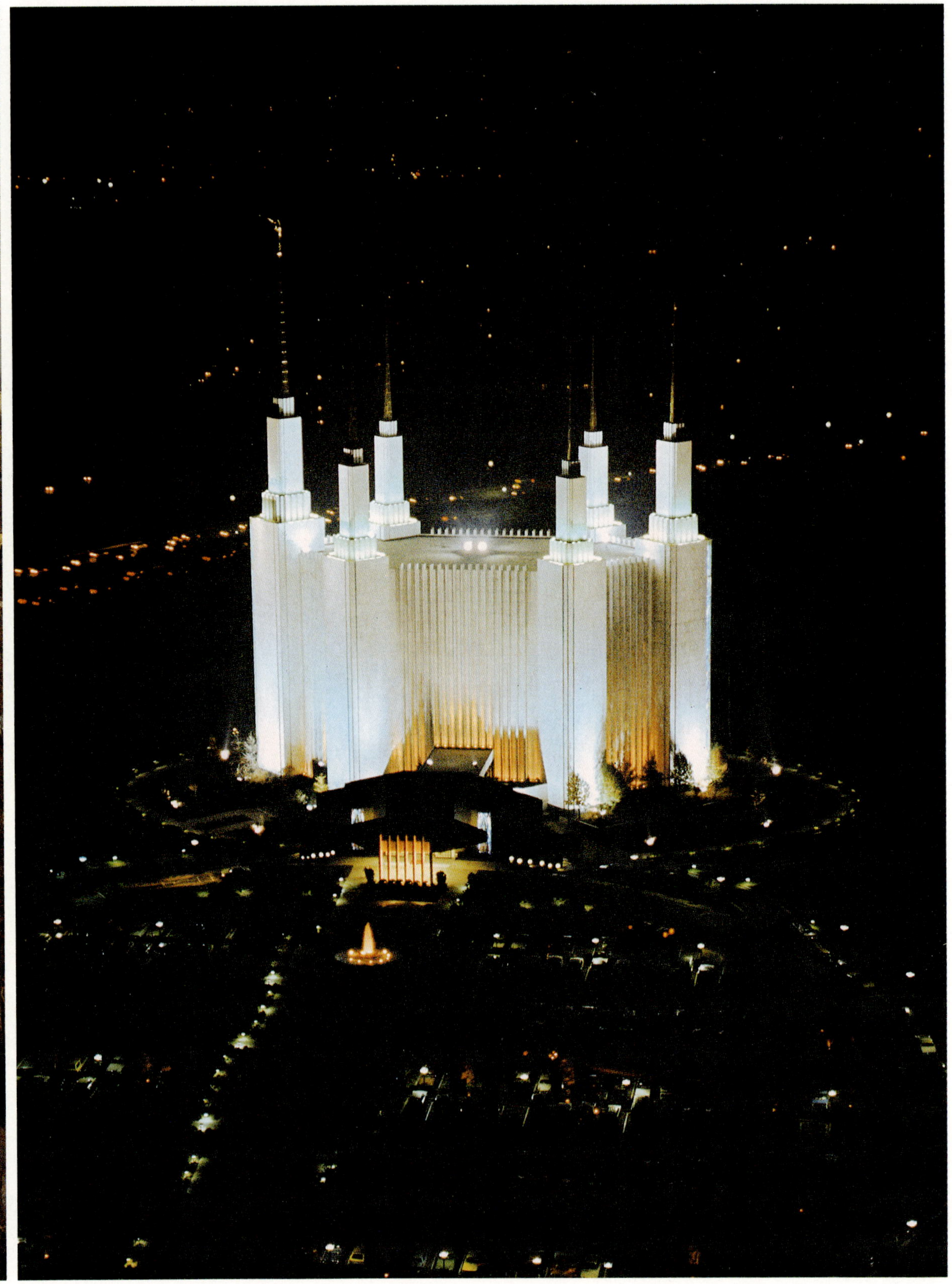

The long covered tank barrel houses systems of wave generation and wind tunnels which make the David Taylor Model Basin a highly sophisticated testing facility for ship design. Models are propelled on interior track under water in exhaustive experimentation. The location is in Cabin John, Maryland.

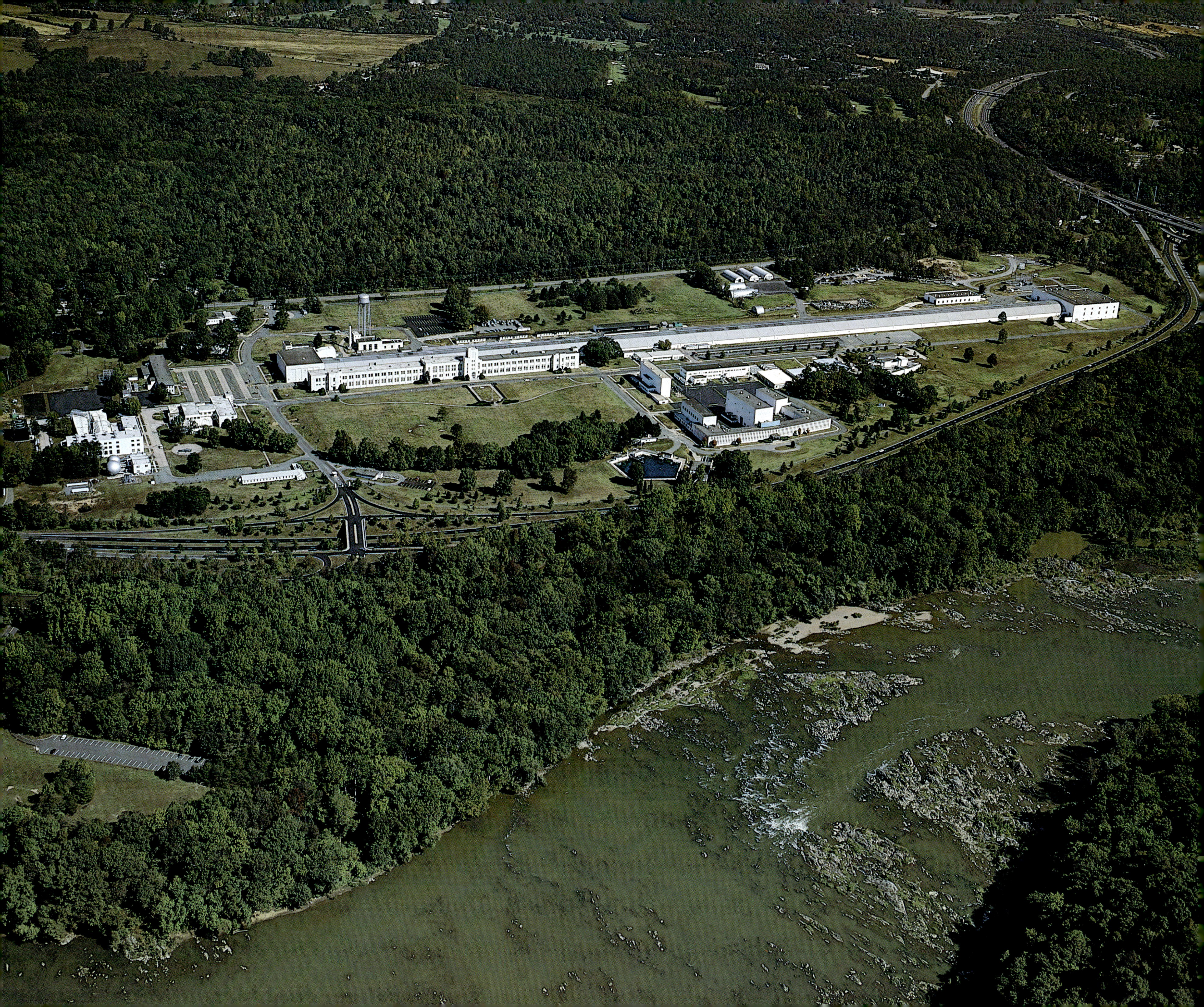

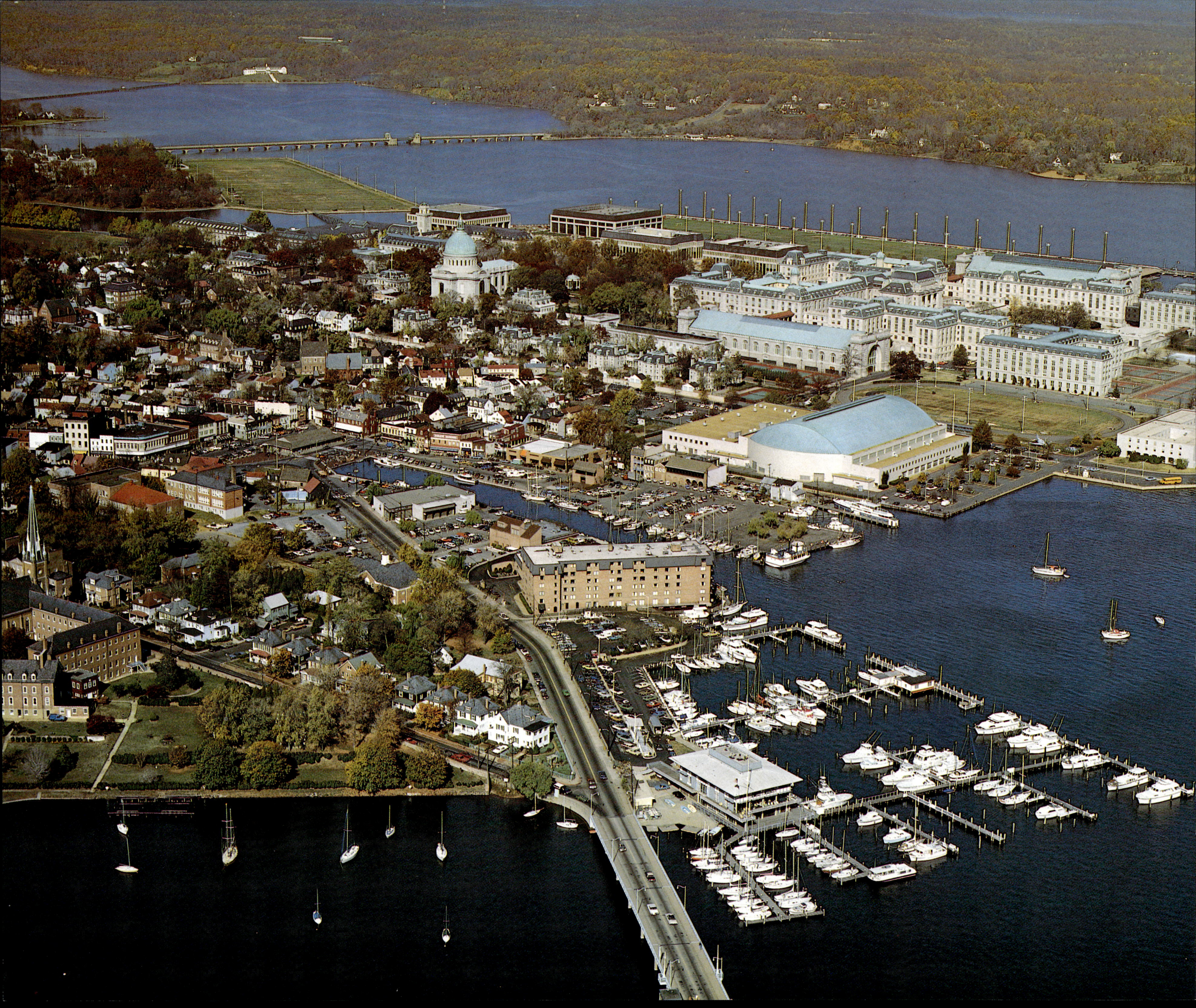

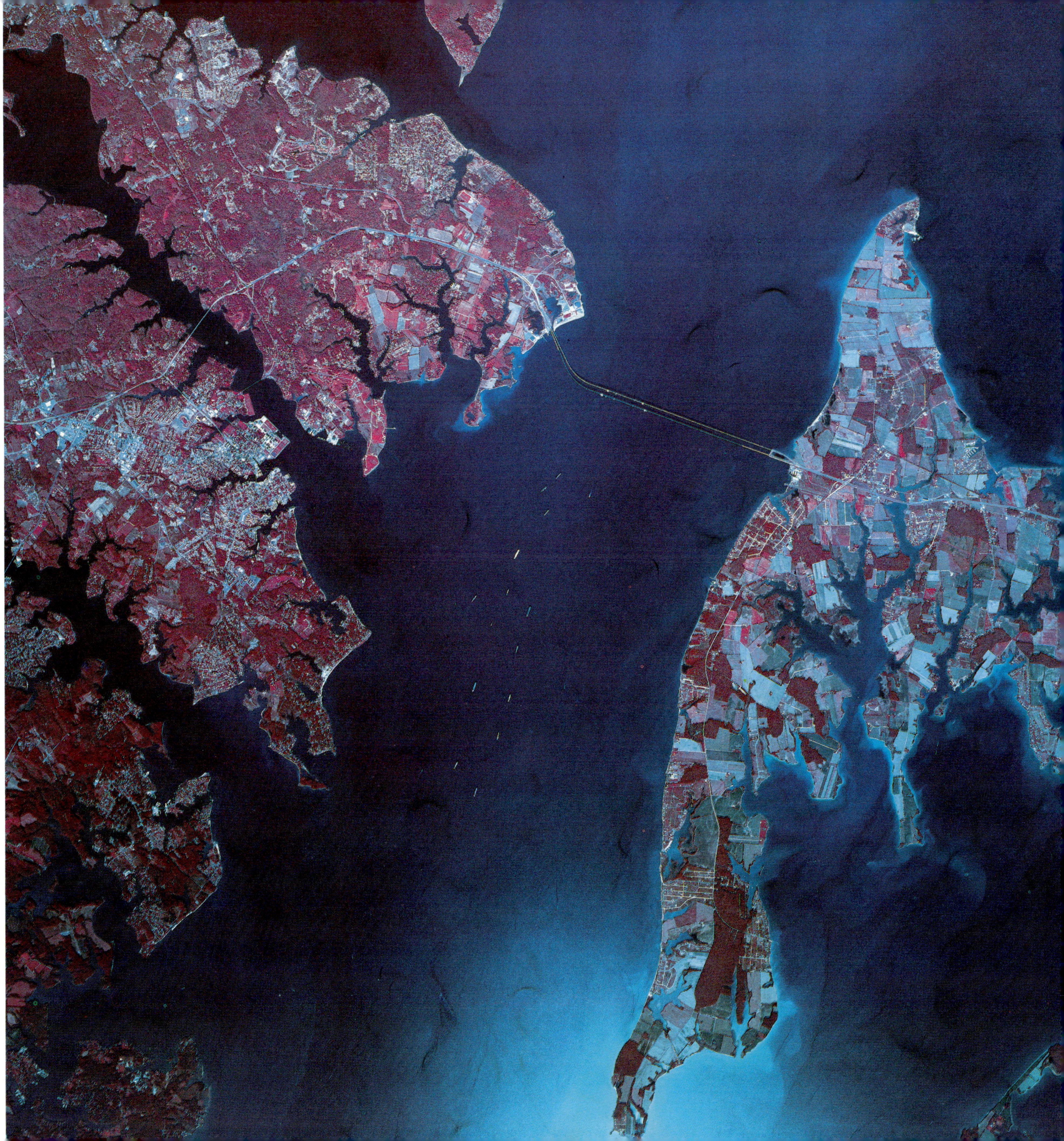

The United States Naval Academy's blue roofs are in spectrum with the beautiful colors of the Severn. The old city of Annapolis has many fine houses remaining from the 18th century. The market at the head of the town's docks is the third on its site, of which the first was built in 1788.

This NASA photograph makes the Annapolis area look tiny indeed from its 65,000 foot vantage point.

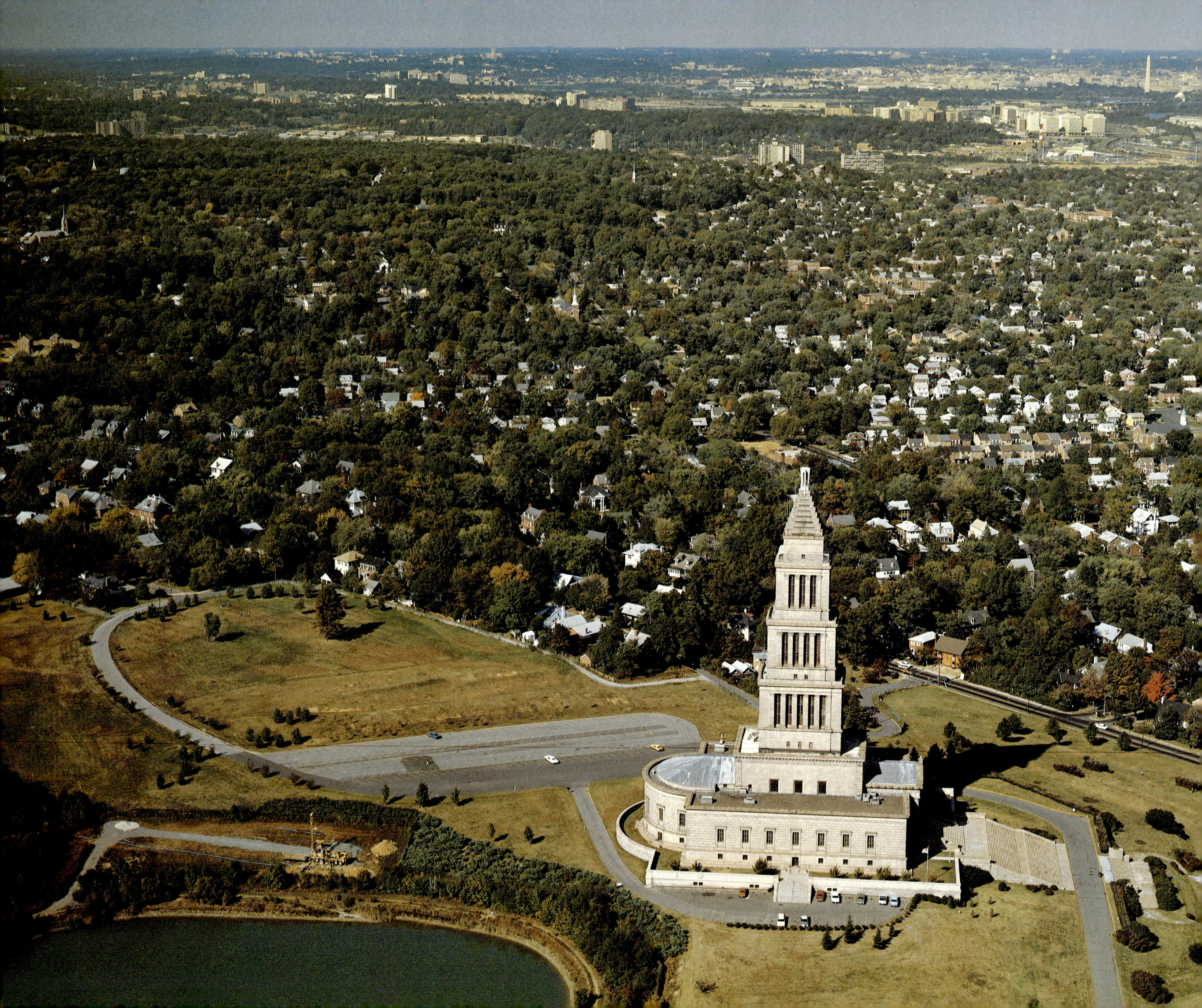

VIRGINIA

It is said Washington attended Scottish Rites at these grounds, Shooter's Hill in Alexandria. The Masonic Temple honors Washington the Mason. The structure was financed by contributions from more than three million members of the order. It contains a remarkable collection including the trowel used by Washington in laying the cornerstone of the Capitol, and the clock that was stopped at the moment of his death.

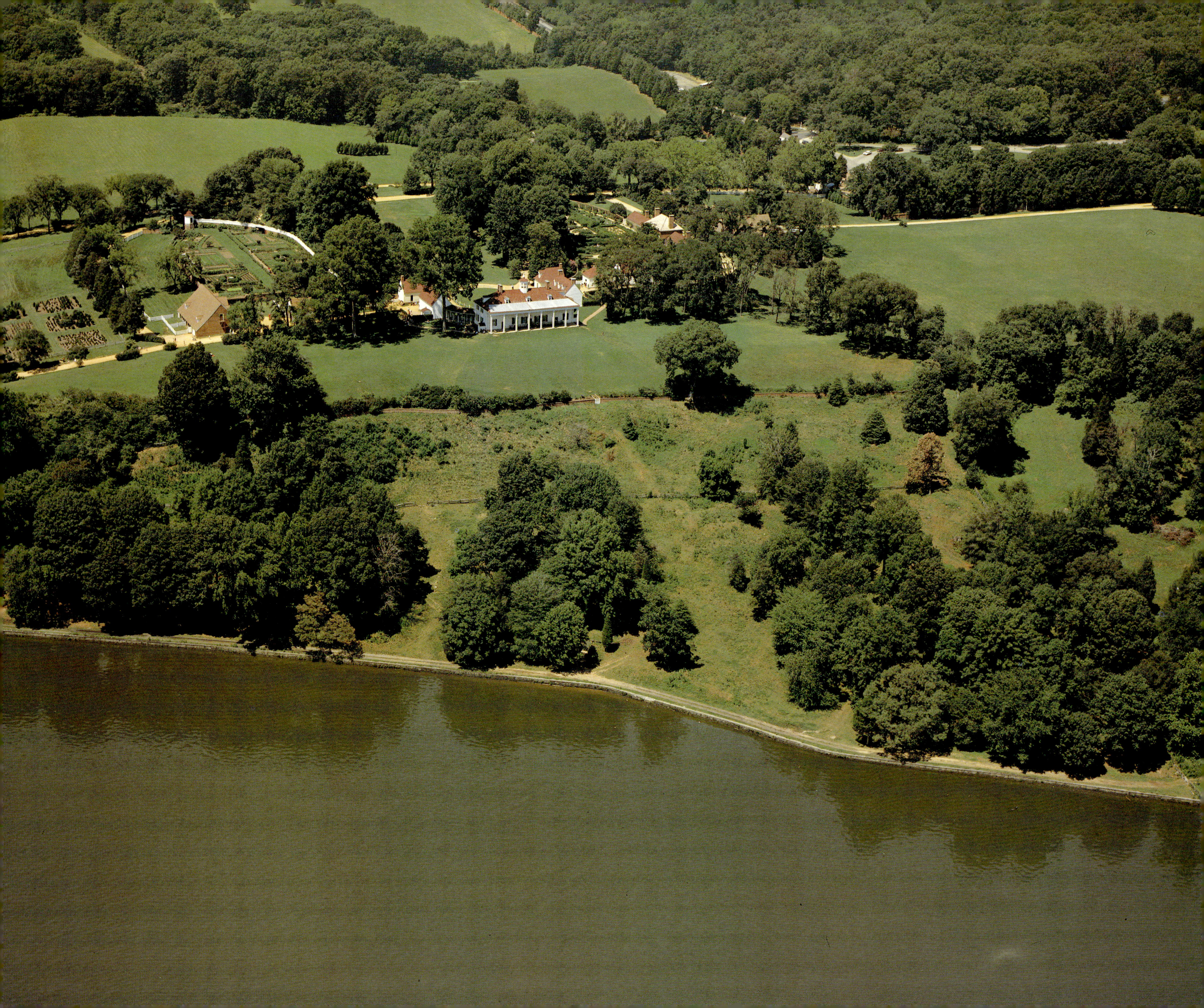

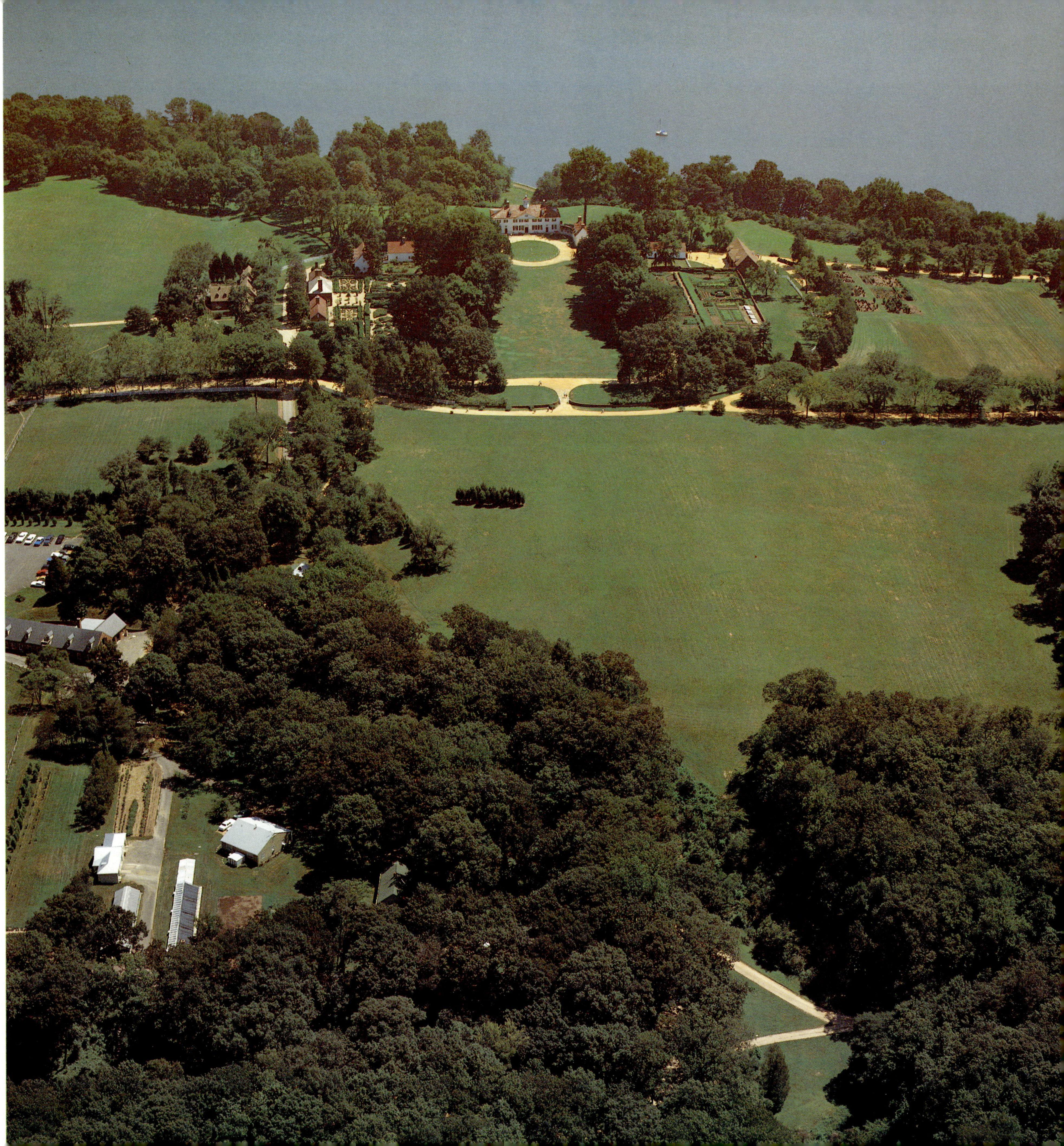

Washington's tomb is at the riverside below the home he loved. The estate remembers him as an individual, a family man. Built in 1743, the house became Washington's in 1759. He acted as his own architect, adding the upper story and the two projecting wings. The planter's life was varied and delightful. Washington recorded the fact that his family did not once sit down to dinner alone in twenty years. Mount Vernon overlooks the Potomac fifteen miles downriver from the capital. Any ship of the US Navy passing lowers the flag to half mast, tolls the ship's bell, and the crew stands at attention.

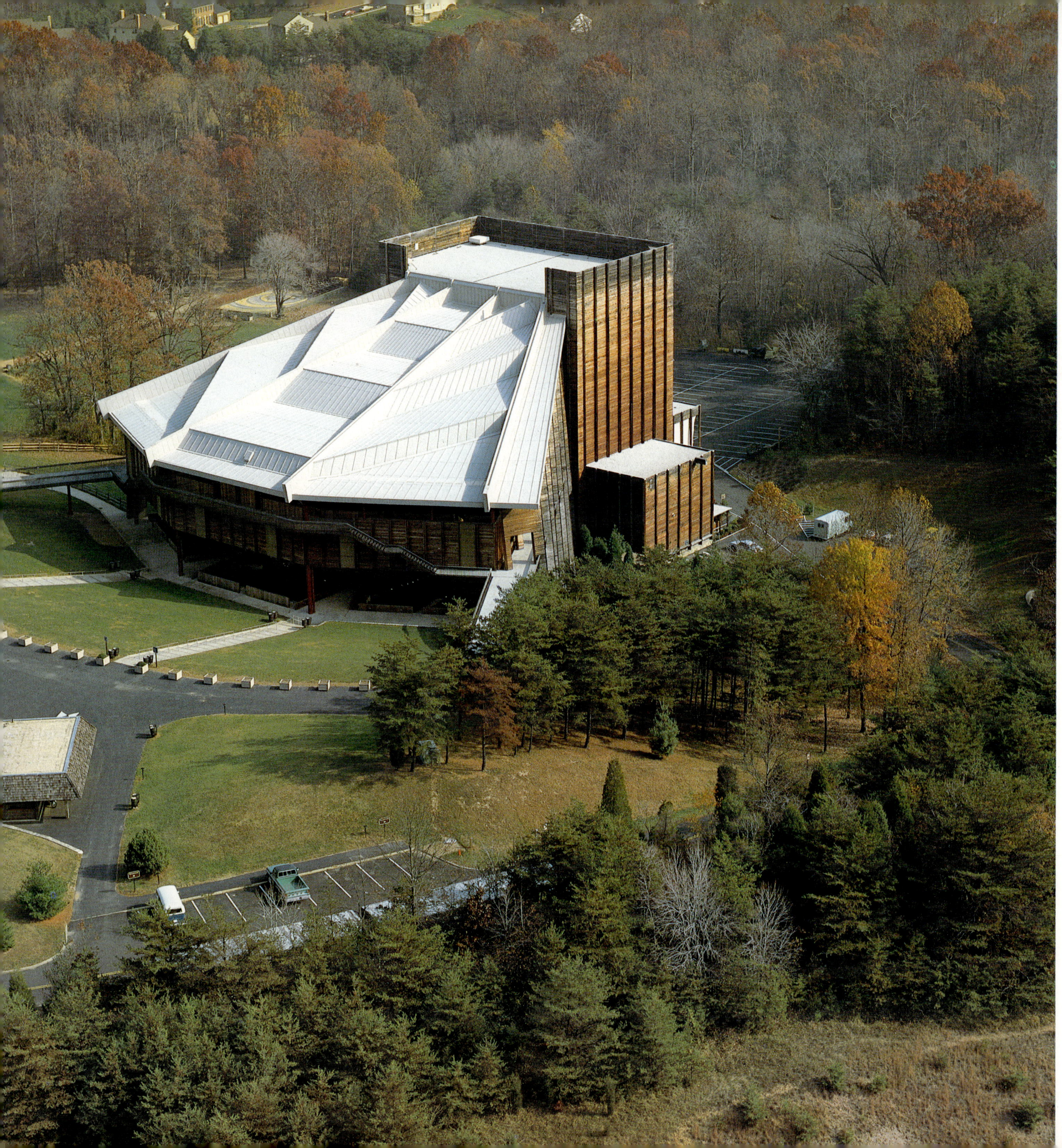

The Filene Center at Wolf Trap seats 3,500 inside and the performances may be seen by some 4,000 more on the lawns. This is a very popular summer attraction in Washington. Concerts and ballets originating here are frequently seen on Public Television throughout the country.

From 1962 to 1972 Reston's population growth was from 500 to 20,000. It is totally self-contained with schools, shopping, job centers, religious and cultural facilities. Lake Anne Center is the central core of this privately developed new town.

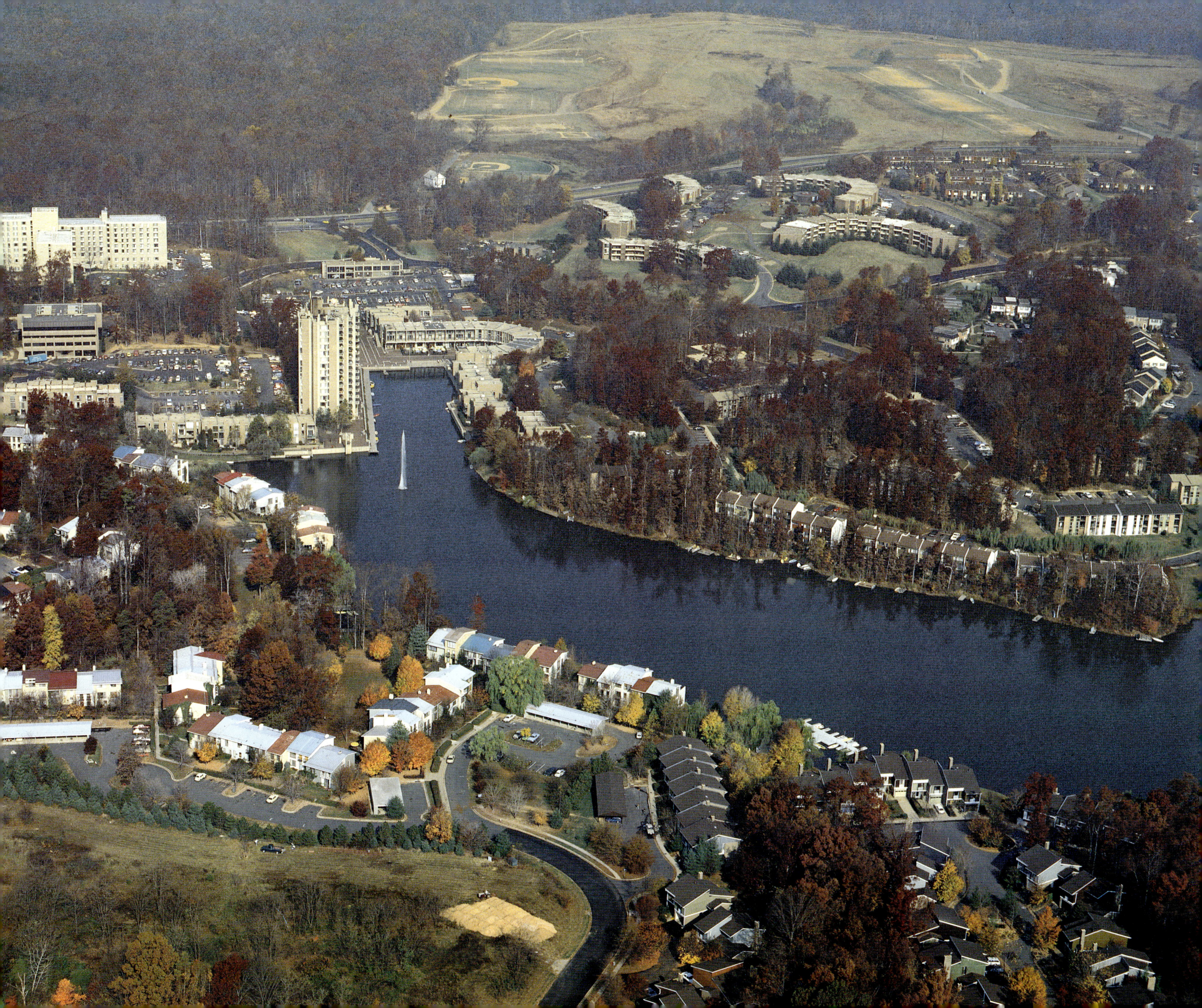

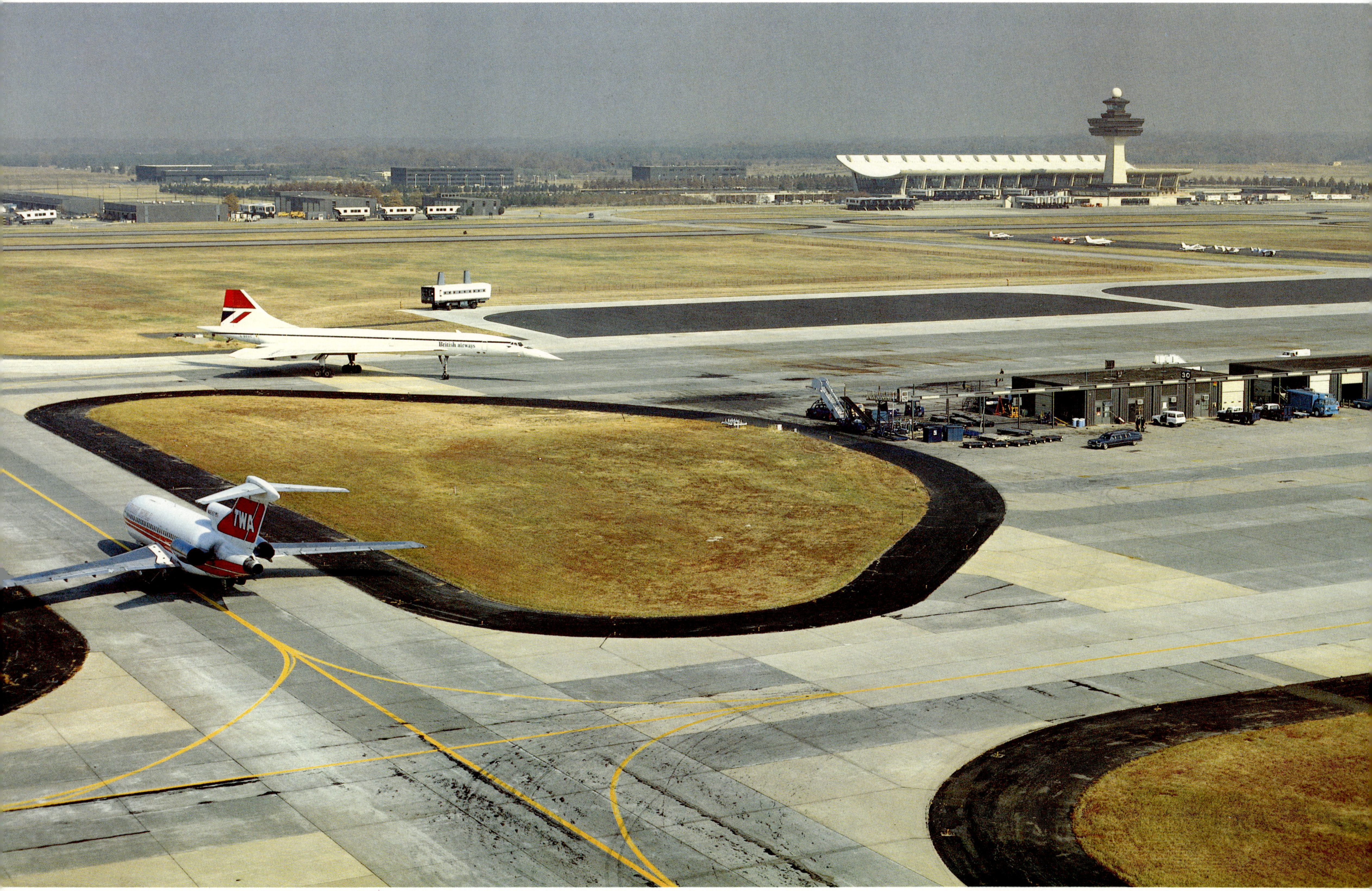

Among low, rolling Virginia hills, Dulles is one of the world's beautiful airports. Coming to it by air, or by car, is a special experience. The great expanses of glass, the swooping suspension roof, designed by Eero Saarinen for this setting and this use, make Dulles an architectural jewel.

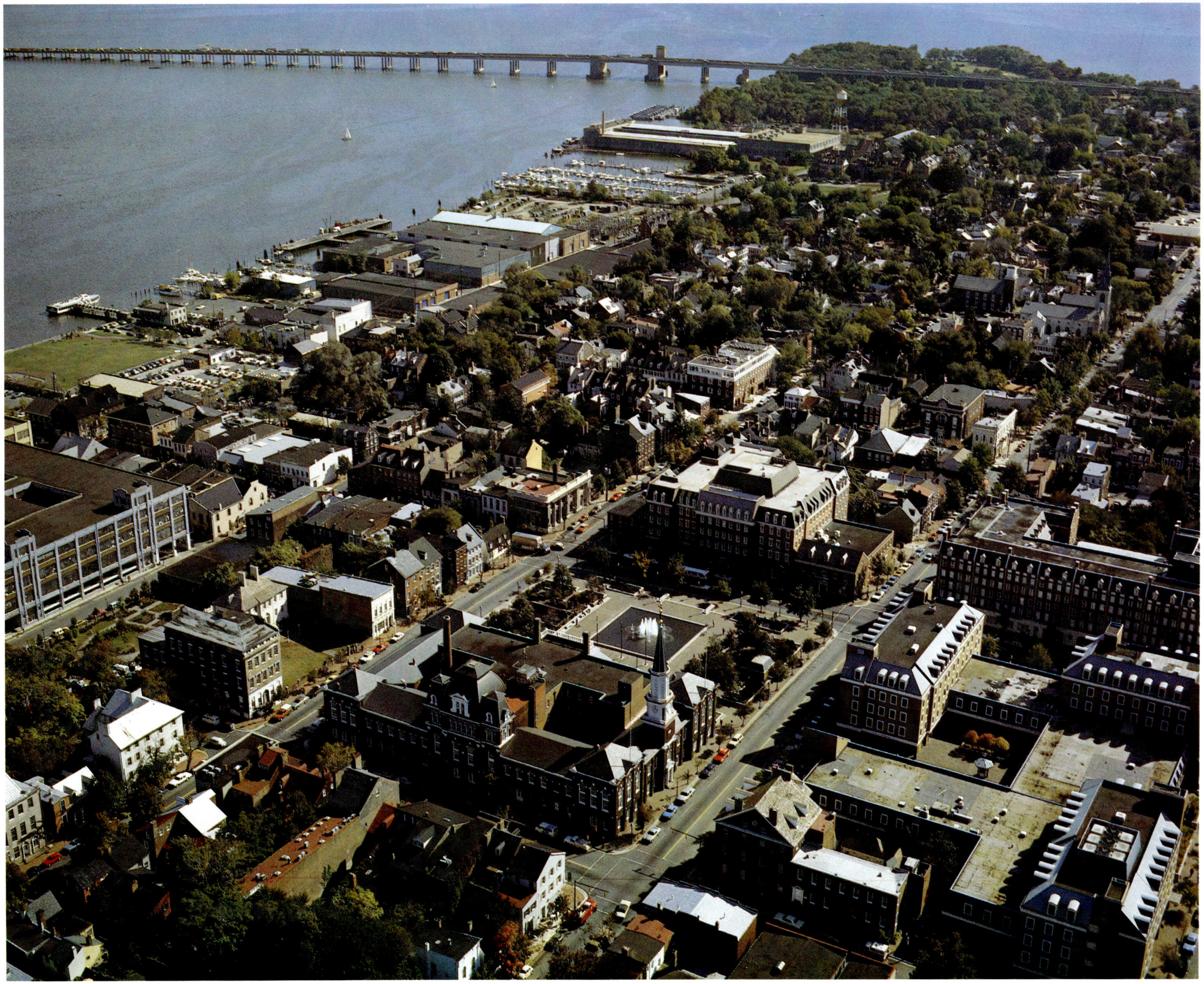

The Alexandria Waterfront was tobacco warehouses and a ferry crossing, which became a natural city in 1749, named for the original owners of the site, the Alexander family. When the District of Columbia was surveyed and granted, Alexandria was a part of the 10 mile square. It was retroceded to Virginia in 1846. It was spared the destruction suffered by many southern cities when it was occupied by union troops in the Civil War. In Market Square, lower center, Washington drilled Virginia Rangers in 1755. The Wilson Bridge carries the Capital Beltway a mile and more across the Potomac.

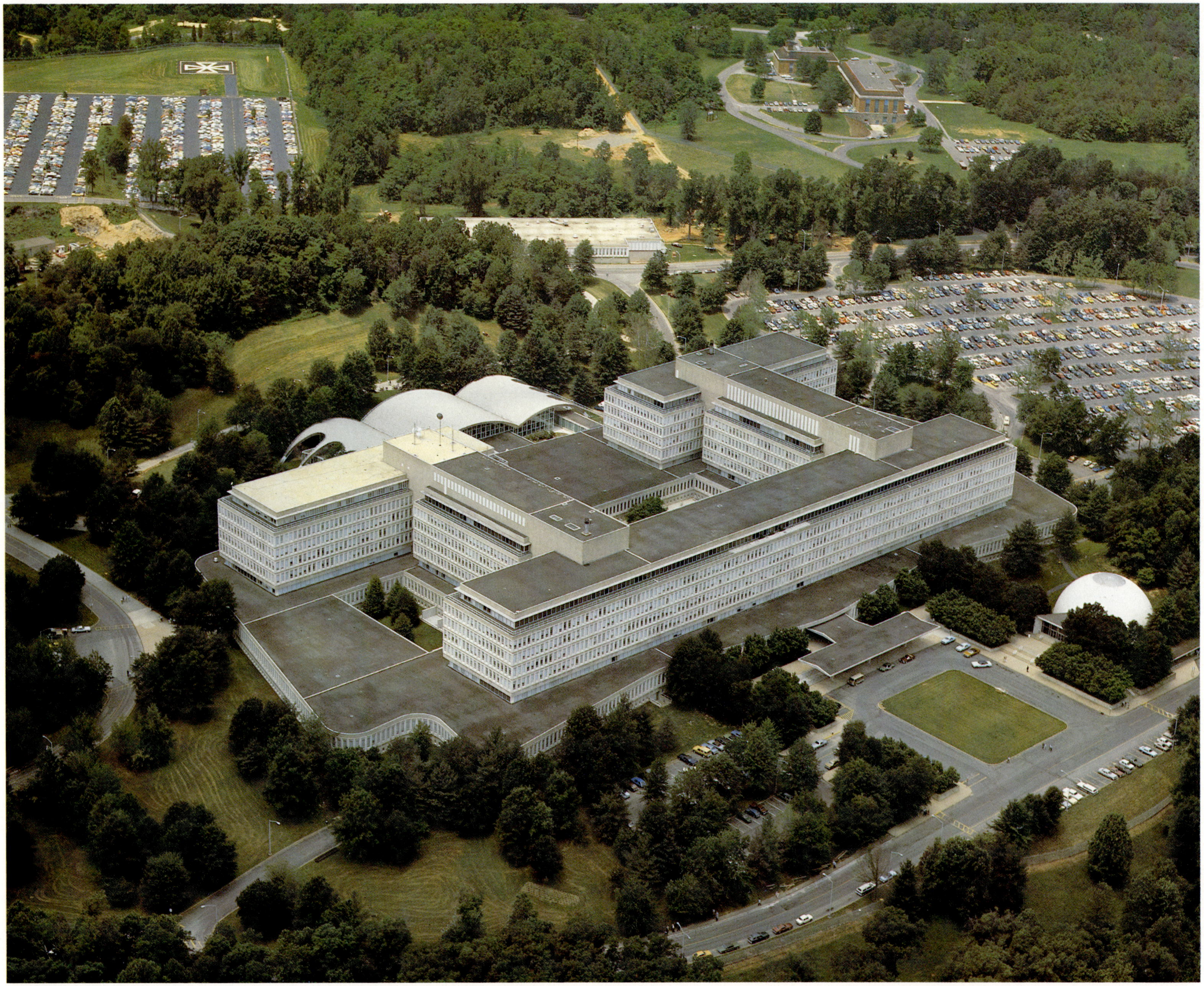

Masked by the fine trees of the Langley area at ground level, the Central Intelligence Agency Headquarters, from the air, is revealed as an orderly relationship of facilities and parking. Until recently, highway exits were unmarked or indicated that you would end up, if you took them, at the **Fairbank** Highway Research **Station**. This is the small brick structure at the upper right.

In Virginia, height limits are less restrictive than in the District of Columbia. This attracts builders to Rosslyn and to other locations, downriver, where land is also less expensive. The Metro, and the Key and Roosevelt Bridges, are the visible access to Georgetown and downtown, from high rise. On the highways Rosslyn vistas to the Potomac and the Capitol are handsome.

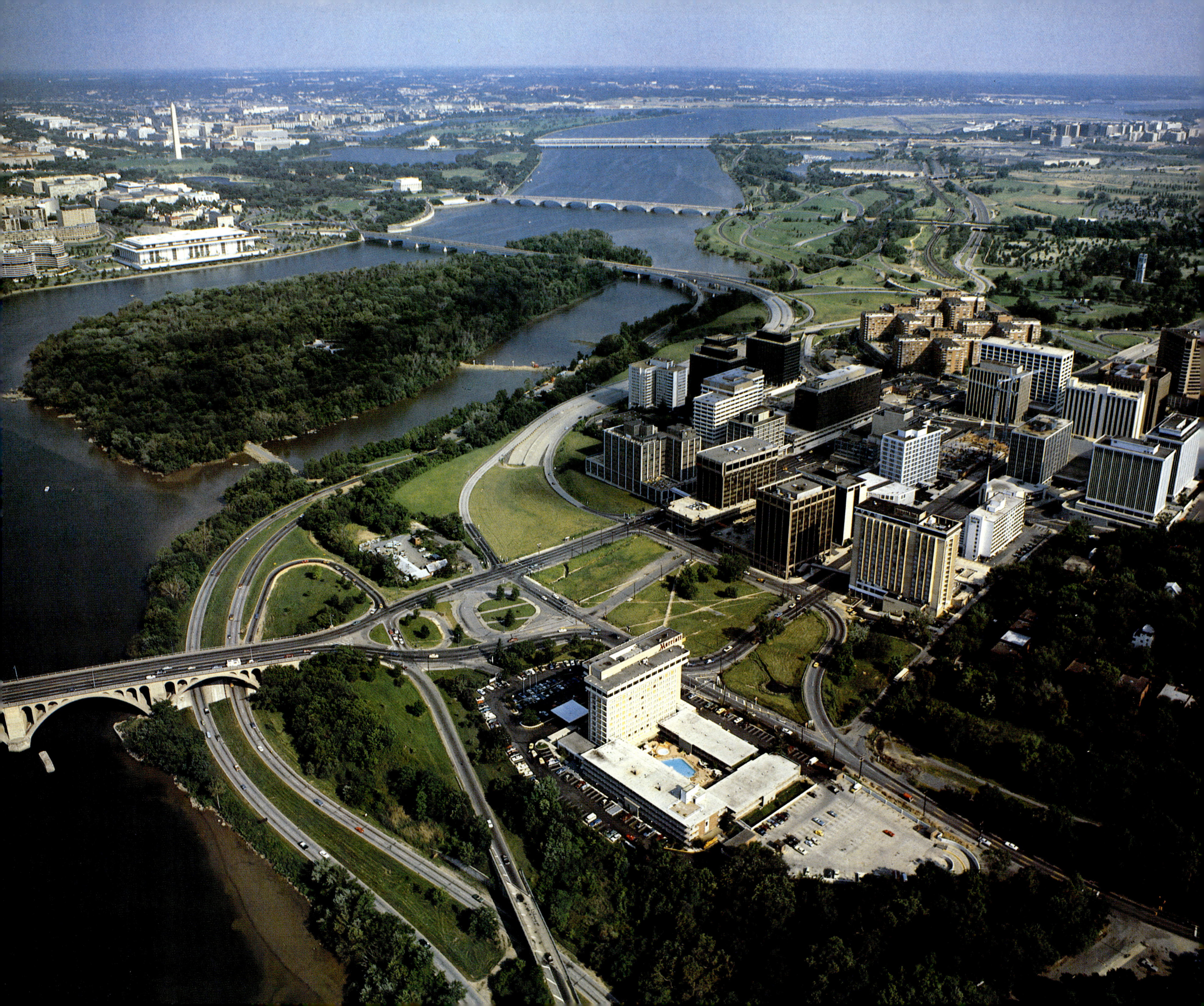

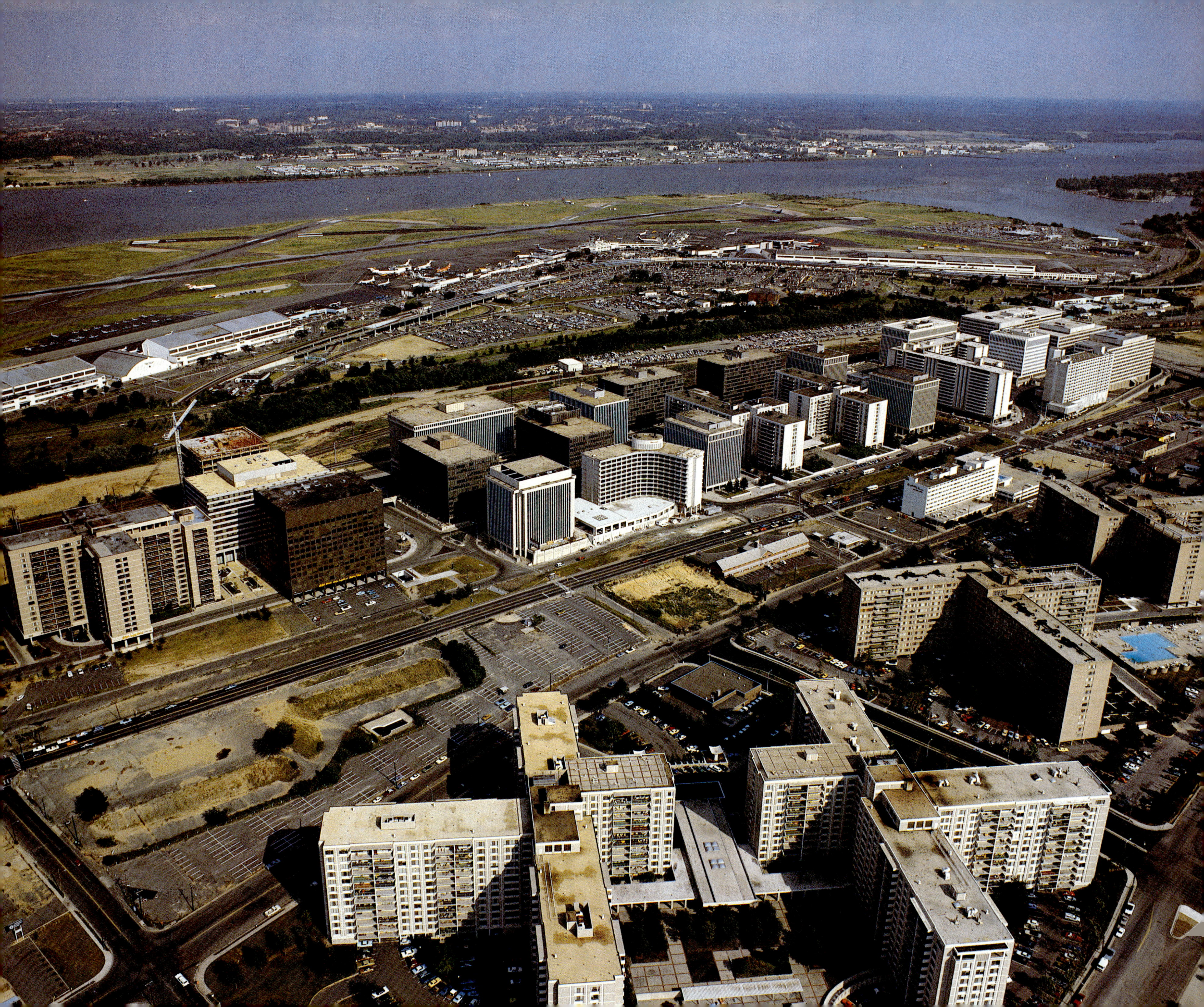

Crystal City looks over Washington National Airport toward Washington beyond the Potomac. The compact integration of office dwellings and commercial facilities, some of the latter in underground malls, means that a resident could go for years without leaving the relatively small area. But the new Metro stop gives it rapid connection to the larger activity and interest of the capital.

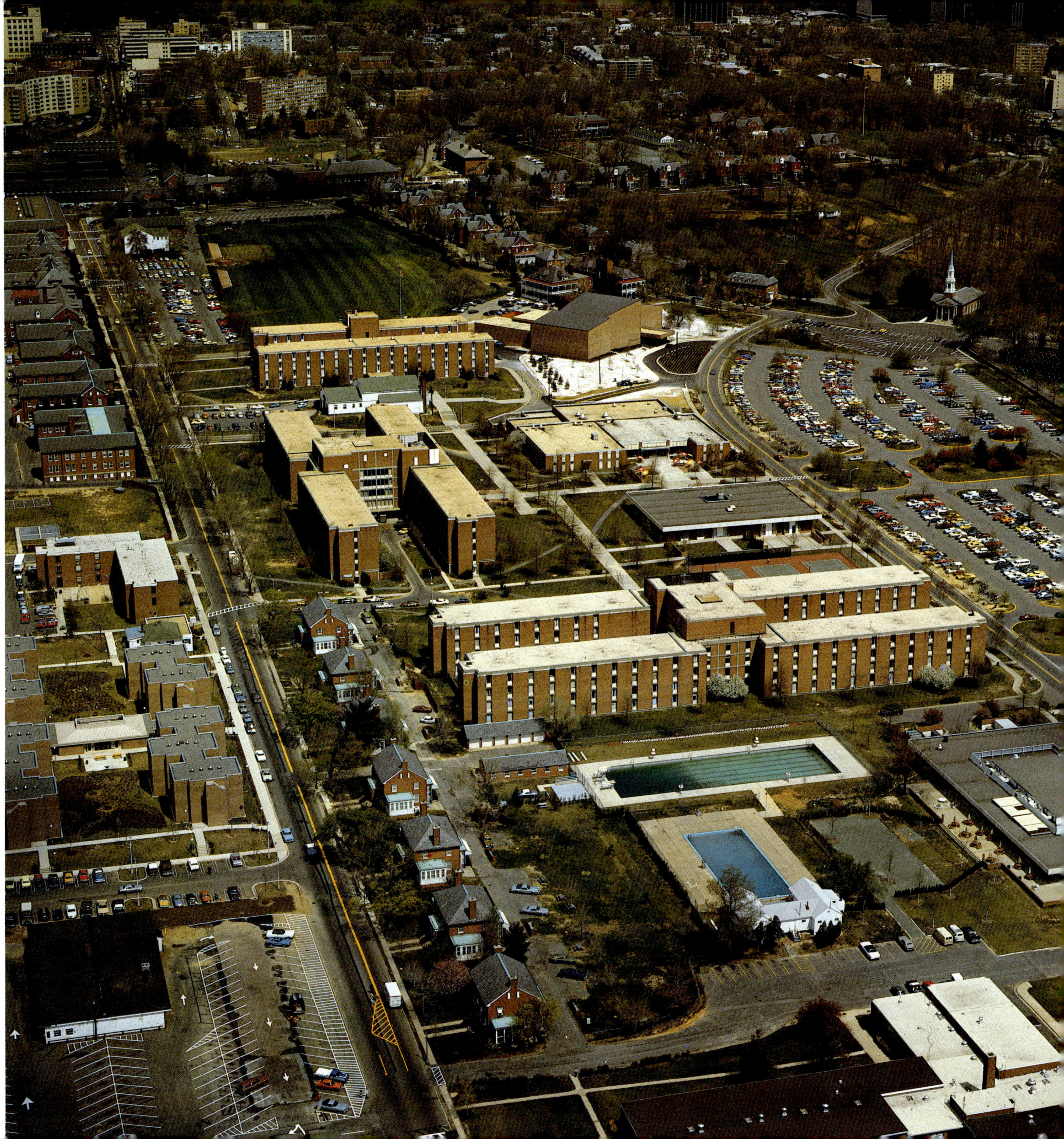

Here at Ft. Myer the Civil War fortifications were once named Fort Whipple in what was once part of the Custis-Lee estate. The Wright brothers used the parade ground for tests after their Kitty Hawk flights. The troops stationed here are active in Washington ceremonial occasions. Blackjack, the riderless horse used in Presidential funeral processions, was stabled here. The chapel at upper right is a popular wedding spot, with ceremonies hourly on Saturday in spring and summer.

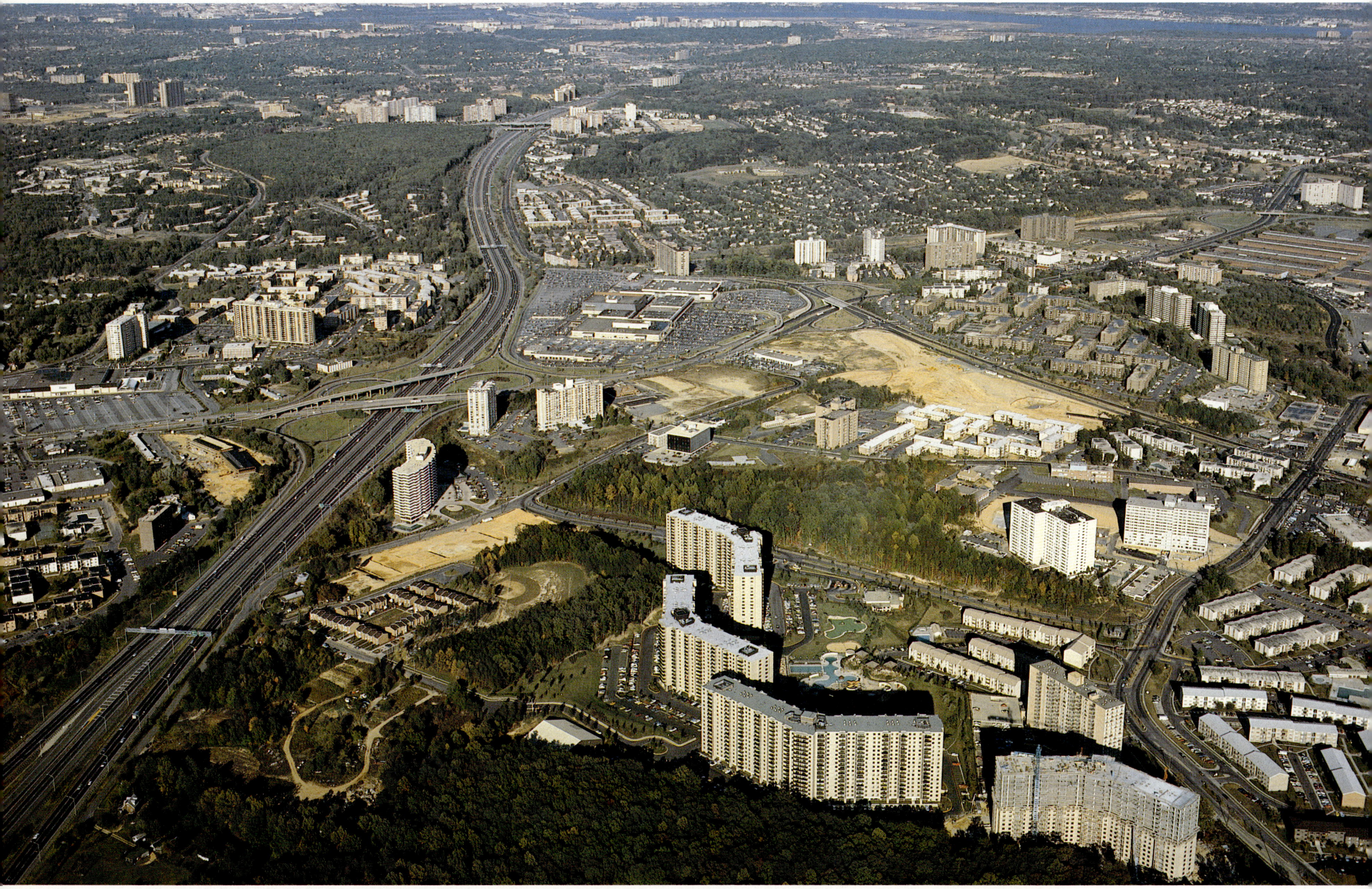

I-95 at left runs south from Washington into this actively developing area of Alexandria. High rise housing and condominiums are in proliferating pattern and extent. The Virginia Theological Seminary, dating from 1859, is just right of center in the photograph.

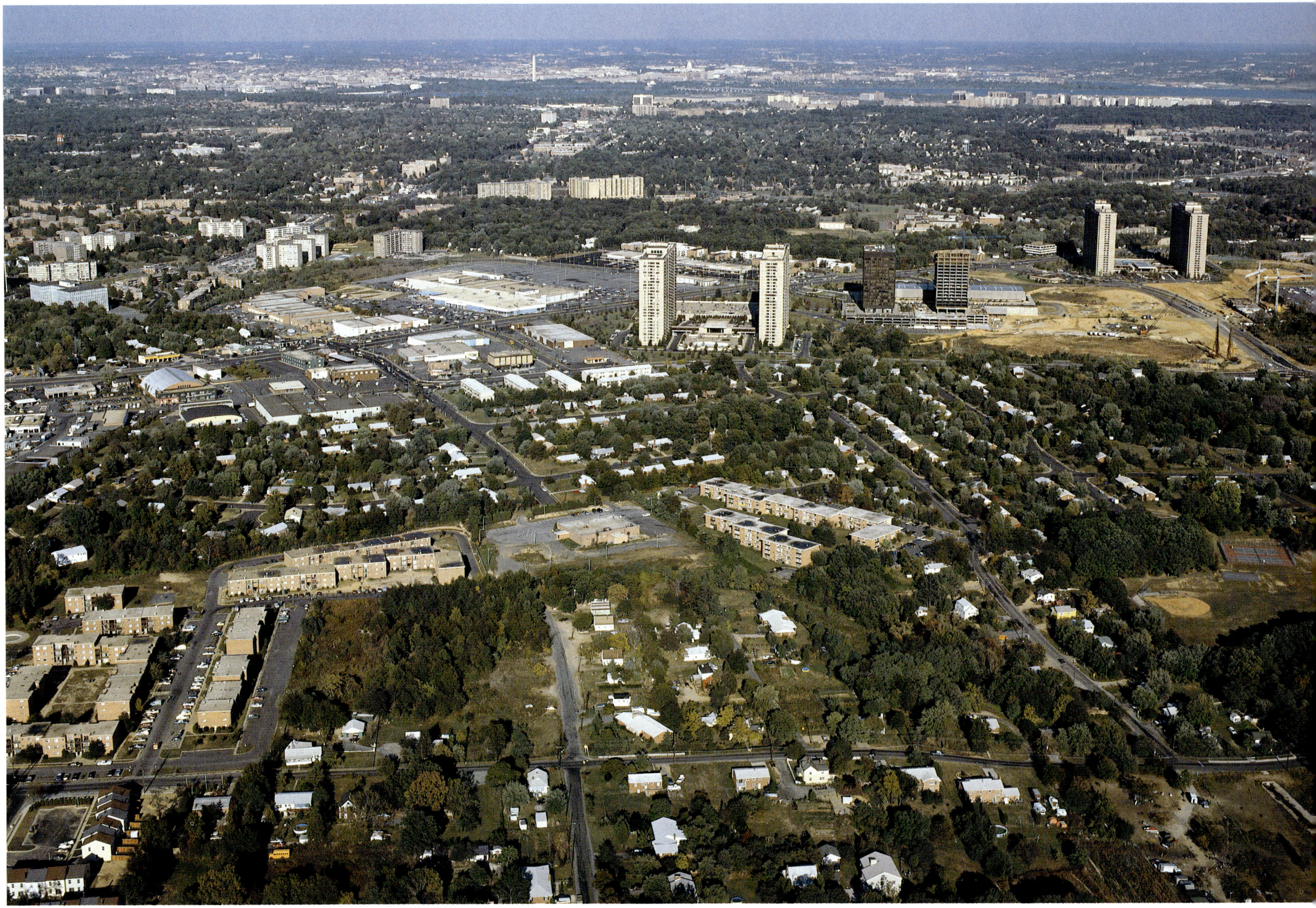

The suburbs in northern Virginia were later in coming than those north of Washington and Maryland, for the most part. Bailey's Crossroads is just outside of Arlington County in Fairfax County, its relative proximity to the capital apparent here, as the monument and Capitol are seen beyond the Potomac.

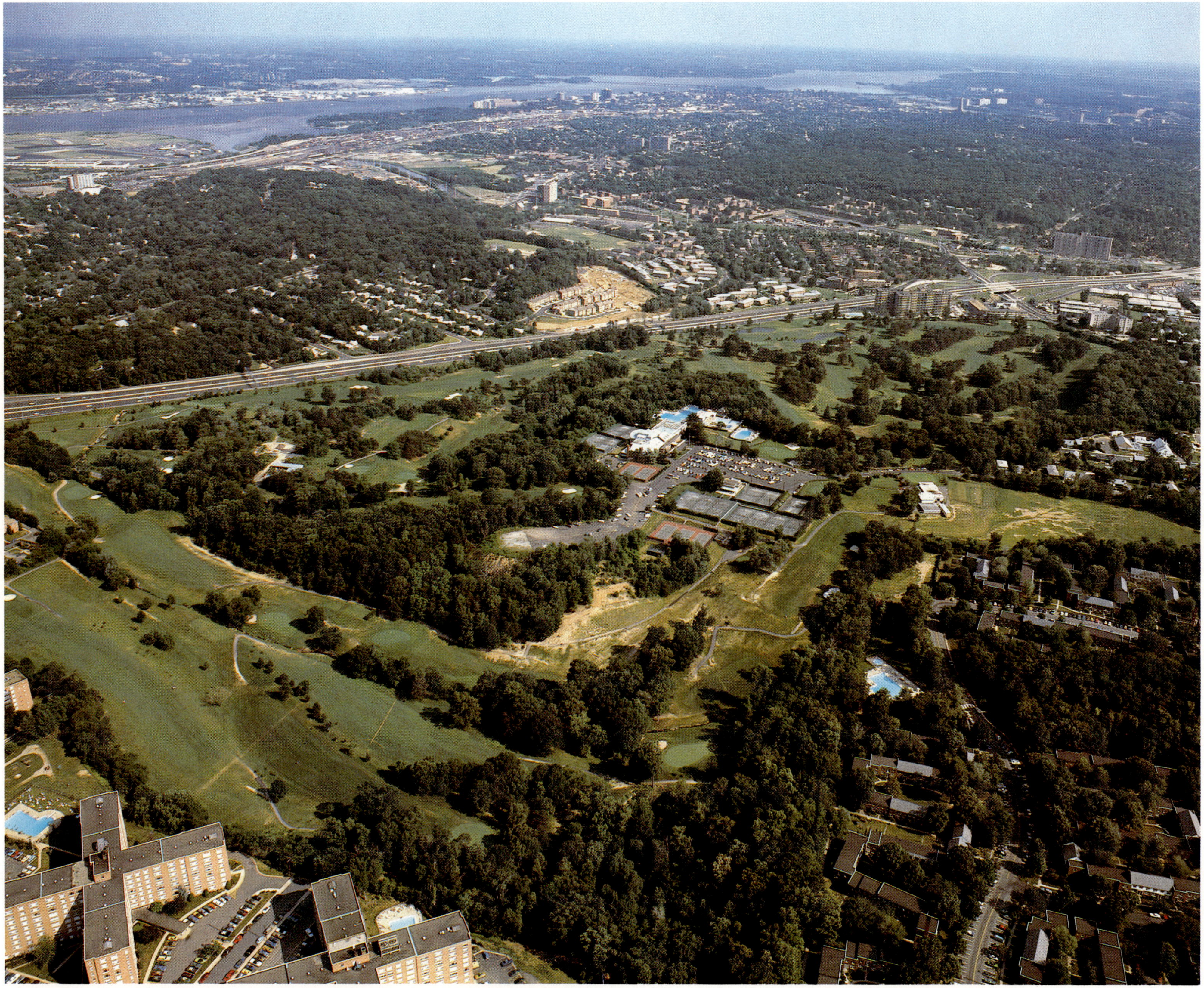

Washington has a large military community. The Army-Navy Country Club has an important place in its recreational accommodation. The Club is near the Arlington Cemetery at Shirley Highway and Glebe Road.

Washington Golf & Country Club is also located in Arlington. This is the Washington area's oldest club, established in 1894. It is close-in, in an older suburb in northern Virginia.

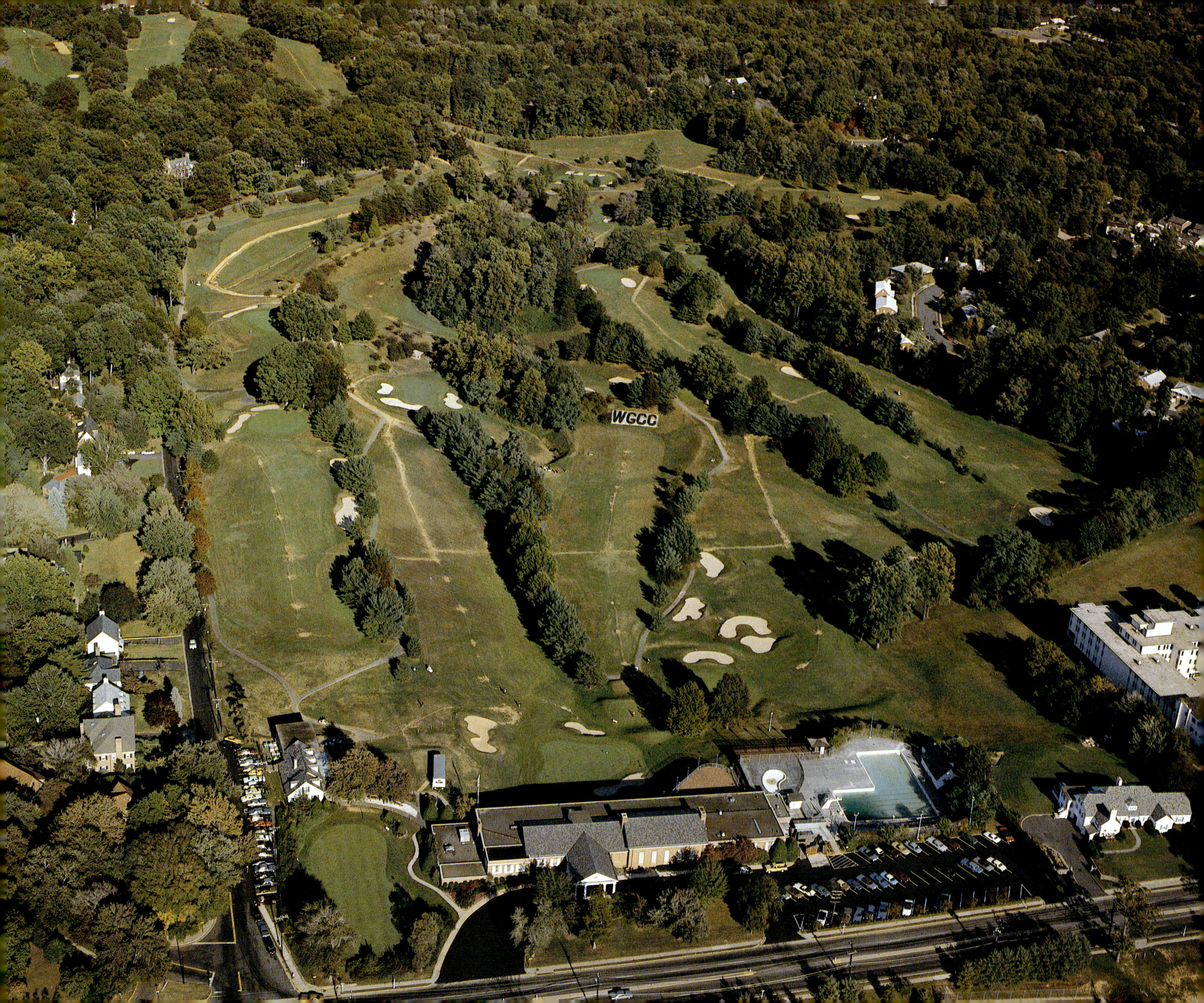
WGCC

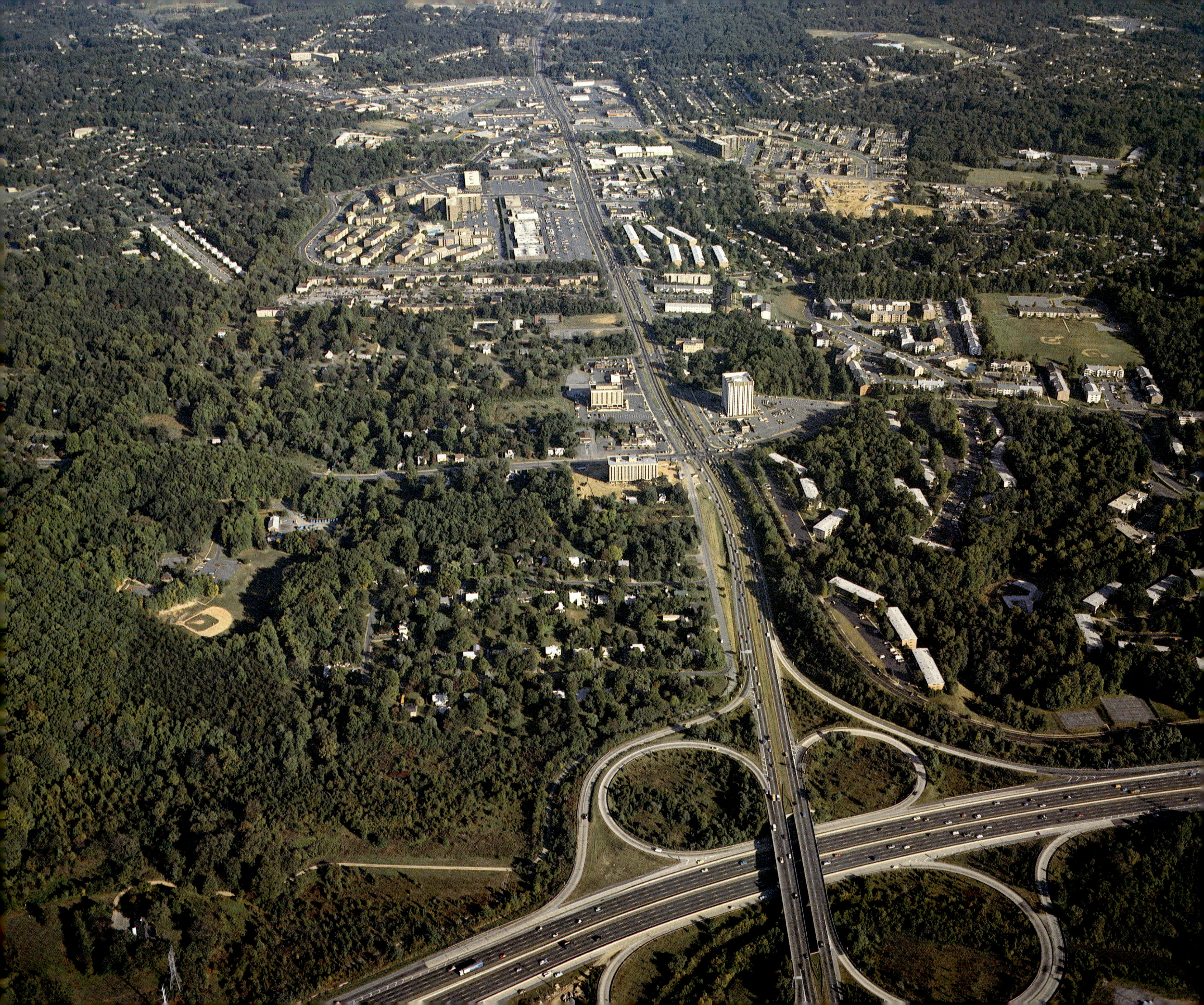

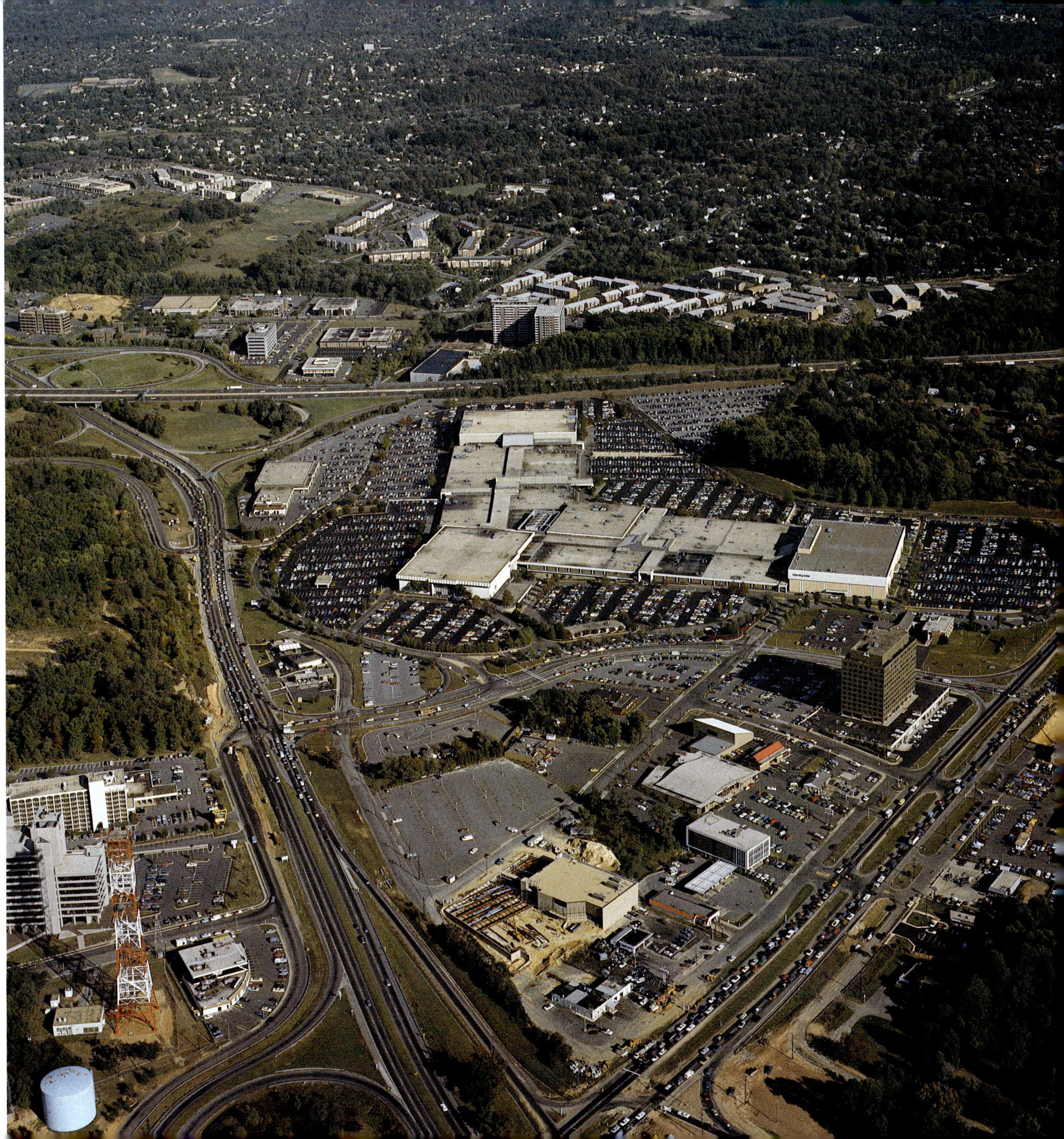

The view east of Annandale is from the beltway along Route 236, Little River Turnpike. Later and slower development in this part of Virginia was owing in part to estate and agricultural continuance through the 1950's. National corporations are now attracted to this area by relatively lower land costs and potential of residential adjacency.

The Tysons Corner Center, erected in the mid-60's was, when constructed, one of the largest indoor shopping malls in the capital area. It caters to nearby residential and corporate communities.

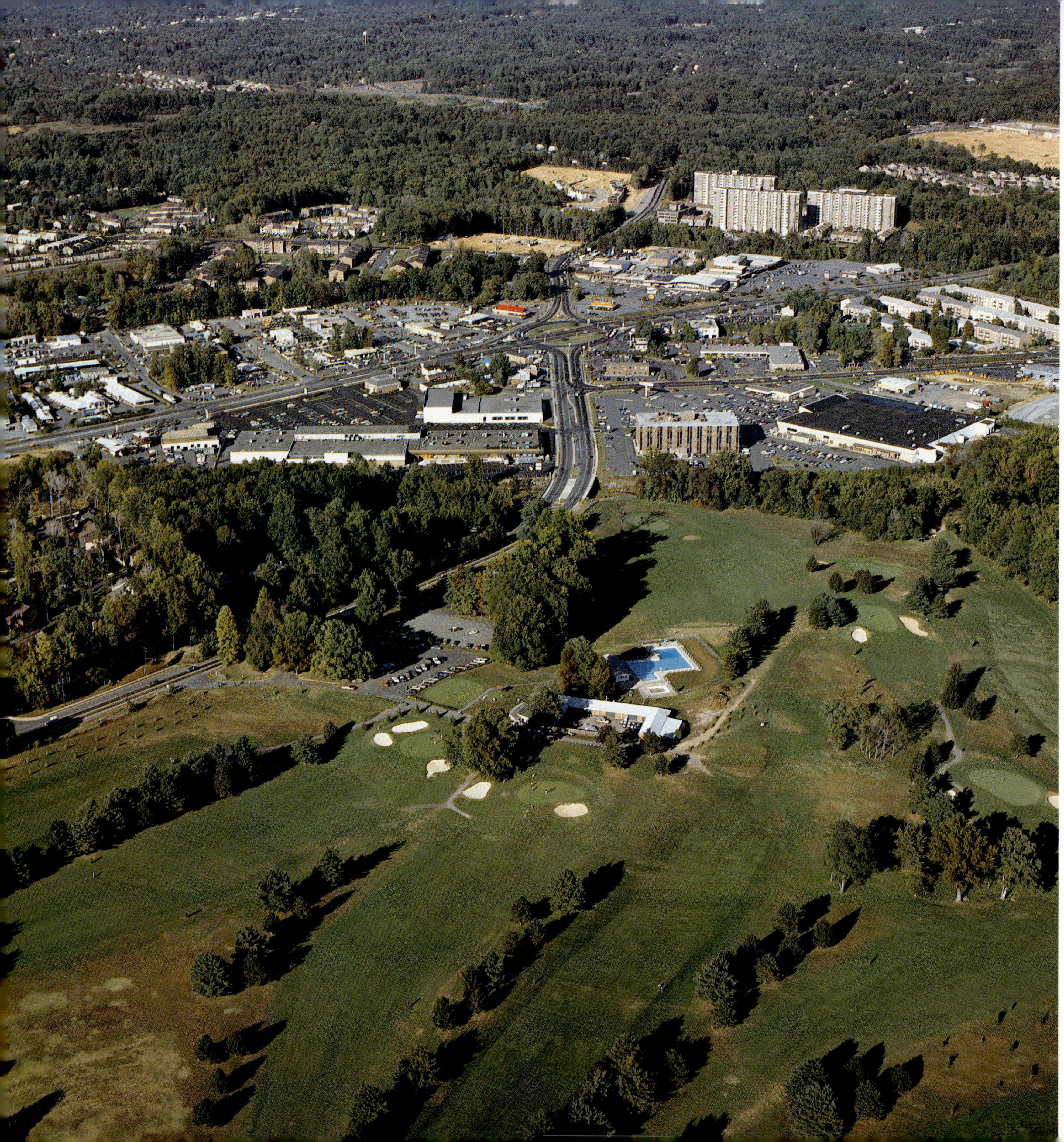

Fairfax Circle was once an old "coaching rest" at the intersection of roads from Georgetown and Alexandria to Kentucky and the west. The Army and Navy Country Club is in the foreground. The old court house still stands, from circa 1800, the county seat of Fairfax County. This is well outside the beltway, on the road to Winchester.

At Seven Corners Leesburg Pike intersects Route 50 and Wilson Boulevard. The small cemetery at lower left is Oakwood. Falls Church lies beyond.

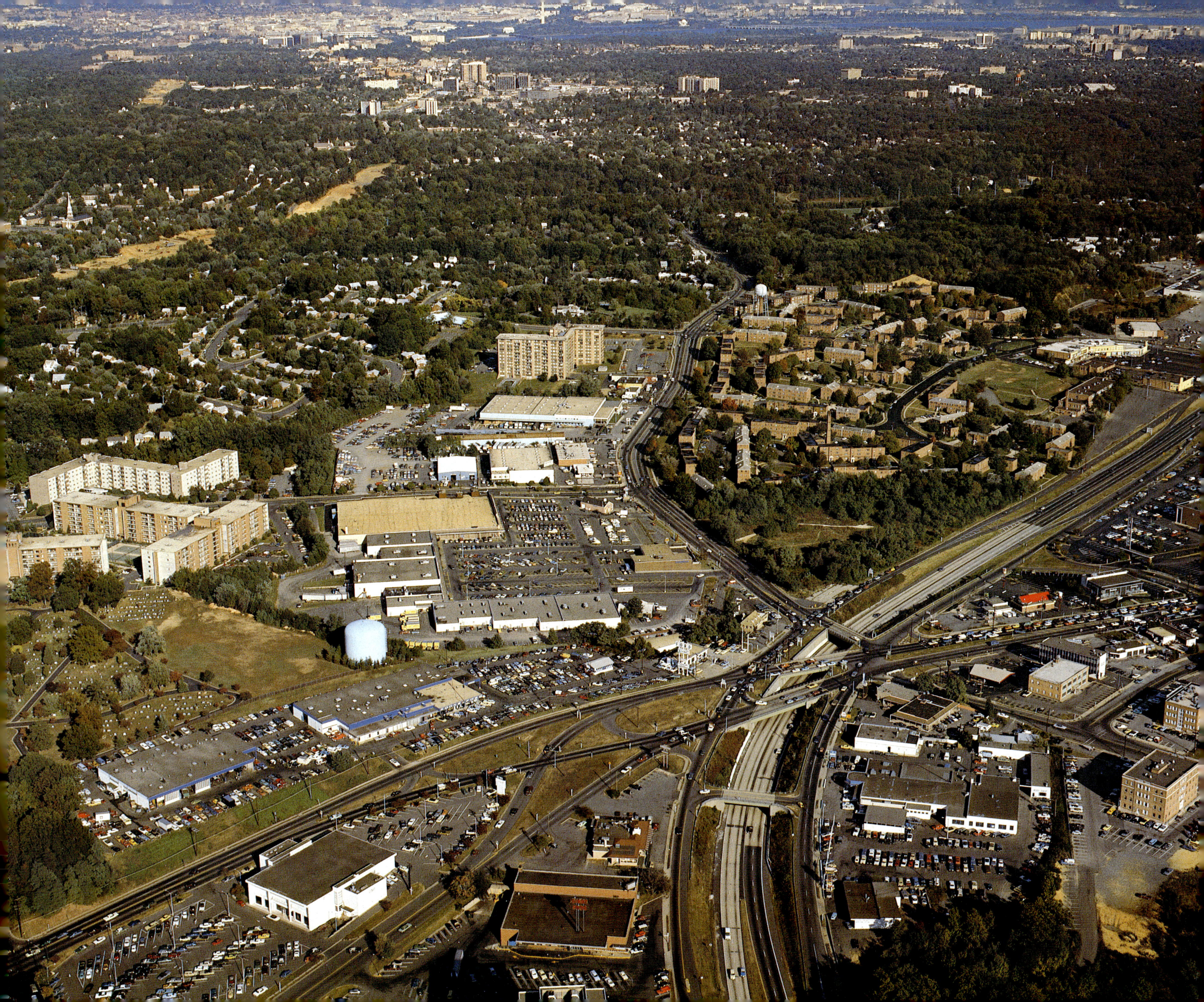

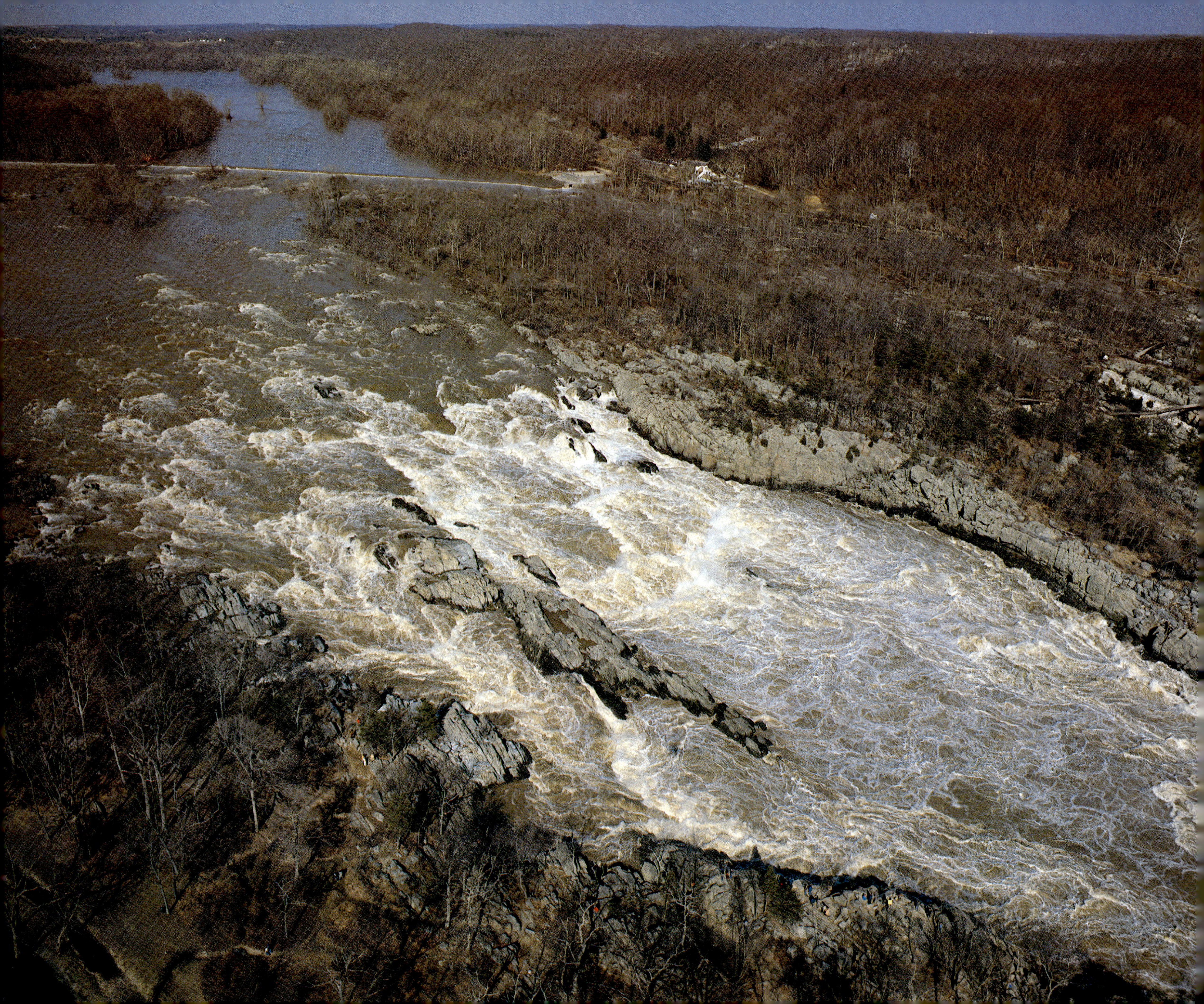

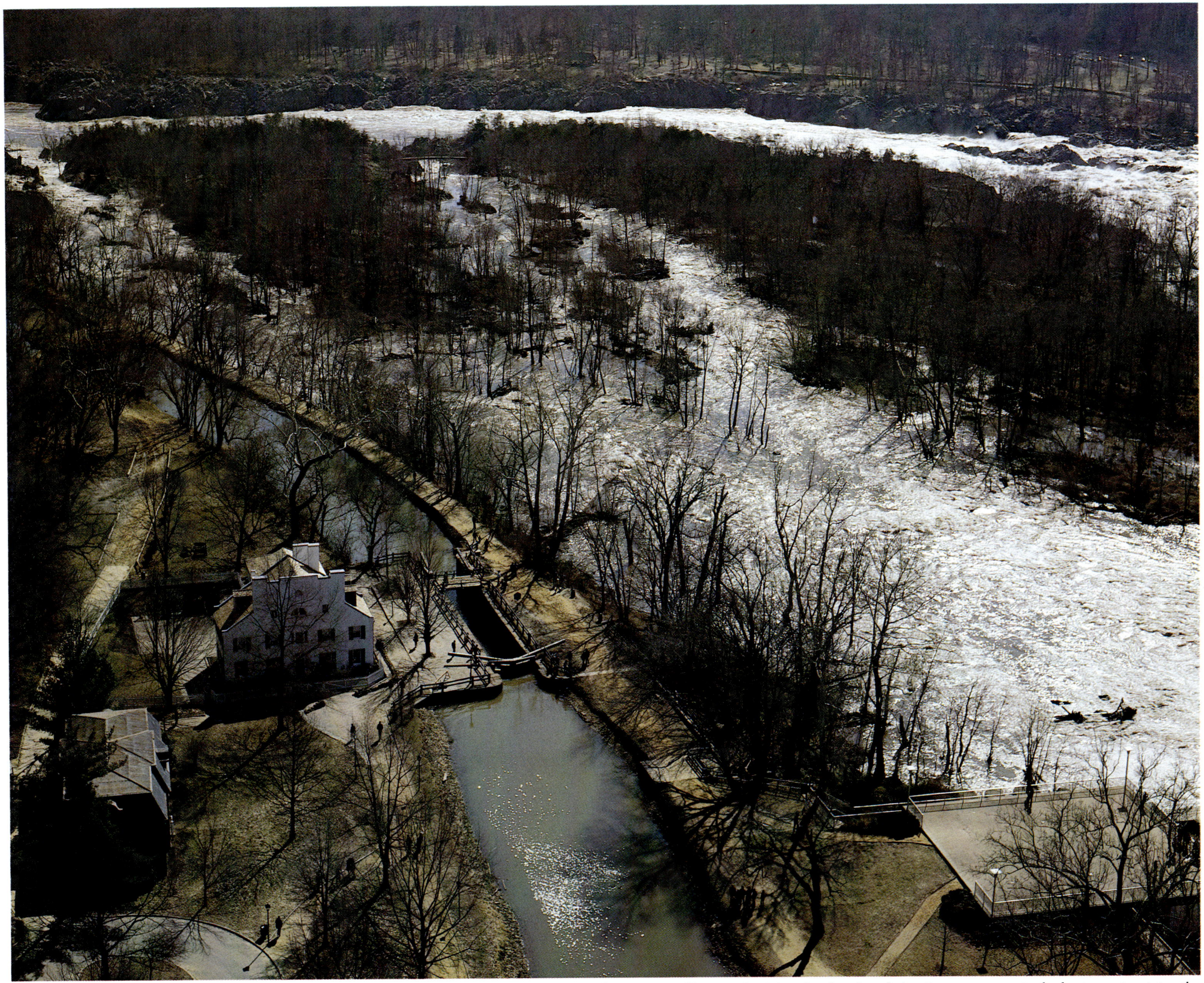

The Great Falls, on the Maryland side of the Potomac are turbulent contrast to the peaceful commerce for which the Chesapeake and Ohio Canal was intended. Begun in 1828, its best year was 1893 when 700 boats were operating. It ran to Cumberland, with 76 locks, 11 acqueducts, and 7 dams. It is now opened to tour barges, canoes, and other recreational craft, and is a favorite of walkers.

Captain John Smith came up the river as far as this in 1608. But no further. The Great Falls are a natural wonder on the Potomac. Although relatively near the capital they are today just as Smith saw them. In good weather on weekends, they offer popular and pleasant Washington outings.

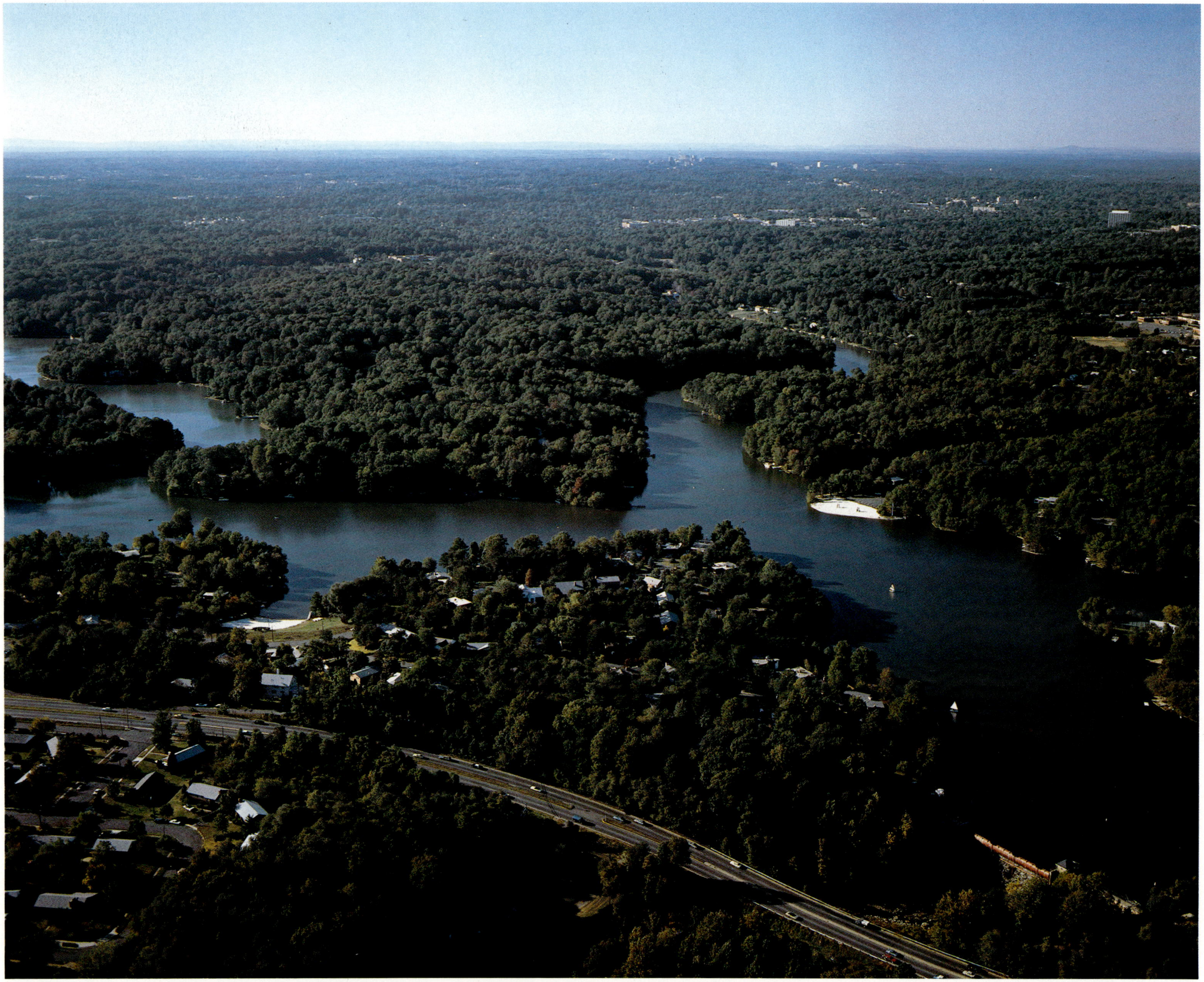

The development near Lake Barcroft at the confluence of Holmes Run and Tripps Run in Fairfax County is idyllically sited and landscaped. Columbia Pike west of Bailey's Crossroads is in the foreground.

Motorists at dusk leave Washington via the George Washington Memorial Parkway along the upper Potomac. Key Bridge spans the Potomac at right.

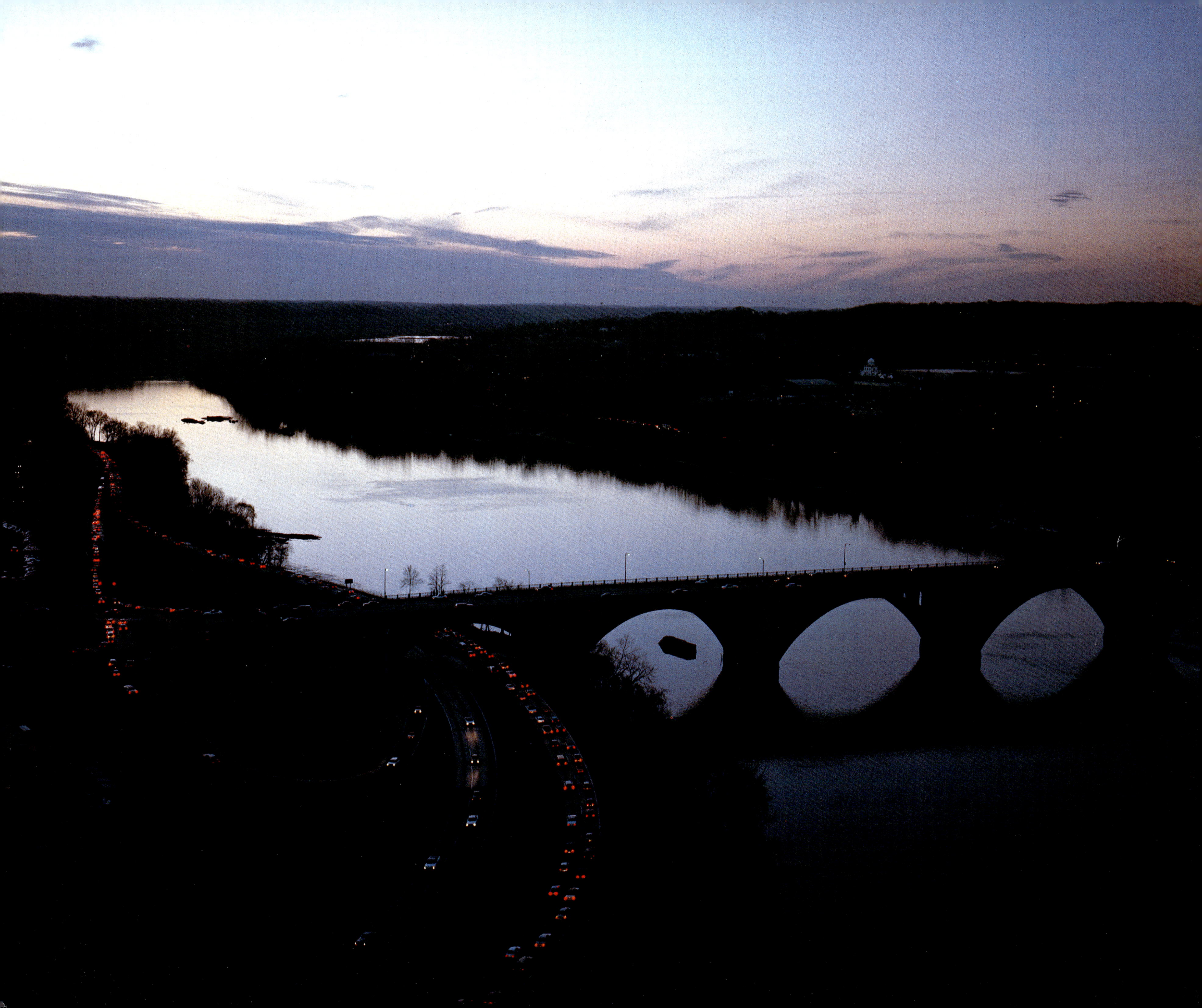